# ACHIEVING A
# PRODUCTIVE AGING
# SOCIETY

# ACHIEVING A PRODUCTIVE AGING SOCIETY

Edited by
## Scott A. Bass, Francis G. Caro, and Yung-Ping Chen

**Auburn House**
Westport, Connecticut • London

Library of Congress Cataloging-in-Publication Data

Achieving a productive aging society / edited by Scott A. Bass,
  Francis G. Caro, and Yung-Ping Chen.
      p.     cm.
  Includes index.
  ISBN 0–86569–032–4 (hc : alk. paper).—ISBN 0–86569–033–2 (pb :
alk. paper)
  1. Aged—United States—Social conditions.   2. Life span,
Productive—United States.   3. Aged—Employment—United States.
4. Aged—Long term care—United States.   5. Aged volunteers—United
States.   6. Aged—Government policy—United States.   I. Bass, Scott
A.   II. Caro, Francis G., 1936–   .   III. Chen, Yung-Ping, 1928–
HQ1064.U5A628      1993
305.26'0973—dc20           92–22757

British Library Cataloguing in Publication Data is available.

Library of Congress Catalog Card Number: 92–22757
ISBN: 0–86569–032–4 (hc); 0–86569–033–2 (pb)

First published in 1993

Auburn House, 88 Post Road West, Westport, CT 06881
An imprint of Greenwood Publishing Group, Inc.

Printed in the United States of America

The paper used in this book complies with the
Permanent Paper Standard issued by the National
Information Standards Organization (Z39.48–1984).

10  9  8  7  6  5  4  3  2  1

# Contents

# Acknowledgments

The editors are indebted to Patrick O'Reilly, who helped identify the contributors for this volume, conducted an initial review of the literature, and organized the working conference on productive aging in Boston, which most of the authors attended; also, the administration of the University of Massachusetts of Boston for its support for this project; Jill R. Norton, who served as managing editor for the book; and James P. O'Brien, who helped edit several chapters and prepared the index.

W. Andrew Achenbaum wishes to thank Scott A. Bass, Fred Bookstein, Harry R. Moody, Thomas R. Cole, Edward Dobihal, and R. Stewart Wood for their helpful suggestions in conceptualizing Chapter 10.

A. Regula Herzog and James N. Morgan thank their colleagues Toni C. Antonucci, James House, James S. Jackson, Robert Kahn, Graham Kalton, James Lepkowski, and Camille Wortman for their collaboration on the Americans' Changing Lives Survey and for comments on an earlier version of Chapter 7.

James S. Jackson, Toni C. Antonucci, and Rose C. Gibson would like to thank Sally Oswald and Keith Hersh for their help in preparing Chapter 14 and Halimah Hassan and Linda Shepard in the analysis that supports the research. Special acknowledgment goes to their colleagues Linda Chatters and Robert Taylor whose research in related domains of aging and human development contributed to the framework of the chapter.

# Preface

Since 1980 the Gerontology Institute of the University of Massachusetts at Boston has examined social and economic roles for older people. The institute's activities have been both academic and practical in nature. At times, they have been designed to provide an impartial research and scholarly understanding to a particular question. At other times, they have been focused on direct advocacy and change-oriented positions.

Our knowledge base emerges from many papers, studies, symposia, lectures, and discussions with others around the United States and from other industrialized nations. We have invested substantial state resources in an undergraduate and two certificate career-training programs for older people who wish to engage in service, policy, or administrative positions in gerontology. These programs have been highlighted by The Commonwealth Fund as among the most promising older-worker training programs in the nation. They have been spotlighted in numerous television and newspaper stories, both nationally and locally, including the American Association for Retired Persons' former television program *Modern Maturity*, the *Chicago Tribune*, the *Los Angeles Times*, and the *Boston Globe*.

At the Gerontology Institute, older people are not merely the subjects of our inquiries; they are active participants as students, staff, and volunteers. For example, our employment discrimination project funded by the Massachusetts Bar Association and the Executive Office of Elder Affairs was established by one of our certificate program graduates. Our perspectives have been significantly influenced by the direct participation of older people in our teaching, service, and research.

This volume follows two other edited books that have been supported by the Gerontology Institute. They are *Retirement Reconsidered* by Robert Morris and Scott A. Bass, which begins to question the institution of retirement; and *Diversity in Aging* by Scott A. Bass, Elizabeth Kutza, and

Fernando Torres-Gil, which examines the increasing heterogeneity of the older population and the need to shape policy reflective of the many different groups that compose the age cluster we call "the old."

In this book, we seek to go beyond our previous efforts and the writings of others—primarily in respect to retirement and the roles that most able-bodied elders play in later life. We discuss the need for some elders—not all—to find options for themselves beyond the traditional leisure activities and family obligations. In discussing alternatives, we look at the larger societal institutions and structures and the ways in which they support or inhibit productive roles for the elderly.

To assist the editors in preparing a collection of chapters around the theme of the impact of institutions on what is called *productive aging*, we convened a working conference in Boston in the summer of 1990. The conference was coordinated by Patrick O'Reilly, a research associate at the Gerontology Institute, who also prepared a literature review on the subject for the meeting. The final set of conference participants came from very different disciplines. Nearly all of the authors represented in this book attended the conference. They struggled with a number of issues reflecting both disciplinary differences and conceptual perspectives. For many of them—familiar with the literature about individual behavior prior to and after retirement—it was a challenge to consider the effects of institutional norms and sanctions on the range of options available to older people. Further, we had to work through definitional issues about the meaning of *productive aging*. Finally, we wrestled with the implications of the productive aging movement for special populations such as women, low-income elders, the frail, the disabled, and people of color.

Despite some remaining differences of opinion, our authors emerged from the Boston meeting with a set of assumptions and a framework for their individual chapters. Throughout the writing process, the editors sought to maintain the original purpose of the volume. This was not only an intellectual exercise but also one in which we tried to be responsive to the hundreds of older people who question the available roles for the aged and who are or have been a part of our activities at the University of Massachusetts at Boston.

Scott A. Bass

# Part I

## The Concept of Productive Aging

# 1

# Introduction: Achieving a Productive Aging Society

## Francis G. Caro, Scott A. Bass, and Yung-Ping Chen

This volume on productive aging builds upon the perspective that older people face a prolonged period in life in which they are relatively healthy and vigorous but lack a recognized role in the economic and social life of the society. Although elders, especially older women, are encouraged to provide support to their extended families, they too frequently are left without a significant role in late adulthood. This ambiguous status of retirement and explicit devaluation may last for a period as long as twenty or thirty years, which in some cases may be as long as a working career.

This book is intended to add to the growing literature that questions the appropriate range of role options available for able older people in a modern industrial society. Our unique contribution, we expect, is the examination of how the policies and practices of major societal institutions—such as education, family, mass media, religion, and work—influence the roles of older people.

A so-called productive aging perspective views older people as a major and valuable resource. In the United States and certain other nations, within this large and diverse group of older individuals, many are becoming increasingly dissatisfied with a life primarily structured around leisure. But even these people too frequently experience serious barriers as they seek significant societal roles.

Most older people are relatively healthy and robust well into their sixties and seventies, and in some cases beyond. Although, as a group, they tend to experience chronic ailments, they are capable of sustaining most of the intellectual and many of the physical activities in which they participated during their fifties.

Ongoing research supported by The Commonwealth Fund is measuring the extent to which older people in the United States are interested in participating in part-time and full-time work, career-related retraining, or meaningful volunteer activities. Initial findings indicate that, after traditional retirement, as many as 5.3 million older Americans are interested in some major roles other than leisure and family obligations (Taylor, Bass, & Hoeffler, 1992; McNaught, Barth, & Henderson, 1989). Although this number represents a relatively small percentage of the elderly, it also represents the potential for major social change.

We have asked contributors to this book to consider the more subtle and ingrained expectations that our major societal institutions have about the elderly. For the most part, the chapters in this book examine the powerful institutions in modern society, such as the family, employment, government, education, and religion. Because institutional forces may affect various populations of the elderly differently, we also commissioned chapters that look at productive aging from the standpoint of special populations, such as women and minorities.

## DEFINING PRODUCTIVE AGING

The term *productive aging* has emerged over the past decade as a rallying cry for elder advocates, policymakers, and academicians dissatisfied with the stereotype of older people as dependent and frail. During the 1970s and well into the early 1980s, it was common to attend major scientific meetings in gerontology and find that almost all of the papers presented concentrated on the problems of a relatively small percentage of the aged population; few were concerned with the experiences and problems of the vast majority of the relatively healthy and able aged. As an alternative to the view of the aged dominated by frailty and dependency, "productive aging," without a clear definition, served as a general unifying concept.

Evidence indicates that the desire to have older people play a more active role as they age actually emerged from older people themselves. For example, Elsie Frank, the seventy-nine-year-old president of the Massachusetts Association for Older Americans, stated in 1984:

Public policies should focus not only on the extension of life but on a healthy, vigorous, empowered, productive old age. Not allowing us to be involved in decisions deprives Americans of all ages of the contribution of many competent and creative persons who are capable of dealing with complex problems. Not allowing us to be involved deprives us of the right to control our destinies, and our lack of access to power results in social and economic discrimination and ofttimes leads to despair and hostility.

As Frank articulates so clearly, some older people feel wrongly excluded from the mainstream of society. By focusing on *productive* aging, elderly activists emphasize the large number of older people who can take an active and positive role in society. This is a powerful message of self-pride and collective value from elder activists, not unlike the aspirations historically attributed to the women's and civil rights movements.

For a growing number of gerontologists today, aging is no longer a corollary to disease. The shift to the exploration of human development and aging has been referred in the literature as "successful aging," "normative aging," or "productive aging." This more positive approach to the examination of aging seeks to identify the changes associated with aging and to maximize the human potential throughout the life course. At the center of the discussion is the fact that, in many activities, chronological age, up and into the advanced ages, is not necessarily a strong predictor of performance. Compelling evidence indicates that the aging process is highly individualistic, with enormous differences in the way various individuals age and in their subsequent performance in physical and mental activities. Some individuals in their seventies and eighties may be very active and produce their most significant contributions, while others in their fifties and sixties may be unable to function fully in society or may choose to withdraw from productive activity. Age as a sole predictor of performance is simply too crude a tool to reflect the actual capability of older people.

*Productive aging*, not unlike other terms such as *successful aging* or *normative aging*, has reflected an intellectual direction or theme that has attempted to attract individuals from many different perspectives. The goal has been to expand the ways in which both the general public and the scientific community approach the discussion of aging—to explore the potential of older people. As long as the term remained relatively flexible, it was a way for people to begin to develop a common language and a tie. And with two words it gave them the means to separate themselves from the common historical descriptions of the elderly.

A few early attempts were made to define the term *productive aging*, but for the most part, as it became more specific, disagreement surfaced. In 1979 (Panel to Review Productivity Statistics, 1979) and again in 1986, the National Research Council recommended that traditional economic analysis of market-oriented productivity be reformulated to incorporate productive activities that take place outside the economy (Committee on an Aging Society, 1986). Robert Butler and Herbert Gleason (1985) also recognized the definitional issue and the need to go beyond a restrictive economic use of the term *productive*, but they did not provide a working definition. In the edited volume *Our Aging Society*, Alan Pifer and Lydia Bronte (1986) base productivity "on accomplishment rather than a monetary compensation, and one that includes full- and part-time volunteer work as well as full- and part-time employment. What is important is that all of the employment can be *productive*—that is, that it contributes something significant to the economy or the quality of life." Robert Morris and Scott A. Bass in an essay in *The Gerontologist* (1986) discussed expanding current roles for older people to include activities that society needs at less than traditional market rates. Later they wrote in *Social Policy* (1988) of an emerging "new class" of able older people without societal function, struggling to find a purpose in modern society. Others (Kerschner & Butler, 1989; Moody, 1988; and Somers, 1988) have also used the term *productive aging* but have not defined it.

James Morgan, in his contribution to the 1986 National Research Council's report on productive aging, proposed a broad definition. Productivity, he stated, is "activities that produce goods and services that otherwise would have to be paid for" (Morgan, 1986). He suggested that productive use of time includes employment; commuting time; strike or unemployment time; time lost from work because of illness; and time spent on housework and child care, on volunteer work, in helping friends and relatives, on household maintenance, and in taking a course or lesson. Morgan also distinguished market transactions (paid labor) from productive effort with expectations of some reciprocal benefit, productive effort with direct benefits (e.g., home repairs), and productive effort with no expectation of a contract for something in return. In a subsequent article, Morgan (1988) reiterated that the definition of productivity should include anything that produces goods and services and that it should reduce the demand on goods or services produced by others. He identified three types of barriers that inhibit the productive activity of older people: (1) economic and legal, (2) social and organizational, and (3) environmental.

More recently, A. Regula Herzog (1989) has defined productive aging as "any activity that produces goods or services, whether paid or not, including activities such as housework, child care, volunteer work, and help to family and friends."

The major difference among the definitions is the range of activities they include. The broadest includes nearly all activities of older people. The most restrictive includes only paid employment and formal volunteer work.

A definition we prefer is the following: Productive aging is any activity by an older individual that produces goods or services, or develops the capacity to produce them, whether they are to be paid for or not. This definition builds on Herzog's by including only voluntary or paid service or goods produced but excluding activities of a personal enrichment nature. Our definition expands upon Herzog's to encompass activities that provide training or skills to enhance one's capacity to perform paid or volunteer work; it does not include education for personal growth as that would not directly contribute to enhanced skills for paid or volunteer labor.

While we acknowledge the many facets of productive aging, we particularly emphasize paid employment and volunteering because they are sectors in which older people experience significant barriers. In other sectors, productive involvement of older people is usually expected. The role of older people in providing long-term care to disabled spouses is a good example. As indicated by Pamela Doty and Baila Miller in Chapter 8 of this volume, healthy spouses of the disabled are *expected* to provide care to their partners. In fact, the public policy issue concerns how public intervention should complement that responsibility. In the case of employment, however, the issue is how to reverse skepticism about the capabilities of older people and even the loss of confidence of older people in their ability to be effective in the world of work. In the employment sector, the issue is also how to address a whole set of institutional forces that encourage early departure from the work force. In the case of volunteering, the question is how volunteer roles can be made significantly more attractive so that volunteering among older people will expand.

The definition we have selected sufficiently excludes many important and constructive activities undertaken by the elderly, such as worshiping, meditation, reflection, reminiscing, reading for pleasure, carrying on correspondence, visiting with family and friends, traveling, and so forth. It is not to say that these are not valuable activities and part of healthy and fulfilling aging experience, as discussed by W. Andrew Achenbaum in Chapter 10; they simply are outside the bounds of productive aging as we define it. Activities undertaken in our definition can be counted, aggregated, and assigned some economic value. Productive aging, therefore, is not for all older people, only for those who are interested, and that interest may vary at different times, ages, or even seasons. In our search for words that embody all that gives aging meaning, *productive aging* may be only one of several components.

As mentioned earlier, other terms such as *successful aging* and *normative aging* seek to present a more positive image of aging. Successful aging as introduced in 1987 by John W. Rowe and Robert L. Kahn in *Science* sought to examine those activities of a subset of the aging population who excel in the dimensions of physical and cognitive functional abilities and who are without the diseases or chronic disorders that traditionally are associated with aging. Rowe and Kahn's thesis is that the disorders associated with aging are highly variable and can be influenced by diet, exercise, personal habits, and psychosocial factors. In successful aging, the extrinsic factors can play a neutral or positive role in later life. Rather than discussing normal aging, Rowe and Kahn highlighted the capacity for a more enhanced aging experience (Rowe & Kahn, 1987).

Although *successful aging* and *productive aging* are representative of a wave of positive thinking about aging, the terms reflect very different perspectives about older people. In productive aging, the emphasis is on the role older people can play in society; in successful aging, the emphasis is on individual physiological and psychological capacity and performance.

Normative aging, not unlike successful aging, seeks to look at the typical and usual development and life experiences in later life. Normative aging usually takes a life course developmental approach, but it too is centered on the individual rather than the role the individual plays in society.

Using our definition, productive aging may not encompass all that is positive about aging, nor is it intended to be prescribed for all older people. At the same time, many scholars and advocates are struggling to find a new frame of reference for Peter Laslett's Third Age (1991)—the last third of life—that does not seek to mimic earlier life stages, that builds upon the strengths and perspectives of earlier stages, but that finds new meaning and purpose in its last stage. The goal of finding a new way of structuring the later years—of finding harmony, inner peace, social purpose, continuity, stature, and opportunity—unique to this period, is certainly beyond the scope of this volume.

We recognize that old age is not merely an extension of earlier life stages but a unique period of personal growth and exploration. The concept of productive aging is intended to expand current opportunities for older people; it is not meant to mandate them or to place an obligation on those who choose not to engage themselves this way.

## HISTORICAL ORIGINS

*Nonproductive* aging, as evidenced by retirement and an absence of a role in late life, is a relatively recent phenomenon in America. In other developed nations, it is a concept that dates back no earlier than the late nineteenth century. Prior to these times and dating back to antiquity, older people were engaged in some form of work until they were unable to continue with it. Throughout the centuries, the old were expected to work or to beg until they were simply too ill or enfeebled, leaving their care to the family, neighboring community, poorhouses, or no one (Axinn & Stern, 1988).

In fact, it might be argued that the contemporary productive aging movement was anticipated by nineteenth-century European utilitarians who promoted sanitary reforms. In several Belgian towns, the elderly poor were enlisted in collecting rubbish to repay part of the community expenditures on them. In one municipality, the elderly were even expected to provide their own wheel barrows unless they could not afford to buy them (Corbin, 1986).

By 1900, Simon Patten argued that there was a time approaching when all societal needs could be met with less and less labor. He hypothesized that, through productivity, technology, and efficiency, there would be a time of surplus labor, when working time would be reduced and leisure increased (Fox, 1967).

The first reported social security system came into being in the 1890s in Bismarck's Germany. By 1913, Australia, Belgium, Great Britain, Denmark, France, New Zealand, and Sweden also had public pension systems for the elderly. The United States was among the last of the industrial nations to institutionalize a national pension program to provide economic security to the elderly. Several western states began modest public pensions as early as 1914, and Montana, Nevada, and Pennsylvania passed voluntary pension laws in 1923. But prior to the establishment of Social Security in 1935, older people, for the most part, were expected to work or to seek shelter and care from almshouses, or they were cared for by their families. Early in the twentieth century, public provision for the income needs of the elderly was a relatively minor issue because the elderly constituted a much smaller percentage of the population than they do now (Achenbaum, 1986; Gerbner, 1980).

In the late nineteenth and early twentieth centuries in the United States, the nonworking elderly were not usually accorded favorable consideration. In fact, David Hackett Fisher (1977) notes that expressions of hostility toward the poor, nonworking elderly continued to grow during the nineteenth century. The opinion at the time was that there was enough work for all who could work. Those who could not placed a burden on the family and society. Little was available other than personal family charity for those who could not work, including the frail aged.

Within the first fifty years of Social Security, a relatively short time in history, all had changed. From a situation where the elderly had no option but to continue to work or be dependent on others, we arrived at a place where retirement had become an institution rather than a luxury (U.S. Senate, 1989). Most older Americans sixty-five and older no longer are in the work force. In 1990, only 14.1 percent of men and only 7.0 percent of women sixty-five and older were in the work force (U.S. Department of Labor, 1989). Despite the availability of Social Security, as recently as 1950, 45.8 percent of men sixty-five and older remained in the work force and 9.7 percent of older women worked outside the home (U.S. Senate, 1990).

Near-universal work for the aged has been replaced by near-universal retirement. The contrast and extremes remain stark. The contemporary pattern of nonparticipation of the elderly in the work force is particularly remarkable in light of the growth of the elderly population and the number of years older people now typically live in retirement. The fact that many elderly are able to live comfortably on the basis of pensions and savings is a reflection of the strength of the economy (Schulz, Borowski, & Crown, 1991). The ability of the U.S. economy to function adequately without the presence of most older people in the work force also is consistent with the assumptions that Patten advanced nearly 100 years ago. But will these assumptions hold true as we look to the economic future of America?

## APPROPRIATENESS OF THE PAST IN TODAY'S POLICY

To what extent is there a labor-supply abundance? Since the late 1960s the economy has absorbed large numbers of new women workers, and new supplies of labor for economic growth are limited as a result of the low birthrate of the 1970s and 1980s and recent restrictions on immigration (Schulz, Borowski, & Crown, 1991). If the nation faces modest economic growth, from where will labor support come? Older people are one nontraditional population to consider (McNaught, Barth, & Henderson, 1989). For the most part, they have good work habits and extensive on-the-job experience. With the older population increasingly in better health, could it not be an important economic resource to the nation (Bass & Barth, 1992)? Further, in light of the vast array of social needs and the declining public willingness to provide tax support for human service programs, could not interested older people be trained to fill certain important, but currently unmet, social needs, and if so, to what extent? We are not advocating that older volunteers replace paid workers, but we do believe that there are societal functions that may be performed by trained older volunteers or stipend workers.

Such a scenario for older people is not without its problems. There are family and societal expectations of the aged. And no equivalent of career counseling is available for those who leave their primary employment at age sixty or sixty-five and seek an alternative. Retirement is thought of as the terminal work experience; in fact, it may be a transitional one. Career planning for paid or volunteer roles after retirement is not yet common. Part-time or flexible work hours which many older workers want remain elusive and are considered unconventional. Training programs and higher educational opportunities are designed for younger people, with little thought to the needs of older workers seeking work past retirement. In many different institutions discussed in this volume, older people frequently are marginalized and moved aside in favor of youth. This volume discusses in some detail examples of barriers and problems older people face in exploring sustained productivity in later life.

## OBSTACLES TO PRODUCTIVE AGING

How is the limited participation of older people in paid work and volunteering to be explained? To what extent do older people prefer not to work and not to volunteer? To what extent are important opportunities for employment and volunteer work denied elders? Are elders tracked out of mainstream roles in subtle and discriminatory ways?

One hypothesis is that the limited participation of older people in paid work and volunteering is the result of "institutional ageism"—that societal institutions have structures, rewards, and sanctions that value certain cultural norms. These idealized and otherwise unspoken values and cultural traditions are inclusive of certain behaviors and groups and exclusive of others. Indeed, some individuals may overcome these barriers, but they are the exceptions rather than the rule.

The forces that exclude older people on bases other than merit are widespread. Some have been documented, such as age discrimination in employment. However, institutional ageism may be such a pervasive aspect of all major institutions in our society that we often do not recognize it. In fact, many older people themselves have internalized ageism. Too often they underestimate their own capabilities and accept the notion that older adults should leave productive roles at certain prescribed ages.

The major force at the root of institutional ageism may be the conflicting interests of the elderly and the nonelderly. Embedded in existing institutional arrangements may be management's desire to remove the elderly from attractive jobs and other positions of power and influence to facilitate greater access for younger people. Conflict theory suggests that such removal can be explained in part by economic competition between the nonelderly and elderly. It hypothesizes that pressure to exclude the elderly is affected by labor market conditions. During recessions, when jobs are scarce, pressure to remove the elderly is expected to increase. In periods of economic boom, when workers are in short supply, conflict theory predicts that older workers will be seen in a much more favorable light and the employment of older people is more likely to be actively encouraged.

Cultural lag is a second potential explanation for the limited participation of older people in attractive paid-work roles. The cultural-lag hypothesis differs from the conflict hypothesis on the basis of its assumptions about the underpinnings of institutional patterns. The cultural-lag hypothesis suggests that, as a society, we are slow to adjust our institutions in response to changing conditions. We may be slow, for example, in modifying our retirement policies moving from an era of labor oversupply to one of labor shortages. We may be slow in reorganizing our educational institutions to provide the lifelong training for work necessary in an economy characterized by sharper competition and rapid technological advances. Further, our society may take too long to recognize that people now have the potential for remaining productive later in life than in the past as a result of their improved health and of reduced physical demands in the workplace.

A third explanation, which might be called the defective-institutions hypothesis, is that employment and volunteer options are so badly flawed that people who can choose to depart from jobs as early as they can and generally avoid extensive volunteer commitments. A factor here is the quality of the work environment itself. In many fields, working people of all ages in this country complain about their work environments and compensation. Further, many of the volunteer assignments are unattractive, having unappealing tasks, insufficient challenges, or heavy demands, and training and support are inadequate.

A fourth explanation, which we will call the alternate preferences hypothesis, is that many older people organize their lives around alternatives to the work ethic. According to this hypothesis, many older people subscribe to values other than those that lead to employment and community service. They find personal expressive activities highly attractive and, when given a choice, are not interested in paid employment or volunteering options. According to this hypothesis, some advocates for productive aging may be overestimating the number of older people currently interested in access to work and volunteer roles.

A pilot study conducted by Ph.D. students at the Gerontology Institute at the University of Massachusetts at Boston provides some evidence of a link between attitudes of the nonelderly toward productivity among the elderly and their own *anticipated* behavior. A sample of 200 working people over forty years of age in the Boston area was surveyed. Anticipated age of retirement and anticipated volunteering after retirement were studied. Anticipated age of retirement was associated with a single attitudinal item: "People should continue to work as long as they are able." (Agreement with the item was associated with projection of "late" retirement; disagreement was associated with an expectation of "early" retirement.) Anticipated volunteering after retirement was *positively* associated with an attitude scale measuring "obligation to be productive." The scale included such items as "Retired people have an obligation to be involved in community activities." Anticipated volunteering after retirement was *negatively* associated with a scale measuring "right to leisure." The scale included such items as "Retired persons should be left alone to relax and do what they want to do" (Gerontology Institute, unpublished data).

Both the conflict and cultural-lag theories can provide explanations of the alternate-preferences hypothesis. Both of these theories would argue that alternate preferences are learned either through the popular culture or through direct experience with the negative aspects of work environments and volunteer opportunities. Both theories predict that older people would regard paid employment more favorably if work environments were made more attractive. Further, as a change strategy, the infusion into the society of more positive views about employment of older people might trigger increased public support for the employment of older people.

Because we suspect that both conflict theory and cultural-lag theory help explain current arrangements that discourage participation of older people in paid employment and meaningful volunteer work, we believe that both confrontation and public education are useful strategies for directed change. Political action may help break down discriminatory policies and practices and create improved employment options for the elderly. Public education also may be effective in encouraging older people to seek to remain active in both paid employment and volunteering, it may stimulate employers and voluntary organizations to be more creative in recognizing older people as resources, and it may lead educational institutions to develop attractive retraining programs.

Preferences among the elderly that cause them to focus their interests and activities on sectors other than paid employment and volunteering must be recognized. Our hypothesis is that, if work and volunteering are made more attractive as later-life options, many more older people would pursue them. How many more people actually would work or volunteer would then depend both on the attractiveness of work and volunteer options and the pull of competing alternatives.

Like any other reform movement, productive aging can have perverse effects on its intended beneficiaries. Our emphasis is on expanded *opportunities* for the elderly for paid employment and volunteering. Others may redirect this theme by calling for greater *obligations* for older people to work or volunteer. Martha Holstein in Chapter 13 develops this concern as an older women's issue and Harry R. Moody in Chapter 12 looks at it from a philosophical perspective. James S. Jackson, Toni C. Antonucci, and Rose C. Gibson, in Chapter 14, develop a life-course perspective of cultural, ethnic, and racial influences. At this point, we would not endorse blanket proposals to expand either work obligations or reduced pensions for the elderly premised on an extended work life. A great deal has to be accomplished in extending work opportunities before there is a sound basis for debating whether work obligations should be increased.

Similarly, we advocate improved volunteer opportunities for older people to address serious human needs that currently are not being met. But we do not regard elderly volunteers as substitutes for paid workers. If efforts to recruit and retain older volunteers were spectacularly successful in some sectors, some might conclude that fewer paid workers are needed in those fields. We prefer to wait until large, effective cadres of older volunteers actually threaten to displace paid workers and debate the specific issues on their merits.

## INSTITUTIONAL SECTORS

The central purpose of this volume is to examine the impact of major institutions in the United States on productive aging. To what extent do they encourage or discourage productive aging? Our premise is that they play a powerful role in setting the context in which older people make the kinds of choices we have just discussed.

### The Economy and Employment

The economy is important as a source of employment opportunities. Because employment is a major arena for productive activity, employment opportunities obviously are critical for older people who want to work. Older people are concerned not only with retention and hiring but also with promotions, demotions, and transfers.

In this context, age discrimination policies and practices are of real concern. To what extent do employers discriminate against older workers in retention and hiring? Do they have equal chances to be promoted? Are demotions and transfers systematically applied to older workers? What forms of discrimination occur most frequently? In what work settings are older workers most vulnerable to discrimination? What measures have been developed to combat age discrimination in the workplace? To what degree and under what circumstances are they effective?

A more fundamental issue is the degree to which the economy permits people to accumulate enough individual wealth so that voluntary departure from work is a viable option. Within the past fifty years the U.S. economy has generated sufficient wealth and distributed it widely enough so that income security is within reach for a majority of older people if they choose to stop working. There is, however, a significant minority that have not accumulated sufficient funds for retirement. In some sectors of the economy more than others, workers are able to accumulate savings and pension credits. Our economy also generates differential employment opportunities for various population groups. Historically, women and racial and ethnic minorities have fared less well in garnering jobs that provide a strong financial base for income security in old age. Some older people, therefore, find themselves under greater pressure to continue to work because of the economic sectors in which they have worked or because of their sex or race.

In Chapter 15, Karen C. Holden projects that future generations of older people will have less accumulated wealth than the younger elderly have today. The effect may be that older people will have to remain in the work force longer.

From a research perspective, useful questions can be raised about the characteristics of various industries, occupations, and work organizations and the degree to which they relate to income security for their workers in their old age. From a policy perspective, important questions can be raised concerning legislation to develop income security for individuals who spend most of their work lives in fields that historically do not permit the accumulation of significant savings or pension benefits.

As Joseph F. Quinn and Richard V. Burkhauser note in Chapter 3, pension programs have been found to be an important force in encouraging workers to leave their jobs. Jobs that are structured to provide older workers with reduced financial incentives for continued employment do precipitate departure from jobs. What, then, are the obstacles to restructuring private pension programs so that they encourage continued employment of older workers?

Higher insurance premiums for older workers are often cited as a reason why some employers prefer younger employees. Both health insurance premiums and worker compensation premiums are involved in these complaints. Under what circumstances are these costs significantly higher when the work force includes greater numbers of older workers? If this barrier to employment of older workers is real, how can it be reduced or removed?

The ways in which work organizations structure the relations among productivity, seniority, and compensation may have important effects on the willingness of employers to retain older workers. In principle, most employers probably prefer to link compensation to length of service, and since individual productivity is difficult to assess in many organizations, compensation is linked to seniority. The premise is that experienced workers are more productive than inexperienced workers. Particularly in many white-collar fields, the expectation is that compensation will increase with seniority, and only under exceptional conditions can employers reduce compensation. Because compensation moves up with seniority, employers eventually may develop the conviction that many of their senior staff are overpaid, an explanation for the emphasis by many employers on early retirement incentives. The relations among productivity, seniority, and compensation in work settings deserve careful research attention. Also of interest is the possibility that compensation packages that more sensitively reflect productivity may increase the interest of employers in older workers. In Chapter 6, W. Andrew Achenbaum and Malcolm H. Morrison discuss the possibility of retired people seeking to return to work through a process they term *unretirement*. Alan Walker and Philip Taylor provide, in Chapter 4, a specific analysis of the impact of labor market changes on older workers.

In our society, we are accustomed to hierarchical relationships linked to age. Some of the resistance to older workers reflects the culture of work organizations but more fundamentally the structure of age relationships in the larger culture. The basic pattern in work organizations is for those in positions of greater authority to be older than their subordinates. The older worker who reports to a younger supervisor challenges traditional expectations about the proper link between age and authority. Too often, neither supervisor nor subordinate may know how to handle the situation. Both may find themselves threatened, and the strain may lead to dissatisfactions that spur the departure of the older worker either from a given assignment or from the organization entirely.

Age is not the only dimension in which there are cultural expectations about authority relationships. Gender and race are dimensions in which there have been similar expectations. Social movements to provide women and minorities with equal employment opportunities have likely added to the distress of some workers in recent years when they have experienced age-authority reversals. For some older white males, for example, reporting to a younger supervisor may be even more difficult when that person is a woman, a minority-group member, or both.

In an increasingly complex and volatile economy and in a work force with greater mixing of younger and older workers, men and women, and minority and majority populations, authority imbalances can be expected to become more common. It is essential, therefore, that our work culture be modified to normalize what is now an anomaly.

Dwindling numbers of older people in the workplace also can be a significant problem for the older workers who remain. Positive interactions between coworkers for many are important nonmonetary reasons for working. But if good relationships with peers are important to workers and those relationships are built entirely on interaction with workers of similar age, older workers can experience significant loneliness when their age peers begin to retire.

Under favorable circumstances, older workers can develop positive relationships with younger peers in the workplace. Sometimes they can become informal mentors to younger workers. This mentor relationship can assist the younger worker to adjust to the workplace; it also can be a source of satisfaction to the older worker. These relationships also can have quasi-maternal and paternal qualities.

Caution in interpreting these mentoring relationships between older and younger workers is in order. In some cases, older workers can draw younger workers into negative aspects of the work culture. Older workers, for example, can be expected to attempt to teach younger workers quickly about the prevailing standards to limit output. Younger workers may not welcome the mentoring or parenting overtures of older workers. Similarly, some older workers may balk when younger workers look to them for mentoring or parenting.

Again in this arena, both basic and action research are needed. Studies are needed to provide a greater understanding of the importance of age relationships among peers in the workplace. Interventions accompanied by evaluation research are needed to find effective ways to modify work cultures both to make them more attractive to older workers and to draw more effectively on older workers in socializing younger workers.

To what extent can the restructuring of jobs lead to the extension of work life? Customarily, in this country, work in an organizational setting is an all-or-nothing matter. Workers typically move from full-time employment directly to total retirement. Yet frequently heard from those leaving full-time jobs is a preference to remain active but on a reduced basis. Some people prefer to continue with the same jobs on a part-time or intermittent basis. Others prefer to take on other assignments that either involve less pressure or provide different intrinsic rewards. For many years, pleas have been heard for the restructuring of jobs so that they will be more accommodating to people of all ages who prefer not to work full-time. In isolated instances, we have examples of programs that make effective use of retired or semiretired workers by making adjustments to their previous jobs. The Travelers Insurance Company, for example, has a successful program that draws in retired workers for a variety of temporary assignments. The retirees are willing workers; management is pleased not only with the quality of their work but also with the fact that they are less expensive than other sources of temporary help. The larger problem, however, is that significant restructuring of jobs to accommodate those unavailable on a full-time basis is so rare. Few major work organizations to date have been willing to introduce significant flexibility into the structuring of their positions on a large scale. Those that do make extensive use of part-time help to avoid hiring full-time workers, thus reducing opportunities for those seeking full-time employment. Compensation levels for part-time workers are typically subpar, and part-time workers enjoy no fringe benefits.

The substantial resistance of employers to restructuring suggests that careful research is needed on the obstacles—real or perceived—that employers face. In the instances in which organizations have restructured successfully to accommodate older workers, careful attention must be paid to the circumstances that made the organization receptive to restructuring. Such studies may provide the key to understanding the basis for achieving restructuring on a more widespread basis.

The potential for more extensive self-employment among older workers deserves attention. As indicated, those older workers who have left managerial or supervisory positions may find self-employment, such as consulting, more attractive than subordinate positions. They may be able to work part-time and work intermittently, for example. Not clear are the circumstances under which older people are able to find as much work as they would like when they are self-employed. Also uncertain is the extent to which older people find it attractive or even tolerable to do all of what self-employed people have to do, including such tasks as marketing, billing, accounting, and so on.

Of interest is the role that intermediary organizations can play in supporting self-employed older people. In the Boston area, for example, a number of cooperative organizations have emerged through which self-employed older people provide and obtain mutual support and aid concerning some of the matters just mentioned (McKibben, 1992).

In a volatile, more sharply competitive, and increasingly technical economy, workers have to expect to change jobs, and even fields, more often during their working lives than in other periods. (The likely effects of technology on employment opportunities for older people are discussed by David C. Mowery and Mark S. Kamlet in Chapter 5.) Even those who remain in jobs for extended periods now have to upgrade their skills regularly to keep pace; otherwise, at mid-life they may face the prospect of becoming technologically obsolete. Large and sophisticated work organizations now often make substantial investments in the upgrading of personnel. Not clear, however, is the extent of the willingness of these employers to invest in upgrading the skills of older workers per se. There is at least a risk that older workers are written off prematurely as unsuitable for retraining either because they are seen as lacking in that capacity or because such retraining is not seen as cost-effective. For the majority of people who are employed in small- and medium-sized organizations that lack the capacity for internal training, retraining takes on another dimension. Also of concern are sources of retraining for those who are changing fields. As part of collective-bargaining agreements, some large firms that close plants subsidize external retraining for workers. However, the vast majority of older workers who need retraining must pay for it without help from their employer.

Relatively little is known about the circumstances under which people over fifty are receptive to retraining. A recent Louis Harris survey conducted by The Commonwealth Fund (in Taylor, Bass, & Hoeffler, 1992) indicates greater interest than was previously thought to exist. Of particular importance are questions about the extent of older people's willingness to invest money and time in their own retraining. Anecdotal evidence suggests that older people have a strong preference for programs that are short and that make no more than modest financial demands. The extent to which older workers are able to combine retraining with current employment, volunteering, and personal obligations also is not clear. Even less is known about the willingness of older people to be retrained to become more effective as volunteers.

### The Family

The family is a major traditional arena of productive activity for older people. The role that families play in long-term care is well documented; a number of studies indicate that families are by far the major source of long-term care in this country (Doty, 1986; Horowitz, 1985). Spouses when present within families tend to be the primary providers of long-term care, so a great many older people can expect at some time to be the primary provider of such care for their partner. The younger elderly also often play a significant role in long-term care for their very old parents. In this volume, the Chapters 8 and 9 by Pamela Doty, Baila Miller, and Laura Katz Olson are concerned with the role of older people as providers of this kind of informal care.

Little attention by comparison has been given to the productive roles that older people play as grandparents and great-grandparents. In some cases, care is regular; in others, it is intermittent but nonetheless significant.

Within the productive aging movement, major emphasis has been on institutional sectors like employment in which older people have been denied opportunities, with focus on strategies that would expand opportunities. Access to opportunities to productive activity within the family has not been viewed as a problem. If anything, the emphasis has been on strategies that would relieve older people of extraordinarily heavy family responsibilities. Most significantly, in the long-term care arena, extensive caregiving has been seen as a potential serious burden on family providers, and some programs are explicitly designed to provide relief to them.

Families also can be important in supporting or discouraging productive activity outside the family setting. Anecdotal evidence exists about people who encourage their spouses to retire at the same time that they retire. These joint retirement decisions may be motivated by a plan to relocate to another area or to initiate extensive leisure travel. In these cases, family pressures may discourage productive activity.

Married couples can be supportive of their partners' efforts to remain productive. A steadily employed husband or wife, for example, can provide the income base that makes it possible for his or her partner to return to school for retraining or to make the transition to self-employment.

Adult children, through their indications of approval or disapproval, can encourage or discourage activities of their aging parents—for instance, by emphasizing the benefits of employment or volunteering or, similarly, by emphasizing health risks or deemphasizing the significance of such activities. Research is needed on the ways in which families support or discourage productive activity outside of the home. Such research should focus not only on the link between family and employment but also on the relations between family and such other areas as volunteering and education.

### Education

Educational organizations have made some efforts to reach older people but have done very little to assist them in preparing for productive roles in later life. As indicated by Harry R. Moody in Chapter 12, most of the emphasis in educational programs for older people is on enrichment or on practical personal assistance in such areas as health and finances. Educational programs for older people have emphasized that this group is *retired*. People in their fifties for whom retraining for employment is highly pertinent have received very little attention (U.S. Department of Education, 1990). Community colleges appear to be well suited to provide extensive retraining of older workers for a number of reasons, as follows: (1) the vast majority of the population in this country is within commuting distance of a community college, (2) these institutions can offer programs at substantially lower cost than four-year institutions, (3) they have shown that they can be flexible in program design, (4) many work closely with local employers and in some cases design programs explicitly for them, and (5) they have extensive experience in working with nontraditional, or older, students. The major problems concern how such institutions can be persuaded to change their perspectives to make the needs of older learners a priority and how they can acquire the development resources to enable them to mount viable retraining programs for older workers (Caro & Morris, 1991).

Much less well understood than these institutions are our less formal vehicles for education. In the professional world, conferences and workshops are a means for disseminating new information, a kind of retraining. In some professions they are sufficiently structured so that credit is given for participation. Certain professionals must acquire credits on a regular basis to retain their licenses. Relatively little is known about the aggregate impact of these forms of retraining, particularly their role in upgrading the skills of older workers.

Journals, books, manuals, and newsletters disseminate material meant to upgrade the skills of older workers. Cumulatively, these are major vehicles for conveying information to people outside of institutions of higher education. How much they actually contribute is uncertain. Formal educational programs are well-established vehicles for assisting students in mastering a complex, new body of knowledge. In some cases, older workers can benefit greatly from specific, well-designed programs to acquire a new set of skills. Sometimes, however, they need only to fine-tune their skills, and less formal educational strategies may be sufficient. Much more needs to be known about the extent to which our less formal educational strategies are adequate for the retraining of older workers and how they can be revised to be more effective (Eurich, 1990).

### Volunteerism

The United States has a long tradition of volunteerism. From its early days, civic life has relied extensively on volunteers. U.S. social services began on a strictly volunteer basis, and even though they have been extensively professionalized, the role of volunteers remains of great importance. With recent declines in the availability of public funds for human services, volunteerism has taken on renewed importance.

Older people potentially are of enormous importance as volunteers (Fischer, Mueller, & Cooper, 1991). With the extension of life, the improvement of general health among the young elderly, and the trend toward early retirement, the healthy nonworking elderly represent an enormous pool that could be making major contributions as volunteers.

As A. Regula Herzog and James N. Morgan indicate in Chapter 7, volunteering among the elderly is significant but hardly developed to its full potential. Most research attention has been on the characteristics of individuals that predict volunteering. We know, for example, that older people who have higher levels of education and who volunteered earlier in their lives are more likely to volunteer in old age (Marriott, 1991). Much less is known about how the opportunities for volunteering affect the extent of volunteering among the elderly. An informal study in the Boston area revealed that service organizations vary greatly in the manner in which they are organized to work with older volunteers in terms of the range of assignments they offer, the training and supervision they provide, the recognition they confer, and the degree to which they extend individualized assistance in placing older people in assignments (McKibben, 1992). Volunteer clearinghouses also are an important part of the volunteer scene, but the assistance they provide is highly uneven. Some argue that older people would volunteer more if volunteer assignments were more meaningful and challenging. With support from The Commonwealth Fund, the Gerontology Institute at the University of Massachusetts at Boston is conducting a study of older people to determine how the structure of volunteer opportunities affects their willingness to volunteer (Caro & Bass, 1991). Additional research is needed in this area. Particularly needed are experimental efforts to make volunteer assignments more attractive with the expectation of increasing participation by older people.

### Religion

Although religious organizations are highly important for vast numbers of older people, the overall implications of religion for productive aging are uncertain. Organized religion has little to say about questions surrounding the employment of older people. Religious groups do tend to support some forms of productive activity of older people, and they tend to be strongly linked both to concerns about family and health. Traditional religious values place heavy emphasis on loyalty to family and care of the sick and, therefore, tend to be highly supportive of the role of older people in providing long-term care to family members.

As indicated by W. Andrew Achenbaum in Chapter 10 of this book, religion is strongly linked to voluntarism. Many churches promote volunteering as an important form of good work. Churches, themselves, rely extensively on volunteers; according to the recent Marriott survey of older volunteers, older people volunteer more often for churches and other religious organizations than they do for any other sector (Marriott, 1991). Some religious denominations place particular value on certain older volunteers; in certain Protestant denominations, those in the lay policymaking body are actually known as "elders." However, the extent to which churches are truly responsive to the interests and energies of potential older volunteers is largely unknown.

Productive activity among older clergy is another dimension of the link between religion and productive aging. Under what circumstances do religious groups encourage older clergy to remain active? What options do religious groups provide for partial retirement? An example of a constructive response by a religious group to these issues is a long-standing arrangement through which the Catholic archdiocese in Boston regularly sends older clergy to the Manning Gerontology Certificate program at the University of Massachusetts at Boston. Participation in the program stimulates clergy to take on a variety of new productive roles in gerontology. How widespread are such arrangements? How can they be replicated?

## Mass Media

Dissemination of information and ideas through the mass media is an important aspect of contemporary American life. Much of our lives is structured around watching television, reading newspapers, and listening to the radio. The mass media can do a great deal to shape the way we think. George Gerbner in Chapter 11 argues that television tends to reinforce traditional, simplistic negative ideas about older people.

What role can the mass media play in restructuring our thinking about the productive potential of older people? How effective in shaping public opinion are well-publicized stories about the positive experiences of work organizations with older workers or of service organizations with older volunteers?

At a more mundane level, the mass media can play an important role in simply transmitting information about the availability of opportunities for older people. In the Boston area, for example, listings of volunteer opportunities in a column for seniors in the *Boston Globe* help recruit necessary volunteers for some organizations. Newspapers are an important vehicle for recruiting older people to the Center for Creative Retirement at the University of North Carolina in Asheville and the University of Massachusetts at Boston's Manning Gerontology Certificate program. A better understanding is needed of the role of various specialized media in transmitting information to older people about opportunities for active participation in contemporary life.

## Government

The public sector has an enormous presence in contemporary societies. Through its interactions with every other sector, government can influence nearly every aspect of productive aging—for example, by prohibiting age discrimination in employment through legislation, by subsidizing retraining, by creating public-service jobs that would include older people, and by funding or operating job-placement services. Government also influences employment of older people through the financing of workers' compensation programs, through the regulation of private pension programs, through the provision of disability benefits, and through its involvement with health insurance. The adequacy of public income-security benefits also affects whether or not older people need to work.

Governmental policies that encourage or discourage continued productive participation by older workers are of major importance because of the vast numbers of people they employ. Local governments rely extensively on volunteers. Not known is the extent to which they rely on older volunteers for assistance, ranging from participation on policymaking bodies to assistance with basic public services. Volunteer fire departments use younger people for fire fighting, for example, but many local libraries count heavily on older people. Local senior centers could not operate without extensive help from them.

The federal government actively promotes volunteering by older people by supporting programs such as the Retired Senior Volunteer Program (RSVP) and the Foster Grandparents program. RSVP not only serves as a broker for volunteer assignments for older people but also subsidizes travel and insurance costs.

Government indirectly affects the forms and intensity of care provided by older informal caregivers through its funding of long-term care services as well as through regulations that determine access. Publicly financed programs take pressure off older informal caregivers. Publicly funded services do not lead to the withdrawal of participation of older informal caregivers, but they lower the demands such caregivers experience. Similarly, public policy concerning various human services can affect the expectations placed on older people to provide help to family members in a variety of sectors. The extent of public funding for child care, for example, affects the expectations placed on grandparents to provide child care. Although the exact relationship between the two is unknown, we can assume that when public funding for child care for low-income families is less available, grandparents will be asked more often to provide child care. These examples are only suggestive of the wide-ranging effects that government policies can have on productive aging.

## CONCLUSION

This book attempts to reflect upon a set of societal changes as they are occurring. A demand for more productive opportunities for certain segments of the older population is growing as we write about it. We all know how difficult it is to describe and understand social change while it is taking place. Only time will tell whether the efforts being made toward expanded opportunities for productive aging will be peripheral to the mainstream of society or whether they will be fundamental. We believe that major changes will take place over the next fifty years regarding the productive roles and functions of older people in this country. To accommodate these roles, powerful institutions must adapt or they will meet resistance.

## REFERENCES

Achenbaum, W. A. (1986). *Social security: Visions and revisions.* New York: Cambridge University Press.

Axinn, J., & Stern, M. J. (1988). *Dependency and poverty: Old problems in a new world.* Lexington, MA: Lexington Books.

Bass, S. A., & Barth, M. (1992). *The next educational opportunity: Career training for older adults*. Draft for the Commonwealth Fund. New York: The Commonwealth Fund.

Butler, R., & Gleason, H. (Eds.). (1985). *Productive aging: Enhancing vitality in later life*. New York: Springer.

Caro, F., & Bass, S. (1991). *Effective structuring of volunteer roles for the elderly*. Paper presented at the Gerontological Society of the American Annual Scientific Meeting, Boston, MA.

Caro, F., & Morris, R. (1991). *Older worker retraining: An important new direction for higher education*. Boston: Gerontology Institute, University of Massachusetts at Boston.

Committee on an Aging Society. (1986). *Productive roles in an aging society*. Washington, DC: National Academic Press.

Corbin, A. (1986). *The foul and the fragrant: Odor and the French social imagination*. Cambridge, MA: Harvard University Press.

Doty, P. (1986). Family care of the elderly: The role of public policy. *Milbank Quarterly, 64*(1), 34–75.

Eurich, N. P. (1990). *The learning industry: Education for adult workers*. Princeton, NJ: Carnegie Foundation for the Advancement of Teaching.

Fischer, L., Mueller, D. P., & Cooper, P. W. (1991). Older volunteers: A discussion of the Minnesota Senior Study. *The Gerontologist, 31*, 183–194.

Fisher, D. H. (1977). *Growing old in America*. New York: Oxford University Press.

Fox, D. (1967). *The discovery of abundance*. Ithaca, NY: Cornell University Press.

Frank, E. (1984). *Do public policies empower the elderly? An elder citizen perspective*. Speech delivered at the Massachusetts Gerontology Association and Villers Foundation conference, Weston, MA. Boston: The Gerontology Institute, University of Massachusetts, Boston.

Gerbner, G., Gross, L., Signorelli, N., & Morgan, M. (1980). Aging with television: Images on television drama and conception of social reality. *Journal of Communication, 30*(2), 37–47.

Herzog, A. R. (1989). Age differences in productive activity. *Journal of Gerontology: Social Sciences, 44*, S129–S138.

Horowitz, A. (1985). Family caregiving to the frail elderly. In C. Eisdorfer, M. P. Lawton, & G. Maddox (Eds.), *Annual review of geriatrics and gerontology*. New York: Springer.

Kerschner, H., & Butler, F. (1989). Productive aging and senior volunteerism: Is the U.S. experience relevant? *Aging International, 15*, 15–19.

Laslett, P. (1991). *A fresh map of life: The emergence of the third age*. Cambridge, MA: Harvard University Press.

McKibben, M. (1992). *Opportunities for older people: Volunteer work and employment resources*. Boston: Gerontology Institute, University of Massachusetts at Boston.

McNaught, W., Barth, M., & Henderson, P. (1989, Winter). The human resource potential of Americans over 50. *Human Resources Management, 28*(4), 455–473.

Marriott Senior Living Services. (1991). *Marriott senior volunteerism study*. Washington, DC: Marriott Senior Living Services.

Moody, H. R. (1988). *Abundance of life: Human development policies for an aging society*. New York: Columbia University Press.

Morgan, J. (1986). Unpaid productive activity over the life course. In Committee on an Aging Society (Ed.), *Productive roles in an older society.* Washington, DC: National Academy Press.

Morgan, J. (1988). The relationship of housing and living arrangements to the productivity of older people. In Committee on an Aging Society, *The social and built environment in an older society* (250–280). Washington, DC: National Academic Press.

Morris, R., & Bass, S. A. (1986). The elderly as surplus people: Is there a role for higher education? *The Gerontologist, 26,* 12–18.

Morris, R., & Bass, S. A. (1988, Spring). A new class in America: A revisionist view of retirement. *Social Policy,* 38–43.

Panel to Review Productivity Statistics. Committee on National Statistics, Assembly of Behavioral and Social Sciences, National Research Council (1979). *Measurement and interpretation of productivity.* Washington, DC: National Academic Press.

Pifer, A., & Bronte, L. (Eds.). (1986). *Our aging society: Paradox and promise.* New York: Norton.

Rowe, J.R., & Kahn, R.L. (1987). Human aging: Usual and successful. *Science, 237,* 143–149.

Schulz, J., Borowski, A., & Crown, W. H. (1991). *Economics of population aging.* New York: Auburn House.

Somers, A. (1988). Aging in the 21st century: Projections, personal preferences, public policies—A consumer view. *Health Policy, 9,* 49–58.

Taylor, H., Bass, R., & Hoeffler, L. (1992). *Productive aging: A survey of Americans age 55 and over.* Study by Louis Harris and Associates for The Commonwealth Fund. New York: Louis Harris and Associates.

U.S. Department of Labor, Bureau of Labor Statistics. (1989). *Handbook of labor statistics.* Washington, DC: U.S. Government Printing Office.

U.S. Department of Education, Center for Education Statistics. (1990). *Digest of aging statistics* (Table 161). Washington, DC: U.S. Government Printing Office.

U.S. Senate, Special Committee on Aging. (1990). *Aging America.* Washington, DC: U.S. Government Printing Office.

# 2

# Age, Productivity, and Transcendence

## Harry R. Moody

### THE IMPERATIVE OF PRODUCTIVITY

"What is honored in a country is cultivated there." In America in the 1990s, no ideal is more widely honored than "productivity." The signs are all around us, and the opinion leaders have spoken. Articles in the *Harvard Business Review* or the *New York Times* warn us that falling productivity will mean future economic downfall for America. Politicians take up the cry that Japan and Germany are overtaking the United States. Pundits across the political spectrum nod their heads and shake their fingers at the hangover of debt and greed now associated with the decade of the 1980s, in much the same spirit that other critics once lamented the excesses of the 1960s. The answer to our problems? Productivity, of course. Now that the Soviets are vanquished, it is only lagging productivity that can prevent us from again being "Number One."

What is more natural in this mood than to imagine that the problems of an aging society also can be vanquished by—what else?—"productive aging." The problem is, first, to define the term and, second, to ask some questions about what "productive aging" really might imply for aging policy and aging society. Only after this philosophical appraisal can we make progress in thinking about specific proposals or programs on behalf of productive aging. What I want to do here is to offer a historical reconstruction and then a philosophical critique of the idea of productive aging so that we can appreciate what is gained, and what is lost, by adopting it as a regulative ideal for later life and as a framework for public policy.

### POST-INDUSTRIAL GERONTOLOGY

We can begin this discussion by locating the problem of productive aging in a specific historical and sociological framework. The framework adopted here is drawn from the categories of "postindustrial society" originally developed by Daniel Bell (1974). Bell notes that modern societies can be described according to a demarcation between three separate spheres—economy, polity, and culture—each dominated by three distinctive values: efficiency, equality, and individual autonomy. In the economic sphere, the driving force is efficiency in maximizing profits, while in politics it is the imperative of equality that holds sway. In the cultural domain, it is maximal freedom—a multiplicity of options—that is the dominant ideal. In Bell's terms, these constitute the "axial values" of modernity.[1]

Table 2.1 sets forth some of the ways in which these three separate spheres give rise to characteristic roles which can be analyzed for their relevance to productive aging. In each instance, there are subcategories and, for each subcategory, distinctive roles that are either "active" or "subsidiary." In each instance, the "active" role is the one that would be emphasized by a philosophy of productive aging, while the "subsidiary" role is the position where older people are cast in a more passive stance: as recipients of services, as objects of manipulation or social control, and in the worst instance as victims and people unable to contribute to the wider society around them.

The difficult problem facing advocates of productive aging is that, in all instances, the active roles here are very poorly structured or integrated, while the subsidiary roles are the object of extensive planning and social control. To understand this point, let us look at the three domains in detail.

### The Economy

The importance of distinctions among axial values can be seen most clearly by looking first at the economic sphere, where the idea of productive aging takes its origin and basic vocabulary. In capitalist societies, the economy is dominated by the marketplace. From the standpoint of the labor market, in advanced industrial societies the distinctive role for older people is not work but retirement, a period when direct economic productivity comes to an end. To the extent that retired people are "unproductive," within the exchange economy they become relegated to the status of consumers of goods and services. Their buying power is supported by savings, by transfer payments, or other subsidized claims on productive members of society. In this subsidiary status the elderly are still of interest to the powers that be. Even in their unproductive status, the elderly become part of a vast "gray market," attracting increasingly greater interest from advertisers and merchandisers.

A postindustrial economy is increasingly an economy dominated by the service sector. As the population ages, many of those services are rendered to the aged, often outside the competitive marketplace in what we call the "human services" sector. In the sector of human services, the position of old age appears distinctly unproductive. Here older people are cast often

Table 2.1
Characteristic Roles in Modern Society

|  |  | ACTIVE | SUBSIDIARY |
|---|---|---|---|
| ECONOMY | Market | Worker | Consumer |
|  | Human Services | Self-Help/ Volunteer | Patient/ Client |
| POLITY | Participation | Citizen | Voter |
|  | Motivation | Steward for Future Generations | Interest-Group Member |
| CULTURE | Self-Cultivation | Creative Artist | Lifelong Learner |
|  | Spirituality | Spiritual Seeker | Church Member |

in the role of the "ill-derly," either as geriatric patients or as clients for gerontological services (Estes, 1979).

Such services are increasingly managed (e.g., "case management") and fall under the control of vast economic machines (the "medical-industrial complex") that have an interest in perpetuating the "sick role" of old people but have little interest in encouraging preventive health care, health promotion, or other forms of self-help. Within the health and social service system, professionals retain control, but volunteerism also has a role as a kind of nonmonetized labor supply, just as mutual self-help serves as a nonmonetized exchange structure to complement the formal service system in ways documented by gerontologists. The fate of old age under professional hegemony in the welfare state is aptly summed up by Habermas's phrase describing the "colonization of the life world" (Habermas, 1984; see also Ingram, 1990).

The point of this analysis is not to repeat familiar observations about older consumers or geriatric medicine but simply to group this whole domain under the economic sphere and to recognize that, by and large, the coming of an aging society in advanced industrial societies has been accompanied by an enlargement of the passive or subsidiary role of older people—as consumers, patients, clients, and so on. This point has been documented by political economy critics of mainstream gerontology. Mainstream gerontology is still overwhelmingly dominated by what Richard Kalish (1979) called the "failure model" of old age. In terms of the analysis offered here, the failure model can be described succinctly as an ideological framework that underwrites professional hegemony. By contrast, moving toward a framework of productive aging would enable older people to take on more active roles (employment, mutual self-help), a move which not only would improve the status and meaning of old age but also would make better use of the vast human resources represented by the growing older population (Moody, 1988).

### The Polity

Let us move now to the second sphere demarcated by Bell—namely, the political sphere. Here again one can distinguish two ideal types of political participation, passive and active, or, roughly speaking, the voter and the citizen. As a purely formal requirement of a democratic society, free elections require the role of the voter. But even in ostensibly free societies the electorate can be notoriously ill-informed, passive, and subject to mystification through mass media. Just such a trend seems to have become pronounced in the United States over the past two decades, as shown by declining voting rates and a general deterioration in the level of public dialogue in elections.

How does political participation relate to productive aging? Interestingly enough, senior citizens, as a group, retain the highest percentage of voting participation and their political involvement remains at high levels (Day, 1990). A high level of political involvement or voting participation, however, is not by itself tantamount to contribution to the wider society, such as we might imagine under one definition of productive aging. Here we can appreciate the contrast between the roles of voter and citizen. The citizen, as opposed to the relatively passive voter, is one who takes a deep and abiding interest in the common good. The difference here is not defined by level of activity per se but by motivation, the second subcategory identified above. Some political participation is motivated by a desire for a better society, some by self-interest. It seems reasonable to think of this broader, altruistic motivation as a form of social productivity and, therefore, as one ingredient of productive aging. We might imagine that older people, as citizens, could have, and do have, an interest in the ongoing well-being of society, of old and young, both today and tomorrow. This ideal is summarized here under the label of "stewardship for future generations." By contrast, much of the politics of old age is based on a picture of older voters simply as one more interest group motivated exclusively by matters such as Social Security benefits—in short, by self-interest.

Viewed in these terms, old age politics can be thought of as an opposition between the "politics of entitlement" and the "politics of productivity" (Moody, 1990). This dichotomy may be oversimplified, but it underscores the extent to which conventional interest-group politics has tended to exclude any attention to the real issues of productive aging. Still worse, to the extent that interest groups representing the elderly have succeeded in protecting age-based entitlements, it is perhaps understandable that some backlash has occurred under the framework of "generational equity" (Longman, 1987). As long as older people are thought of as inherently "unproductive," conventional analysis will tend to relegate the politics of aging to the specter of a "gray lobby" devouring an ever-increasing share of the federal budget— hardly a positive image of the future (Torres-Gil, 1992).

### Culture

Last, we turn to the cultural sphere where again we can distinguish between active and subsidiary roles for older people. One of the most important cultural ideals today is self-cultivation, the ideal of the self open to continued growth and development over the full span of life. Corresponding to that ideal is the emerging role of the lifelong learner, whether tied to the higher education system (e.g., Elderhostel) or to many new opportunities for lifelong learning available through travel or, indirectly, through the media of an information society.

The problem with late-life learning in an information society is that the nature of commodified information—purveyed through television, for example—tends to be inhospitable to the accumulated experience of old age. When media set the terms for cultural productivity, the old almost always will be at a disadvantage. Insofar as an ideal of self-cultivation or self-development is defined and controlled by the dominant values of modern society, the life experience of the old will be devalued in favor of novelty. Under such circumstances, lifelong learning becomes less of an opportunity and more of an obligation, lest older people be "left out" by changes in contemporary culture or technology. Even when committed to lifelong learning as a cultural ideal, the old person ultimately is passive in the face of an environment where obsolescence is the watchword for all activities in the cultural sphere.

Potentially different is the more active ideal represented by the creative artist. Here, one of the most striking examples of productive aging is provided by the case of artists who have remained fully creative far into the later years, even when their physical vigor has been impaired. Among the old masters, we can find examples such as Michelangelo, Titian, and Rembrandt. Among contemporary artists, we can point to figures such as Picasso, Matisse, Louise Nevelson, and Georgia O'Keeffe. A pitfall for contemporary artists remains the seductive power of the art market to define aesthetic values in terms of novelty. But precisely here, the four modern artists cited are instances of creative people who maintained the integrity of their own style into advanced age, continuing to develop but not succumbing to fashion or the lure of novelty for its own sake. Instead of becoming culturally obsolescent, they became heroic models of what productive aging might mean, with implications far beyond the sphere of art.

The difference between lifelong learning and late-life creativity is the difference between a fundamentally passive and a fundamentally self-generative approach to culture. Nor is the late-life creativity of a Rembrandt or a Nevelson of significance only for the most gifted persons or artists alone. This point was made by the great art critic Ananda Coomaraswamy when he remarked that it is not that the artist is a special kind of man but that each man is a special kind of artist. The aim of this contrast, of course, is not to celebrate art over adult education. Both remain valid and important vehicles for self-development in late life.

But in the sphere of culture, as of the economy and the polity, we need to recognize that not all roles in old age involve opportunities for comparable levels of productivity. Some artists, like Picasso, in their later years, maintained "productivity" in a quantitative fashion, multiplying the amount they produced even if the quality was uncertain (Schiff, 1983). Others—Matisse is the great example here—coped with undeniable physical frailty by shifting to a qualitatively different kind of artistic productivity (Wheeler, 1961). The difference between quantitative and qualitative shifts in late-life productivity suggests analogies for creative or productive roles for the old in other occupations and modes of activity.

The same kind of distinction can be found in the last subcategory—spirituality. Much of the sociological literature on religion and old age has tended to trivialize the subject by focusing on purely behavioral or attitudinal measures adopted by mainstream social science methodology. This methodological approach goes hand in hand with a view of late-life spirituality that measures productive aging by items such as voluntarism, church membership statistics, or participation in religious activities. These forms of measurement are congenial to the behavioral and quantitative outlook of the social sciences. But they tend to diminish and misunderstand what late life spirituality is all about—qualitative growth of selfhood in the face of death and finitude. Further, all such behavioral forms of activity or participation tend to perpetuate the fundamentally passive role of the churchgoer rather than the spiritual seeker.

An alternative view of religion and aging is offered by the mystical and spiritual traditions of both the East and the West. In traditional Hinduism, for example, later life is understood as a period of responsible detachment ("disengagement") from previous roles in favor of meditation on ultimate or transcendent matters (Kakar, 1968). In the spiritual traditions of the West, too, it is not unusual for mid-life or later life to involve a turning inward as people confront questions about the meaning of their lives (O'Conner, 1978; Fowler, 1981). In the narratives of the founders of great religions, such as Jesus or Buddha, we find the archetypal story of the spiritual seeker who is dissatisfied with conventional answers and goes forth on the spiritual journey.

This process of searching for a transcendent source of meaning seems the opposite of productive aging as we ordinarily describe it. Aren't contemplation and activity opposing positions? Yet the statement in the Tao Te Ching concerning the Perfect Man (the Saint) also remains true: "The Perfect Man (Ruler) does not act. Yet nothing remains undone." To take up the role of the spiritual seeker in later life demands a passionate commitment to make each moment of remaining life as "productive" as possible. But, again, such productivity represents more an inner stance toward the universe: the attitude of one who is detached and engaged at one and the same time.

## AXIAL VALUES OF MODERNITY

Having outlined the significance of the three spheres for productive aging, let us consider how the basic or axial values of modern society can be understood with respect to old age itself. In each case, as we shall see, the axial values of autonomy, equality, and efficiency constitute a two-edged sword. They can serve to diminish or to enhance the value we place on old age and the possibilities that we can imagine for what "productive aging" might mean.

Consider the cultural sphere first, which is dominated, argues Bell (1974), by a fundamentally antinomian value: individual autonomy or removal of all cultural restraints. Insofar as this axial value of autonomy entails a repudiation of tradition and community, it reinforces the culture of the individual, which in old age is so hard to bear (Lasch, 1985).[2] Yet there is another side to "individualism," disclosed by the spiritual idea of detachment. The ideal of autonomy corresponds to a measure of disengagement from dominant social norms, and it corresponds to what Carl Jung described as the fundamental dynamic of late-life development: the drive for individuation and spiritual wholeness (Chinen, 1990; also see Chinen, 1985). The task of finding a proper balance between the claims of tradition and individuality at every stage of life is a challenge for advanced societies at the close of the twentieth century.

What of the political sphere? Once again, the ideal of equality becomes a distinctly two-edged sword, conferring and taking away benefits at the same time. Insofar as the axial value of equality means that all stages of life are strictly equal in their moral status, then equality denies any superior wisdom to old age and perhaps denies any sense that the stages of life represent something more than a mere succession of different values. Old age, the last stage of life, is simply "more of the same." In the political struggle, the elderly may become just one more "interest group." Here, we confront the dilemma of a liberal politics of aging, committed at one and the same time to age-based entitlements (social insurance) and universalist social welfare ideals.[3] To the extent that the value of equality means that all age groups, and even all historical cohorts, are to be given equal consideration and fair treatment, then equality could become a motivating value for an ecological sense of stewardship on the part of elders who can protect and preserve natural and cultural heritage for future generations. If the old merely follow the dictates of "interest-group liberalism," then they may be easily caricatured as "greedy geezers," however unfair this may seem to advocates for the elderly. But if the motivation for participation in politics extends concern to other age groups and other cohorts, then the politics of aging could become the basis for a renewal of the liberal ideal beyond equality and toward intergenerational solidarity.[4]

Finally, we come to the economic sphere, which is the origin of the idea of productivity as an influential ideal. Insofar as the value of efficiency grades human beings according to productive power or contribution to collective material welfare, the old will fall short and will tend to feel useless, uneasy in any prosperity or benefits gained, and vulnerable in times of cutbacks. Here, then, lies the problem. By insisting on the productivity of the old, we put the last stage of life at the same level as the other stages. This transposition implicitly sets up a kind of competition or struggle (who can be the most productive?) which the old are doomed to lose as frailty increases. By celebrating efficiency, productivity or power, we subordinate any moral claim for the last stage of life in favor of values that ultimately depreciate the meaning of old age.[5] Productivity, in its essence, is simply an instrumental value, an augmentation of human power to accomplish unnamed purposes. We can then imagine no other role beyond the struggle or will to power celebrated by Nietzsche, who understood this drive to be the secret subterranean force behind the modern world.

But the dialectic here must have its answer. And the countervailing view—

in favor of productivity and of productive aging—also has its claim, and there lies the paradox of productive aging. In a social world that increasingly prizes only instrumental values, productive aging represents a vindication of the continued vitality and social contribution of older people. Without any hope of productivity, we too often consign the old to the status of bystanders, victims, dependents, or recipients of transfer payments. Hence we find the need to affirm the validity of productive aging as a regulative ideal but, at the same time, to critique the ideal by exposing its limitations.

In this brief discussion, we have looked at some alternative "active" roles for later life. But can these alternative roles be collapsed into a single category called "productive aging"? These roles are inspired by values such as altruism, citizenship, stewardship, creativity, and the search for meaning or salvation. All of them do have something important in common—they are different ways of "outliving the self" (Kotre, 1984). They are answers to what Peck described as the basic psychological dichotomy of old age: ego preoccupation versus ego transcendence (Peck, 1968). In short, these ideals all represent varieties of transcendence that offer themselves as regulative ideals, goals that make life worth living at whatever age.

Can we describe productivity that way, too? In a certain way we can. It was Baudelaire who remarked that "work is less boring than pleasure." It remains true that for many high-achieving individuals in our society work is the ultimate addiction. For those individuals, retirement can seem only a horrible fate, no matter how pleasurable (and thus boring) its enticements. The point is that for those passionately attached to their work continued productivity in later life also represents a legitimate form of transcendence. For high-performing individuals in that category, such as chief executive officers of large corporations, the hour of departure from power can constitute a kind of social death, a phenomenon that can be described as the late-life "King Lear" complex, analogous to the Oedipus complex of early childhood (Sonnenfeld, 1988).

Old age today holds no interest for dominant elites in the most productive sectors of society. Old age remains marginal, in much the same way that underdeveloped countries of the Third World appear marginal when they are not yet integrated into the international market system. Is the solution, then, a kind of "colonization" of old age, to absorb it into the mainstream domains of the culture, polity, and economy? Will the solution most attractive to policymakers be to integrate the last stage of life into those systems of control that dominate education and work? The danger is that we will too quickly adopt a market or human services model and thereby try to integrate old age into the hegemony of a service economy where all elements of the life world become transactions dominated by the instrumental logic of productivity. Too late we will discover that productivity has become an idol to which the last stage of life, like all others, must be sacrificed.

The problem comes when we try to extend one particular form of transcendence—productivity—as a model for all forms of transcendence in later life. Productive aging constitutes a reformulation of what later life should be in terms of the dominant values of the Modern Age: growth, energy, activity, accumulation, and efficacy in shaping the world around us. Productive aging, in its most elemental meaning, is an economic ideal, as the words *productive* and *productivity* surely suggest.

But, more deeply than economics, the notion of anything as "productive" betrays a fundamentally instrumental orientation toward the world. Instrumentality means, above all, to see all things, objects in the world or human lives, in terms of our ability to act or to effect other things around us. It constitutes an orientation toward life that transcends the self through activity but denies any meaning to life itself without such activity (de Beauvoir, 1972). This ideal, attractive though it must be, is one that can have only provisional validity—that is, a validity for certain practical or policy purposes. In no way does it exhaust or even reach the most serious questions about the meaning of life or the meaning of old age.

## POLICY SIGNIFICANCE OF PRODUCTIVE AGING

We have argued that "productive aging" is a regulative ideal, a statement of the kind of life we might aspire to in old age. But can it have relevance for public policy purposes? Does productive aging, in short, have any "teeth" as an ideal for public policy? It is just at this point that some advocates of productive aging are likely to become nervous. Yes, they will argue, public policy ought to be recast in terms more congenial to productive aging. But most advocates of productive aging are also good liberals—that is, people who are suspicious of the power of the state to impose limiting purposes on human liberty. Liberals must be distinctly uncomfortable with the idea of using government power to enforce values, as we have seen in recent debates over abortion, euthanasia, and so forth.

The liberal stance toward productive aging, then, would from the very first insist that, whatever it means, productive aging must not become coercive. Productive aging, even if an ideal, should remain only an option, a matter of opportunity, but not something we force on people. For example, expanded employment should be offered as an opportunity (hence arguments against age discrimination) but not something imposed on people who want a conventional retirement and have no desire to be "productive" in any of the various meanings of the term.

This liberal response to the matter is attractive but probably inadequate. Simply to talk about options is not enough. Unless the productive aging movement has decisive consequences for policymakers, it is unlikely to be taken seriously in debates about aging policy. Moreover, we can distinguish several different modes in which productive aging could serve as an ideal for a new framework for aging policy. These modes are distinguished in the economic sphere here using examples of recent policy changes in work and retirement, but similar points could be made about politics and culture.

*Permissive Mode* Productive aging could be salient for policy purposes insofar as it directs us to remove barriers, such as age discrimination, that prevent older people from being productive. An example: federal laws banning mandatory retirement in most jobs.

*Facilitative Mode* Productive aging could be part of policies that are empowering for older people; for example, giving older people job retraining, counseling, or placement services enabling them to move into more contributive roles. An example: the Job Training Partnership Act, which has set aside a portion of funding for older workers.

*Programmatic Mode* Productive aging could provide a basis for creating new programs that would underwrite public service jobs or offer subsidies to encourage expanded use of older volunteers. An example: Title V of the Older Americans Act provides community-service jobs to older people on a means-tested basis.

*Benefit Incentives Mode* Productive aging could be part of a benefit scheme that ties failure to be "productive" with loss of benefits, as with certain welfare policies ("workfare") for younger people. In fact, something like this for older workers already has become public policy. An example: the 1983 Social Security Amendment which will begin raising the age of eligibility for Social Security (after 2005), thus providing a clear incentive for older workers to stay on the job longer before retirement. The 1983 Social Security Amendments are squarely on the side of "productive aging." In short, Congress has endorsed the ideal without quite saying so publicly.

The future of productive aging may be promising, but perhaps for reasons that will dismay its advocates. It is likely that the productive aging movement will be taken seriously by policymakers who seek (1) a reduction in costs (from "surplus dependency"); (2) an expansion of the labor supply (responding to the anticipated labor shortage of the 1990s); and (3) a drive to displace human services out of the welfare state and into the private sphere, prodded in turn by public resistance to tax increases. These forces will tend to keep productive aging within the policy agenda, though often in covert forms. Productive aging can appear in permissive, facilitative, programmatic, or benefit-based forms that look very different from the "coercion" much feared by liberals. But in any of these forms, productive aging easily can become a subtle means of social control and simply a modification of the "bureaucratized" life course, and in ways that at present remain imponderable. It is just for that reason that we now ought to debate and examine critically the multiple meanings of productive aging.

## CONCLUSION: TWO (NOT THREE) CHEERS FOR PRODUCTIVE AGING

Is productive aging a good thing, or is it not? Does it represent an appropriate ideal for the last stage of life for human beings at the close of the twentieth century? What, finally, is the connection between productive aging as a regulative ideal and specific public policies that might encourage a more productive use of time in later life? These are some of the questions that need to be considered as more and more enthusiasm greets any of the many meanings of productive aging.

To speak of productive aging at all is to set forth an ideal image for the last stage of life. The first point is to recognize the inescapable semantic significance of the term. *Productive aging*, inevitably, has connotations of a mode of existence that is active, successful, vitally engaged, and contributive to the wider community. Like *successful aging*, the term *productive aging* means to assign a positive value and connotation to age, quite in contrast to stereotypical ideas that associate old age with decrepitude, passivity, or decline.

But the idea of productive aging is not merely a matter of semantics. It also represents a substantive answer to a question that, until recently, has not even been asked: what is later life for? This question is not a matter of connotations or semantics but a matter of the purpose of a specific stage of life, recently called the "third quarter of life" (Pifer & Bronte, 1986) or "the Third Age" (Laslett, 1991). Productivity, or productive aging, then represents a definitive answer to the question of what this stage or period of life is all about.

We need to recognize here that productive aging is not the only imaginable ideal for what the last stage of life might mean. We certainly can imagine other positive alternatives to be considered. If at first glance productive aging seems to be a self-evident good thing, an indisputable goal at which we might aim, then perhaps we would do well to question the goal itself. What does it really mean? What would its opposite be? Why does productive aging hold such attraction for us in late twentieth-century America, at this time and place?

"What is honored in a country is cultivated there." As a society, we honor productivity and success. We despise failure and weakness. We measure accomplishment by money, achievement, fame, and power. Our celebration of these values is precisely why old age at last presents us with such a problem. When the capacity for productivity begins to fail, as it tends to do for all of us if only we live long enough, then we are tempted to avoid facing the truth about our ideals or ourselves.

Let us be blunt about it. It is too easy to talk about the "need to be needed." When each of us, alas, is no longer needed, no longer "productive," then the very ideal of productivity we have pursued will ensnare us and defeat us. The ideal becomes a temptation to despair, to a feeling of uselessness all too common among the very old. We need instead a wider vision of what late-life productivity may mean, a vision that includes values such as altruism, citizenship, stewardship, creativity, and the search for faith. We need to honor and to cultivate these values as they appear in all the forms of transcendence by which both young and old celebrate and find meaning in the gift of life.

## NOTES

1. Note that the advent of so-called postmodern culture in no way diminishes the dominant forces of "autonomy" and "freedom." On the contrary, the ecclecticism and relativism of the postmodern ethos can itself be seen as a macrocultural projection of the ideal of going beyond all limits, including the "progressivist" ideal of modernity. From another standpoint, postmodernism is simply a phase of modernism itself. For an examination of this issue, especially in relation to the category of postindustrialism, see Rose, 1991, and Harvey, 1990.

2. But, on the idealization of traditional and communal values in the past, see also Laslett, 1971.

3. Equality remains the dominant ideal of liberal politics. But the ambivalent meaning of "equality" in considering the claims of different age groups can be seen in the application of the ideas of John Rawls, the foremost philosopher of liberalism, to the problem of justice between age groups. On this issue, see Daniels, 1987.

4. For a more extensive argument in defense of this point, see the section "Justice between Generations" in Moody, 1992.

5. On the historical origins of this trend, see Cole, 1991.

## REFERENCES

Bell, D. (1974). *The coming of post-industrial society*. New York: Basic Books.

Chinen, A. (1985). Fairy tales and transpersonal development in later life. *Journal of Transpersonal Psychology, 17*(2), 99–122.

Chinen, A. (1990). *In the ever after: Fairy tales and the second half of life*. Wilmette, IL: Chiron.

Cole, T. (1991). *The journey of life*. New York: Cambridge University Press.

Daniels, N. (1987). *Am I my parents' keeper?* New York: Oxford University Press.

Day, C. L. (1990). *What older Americans think: Interest groups and aging policy*. Princeton, NJ: Princeton University Press.

De Beauvoir, S. (1972). *The coming of age*. New York: Putnam.

Estes, C. (1979). *The aging enterprise*. San Francisco: Jossey-Bass.

Fowler, J. W. (1981). *Stages of faith: The psychology of human development & the quest for meaning*. New York: Harper & Row.

Habermas, J. (Ed.). *Observations on "The spiritual situation of the age"* (A. Buchwalter, trans.). Cambridge, MA: MIT Press.

Harvey, D. (1990). *The condition of postmodernity*. London: Basil Blackwell.

Ingram, D. (1990). *Critical theory and philosophy*. New York: Paragon House.

Kakar, S. (1968, July). The human life cycle: The traditional Hindu view and the psychology of Erik Erikson. *Philosophy East & West, 18*, 127–136.

Kalish, R. A. (1979). The new ageism and the failure models: A polemic. *The Gerontologist, 19*, 398–402.

Kotre, J. (1984). *Outliving the self: Generativity and the interpretation of lives*. Baltimore, MD: Johns Hopkins University Press.

Lasch, C. (1985). *The one and only heaven: Progress and its critics.* New York: Norton.

Laslett, P. (1971). *The world we have lost.* New York: Scribners.

Laslett, P. (1991). *A fresh map of life: The emergence of the third age.* Cambridge, MA: Harvard University Press.

Longman, P. (1987). *Born to pay.* Boston: Houghton Mifflin.

Moody, H. R. (1988). *Abundance of life: Human development policies for an aging society.* New York: Columbia University Press.

Moody, H. R. (1990). The politics of entitlement and the politics of productivity. In S. Bass, E. Kutza, & F. Torres-Gil, *Diversity in aging* (pp. 129–150). Glenview, IL: Scott, Foresman.

Moody, H. R. (1992). *Ethics and the aging society.* Baltimore, MD: Johns Hopkins University Press.

O'Connor, G. (1978). *The second journey: Spiritual awareness and the mid-life crisis.* Ramsey, NJ: Paulist Press.

Peck, R. C. (1968). Psychological development in the second half of life. In B. Neugarten (Ed.), *Middle age and aging.* Chicago: University of Chicago Press.

Pifer, A., & Bronte, L. (Eds.). (1986). *Our aging society: Paradox and promise.* New York: Norton.

Rose, M. (1991). *The post modern and the post industrial.* Cambridge: Cambridge University Press.

Schiff, G. (1983). *Picasso: The last years, 1963–1973.* New York: George Braziller.

Sonnenfeld, J. (1988). *The hero's farewell: What happens when CEO's retire.* New York: Oxford University Press.

Torres-Gil, F. (1992). *The new aging: Politics and change in America.* New York: Auburn House.

Wheeler, M. (1961). *The last works of Henri Matisse.* New York: Museum of Modern Art.

# Part II

## Employment

# 3

# Labor Market Obstacles to Aging Productively

*Joseph F. Quinn and Richard V. Burkhauser*

American employment patterns have changed dramatically in the past few decades. Women have entered the labor market in unprecedented numbers, and men are retiring much earlier than they did only a short while ago. Additional important demographic changes are on the horizon. The nation is aging, and an increasing proportion of the population soon will be nearing retirement age.

Many people continue to leave the labor force in the traditional manner—they move directly from full-time work on a career job to complete retirement. Others use more complex exit routes, with periods of partial retirement or second careers; some exit and later reenter the work force. Surveys suggest that more workers would like to ease gradually into retirement. Unfortunately, there are significant obstacles to doing so.

In this chapter, we discuss the plans and preferences of older Americans and conclude that society could make better use of its experienced, older work force. Obstacles to productive aging exist, but some encouraging changes already are under way. In the end, employers will capitalize on these willing and able older workers only when they are convinced that it is in their financial best interest to do so.

## PLANS AND PREFERENCES OF THE ELDERLY

A recent survey sponsored By The Commonwealth Fund has shed valuable light on the plans and preferences of older Americans. More than 3,500 women (aged fifty to fifty-nine) and men (aged fifty-five to sixty-four) were interviewed in 1989 and asked detailed questions about their work status and history, plans and expectations, qualifications and skills, health, finances, and attitudes toward work and leisure. About 2,000 of these respondents were working and the other 1,500 were not. A major conclusion of the study was that a substantial minority of these older Americans were willing and able to work longer than they had (if they already were retired) or than they planned to (if they still were working).

William McNaught, Michael Barth, and Peter Henderson (1989; 1991) analyzed those who were not employed at the time of the survey. Nearly a quarter, representing nearly two million men and women in these age groups, said that they preferred to be working and were capable of doing so were a suitable job available. The authors then narrowed this sample by requiring that the respondents also pass a number of specific labor market commitment tests.[1] Even with these additional requirements, respondents representing over one million older Americans indicated that they were willing and able to work. This figure represents a minority, but a substantial one—nearly 14 percent of those not employed in these age groups.

The members of this potential labor pool had backgrounds and skills comparable to those still at work. Three-quarters had high school degrees and one-third had attended college. Nearly half had professional or technical degrees, licenses, or certificates; and 60 percent had spent at least five years at their last job. They expressed considerable flexibility with respect to jobs. A majority said that they were willing to work alone, take seasonal work, commute more than thirty minutes, or work evenings and weekends. Two-thirds said they would work full-time, and nearly seven-eighths said they would work part-time if they had the opportunity to do so.

We have analyzed the wage and salary workers who were still employed at the time of the survey (Quinn & Burkhauser, 1990). Sizeable minorities (10 percent of the men and 13 percent of the women, representing over one million people overall) said that they expected to stop working earlier than they wanted. Comparing the exact age at which they thought they would stop working (plans) with the age at which they would like to stop working (preferences), we calculated the number of additional years they wanted to work. Some said just one or two years, but more than 40 percent claimed that they would like to stay employed for another three to five years. A few said six to ten years; another large group (about 40 percent of the men and a third of the women) implied that they would like to work as long as they could. Even if these optimistic claims are viewed with some suspicion, there is evidence that those who want to work longer often would like to do so for a substantial number of years.

It is not obvious what these divergent plans and preferences mean. If workers prefer to continue working longer than they plan to, why do they not just do so? Mandatory retirement rules once might have explained this, but mandatory retirement is now outlawed for nearly all American workers. One interpretation is that the retired workers did not want to continue under the terms and conditions of employment that they expected to face but would have liked to stay on under different circumstances. This view is consistent with the fact that retirement plans often penalize older workers who remain by reducing the value of their pension rights, as we will discuss.

The Commonwealth Fund survey asked several questions about employment preferences under alternative scenarios. Employees were asked whether they would work longer if employer pension contributions continued at the same level after age sixty-five, or if they were offered a job at somewhat lower pay but with reduced hours and responsibilities. They also were asked whether they would accept a job that required retraining and that had different responsibilities and tasks but had the same hours and salary.

Responses from the entire sample of employed wage-and-salary workers suggest that 2.4 million older workers in these age categories would work longer if pension contributions continued. Nearly three million would work longer with fewer hours and responsibilities, and 3.5 million would accept retraining. There was considerable overlap in the answers. Overall, more than half of these older workers answered "yes" to at least one of the questions. This implies that more than five million men and women were willing to extend their work careers under one or more of the circumstances just mentioned.

Why? Although the survey did not address their motivations directly, it did ask the employed for the most important reason that they held their current jobs. About 60 percent of the wage-and-salary workers implied that they needed their jobs for financial reasons.[2] The remainder wanted their jobs for quite different reasons—they enjoyed their work, found it challenging, would have been bored otherwise, or wanted to do something useful. But among the million who wanted to keep working longer than they expected they would, the majority implied that they worked because they wanted to, not because financial interests were key. This is not surprising since work often provides many benefits in addition to financial remuneration.

This recent survey suggests that many older Americans are willing and able to work longer than they currently do. The one million to two million retirees who claimed they were willing to work longer represent 13 percent to 23 percent of all retired workers their ages. The one million workers who planned to stop working before they wanted to represent about 12 percent of those older employees, and the five million who claimed they would work longer under various hypothetical scenarios is over half of this employed cohort.

There are reasons to be skeptical of questionnaire responses. It is easier to say that one would work longer than it is to do so. Economists usually prefer to analyze what people actually do rather than what they say they will do. When we do this, we find that workers retire in a number of interesting ways and that retirement choices depend, among other things, on the financial options that older workers face.

## EXIT PATTERNS FROM CAREER JOBS

Several authors have analyzed exit patterns from career jobs using the Social Security Administration's Retirement History Study (RHS), which followed a cohort of 11,000 older Americans through the 1970s (Quinn, Burkhauser, & Myers, 1990; Ruhm, 1990b). The results, though now somewhat dated, are interesting. Christopher Ruhm (1990a) also studied the withdrawal patterns of the respondents in the 1989 Commonwealth Fund survey, and his conclusions confirm the earlier results.

Despite the fact that most of the economic literature on retirement treats retirement status as dichotomous, Americans leave their career jobs in many and varied ways. We define a career job as full-time employment held for at least ten years. Following the RHS sample from 1969, when the respondents were fifty-eight to sixty-three years old, until 1979, when the biennial surveys ended, we found that a substantial minority did not leave the labor force when they left full-time status on their career jobs. Among the wage-and-salary population, a quarter did something else—about 20 percent found new employment, and a few dropped to part-time hours on their career jobs. Among the self-employed, who have more control over the amount and kind of work they do, only half left the labor force. A quarter of the self-employed remained part-time on the same job, and the other quarter found new work.

These transitional jobs generally lasted long enough to be interesting. Of those who switched employers, nearly three-quarters were still on the job a year later, and nearly 60 percent remained after two years. A comparison of the career and new jobs revealed that most of the transitions involved different occupations and industries. More people moved down the socioeconomic ladder—from skilled to unskilled jobs and from white-collar to blue-collar jobs—than moved up. There were more pay cuts than wage increases. This was especially true when the new job was part-time, with the exception of those who were able to shift from full-time to part-time employment on their career jobs. There was weak evidence that those at the two ends of the economic spectrum were more likely to stay in the labor force after leaving career employment—the poor probably because they had to and the rich because they wanted to.

Ruhm (1990b) defines a career job as the longest job held, regardless of when it was held, and therefore has found more postcareer "bridge employment" than we have. He estimates that less than half of the RHS sample retired directly from a career job. Of those who moved to another job, only a quarter stayed in the same industry and occupation.

The RHS data suggest that many people actually do behave as the Commonwealth respondents said they would like to. Many older Americans keep working after they leave full-time career employment. Those with the most flexible options, the self-employed, are the most likely to do so. Workers who stay in the labor market are willing to move into new industries and occupations, work fewer hours, and take pay cuts.

Ruhm's (1990a) analysis of the 1989 Commonwealth Fund sample (men aged fifty-five to sixty-four and women aged fifty to fifty-nine) found approximately equal numbers employed in career and bridge jobs. Bridge jobs were more likely to be part-time and more likely to involve self-employment. Nearly 60 percent of those in bridge jobs said that their new job was the most enjoyable one they had ever had.

Research has shown that there are many patterns of withdrawal from the labor force. The stereotypical retirement—from full-time work to full-time leisure—is only a part of the story. Depending on one's definition of a career job, between a quarter and a half of all older Americans remain in the labor force after they leave their career jobs. These patterns are a result of many factors—individual preferences, financial incentives, and job opportunities. Survey and econometric evidence indicates that people do respond to changes in the options they face. Our current system often discourages continued employment late in life. To consider the elderly as a possible additional labor supply will require increased work incentives and additional flexibility on the part of employers.

## INSTITUTIONAL BARRIERS TO PRODUCTIVE AGING

### Social Security and Pension Incentives

Research over the past decade has shown that strong work disincentives exist in many American retirement income programs (Quinn, Burkhauser, & Myers, 1990). At a certain point, at age sixty-five for Social Security and at various ages for defined-benefit employer pensions, the value of retirement entitlements begins to decline if one remains on the job. This loss in retirement wealth is equivalent to a pay cut, and many workers respond exactly as economic theory and common sense would predict they would—they leave the job and sometimes retire.

The key to this research is the insight that pensions are multiperiod in nature. Contributions are made during the working years and benefits are paid later. The value of any stream of benefits can be summarized by its asset, or wealth, equivalent—the present discounted value of the future payments. This is the stock of money today that, if invested at market interest rates, could provide exactly the promised income stream.

When one delays receipt of retirement benefits (e.g., by continuing to work after the age of eligibility), two things happen. The bad news is that one foregoes pension income in the present—the benefit one could have claimed. The good news is that future annual benefits usually are higher. For Social Security, they increase both because average monthly earnings (on which benefits are based) rise and because Social Security adds a delayed retirement credit to all future checks. For defined benefit pensions, benefits usually are based on some combination of last or highest earnings and years of service, both of which are likely to rise with continued work. The choice, then, is not simply between a pension check and no pension check in the hypothetical year in which one is considering retirement; rather, it is between two streams of income, one starting immediately, but with smaller annual amounts, and another commencing later, with higher benefits. Which is worth more, more small checks or fewer large ones?

The answer depends on whether the future increments are sufficient to compensate for the pension income initially forgone. If the increments just compensate, the pension is called actuarially fair. If the future additions are more than sufficient, then one gains twice by working another year, both through the paycheck and through the increase in pension or Social Security wealth. But if the future increments are worth less than the benefits forgone, then one loses pension wealth while working. In this case, one's true compensation is less than the paycheck by the amount of the wealth loss.

Research has shown that the last scenario describes many American retirement-income plans. At some age, workers who stay on the job begin to lose retirement wealth and, in essence, suffer a pay cut.[3] At age sixty-five, the Social Security delayed retirement credit falls from about 7 percent per year of delay to only 3.5 percent. The latter is less than actuarially fair. It is more difficult to generalize about pensions, since there are so many of them, each with its own rules and regulations. But the authors of the largest study of individual pension plan incentives conclude:

Typical pension provisions provide a strong incentive for retirement after the age of plan normal retirement, and a large proportion of plans provide a strong incentive for retirement after the age of early retirement.... [I]t would not be unusual for the reduction in pension benefit accrual after the age of early retirement to be equivalent to a 30% reduction in wage earnings. (Kotlikoff & Wise, 1989, p. 54)

Strong retirement incentives exist, and they influence behavior. Although this is only one of many important factors in the individual retirement decision, those facing significant work disincentives, *ceteris paribus*, are more likely than others to leave their career jobs and the labor force.[4]

These financial incentives have the same effect as mandatory retirement. The latter (the stick) has forced people to leave a job; the former (the carrot) merely makes them an offer they are unlikely to refuse. Prior to the 1978 amendments to the Age Discrimination in Employment Act, sixty-five was the most common age of mandatory retirement; it also was the age at which strong Social Security (and often pension) incentives took effect.[5] In fact, much of what looked like a mandatory retirement effect really was due to pension and Social Security incentives; therefore, the effect of delaying and later eliminating mandatory retirement was less than a simple comparison of those with and without the constraint would have suggested (Burkhauser & Quinn, 1983). There is some evidence that employers increased pension retirement incentives while mandatory retirement was being dismantled (Mitchell & Luzadis, 1988; Luzadis & Mitchell, 1991). Faced with the loss of the stick, they sweetened the carrot.

Workers eventually face three choices as they age. They can remain on their career jobs and eventually suffer surreptitious pay cuts via losses in Social Security and/or pension wealth; they can move to another job, often at substantially lower pay; or they can leave the labor force. As we have seen, people do all three.

These insights may help explain the responses of the workers in The Commonwealth Fund study. Many respondents said that they wanted to work longer than they actually planned to. The appropriate interpretation may be that they did not plan to remain employed given the incentives they saw ahead but would have been willing and able to remain employed under more favorable terms of employment.

Most of the literature on older workers deals with the supply side of the market—the choices that workers make. We know much less about the demand side—the number and the nature of the jobs available to older workers. Evidence suggests that there are too few jobs with the characteristics that older workers want and that many older Americans who are not working would like to be.

## Unemployment

The official unemployment rate traditionally has been low for older workers. In 1990, about 250,000 Americans aged sixty and older were not employed and were actively searching for work. This is about 3 percent of the labor force this age and well less than 1 percent of the sixty and older population. In addition, however, nearly 600,000 of those not in the labor force (i.e., not employed and not actively searching for a job) said that they wanted one.[6] When asked why they were not looking for one, about half said that they were ill, had home responsibilities, or had other personal reasons why they could not get a job, leaving about 280,000 people who actually might have been able to take a job were one available. These discouraged and unemployed workers total over a half million potential workers aged sixty and over.[7]

Once unemployed, older workers are known to stay unemployed longer. In 1990, the mean unemployment duration overall was twelve weeks, but it was about eighteen weeks for those aged fifty-five and over, and over twenty weeks for men in this age category (U.S. Bureau of Labor Statistics, January 1991, Table 15).

## Full-time/Part-time Mix

An additional problem may be the full-time/part-time mix of jobs available. Surveys indicate that many older workers would like to retire gradually, which usually means a period of part-time work before complete retirement (U.S. Senate, 1990, p. 73). In a recent survey of union retirees, only 13 percent of those who worked or would like to work preferred full-time employment (Applebaum & Gregory, 1990). In The Commonwealth Fund study, more of the "willing-and-able retired" were willing to work part-time than full-time. Among those still working, 21 percent of the men and 43 percent of the women wanted to be working part-time (and the proportion rose with age), whereas only 6 percent and 19 percent actually were. Social Security rules encourage part-time work, since earnings reduce benefits after an exempt amount—in 1992, $7,440 for those aged sixty-two to sixty-four and $10,200 for those sixty-five to sixty-nine.[8]

Given these preferences, why are more older Americans not working part-time? There are two related sets of answers. Compensation is often poor on the jobs that are available, and many employers are reluctant to hire older workers at all.

### Compensation

There is little doubt that workers who move from full-time to part-time work usually do so at considerably lower hourly wages. Alan Gustman and Thomas Steinmeier (1985), using the RHS, found that workers who were partially retired suffered hourly wage losses of about 10 percent when they stayed with their previous full-time employer and 30 percent when they switched employers. Joseph Quinn, Richard Burkhauser, and Daniel Myers (1990), also using the RHS, found that wage and salary workers who switched jobs were much more likely to suffer hourly pay cuts than enjoy pay gains. James Jondrow, Frank Brechling, and Alan Marcus (1987) mentioned several studies that report pay declines of 30 percent to 40 percent.

Lower pay for older workers in part-time work is not necessarily evidence of discrimination. Workers who switch jobs lose specific human capital—the expertise built up on the old job that is not relevant on the new one.[9] Their productivity, therefore, can decline when they move, but for reasons having nothing to do with age. Fixed hiring, training, and fringe costs are amortized over fewer hours, both because of their part-time status and because older workers have fewer years of service to offer the firm (Hutchens, 1988). Firms may have to offer lower wages in order to make the arrangement profitable. Finally, many high-paid jobs are complicated, as are the supervisory and coordination tasks that go with them. These problems are magnified when two people cover a job part-time that one could handle full-time.

As a result, firms often offer part-time employment in jobs that require relatively little supervision or training, and they exclude fixed-cost fringes (like medical or life insurance) from the compensation package. John Owen (1978), with some data from the late 1970s, estimated that about two-thirds of the wage gap between full-time and part-time workers was due to the concentration of part-timers in sectors of the economy where all workers were paid poorly. Mark Montgomery (1988), with 1980 data on more than 5,000 employers, showed that the proportion of the work force that is part-time declines with the size of the firm and with the importance of hiring and training costs.

## Employer Attitudes

Richard Belous (1990) conducted over fifty case studies with U.S. employers, focusing on flexible employment opportunities. Although executives thought that older workers had many desirable characteristics (like a strong work ethic and appropriate cultural values), they were concerned that the elderly might fear the technological aspects of many jobs. Others reported difficulties recruiting older workers and found it easier to attract youth and middle-aged women.

In 1989, the American Association of Retired Persons commissioned a study of business attitudes toward workers aged fifty and older, an update of a similar survey done in 1985. They interviewed human resource decision makers in a random sample of 400 firms—100 in each of four size categories. The results reveal generally positive attitudes toward older workers. In the four years since the last survey, an increased proportion of managers rated older workers "excellent" or "very good" on attendance and punctuality (91 percent), commitment to quality (89 percent), loyalty and dedication to the company (86 percent), practical knowledge (85 percent), and emotional stability (71 percent). The rankings tended to be lower, however, in the largest firms—those with over 1,000 employees. In contrast, the ratings were much lower on older workers' educational backgrounds (36 percent), physical agility (29 percent), desire to get ahead (27 percent), and feeling comfortable with new technologies (22 percent).

This last category is very important, since 81 percent of these managers rated maintaining or increasing productivity as a top corporate priority, and 43 percent (70 percent in the largest firms) mentioned the introduction of new technology. Although the rating of older employees regarding comfort with new technology had risen from 10 percent to 22 percent during the four-year interval, the relative importance of this issue has risen even faster. Older workers also were judged deficient on their willingness to be flexible about doing different tasks. Fewer than half of the managers rated them excellent or very good (and only a third in firms with over 1,000 employees), while nearly three-quarters thought this an essential or very important employee attribute.

Rising health care and health insurance costs are major concerns for employers. Seventy percent of those interviewed said that these issues were receiving a great deal of attention in their firm, and a quarter named benefit costs as the most pressing issue facing human resource managers. Those who provided cost figures estimated that an older worker cost 15 percent more than average to insure. In the largest companies, a fifty-five-year-old male was judged to be more expensive to insure than a thirty-year-old male or female with two dependents. These perceptions are particularly important since about 60 percent of these firms provided health insurance to their retirees and over 40 percent provided full coverage.

Relatively few of these companies had implemented specific skill training programs for new employees (29 percent) or had educated managers about ways to utilize older workers (28 percent). Although 45 percent thought that phased retirement (keeping older workers on part-time) was an effective way to utilize older workers, only 18 percent actually had implemented this idea. Even fewer (9 percent) had implemented programs to reduce the level of responsibilities and pay of older workers.

In summary, workers who want to retire gradually, with an interim period of part-time employment, face a number of hurdles. Pension plans rarely allow a benefit recipient to continue working for the firm. Social Security lowers benefits for earnings over an exempt amount, and the delayed retirement credit for those who forgo earnings is less than actuarially fair after age 65. Although employers' attitudes about older workers generally are positive, managers fear that the elderly are not sufficiently flexible to adapt to new technologies and are concerned about relative health care costs. Despite these obstacles, a substantial minority of older workers do remain in the labor force after leaving their career jobs, and many more say that they would like to.

By age sixty-two, about half of all American men are out of the labor force. Only one in six continues to work beyond age sixty-five. The participation rates are even lower for older American women. The majority of these people seem to have left the work force voluntarily and express no desire to return to work.[10] But a sizeable minority of those out of the labor force are willing and able to return to work, and many of those still employed would be willing to work longer than they currently plan to if alternative terms and conditions of employment were to be offered.

The age distribution of the population is changing and will do so dramatically early in the next century. Some analysts anticipate labor shortages caused by declining numbers of the young and declining labor force participation of the old. If so, a partial solution can be found in this pool of experienced older workers.

Currently, human resources are being wasted. Recent studies suggest that labor market productivity declines little as workers age. Olivia Mitchell (1990) surveyed the literature on worker output and health and found "little support for a link between aging, job performance and health." Mary Jablonski, Kent Kunze, and Larry Rosenblum (1990) looked at piece-rate studies and earnings patterns over the life cycle and concluded that "according to the studies cited, worker productivity exceeds 90 percent of peak performance (with one exception) for both men and women near age 60 and exceeds 80 percent for those aged 65 and over."

Older workers have much to offer. What is being done and what more can be done to take them up on this offer? What is the appropriate mix of governmental and private-sector initiatives to bring needed changes about?

## RETIREMENT INCENTIVES

Two trends already under way set the stage for increased utilization of the elderly work force. Both diminish the financial disincentives that currently discourage older workers.

### Social Security

Recent amendments to the Social Security Act are increasing the reward for continued work. In 1990, the delayed retirement credit increased from 3 percent to 3.5 percent per year of delay after age sixty-five and will continue to increase by one-half percentage point intervals every other year until it reaches 8 percent in 2010. This will be near actuarially fair and will make Social Security close to age-neutral; that is, the asset value of the benefits will no longer depend significantly on when they are claimed. In addition, the exempt amount of earnings after which benefits are reduced rises annually. It has been increased further for those aged sixty-five to sixty-nine, and their benefit reduction rate after the exempt amount has been decreased from one-half (which it still is for those aged sixty-two to sixty-four) to one-third.[11]

Simulations of the labor market impact of changes such as these suggest that they will induce later retirement but that the average delay will be modest, on the order of months, not years (Quinn, Burkhauser, & Myers, 1990, pp. 108–111). Many analysts think that pension changes potentially are much more influential.

### Employer Pensions

In the private sector, the relative importance of defined-benefit and defined-contribution plans is changing. Only the former contain the retirement incentives emphasized above. The latter really are just savings accounts with tax advantages and are by their very nature age-neutral. The proportion of pension participants whose primary coverage is from a defined-contribution plan is on the rise; it increased from 13 percent to 29 percent between 1975 and 1985. Virtually all supplementary coverage is defined contribution. Overall, the proportion of active participants in defined-benefit plans fell from 71 percent to 47 percent in the decade ending in 1985 (Turner & Beller, 1989, Tables 4.11 and 4.12).

But defined-benefit plans are still very important, since they continue to provide the majority of primary pension coverage. How will their incentives change in response to the elimination of mandatory retirement and the gradual loss of Social Security work disincentives? Will they go along and reduce their work penalties as well, or will they try to compensate for the Social Security changes and increase their incentives for early retirement? Although we do not know what these decisions will be, we know that they will be important. It is unrealistic to think that many older workers will stay on their career jobs in the face of incentives that penalize those who do.

An intriguing idea is the partial pension, a program in which an employee can work part-time and receive a proportional pension benefit. This, in essence, is the arrangement under Social Security, but few employer pension plans follow suit. This is one reason why many workers leave their career jobs but remain in the labor force.

Sweden has been a leader in this regard. Under a plan introduced in 1976, eligible workers aged sixty to sixty-four who move to part-time work have 65 percent of their earnings loss made up by a partial pension (Kruse & Soderstrom, 1989; Laczko, 1988). Because of the high Swedish tax rates, the loss in net pay is small. The program is popular with business firms, unions, and workers; between 12 percent and 27 percent of those eligible have taken advantage of it each year. Nearly all of the workers stay with the same employer and on the same job.

## THE PUBLIC AND PRIVATE SECTORS' ROLES

Full utilization of the older work force will occur only if employers see that it is in their interest to encourage it. The government can do much to set the stage for this to occur. To some extent, it already has. Mandatory retirement has been almost entirely eliminated, and Social Security is becoming more age-neutral. Firms must now continue to apply pension accrual rules to those who work beyond normal retirement age. Government training programs can help, and macroeconomic efforts to encourage full employment are essential. But the actual personnel decisions will be made at the micro level, by individual employers who decide that older workers are a good deal.

Many already have. Jerome Rosow (1990) lists a number of examples of innovative policies by employers. The Wichita, Kansas, Board of Education allows job sharing for teachers, with two people each receiving half pay and half benefits. State law allows board employees to retire at age sixty, receive their pensions, and then be rehired. The Wrigley Company allows workers to start tapering off the length of their work year at age sixty-two, dropping an additional month off (without pay) each year until age sixty-five. Subsequent pension increases offset part of the lost wages. The New England Mutual Life Insurance Company grants additional paid vacation leave after age sixty-two. A number of corporations call back retirees to handle peak-load problems or to fill in during popular vacation periods.

Peter Libassi (1991) has described the Travelers Companies' innovative retiree job bank. More than 750 older workers are on file as employees and about 250 are working at any given time—about two-thirds of the firm's temporary work needs. The Travelers has adjusted its pension plan so that retirees can work up to 960 hours without losing any benefits. They have found older workers eager to learn and able to adapt quickly to new computer technology.

William McNaught and Michael Barth (1990) have analyzed the experience of Days Inn of America, a major hotel chain that solved a labor shortage and turnover problem at their national reservations center by hiring older workers. They obtained data on wage and benefit costs, training performance, productivity, and retention experience for younger (nearly all under thirty-five) and older (fifty and older) workers on identical jobs between 1986 and 1990. The jobs involved handling reservations inquiries with a state-of-the-art, menu-driven computer system. The authors found that older workers initially took longer to train but that with experience instructors could train young and old workers in the same time. Medical costs were similar (because of fewer dependents among the elderly), but pension and recruitment costs were higher for older workers. Turnover rates of older workers were much lower. Older workers tended to spend more time on each call but they converted a higher percentage of calls into reservations. When all the pros and cons were compared, older workers were a little more expensive but a little more productive, because of their higher conversion ratios. In a simulation of hypothetical reservation centers staffed entirely by younger workers and entirely by older workers, net revenues were almost identical.

The Days Inn experience is interesting because the jobs involved the use of modern technical equipment. But this and the other examples mentioned here are isolated examples. Their results will apply in some industries and occupations but not in others. The federal government can further the cause of older employees by making sure that federal incentives do not discourage work, by maintaining transitional training programs and by funding research and disseminating information on the costs and benefits of hiring experienced workers.[12]

## CONCLUSION

Older workers are a valuable resource. Although many people are eager to leave the labor force and retire, a substantial number of other workers are willing and able to work longer than they currently do. They are discouraged from doing so by financial disincentives, by certain negative employer attitudes, and by an inadequate supply of part-time employment opportunities. Employers with flexibility on hours and levels of responsibility will be in the best position to capitalize on these underutilized resources.

For many older workers, the ideal option would be the opportunity to remain on the career job part-time. This utilizes their specific human capital, maintains their seniority, and minimizes the wage loss associated with the change. It decreases uncertainty, since the worker knows the firm and the firm knows the worker. But this would require changes in many defined-benefit plan provisions, which usually do not permit one to stay on the job and collect a pension, inadequately reward workers for delayed benefits, and base benefits on final earnings.

Pension incentives have changed in the past in response to labor market conditions, and we suspect that they will again in the future. If labor shortages occur, firms can call on experienced workers by structuring employment and compensation packages that make the work worth their while.

## NOTES

1. In particular, respondents had to be willing to work in the kind of jobs generally available to older workers, need a job for financial reasons, be able to perform a series of specific physical tasks, be seeking work and have reasonable wage expectations, and be willing to accept difficult job conditions.

2. They said that they needed the money in general, needed the health insurance, or had medical bills to pay. It is worth remembering that these responses are based on respondents who were still employed at ages 50 to 59 for the women, and ages 55 to 64 for the men. The attitudes of those who had already left the labor force might be very different.

3. See Quinn, Burkhauser & Myers, 1990, Chapter 3, for a review of this extensive literature. It is not even necessary for pension wealth to decline for one to suffer a pay cut. If pension wealth continues to increase, but at a slower rate than previously, then one's net compensation falls.

4. This literature is also reviewed in Quinn, Burkhauser & Myers, 1990, Chapter 3.

5. In those days, the delayed retirement credit for work beyond age 65 was only 1 percent per year of delay, which made the drop from 7 percent (for ages 62 to 64) even more severe than it is today.

6. These numbers are averages for the months of 1990. See U.S. Bureau of Labor Statistics, 1991, Tables 3 and 35.

7. These numbers cannot be compared directly to the Commonwealth Fund estimates because the age categories are different. What can be compared are the Bureau of Labor Statistics (BLS) unemployment estimates for women aged 50–59 and men aged 55–64. (The BLS discouraged workers' estimates are aggregated for those aged "60 years and over.") In 1989 an average of 740,000 people in these

age categories were unemployed (U.S. Bureau of Labor Statistics, 1990, Table 3), compared to 1.1 or 1.9 million people "willing and able" in the 1989 Commonwealth study. The latter include discouraged workers and are based on different questions than the BLS numbers. See McNaught, Barth & Henderson, 1991, pp. 104–105, for a discussion of the differences.

8. The benefit reduction rate is ½ for those aged 62 to 64, and ⅓ for those 65 to 69. At age 70, the earnings test disappears, and one can draw full benefits regardless of earnings.

9. Shapiro & Sandell (1985) studied wage declines among older workers who were forced to look for new jobs and concluded that about 90 percent of the earnings decline reflected the loss of specific human capital and seniority.

10. For a historical view of voluntary versus involuntary retirement, see Quinn, 1991.

11. The exempt amount for those aged 65 to 69 rose to $10,200 in 1992 and was scheduled to rise to $10,800 in 1993. The Bush Administration proposed that it increase an additional $800 in 1992 and $200 more in 1993. Senator Robert Dole introduced legislation that would phase out the earnings test for those 65 and older over the next five years (National Academy of Social Insurance, 1991, pp. 3 and 10).

12. McNaught and Barth (1990) found that the Days Inn employees who had been exposed to computer courses at local senior citizens centers performed significantly better in training sessions.

## REFERENCES

American Association of Retired Persons. (1989). *Business and older workers: Current perceptions and new directions for the 1990s.* Washington, DC: American Association of Retired Persons.

Applebaum, E., & Gregory, J. (1990). Flexible employment: Union perspective. In P. B. Doeringer (Ed.), *Bridges to retirement: Older workers in a changing labor market* (pp. 130–145). Ithaca, NY: ILR Press.

Belous, R. S. (1990). Flexible employment: The employer's point of view. In P. B. Doeringer (Ed.), *Bridges to retirement: Older workers in a changing labor market* (pp. 111–129). Ithaca, NY: ILR Press.

Burkhauser, R. V., & Quinn, J. F. (1983). Is mandatory retirement overrated? Evidence from the 1970s. *Journal of Human Resources, 18*(3), 337–358.

Gustman, A. A., & Steinmeier, T. L. (1985). The effects of partial retirement on the wage profiles of older workers. *Industrial Relations Review, 24*(2), 257–265.

Hutchens, R. M. (1988). Do job opportunities decline with age? *Industrial and Labor Relations Review, 42*(1), 89–99.

Jablonski, M., Kunze, K., & Rosenblum, L. (1990). Productivity, age, and labor compositional changes in the U.S. labor force. In I. Bluestone, R. Montgomery, & J. Owen (Eds.), *The aging of the American work force* (pp. 304–338). Detroit, MI: Wayne State University.

Jondrow, J., Brechling, F., & Marcus, A. (1987). Older workers in the market for part-time employment. In S. H. Sandell (Ed.), *The problem isn't age: Work and older Americans* (pp. 84–99). New York: Praeger.

Kotlikoff, L. J., & Wise, D. A. (1989). *The wage carrot and the pension stick.* Kalamazoo, MI: W. E. Upjohn Institute for Employment Research.

Kruse, A., & Soderstrom, L. (1989). Early retirement in Sweden. In W. Schmahl (Ed.), *Redefining the process of retirement: An international perspective* (pp. 39–61). Berlin: Springer Verlag.

Laczko, F. (1988). Partial retirement: An alternative to early retirement? A comparison of phased retirement schemes in the United Kingdom, France, and Scandinavia. *International Social Security Review, 41*(2), 149–169.

Libassi, F. P. (1991). Mobilize the private sector's economic self-interest. In A. H. Munnell (Ed.), *Retirement and public policy* (pp. 185–191). Dubuque, IA: Kendall/Hunt.

Luzadis, R., & Mitchell, O. S. (1991). Explaining pension dynamics, *Journal of Human Resources.*

McNaught, W., & Barth, M. C. (1990, July). Are older workers a "good buy"? A cast study of Days Inn of America. Mimeo. ICF Inc., Fairfax, VA.

McNaught, W., Barth, M. C., & Henderson, P. H. (1989). The human resources potential of Americans over 50. *Human Resources Management, 28*(4), 455–473.

McNaught, W., Barth, M. C., & Henderson, P. H. (1991). Older Americans: Willing and able to work. In A. H. Munnell (Ed.), *Retirement and public policy* (pp. 101–114). Dubuque, IA: Kendall/Hunt.

Mitchell, O. S. (1990). Aging, job satisfaction, and job performance. In I. Bluestone, R. Montgomery, & J. Owen (Eds.), *The aging of the American work force* (pp. 242–272). Detroit, MI: Wayne State University Press.

Mitchell, O. S., & Luzadis, R. (1988). Changes in pension incentives through time. *Industrial and Labor Relations Review, 42*(1), 100–108.

Montgomery, M. (1988). On the determinants of employer demand for part-time workers. *Review of Economics and Statistics, 70*(1), 112–117.

National Academy of Social Insurance. (1991, February). *Update.* Washington, DC: National Academy of Social Insurance.

Owen, J. D. (1978). Why part-time workers tend to be in low-wage jobs. *Monthly Labor Review, 101*(6), 11–14.

Quinn, J. F. (1991). The nature of retirement: Survey and econometric evidence. In A. H. Munnell (Ed.), *Retirement and public policy* (pp. 115–137). Dubuque, IA: Kendall/Hunt.

Quinn, J. F., & Burkhauser, R. V. (1990, October). Retirement preferences and plans of older American workers. Mimeo. Boston College, Chestnut Hill, MA.

Quinn, J. F., Burkhauser, R. V., & Myers, D. A. (1990). *Passing the torch: The influence of economic incentives on work and retirement.* Kalamazoo, MI: W. E. Upjohn Institute for Employment Research.

Rosow, J. M. (1990). Extending work life. In I. Bluestone, R. Montgomery, & J. Owens (Eds.), *The aging of the American work force* (pp. 399–418). Detroit, MI: Wayne State University Press.

Ruhm, C. J. (1990a, July). Bridge employment and job stopping in the 1980s. Mimeo. Boston University, Boston, MA.

Ruhm, C. J. (1990b). Career jobs, bridge employment, and retirement. In P. J. Doeringer (Ed.), *Bridges to retirement: Older workers in a changing labor market* (pp. 92–107). Ithaca, NY: ILR Press.

Shapiro, D., & Sandell, S. H. (1985). Age discrimination in wages and displaced older workers. *Southern Economic Journal, 52*(1), 90–102.

Turner, J. A., & Beller, D. J. (1989). *Trends in pensions.* Washington, DC: U.S. Government Printing Office.

U.S. Bureau of Labor Statistics. (1990, January; 1991, January). *Employment and earnings.*

U.S. Senate, Special Committee on Aging. (1990). *Aging America: Trends and projections.* Washington, DC: U.S. Government Printing Office.

# 4

# Ageism versus Productive Aging: The Challenge of Age Discrimination in the Labor Market

*Alan Walker and Philip Taylor*

This chapter focuses on the prospects for productive aging through the labor market and has two main aims. First, we examine the structural barriers to productive aging. Recent research is used to illustrate the social processes and policies whereby economic insecurity among older workers is created and, as a corollary, their opportunities for productive aging are constrained. Specifically, we draw on the results of two studies of older workers that we have carried out in Sheffield, England. The first of these was conducted in the early 1980s among a group of 400 redundant steelworkers; the second, conducted in 1990, consisted of in-depth interviews with 140 older workers from a large, representative household survey. This data is used to explore the operation of age discrimination, both formal and informal, in all of the main sections of the labor market. In the first part of this chapter we argue that there is an inherent conflict between ageism and productive aging.

Second, we discuss the policies required to overcome discrimination in the labor market and the institutional barriers to realizing the productive potential of older people. This discussion highlights the unique opportunities offered by current demographic changes to enhance the economic status of older people while at the same time responding to national labor shortages.

## THE SOCIAL CONSTRUCTION OF ECONOMIC INSECURITY

Over the course of this century, the numbers of older workers engaged in economic activity have been contracting, and since the mid–1970s this contraction has been rapid. In Britain at the turn of the century more than two-thirds of men aged sixty-five and over were in the labor force. By 1951 this proportion had halved and by 1989 it had fallen to only 9 percent. Moreover, as Table 4.1 shows, since the mid–1970s the decline in labor

Table 4.1

Labor Force Participation of Older Men in Britain, 1951–1989

| | 1951 | 1961 | 1971 | 1975 | 1981 | 1985 | 1989 |
|---|---|---|---|---|---|---|---|
| Age: | | | | | | | |
| 55–59 | 95.0 | 97.1 | 95.3 | 93.0 | 89.4 | 82.0 | 80.2 |
| 60–64 | 87.7 | 91.0 | 86.6 | 82.3 | 69.3 | 54.4 | 54.6 |
| 65+ | 31.1 | 25.0 | 23.5 | 19.2 | 10.3 | 8.2 | 9.1 |

*Sources*: 1951–1971 Census of Population for England and Wales and for Scotland; 1975–1989 Department of Employment, *Gazette* (various).

force participation among older men has spread into the age groups below pension age (sixty-five for men and sixty for women).

A similar picture may be found in all Organization for Economic Cooperation and Development (OECD) countries though the rate of decline among countries differs markedly. Thus, in 1985, Norway still had 44 percent of men aged sixty-five and over in its labor force and Japan 37 percent, compared with 15 percent in the United States and 5 percent in France and Germany (Holzmann, 1988). Two-thirds of men aged fifty-five to sixty-four were economically active in Britain in 1985 compared with 67 percent in the United States, 83 percent in Japan, 76 percent in Sweden, and 19 percent in Austria. Overall, the labor force participation of older women in OECD countries followed the male pattern, but the decline has been less steep; and in some countries, such as Britain, Canada, Sweden, and the United States, there has been an *increase* in the economic activity rates of women aged fifty-five to sixty-four since the early 1960s (Holzmann, 1988; see also Dex & Phillipson, 1986). The general decrease in labor force participation among older people has meant that the average age of retirement has fallen in all OECD countries over the past thirty years (Holzmann, 1988, p. 78).

What explains this downward trend in economic activity on the part of older workers? A thorough answer to this question would highlight the interplay of both individual-level preferences on the part of successive cohorts of older people and the operation of the labor market (Walker, 1985). In contrast to the popular image of older people choosing freely to leave employment in order to enjoy retirement or early retirement, research suggests that demand-side factors exert a dominant influence on labor market exit (Casey & Laczko, 1989; Trinder, 1990; Walker, 1985).

## Redundancy and Economic Insecurity

The main reason for the especially large fall in labor force participation rates among older workers in the late 1970s and early 1980s was economic recession, which had the effect of accelerating an already well entrenched trend. The majority of unemployed and discouraged men aged sixty to sixty-four either were dismissed or made redundant (Laczko, Dale, Arber, & Gilbert, 1988). Among the early retired, the main reason given for leaving a person's last job was that his employer had introduced an early retirement scheme in order to reduce staff. This indicates that the vast majority of men aged sixty to sixty-four had left their last job involuntarily, and the proportion of fifty-five- to fifty-nine-year-olds doing so was even higher. Furthermore, although the effects of the shake-out of labor, particularly in the manufacturing sector, were felt by all age groups, older people were more likely than younger ones to be made redundant.

Why were older workers more likely than younger ones to experience redundancy (Trinder, 1990, p. 10)? There are three main reasons. First, older workers tended to be overrepresented in industries that suffered the largest decline in employment between 1975 and 1985. Second, older workers were more likely to be dismissed than younger workers as a result of various factors including the age-related state redundancy payments scheme and negative attitudes toward older workers on the part of some employers. Subsequently, they were less likely to find employment if they were made redundant. This necessitated occupational downgrading in the search for work; older people became even more vulnerable to redundancy. Third, for firms needing to shed staff quickly, it was relatively easy to negotiate early retirement for those close to retirement age. In other words, to suggest that the fall in economic activity rates among older workers is simply indicative of a trend toward early retirement is potentially misleading. Early retirement, in the form of withdrawal from the labor market as a result of recession and associated redundancies, is better understood as unemployment rather than as a form of retirement (Westergaard, Noble, & Walker, 1989).

The greater immediate and lasting impact of redundancy on older rather than younger workers may be illustrated by reference to the findings of research among ex-steelworkers in Sheffield, England. Some 400 former employees of a Sheffield steel company were followed up three years after being made redundant during the first wave of deindustrialization in Britain in 1979. The majority were older workers with long service records (Westergaard, Noble, & Walker, 1989).

Three in every four older people (fifty-five and older) were without paid employment three years after their last full-time job. Unemployment, by conventional definition, was sizeable, yet only the large tip of the iceberg: about one-fifth of those aged fifty-five and over had no job and were still

Figure 4.1
Employment Status of Older Male Workers Following Redundancy According to
Age at Time of Redundancy

a) men 55-59

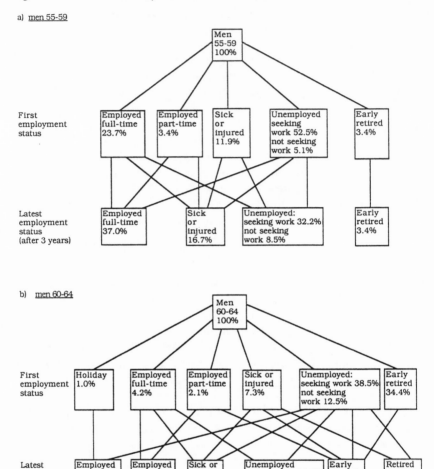

*Source*: Westergaard, Noble, & Walker (1989), Note 8, p. 107.

looking for one. The rest of the ex-steelworkers had *withdrawn* from the labor market. In fact, economic inactivity—effective withdrawal from the labor market—accounted for more of the *nonemployment* than did *unemployment* (average nonemployment was twice the level of unemployment).

Figure 4.1 shows the distribution of postredundancy activity statuses for the two different age groups of male older workers immediately following redundancy and three years later. This figure demonstrates the remarkable impact of redundancy on a previously very stable work force. Redundancy also had a differential impact according to age group, not only among older workers themselves but between them and younger adults. As Figure 4.1 shows, the sixty- to sixty-four-year-olds were ten times more likely than the fifty-five- to fifty-nine-year-olds to exit immediately from the labor market; for the latter group the route out of economic activity more typically consisted of unemployment and a long period of increasing discouragement prior to exit. Two-thirds of those younger than forty were reemployed full-time immediately after being made redundant (compared with an average 17 percent of those aged fifty-five and over). The deeper impact of redundancy on older compared with younger workers is emphasized by looking at the incidence of nonemployment over the whole three-year period. Nearly two in every three older workers held paid employment for less than half of the three-year period, a nonemployment rate more than double that of young and middle-aged adults.

These differences based on age were offset slightly by a gender impact; there was a preponderance of female discouraged workers in the younger age group. The small proportion of women in the study were concentrated in the under-forty age group and, immediately following redundancy, 4 percent of this age group classified themselves as "housewives" or "looking after family." Three years later, 11 percent were in this category.

What did the experience of economic insecurity entail for older workers? As we have seen, it meant, first of all, the concentration of unemployment, experienced as a series of separate spells or as a single long-term one, as well as other forms of nonemployment. Second, as a result of redundancy and nonemployment, older workers had lower incomes than younger ones (who were more likely to be in employment). Among older workers, the employed were, not surprisingly, considerably better off financially than others, whereas the unemployed were most likely to experience poverty. The mean total income of unemployed income units aged sixty to sixty-four was 45 percent of that of the employed, while mean total income of early retired income units was 64 percent of that of employed income units. Not surprisingly, therefore, the proportion of unemployed people who reported having to cut down severely on their expenditures since being made redundant was three times that of the employed. Moreover, the general process of involuntary disengagement among the nonemployed following redundancy, particularly withdrawal from social life, was acute among the unemployed. These findings are supported by national survey data for the years 1980–1982. Among manual-class men aged sixty to sixty-four and their wives, only 9 percent of the employed were living in poverty or on its margins, compared with an average of 54 percent for the nonemployed groups, which extended to 66 percent among the unemployed (Laczko, Dale, Arber, & Gilbert, 1988, p. 327).

Third, the concentration of economic insecurity on older workers was revealed by their greater likelihood to suffer symptoms of psychological distress. Using Norman Bradburn's measure of "negative affect,"[1] it was found that older workers were most prone to psychological distress, and it was the fifty-five- to fifty-nine-year-olds who were slightly more likely than the sixty- to sixty-four-year-olds to experience distress.

Fourth, economic insecurity in the labor market meant more than difficulty in finding employment. When older workers were successful in finding a job, it was not necessarily of the same type or grade as the one they had held previously. In other words, occupational downgrading was commonplace among those in employment. Moreover, once downgraded they became vulnerable to a second redundancy; 27 percent of the employed found themselves in this position. This group, once regarded as being part of the "aristocracy" of skilled labor, when they were eventually pressed out of the labor market were in virtually the same position as their semiskilled and unskilled counterparts had been all along.

These various dimensions of economic insecurity were reflected in the subjective responses of older workers. For example, older workers were much more likely than younger ones to regard their status as insecure. Focusing on the unemployed, four out of five of those aged fifty-five and over rated their prospects of finding a job as poor compared with one in four of those under forty.

So, during the late 1970s and early 1980s redundancy was a major factor in involuntary exit from employment, and there appeared to be an active policy of discrimination in favor of older workers as candidates for dismissal. Moreover, once they were back in the labor market, older workers were at a considerable disadvantage compared with younger ones as a result of ageism in recruitment.

### Ageism in the Internal Labor Market

The first major obstacle to productive aging, therefore, is the apparent attitude of employers—reinforced by official redundancy payment regulations—that it is more acceptable to make older workers redundant than younger ones.

The research among ex-steelworkers in Sheffield distinguished two distinct pathways into early retirement following redundancy. One the one hand, there were those who chose willingly to exit from the labor market and, to some extent, were relieved to do so; on the other hand, there were those who were forced into early retirement by the lack of alternatives, sometimes following prolonged unemployment, and who gave up employment reluctantly (Walker, 1985, p. 226). The population of redundant older steelworkers was divided almost equally between these two groups. But even among those older workers who reported that they gave up employment voluntarily, there seems to have been pressure exerted on them to leave the organization. In the case of the ex-steelworkers in Sheffield, this pressure took the form of redundancy, especially during the phase leading up to the plant closure when older workers repeatedly were encouraged to accept the company's early retirement package.

Similarly, research among older automobile workers has found that those facing or merely anticipating on-the-job changes are more apt to retire early given the opportunity than others not facing such changes (Pollman & Johnson, 1974). That the "finances were right" was the most frequently cited reason for the decision to take early retirement by a sample of ex-professional and managerial employees. This was followed by feelings that they had worked long enough and deserved retirement, a desire for more free time, and the state of their health. In addition, unsatisfactory job factors were cited, and these included job changes, feelings of insecurity in their posts, management, and the stresses and strains of the job (McGoldrick & Cooper, 1980). In the words of the researchers, Ann McGoldrick and Cary Cooper:

While the majority felt that they had made their decision in an entirely unpressured way, certain "influences" were noted by retirees. Some had felt influenced by company pressure or the feeling that they were not indispensable, pressure from union or fellow workers and the belief that they were expected to retire to prevent younger workers being made redundant. Close-downs and redundancies caused insecurity. Volunteers sometimes felt that they might later be forced to leave with reduced financial benefits, or at a time when it would be more difficult to find alternative employment (McGoldrick & Cooper, 1980, p. 860).

The second group—those who reluctantly exited the labor market—was concentrated among lower socioeconomic classes, but by no means exclusively so. While some professional older workers may leave employment on relatively favorable terms, those in semiskilled or unskilled jobs may enter a period of unemployment with little more to live on than social security payments and a modest redundancy settlement. Such workers are likely to remain anxious to find employment and suffer particularly from depression and low morale.

Employers also may discriminate against older workers within the internal labor market in terms of performance appraisal. Appraisers may make stereotyped judgments based on a limited set of characteristics—for example, educational level, age, sex, and their supposed relationships to job performance (Davies & Sparrow, 1985). These ratings often reflect the rater's bias rather than the employee's performance (Stagner, 1979). In support of this notion, other research (Cleveland & Landy, 1981) found that when managers were appraised on eight attributes, the correlations of ratings with the manager's age were less for experienced appraisers than for inexperienced ones.

Older workers also may get passed over in preference to younger people when promotion decisions are made. For example, research among a sample of aerospace employees aged forty-five and over, found that 22 percent personally had experienced an inability to advance in a job because of their age, while 22 percent said that their friends had faced such a problem (Kasschau, 1976). Similarly, there is the reported case of an insurance company where management held a very negative attitude toward older workers. There were few promotion opportunities open to older people and, as a result, ambitious workers over the age of fifty-five left in substantial numbers (Hirshorn, 1988).

In employment, the amount of training an older worker receives declines with his or her age. A recent Department of Employment survey found that, of those who had received any form of training in the four weeks prior to being interviewed, only 4.5 percent were people aged fifty to fifty-nine while the sixty- to sixty-four-year-olds comprised only 1.9 percent (Department of Employment, 1988). In addition, a higher proportion of older employers lack qualifications. Other research has shown that, even though older workers are less likely than younger ones to be willing to consider vocational education or training, a majority of them either are actively considering it or, more likely, would be willing to do so (Coulson-Thomas, 1989). Older workers may be by-passed because of supposed fewer future years of service or because it is felt that they would not want to retrain. As noted above, employers also may consider older people less trainable. According to Colin Coulson-Thomas (1989, p. 17),

Too many staff are plateaued because their managers lack the imagination and motivation to provide new challenges and opportunities. In this respect younger employees are sometimes less hassle to manage, and are hence preferred.

In the words of a fifty-five-year-old male design engineer who we interviewed: "Too old to retrain for computers. I wanted to, they wouldn't allow me." The obvious dangers associated with this discrimination with respect to training is that a gap in skill levels will develop between older and younger employees. As a result, older workers may become dissatisfied and demotivated and feel under pressure to retire or accept redundancy. Those seeking work subsequently will have outdated skills and consequently less to offer prospective employers.

As well as the more overt examples of ageism above, employer policy inadvertently may discriminate against older workers. For example, there is a growing body of evidence that labor market orientation and participation are affected directly by obligations in the informal sector (see, for example, Berger, 1983; Bytheway, 1986; Qureshi & Walker, 1989; Scharlach & Boyd, 1989). For example, Mark Berger (1983) found that both the probability of being in the labor force and the annual working hours of women increased in response to the poor health or death of their partner; men reduced both their participation and hours of work when their partner died or suffered a deterioration in health. Evidence suggests that the caring role often has a negative impact on well-being, finances, quality of life, and career opportunities (Scharlack & Boyd, 1989). Thus, a failure to recognize the need for provision to assist older employees in these circumstances can, in effect, be discriminatory.

## Ageism in the External Labor Market

Older workers are more likely to experience redundancy than younger ones and, once in the labor market, they are faced with formidable barriers. For example, they are more prone to illness and disability than younger people, manual workers more so than nonmanual ones. Reductions in working capacity on this score may remain invisible or be condoned by a long-term employer, but once the individual is unemployed, they become a barrier to finding a new job. Older workers also are at a great disadvantage because of age discriminatory recruitment practices. Most of the ex-steelworkers we studied in the sixty- to sixty-four-year-old age group who were unemployed had more or less given up looking for a job, in the words of one 63-year-old man "because I'm sick of trying and being told I'm too old."

It is not surprising, therefore, that older unemployed workers have a low expectation of regaining employment and may prefer to define themselves as disabled or early retired (Bytheway, 1987; Laczko, 1987; Piachaud, 1986; Rosenblum, 1975; Walker, 1985). Many feel discouraged from seeking employment. Some regard themselves as having effectively retired, despite being in their fifties or early sixties, and become resigned to the fact that they will not work again.

Age restrictions in job advertisements often are cited by older workers as one of the main barriers to employment. A recent study carried out by the Department of Employment on advertisements placed in Job Centres[2] showed that 11 percent of vacancies were not open to people aged sixty years and over (Jones & Longstone, 1990). Another recent survey of advertisements placed in the national press showed that age bars to recruitment most likely were found in sales and marketing posts, access being restricted to those people in their early twenties to late thirties (Tillsley, 1990), despite evidence that performance in such jobs is least likely to decrease with age (Davies & Sparrow, 1985).

Without actually specifying age bars in advertisements, recruitment practices may discriminate unwittingly against older people. For example, the unnecessary specification of education qualification and types of experience that could be gained only by recent labor market entrants can restrict applicants to a desired age range. The age of the person doing the interview also is cited by older people as a factor in getting turned down for jobs. In the words of a fifty-eight-year-old man recently interviewed: "The more I look at jobs and the age requirements, the more I consider myself at retirement age now."

A larger number of potential working years, paper qualifications, and purported greater adaptability are cited by older people as reasons employers might give for preferring to employ younger people, although older workers themselves think they are more reliable. Other reasons given are that employers are not willing to train older people. Another barrier to employment identified by older people is that employers have concerns that an older person might not be fit to do a job. Many older people also feel that the only jobs open to them are extremely low paid. These are some examples from our recent interviews:

Not at all interested. They'll get a longer working life out of younger ones. They'd not dream of training anyone fifty to sixty. They've no great regard for setting [taking] on anyone older but if they've been with the firm they know they are loyal. But not to start them working for them. [Man, sixty-four]

They are eager to set people on until they find their age—they have to pay older workers more. They don't trust them to be fit to do the job. [Man, fifty-nine]

The results of a survey of employers, carried out to examine whether attitudes and practices toward older workers are altering in response to demographic changes, revealed that employers were taking more active steps to recruit more older people. However, employers felt that older people were suitable for employment only in low-skill, low-responsibility, and repetitive jobs, while physically demanding, time-pressured, or information technology–based jobs were deemed unsuitable. Employers also considered older workers less trainable. Methods used by companies to recruit more older workers included creating more part-time jobs and giving all part-timers status and pension rights in order to make these jobs more attractive (Metcalf & Thompson, 1990). This policy would seem to preclude those nonworking older people who require full-time employment and the income it would provide.

It is not only employers that erect discriminatory barriers to the recruitment of older people. In both of the Sheffield studies, official labor market intermediaries, working in Job Centres and Department of Social Security offices, were important sources of discouragement. Many older workers simply were not interviewed and, if they were, they were told that their job prospects were zero. Others had experienced a negative approach by staff at the Job Centre. Thus, many do not even reach the stage of applying for jobs. In the words of a sixty-three-year-old man: "When I went to the Job Centre they said they couldn't do anything for me at my age." According to another man, aged sixty: "They told me at the Unemployment Office not to bother now that I'd reached sixty—that I'd got no chance of a job anyway now. Nothing would prompt me now having being told not to bother."

In addition, several of the people in our 1990 study had attended Restart interviews at their local Job Centre (these are compulsory for anyone who has been unemployed for six months).[3] Again, it would appear that older people often are told that because of their age the prospects of them regaining employment are remote, and they are advised to discontinue their job search:

I was only in for ten minutes. Jobs were never discussed. Sixteen of us about the same age went in together. Just said at your age don't bother and come back in six months. They couldn't change anything. It all comes back to being too old at sixty for anything. [Man, sixty]

The results are consistent with an earlier survey of Job Centre staff, which found that fifty-year-olds were rated by officials as the most difficult to place during a recession, the most difficult for an employer to train, and the slowest and least able to maintain production schedules (Britton & Thomas, 1973).

Older workers also are discriminated against in terms of access to government training schemes. For example, a Department of Employment guide to the Employment Training Scheme for unemployed adults gives the following information about eligibility:

Employment training aims to help a wide range of people's needs. First priority will be given to people aged between 18 and 24 unemployed between 6 and 12 months; next to those people aged between 18 and 50 unemployed for more than two years. But as long as there are enough places available the needs of all people eligible for the program will be catered for.

It is clear from this statement that the lowest priority for training is given to those people aged over fifty, although the evidence is that they already possess less education and training than younger adults. Thus, older people are confronted with a variation of Catch–22. They are discriminated against by employers on various age-related grounds but, at the same time, are denied access to the programs designed to overcome such barriers in the labor market on exactly the same grounds.

## The Social Construction of Ageism

The above review, based largely on British research, shows that older people may be discriminated against in both internal and external labor markets and that this discrimination can take overt and covert forms. However, many of the barriers to employment facing older people appear to be based on inaccurate stereotypes. Previous research has shown that older workers are rated as more likely to be in poorer health, less likely to be with a company for a long period, more resistant to change, less creative, more cautious, having a lower physical capacity, less interested in technological change, less trainable, displaying less autonomy, more accident prone, less effective, and less personally acceptable (Craft, Doctors, Shkop, & Benecki, 1979; Rosen & Jerdee, 1976a, 1976b). Despite evidence to the contrary, it would appear that such stereotypes are still commonplace.

While stereotypes of older workers may affect the decision to hire or retrain them, other ageist motivations can influence policy and practice with regard to this group. For example, the organization may wish to present a young image to its customers. It is not necessarily that younger employees are valued for what they bring to the organization but rather for what they can do to enhance a company's profile in a youth-oriented society.

This endemic ageism is not simply a matter of individual prejudice (if it were, it would be relatively easy to tackle); it is institutionalized in the labor market and other social and economic systems. It is reproduced at both macro and micro levels by social policies. Thus, retirement may be said to be both the leading form of age discrimination and the driving force behind the wider development of ageism in modern societies (Walker, 1980, 1981). The long-term decline in the participation of older people, particularly older men, in the work force cannot be attributed to changes in the individual characteristics of older people themselves—their health, attitudes toward work, and so on. Nor can this trend be understood simply on the basis of the preferences expressed by older workers. In Britain and other industrial societies, retirement has been used by employers, including government, to reduce and restructure their work forces in response to both the constant pressure to increase productivity and cyclical changes in the demand for labor (Graebner, 1980; Guillemard, 1980; Myles, 1984; Phillipson, 1982; Walker, 1980). Thus, retirement may be interpreted, in large measure, as an age discriminatory social process designed to exclude older people en masse from the work force. Retirement conditions attached to both public and private pensions are key elements of this process. Much of the impetus behind the development of retirement was provided by economic, medical, and managerial theories of the late nineteenth and early twentieth centuries concerning the industrial efficiency of younger and older workers. The most notable example of this was Frederick Taylor's (1947) theory of scientific management. Although these early scientific and quasi-scientific theories about declining productivity in older age groups are discredited, as we have seen, they still exert a powerful influence in labor markets.

In the post–World War II period, employers have used redundancy like retirement to restructure their work forces by "buying out" those regarded as the least efficient. This restructuring has been concentrated on older workers and, as we have seen, for some it has effectively reduced their retirement age. In Britain, this process has been encouraged by public policy—for example, because redundancy payments are based on a formula that renders awards based on the length of service. This has both encouraged the view that it is more acceptable to make older workers redundant than younger ones and legitimated the use of age, by employers and trade unions, as a basis for redundancy. In the Sheffield study of ex-steel workers, the redundancy package was designed to appeal to older workers. There is plenty of evidence from this and other research to demonstrate that older people often come under intense managerial and peer group pressure to take redundancy or early retirement. An important aspect of this coercion is the financial inducement of a lump-sum redundancy payment. In the words of one fifty-eight-year-old office worker, who took early retirement from the steel company we studied:

I saw the writing on the wall. Despite promises people were losing their jobs or being moved to uncongenial jobs, I think on purpose to make them leave. I don't think any staff were sacked, but things were made uncomfortable and if I hadn't accepted the generous offer I might have been given the push one or two years later without the extra redundancy pay.

Our research shows that age discrimination operates across all socioeconomic groups but that its impact is greatest on the manual group. Therefore, redundancy has the effect of exposing the disadvantages associated with social class and age that influence other aspects of a person's economic life when in employment—such as poor working conditions (resulting in poor health), low levels of education and training, and lack of opportunities for skill enhancement and promotion—as well as opening the door to new age-related ones.

In the face of financial hardship and constant rebuttal from employers, it may seem remarkable that so many older people hold on tenaciously to the labor market. Yet, for many, especially those in the fifty-five- to fifty-nine-year-old age group, there is little choice. They are caught in a painful dilemma. On the one hand, there are the pressures associated with poverty and low incomes and the force of the paid employment ethic of capitalist societies pushing them to search for a job or to accept an insecure one; on the other hand, there is the reality of an age-segmented labor market. In other words, the economic insecurity experienced by older workers is a function of social policies with regard to employment, social security, and retirement, with public policy playing a leading role. The end result of this socially constructed relationship between old age and the labor market is the economic hardship and psychological stress, outlined earlier, which is borne individually by older people and their families.

## TOWARD PRODUCTIVE AGING?

What changes are necessary to overcome ageism and enhance the possibility of productive aging? Although we would favor a broad definition of productive aging, encompassing all personally rewarding pursuits, we accept the need for the rather narrower definition—entailing the greater involvement of older people in paid employment and community service— for the purposes of this volume. However, before proceeding to outline specific policy proposals, it is important to emphasize two cautions concerning the promise of productive ageing.

First, the assumptions underlying the concept of productive aging—that there is a vital connection between health and productivity and, therefore, that the employment of older people is both good for them and society (Butler, Oberlink, & Schecter, 1990, p. 201)—are problematic. These assumptions are questionable with regard to certain kinds of jobs, especially those of a physically arduous or mentally debilitating nature. Because of wide variations in the quality of the labor that individuals are engaged in during their early and middle years, some people's bodies, quite simply, wear out sooner than others. If society assumes that productivity is necessarily good for the older person, it may compound inequalities in poor health and disability created by socioeconomic status in the workplace. This has obvious policy implications: it would be detrimental to the interests of some older workers if policy shifted from the ageist assumption that older people should be made redundant or not reemployed simply because of their age to an unsophisticated productive aging "ethic," which states that they *must* be in employment or community service for their own good and that of society. It is vital, therefore, that any policy based on the idea of productive aging is sensitive to individual circumstances and does not stigmatize people for not being productive. Furthermore, action must be taken to change work processes that create poor health and disability.

Second, in the past the processes of social exclusion and ageism in the labor market have been consciously manipulated by policymakers in response to changes in the demand for labor. Therefore, it is important to ensure that productive aging is not used by policymakers as a slogan to encourage older people to stay in, or return to, the labor force to solve short-term labor shortages only for them to be jettisoned when these shortages disappear.

In Britain, for example, over the past forty-five years or so older men have been used as a labor reserve. In the period immediately after World War II, people of pension ages were urged *not* to retire but to work longer and enjoy a happier old age. Special measures were introduced by the government to encourage them to do so. Moreover, medical and social science research began to indicate that retirement had detrimental effects. In contrast, as unemployment rose in the mid–1970s, policymakers began to encourage older workers to retire early in order to enjoy a happier old age. In 1977, the Job Release Scheme was introduced, as a temporary measure, to alleviate unemployment among younger workers by providing allowances for older workers to take early retirement and be replaced by younger ones.

The scheme reached its peak, along with unemployment, in 1984–1985 when 90,000 older people were receiving allowances. In 1981, unemployed men aged sixty to sixty-four were awarded an additional social assistance premium if they withdrew from the unemployment register. Since the late 1980s, reductions in the numbers of young entrants to the labor force have led to changes in policies aimed at older people. A series of measures have been introduced to encourage older people to remain in or to reenter the labor force. These include the 50-plus Job Start Allowance Scheme, whereby an older person receives an extra amount on top of the wage or salary paid by the employer (the scheme was abandoned in February 1991 because of low participation); the abolition of restrictions on the amount older people could earn if they were still working beyond the state pension age before their pension would be reduced; and, more recently, changes to regulations concerning the registration for benefits of those over fifty so that in the future they will be required to register for state benefits every two weeks instead of every three months. As a result of this fluctuating experience over many years, older men would have good reason to be skeptical initially about policies promising them a more productive aging. With these cautions in mind then, what can be done to overcome the barriers within the external and internal labor markets outlined in the main part of this chapter?

## Promoting Productive Aging

In the first place, it is necessary to recognize that a narrow focus on paid employment will not be sufficient to ensure equal opportunities for older people. For example, as indicated earlier, it is important for action to be taken with respect to work processes that debilitate many older workers *prior to* pension age and, thereby, foreclose any other options apart from exit from the labor force. This requires monumental efforts on the part of advanced industrial societies and levels of government intervention that some, such as the United States, might find unpalatable. If such action is not taken, however, it must be accepted that the idea of productive aging will have very little meaning for, and may even be offensive to, some older people prevented by disability from participating.

Another example is that many older people outside of the labor force already are providing vital services in the informal sector, either in a voluntary capacity in the community or in caring roles within the family. Some of these tasks, such as the care of grandchildren, are supporting other productive workers and may be crucial to their involvement in the labor force. Thus, it is important to extend the meaning of productive aging to include these sorts of informal caring and tending tasks. If the basic tenets of productive aging are correct—that productivity preserves health and vice versa—then those older people engaged in a range of educational and leisure activities also must be accorded social recognition and not be subjected to stigma, because what they are engaged in does not conform to a narrow conception of production.

Second, if institutional ageism is to be overcome, then governments must take a lead in both legislative and promotional terms. As experience under the 1967 Age Discrimination in Employment Act in the United States indicates, legislation by itself will not alter institutional norms and practices. It does, however, have symbolic importance; furthermore, lessons can be learned from the restricted operation of the U.S. legislation to ensure that subsequent attempts to outlaw age discrimination have a greater impact on the labor market. In the first instance, the state should ensure that its own policies and agencies do not discriminate on age grounds. Then policy could extend further to encourage, by a combination of carrot and stick, compliance on the part of all employers. In a British context, this would entail giving specific responsibilities to staff in Job Centres to combat age discrimination (Laczko & Phillipson, 1990). Again, however, it must be recognized that promotional campaigns alone will not ensure compliance, as demonstrated by experience in different countries with quota schemes for the employment of people with disabilities.

Third, the whole process of retirement must be made more flexible. This entails the abolition of age-barrier retirement and the introduction of partial pensions, as in Sweden, to allow some older employees to work part-time and receive reduced pensions and so adjust their working time gradually, at their own pace (Schuller & Walker, 1990).

Finally, at the level of the workplace, employers and trade unions both face the challenge of age discrimination in all its various overt and covert forms. It is only when concerted action is taken at the plant as well as the national level that it will be possible to begin to overcome assumptions about older people which have been made so regularly and for so long that they have achieved the status of conventional wisdom. Examples of the policies required at the plant level include not using age as a primary means of selection in recruitment, promotion, and training; challenging the use of all age bars in employment; the provision of career guidance and counseling for older workers; educational leave schemes; and the targeting of in-house training schemes on older people.

As well as proposing a package of policy measures such as this, it is necessary to acknowledge the considerable institutional barriers to its introduction. These include the reluctance of governments to intervene in what is widely regarded in capitalist societies as a private contract between employer and employee. An ideological belief in the free market merely emphasizes this reluctance. Thus, according to the Department of Employment in Britain,

There is currently no legislation in this country to prevent age discrimination in employment and the government's view is that it would be neither beneficial nor practical to do so. Employers should be free to recruit the most suitable workers and not be restricted from doing so by legislation and regulation.

Employers and trade unions too have colluded in the promotion of re-tirement and more recently early retirement, believing it to be in the best interests of their companies and their members respectively. The trend to-ward early retirement in all advanced industrial societies will be difficult to reverse. The production process itself acts as a barrier to change to the extent that it can create a major disincentive to continued employment and, in some cases, can produce alienation.

## CONCLUSION

The mainly British research evidence reviewed in this chapter suggests that the prospects for productive aging in the late twentieth and early twenty-first centuries are constrained severely by age discriminatory practices in different sections of the labor market and sectors of employment. In other words, there is a direct conflict between ageism and productive aging: the former must be overcome if the latter is to become a reality. The aging of the population and shortages in the supply of labor experienced by some countries, such as Britain, offer a unique historical opportunity for this goal to be realized. But the barriers to change are formidable because ageist policies and attitudes are deeply ingrained institutionally as well as cultur-ally. Thus, if age discrimination in the labor market is to be combated, it must first be recognized by all parties as a challenge.

## NOTES

1. Norman Bradburn (see Warr, Barter, & Brownbridge, 1983) has measured psychological well-being in terms of two separate five-item scales of positive and negative affect. Each item asks whether in the past few weeks the respondent has felt (yes or no), for example, "very lonely or remote from other people." Each scale is scored in terms of the number of positive or negative feelings over this time period.

2. Job Centres are a national network of official employment bureaus operated by the Department of Employment.

3. The Restart Programme is intended to encourage the long-term unemployed to seek work.

## REFERENCES

Berger, M. (1983). Labour supply and spouse's health: The effect of illness, disability and mortality. *Social Science Quarterly, 64*(3), 494–509.

Bradburn, N. M. (1969). *The structure of psychological well-being*. Chicago, IL: Aldine.

Britton, J. O., & Thomas, K. R. (1973). Age and sex as employment variables:

Views of employment service interviewers. *Journal of Employment Counselling, 10*, 180–186.

Butler, R., Oberlink, M., & Schecter, M. (Eds.). (1990). *The promise of productive aging.* New York: Springer.

Bytheway, B. (1986). *Early retirement and the care of dependent elderly people.* Paper presented to the British Sociological Association's Annual Conference, Loughborough, England.

Bytheway, B. (1987). Redundancy and the older worker. In R. M. Lee (Ed.), *Redundancy, layoffs and plant closures* (pp. 84–115). Beckenham, England: Croom Helm.

Casey, B., & Laczko, F. (1989). Early retired or long-term unemployed? The situation of non-working men aged 55–64 from 1976 to 1986. *Work, Employment and Society 1*(4), 509–526.

Cleveland, J. N., & Landy, F. J. (1981). Influence of rater and ratee age on two performance judgments. Personnel Psychology, *34*, 19–30.

Coulson-Thomas, C. (1989). *Too old at 40.* London: British Institute of Management.

Craft, J. A., Doctors, S. I., Shkop, V. M., & Benecki, T. J. (1979, Spring). Simulated management perceptions, hiring decisions and age. *Aging and Work,* 95–102.

Davies, D. R., & Sparrow, P. R. (1985). Age and work behaviour. In N. Charness (Ed.), *Aging and human performance* (pp. 293–332). London: Wiley.

Department of Employment. (1988). Training in Britain: Key statistics. *Employment Gazette, 96*(3), 130–143.

Dex, S., & Phillipson, C. (1986). Social policy and the older worker. In C. Phillipson & A. Walker (Eds.), *Ageing and social policy.* Aldershot, England: Gower.

Graebner, W. (1980). *A history of retirement.* New Haven, CT: Yale University Press.

Guillemard, A-M. (1980). La viellesse et l'état. Paris: PUF.

Hirshorn, B. A. (1988). Organisational behaviour regarding older workers: Prototypical responses. *Journal of Aging Studies, 2*(3), 199–215.

Holzmann, R. (1988). *Reforming public pensions* (pp. 144–145). Paris: Organization for Economic Cooperation and Development.

Jones, A., & Longstone, L. (1990, March). *A survey of restrictions on Job Centre vacancies.* London: Department of Employment Service.

Kasschau, P. L. (1976). Perceived age discrimination in a sample of aerospace employees. *The Gerontologist, 16*, 166–173.

Laczko, F. (1987). Older workers, unemployment, and the discouraged worker effect. In S. DiGregorio (Ed.), *Social gerontology: New directions* (pp. 239–251). Beckenham, England: Croom Helm.

Laczko, F., Dale, A., Arber, S., & Gilbert, G. N. (1988). Early retirement in a period of high unemployment. *Journal of Social Policy, 17*(3), 313–333.

Laczko, F., & Phillipson, C. (1990). Defending the right to work. In E. McEwan (Ed.), *Age: The unrecognised discrimination* (pp. 84–96). London: Age Concern.

McGoldrick, A., & Cooper, C. L. (1980, August). Voluntary early retirement—Taking the decision. *Employment Gazette,* pp. 859–864.

Metcalf, H., & Thompson, M. (1990). *Older workers: Employers' attitudes and practices.* Sussex, England: Institute for Manpower Studies.

Myles, J. (1984). *Old age in the welfare state.* Boston: Little, Brown.

Phillipson, C. (1982). *Capitalism and the construction of old age.* London: Macmillan.

Piachaud, D. (1986). Disability, retirement and unemployment of older men. *Journal of Social Policy, 15*(2), 145–162.

Pollman, A. W., & Johnson, A. C. (1974). Resistance to change, early retirement and managerial decisions. *Industrial Gerontology, 1*(1), 33–41.

Qureshi, H., & Walker, A. (1989). *The caring relationship.* Philadelphia: Temple University Press.

Rosen, B., & Jerdee, T. H. (1976a). The nature of job-related age stereotypes. *Journal of Applied Psychology, 61*(2), 180–183.

Rosen, B., & Jerdee, T. H. (1976b). The influence of age stereotypes on managerial decisions. *Journal of Applied Psychology, 61*(2), 428–432.

Rosenblum, M. (1975). The last push: From discouraged worker to involuntary retirement. *Industrial Gerontology, 2,* 14–22.

Scharlach, A. E., & Boyd, S. L. (1989). Caregiving and employment: Results of an employee survey. *The Gerontologist, 29*(3), 382–387.

Schuller, T., & Walker, A. (1990). *The time of our life.* London: Institute for Public Policy Research.

Stagner, R. (1979). Ageing in industry. In J. E. Birren & K. W. Schaie (Eds.), *Handbook of psychology of aging* (pp. 789–817). New York: Van Nostrand Reinhold.

Taylor, F. W. (1947). *Scientific management.* New York: Harper & Row.

Tillsley, C. (1990). *The impact of age upon employment.* Coventry, England: University of Warwick.

Trinder, C. (1990). *Employment after 55.* London: National Institute for Economic and Social Research.

Walker, A. (1980). The social creation of poverty and dependency in old age. *Journal of Social Policy, 9*(1), 49–75.

Walker, A. (1981). Towards a political economy of old age. *Ageing and Society, 1*(1), 73–94.

Walker, A. (1985). Early retirement: Release or refuge from the labour market? *Quarterly Journal of Social Affairs, 1*(3), 211–219.

Warr, P., Barter, J. & Brownbridge, B. (1983). On the independence of positive and negative affect. *Journal of Personality and Social Psychology, 44*(3), 644–651.

Westergaard, J., Noble, I., & Walker, A. (1989). *After redundancy.* Oxford: Polity Press.

# 5

# New Technologies and the Aging Work Force

## David C. Mowery and Mark S. Kamlet

Forecasting the effects of new technologies on the older worker in the future U.S. economy is a complex task. Projections of the direction and rate of technological development themselves are notorious for their inaccuracy. In addition, the implications of new technologies for the skills needed by the work force are often uncertain and subject to considerable change. Finally, any assessment of technology's effects on the older worker must take into account the retirement behavior of workers within an aging U.S. work force that is likely to experience lower rates of lifetime earnings growth and wealth accumulation than their parents or grandparents. As a result, historic trends in retirement behavior, which have been compiled against a background of steady growth in income and wealth and rapid growth in the U.S. labor force, may be inaccurate predictors of future behavior.

In view of these uncertainties, this chapter does not attempt to predict the future. Instead, we describe the range of possibilities and raise the issues that will require attention regarding the response of an aging work force to new workplace technologies. We begin by outlining a simple framework for understanding the process of technological change. Among other things, this perspective challenges the widely held characterization of technological change and technological adoption as rapid processes that can suddenly displace large segments of the work force. We then consider the limited and contradictory evidence on the skill effects of new technologies, review the evidence on the retirement behavior of U.S. workers to provide some information on future behavior, and, finally, make an assessment of the possible effects of new technologies on older workers.

The primary technologies that we are considering in this chapter are the computer-based technologies of office and factory automation frequently categorized as "information technology." Information technology and its related applications have grown and changed dramatically during the past decade, reflecting rapid rates of innovation in microelectronic components and software. We include in our discussion of information technology the application of computers within offices and manufacturing establishments, as well as telecommunications and advanced information storage and retrieval technologies. In our definition, such technologies as robotics, computer-aided design (CAD), and computer-integrated manufacturing (CIM) are all part of the information technology cluster.

One of the most important conclusions can be noted immediately. Technology, especially the new technologies being adopted within this nation's factories and offices, rarely exerts a strong, autonomous, deterministic influence on workplace organization or worker skill requirements. Instead, new technologies are relatively plastic, and the economic and skill implications of their diffusion within an economy depend critically on managerial decisions and organizational structure. A better-informed population of workers, managers, and policymakers can contribute to more intelligent decision making and improved working and economic conditions for older workers and for all U.S. workers.

## UNDERSTANDING THE PROCESS OF TECHNOLOGICAL CHANGE[1]

Although popular accounts frequently portray technological change as a force that operates with rapidity, in fact, it consists of several processes, each of which varies in speed, sensitivity to external shocks, and resource requirements. These processes overlap in time and often interact in complex ways.

The invention phase of the process of technological change typically covers basic research and includes the discovery of scientific or technological advances and the translation of these discoveries into operational principles or prototypes. Innovation follows invention and includes the development of a prototype into a commercial-scale machine or production process. In the case of the transistor, which underpins information technologies, the process of invention spanned the period from the late 1930s, when Bell Telephone Laboratories launched a research effort in solid-state physics, through 1947, when Bardeen, Brittain, and Schockley first produced their model of a point-contact transistor. The innovation phase for the transistor spanned the period from 1947 to 1954 and resulted in the development of a commercially produced device. Development of the commercially feasible version of the transistor required significant advances in the science and technology of materials, primarily pure silicon crystals, and in the theory of semiconductors.

In most instances, the costs of research increase steeply as one moves from the invention into the innovation phases because of the growing share of costs devoted to capital equipment and production facilities. The individual or firm responsible for the invention of a new product or process need not be the firm or individual that eventually is successful at innovation, translating the advance into a commercially successful product. Many of the important innovations introduced by the DuPont Corporation during the 1920s and 1930s (other than nylon), for example, were inventions purchased from other firms (in many instances, acquired with the firm) or individuals and "scaled up" and commercialized by DuPont.

The phase of the process of technological change that is most important for the concerns of this chapter is the diffusion of new technologies within an economy, the adoption by users of a new technology. The effects of new technologies on employment, working conditions, and productivity obviously are influenced by the rate and extent of their adoption by users. Technological diffusion typically is a relatively gradual and extended process—it can take decades for all of the firms within a specific industry to adopt a new technology.[2] Moreover, there are few indications that the rate of diffusion of new technologies within the U.S. economy has accelerated in recent years. Indeed, it has been argued that one source of lagging U.S. competitiveness is the slow pace with which such advanced manufacturing technologies as robotics or CIM are being adopted by U.S. manufacturing firms. The slow pace of diffusion reflects the imperfect information available to prospective adopters about the new technology, the high costs of early adoption, and other factors.

One important influence on the pace of adoption of new technologies is the skills of the work force. Although causality cannot be established from the available data, some portion of the relatively slow adoption of new manufacturing technologies by U.S. firms may be linked to lower levels of private and public investment in production worker skills (e.g., through training, primary and secondary education, etc.). Worker skills are especially important to early adoption of new technologies, since in their initial versions new technologies often have much more demanding skill requirements. The level of worker skills needed to operate the IBM mainframe computers of the early 1960s considerably exceed those required to operate an Apple Macintosh personal computer in the 1990s. Computer technology now includes a number of segments, some of which have much less demanding operator skill requirements than those of earlier computer technologies. Early adoption of new technologies thus may require a more highly skilled production work force.

Still another important characteristic of the diffusion phase of the process of technological change is the tendency for new technologies to undergo considerable modification and improvement during the period of their adoption. These modifications reflect the fact that a great deal of learning occurs during the early period of their use, and the results of this "debugging" are gradually incorporated into improved versions of a specific innovation. In the case of the transistor, for example, one might classify the period of "diffusion" as extending from 1954 to the present. During this period, the performance, complexity, and reliability of this component all have improved dramatically.

The fact that technological diffusion within an economy is typically an extended process has very important implications for the employment and skill effects of new technologies. Since this process is a gradual one, the all-too-frequent predictions of massive worker displacements that have pervaded the literature on technology and employment since the 1930s rarely have been validated by experience. Moreover, the economic and skill effects of new technologies also are realized gradually within an economy. As a matter of methodology, it is inappropriate to infer the employment or skills effects of new technologies from the observed capabilities of laboratory versions of these innovations. Among other things, such an approach ignores the lengthy time period needed to adopt these innovations. In addition, the analysis overlooks the tendency for these innovations to be modified considerably in the course of their diffusion.

A final important point is the fact that technology adoption very frequently involves significant organizational change. The interdependence of technological and organizational innovation is especially pronounced for the information technologies that are the focus of this chapter. Technological change creates new options for the performance of specific production or information-processing activities. But the precise organization of these activities and their skill requirements rarely are determined solely by the technology—they are influenced to a considerable degree by the organization of the workplace. Organizational factors heavily affect the implementation of new technologies and their effects on skill requirements, quality of work life, productivity, and profitability. Indeed, the potential improvements offered by many innovations often can be realized only through complementary reorganization of production processes in factories or offices. Both manufacturing plants and their products have to be redesigned to exploit the potential of computer-integrated processes.

## EVIDENCE ON THE SKILL EFFECTS OF NEW TECHNOLOGIES

We begin our discussion of the skill effects of new workplace technologies with an examination of the evidence concerning technology's effects on skill requirements, followed by a consideration of the relationship between technology and workplace organization. We follow scholarly convention in distinguishing between the *basic skills* of literacy, problem-solving, numerical reasoning, and written communication, and *job-related skills*, which generally are highly specific to a given occupation or function. Historically, U.S. workers have relied on publicly supported primary, secondary, and adult education for the acquisition of basic skills, and much of the training in job-related skills has been provided by employers.

As Kenneth Spenner (1988) has pointed out in his recent review of the extensive literature on new technologies and worker skill requirements, "Much of what we do know suggests an uncertain, complicated, and contradictory relationship between technological change and the skill requirements of work" (p. 131). There are several reasons for the uncertain verdict of this large literature. Many studies of the skill effects of new technologies have employed methodologies and/or data that are weak, imprecise, and often conflict with those employed in other studies. Among other things, within this literature, the definition (and therefore the measurement) of job-related skills is the subject of widespread disagreement.

Longitudinal studies of change in the skill requirements and occupational structure of employment also require reliable data on occupational structure, which is difficult to obtain. The U.S. Department of Labor's *Dictionary of Occupational Titles*, for example, is plagued by significant change over time in the definition of the content and skills associated with specific occupations. Case studies of the skill effects of new technologies also rarely contain a significant longitudinal component, thus making it very difficult to detect changes over time in the skill requirements associated with a specific technology. Yet casual and scholarly empirical evidence suggest that such changes over time can be quite significant. Finally, many studies suggest that the skill effects of new technologies are quite sensitive to managerial decisions concerning their implementation. Identical technologies can have very different effects on skill requirements in differently organized workplaces. Moreover, managers appear to have considerable discretion in the ways in which they organize the implementation of new technologies. Part of the interdependence between the adoption of new technologies and their skill effects, indeed, stems from the ability of managers to adapt workplace organization and technology deployment to accommodate the available skills of the work force.

Although the empirical evidence on the skill effects of new technologies is too fragmentary and mixed to support strong predictions of aggregate skill impacts, most suggests that the entry-level skill requirements for the jobs of the future will not rise significantly from their current levels. As more intelligence is embedded in the computer-based hardware and software employed in the nation's offices and factories, for example, users are likely to require less computer literacy to operate a particular piece of equipment. Nevertheless, the requirements of the jobs of the future will require stronger basic skills. Basic skills provide an important foundation for acquiring the job-related skills to operate new technologies, skills that increasingly will be mental, rather than physical, in character. As we note below, the very limited evidence on the basic skills preparation of older workers in the U.S.

population suggests some basis for concern about their ability to adapt to new workplace technologies.

Another important conclusion from the evidence is the uncertainty that pervades all forecasts of the specific skill requirements of the jobs of the future. Public policymakers responding to the challenges of new workplace technologies are well advised to avoid massive commitments to a particular vision of the occupational structure and job-specific skill requirements of the jobs of the future. Historically, forecasts of both have been unreliable. Rather than making large commitments of public resources to such specific visions, a wiser investment strategy may be to target the basic skills of labor force entrants, as well as employed and displaced workers.

The organizational effects of computer-based office automation and manufacturing technologies are worth brief discussion, to provide some basis for understanding their potential effects on older workers, whether the future can be predicted or not. Much high-volume production activity in U.S. factories and offices (especially in the data-processing and information entry "back rooms" of banks and insurance companies) historically has been organized according to principles pioneered by Frederick Taylor in the early twentieth century.[3]

Taylor's principles were formulated in part as a way to manage a large, ethnically heterogeneous work force with limited skills. Taylorism relied on the definition by management of a "best way" to perform a specific function and the obedience of production workers to this definition. Workers, in other words, were appendages to machines, and efficiency was achieved through a reduction in the contribution of direct labor to output and costs. Production jobs were defined very narrowly and involved very little worker discretion and skill, a large middle-management organization exercised very close supervision over workers, and the extensive use of highly specialized machinery meant that production runs of a single model or product were long and inventories of "work in progress" and inputs were large. Inventories "buffered" the production process against interruptions in supply, breakdowns in a specific function, or defects in output quality.

This approach to work organization substitutes technology for human skill and effort. In the automobile industry, for example, the extensive deployment of advanced manufacturing technologies during the 1950s frequently resulted in the "de-skilling" of jobs. A Taylorist approach to production organization and management also has been used in the adoption of computer-based office automation and production technologies. Indeed, the coexistence of Taylorist approaches to production organization and computer-numerically-controlled (CNC) machine tools, for example, is one reason for the widely cited finding by Maryellen Kelley (1986) that the skill effects of CNC machine tools depended on more than simply the adoption of this technology. Taylorism was developed in the United States and adopted more widely in U.S. manufacturing than in the manufacturing industries of Western Europe or Japan during the post–World War II period.

Computer-based office automation and manufacturing technologies have important organizational implications that challenge some of the tenets of Taylorism. As Paul Osterman (1989) has argued, computer and information technologies allow different functions within the organization and different activities within the office or factory to be integrated far more tightly. Databases can be shared in real time among different functions, for example, enabling design changeovers and adjustments in work flows to be made much more quickly. In addition, the increased availability and quality of information means that production and other operations can be monitored by a smaller cadre of middle managers or, in some instances, by senior management alone. A related consequence of the deployment of these technologies is increased speed in the production process. Increased speed and interdependence, however, mean that breakdowns in any single step of a factory or office production process are more disruptive than is the case in a Taylorist system that is well buffered by inventories and work in progress.

In a "non-Taylorist" approach to work organization that takes advantage of the characteristics of computer-based production technologies, production workers assume far more responsibility for monitoring production flow, pace, and product quality, assuming many of the functions previously performed by supervisory managers. The jobs of individual production workers also are broadened, and teams and/or "multiskilled" job descriptions are employed widely. Fewer middle managers are needed and monitoring of production operations is performed by senior managers or a far smaller middle-management group. The adoption of new technologies in this work organization often results in a considerable expansion of and increase in the skills associated with individual workers' jobs. So-called high commitment production organizations increasingly are recommended by students of labor relations and technology (e.g., Walton & McKersie, 1989) as a more effective route for exploiting the potential of computer-based technologies to improve product quality, productivity, work-life quality, and profit.

In these organizations, investments in training must be more substantial and continuous, workers are required to invest more mental effort in the performance of their jobs and in the management of the overall production process, and change in the content of a production worker's job over the course of a career is far more likely. Unfortunately, the limited evidence on training in job-related skills suggests that blue-collar workers of all ages are not well served. Employers are by far the most important source of training in job-related skills once a worker has entered the U.S. work force. According to Anthony Carnivale and Harold Goldstein (1983), more than 70 percent of training in skills improvement is conducted at a worker's place of employment. Unfortunately, employer-provided training tends to increase any differences in the educational attainment of workers that are present when they enter the work force. Michael L. Tierney (1983) found that workers with some graduate training beyond their college degrees were seven times as likely to have received this kind of training as those with less than a high school education. Employees in small firms also receive much less training than those in large firms. Seymour Lusterman (1977) reported that firms with 10,000 or more workers spent an average of $86 per worker on training annually, while smaller firms (500 to 999 employees) spent an average of $27.

For older workers with levels of educational attainment that are, on average, lower than those of recent entrants to the work force, employer-provided training in job-related skills thus may have important deficiencies. Unfortunately, public agencies from the federal, state, and local government levels in the United States provide little or no financial support for training in job-related skills for currently employed workers. Existing (and seriously deficient) programs for the support of such training focus mainly on displaced workers. There is no lack of U.S. public institutions to provide such training, ranging from universities to community colleges. Financial support for this training is needed, however, as well as significant innovations in the delivery of training. Older workers with limited formal education are especially unlikely to approach classroom teaching techniques with enthusiasm, but public institutions have been remarkably slow to adopt proven techniques and technologies for self-paced, individualized instruction. As we note below, these deficiencies in the U.S. training "system" are, if anything, most serious in the provision of basic skills training for older workers.

Unfortunately, very little is known about the response of older workers to these challenges. The employment and other effects of new workplace technologies on older workers are not well documented in public surveys of worker displacement or skills (the absence of reliable data on these issues for older workers reflects the general paucity of public data on the employment effects of new technology). The evidence from the "displaced worker" (defined as workers suffering permanent job losses) surveys of the 1980s suggests that older workers are especially hard hit by displacement. Michael Podgursky's (1988) analysis of the results of the 1984 Bureau of Labor Statistics survey of displaced workers has yielded several important findings on older displaced workers. Unfortunately, the 1984 survey did not include a well-designed set of questions to determine the *causes* of displacement. Accordingly, the sample of displaced workers discussed below includes workers displaced for a number of reasons, among which technology is only one. Since the survey was conducted in the immediate aftermath of the worst recession since the Great Depression, it is very likely that the dominant causes of the displacement of this sample of workers were macroeconomic, rather than technology related.

Older workers were somewhat less likely to be displaced, which reflects the "last-hired, first-fired" principle of seniority that is particularly significant in the unionized, manufacturing industries that experienced considerable worker displacement in the early 1980s. Once they lost their jobs, however, older workers were unemployed for longer periods and experienced more severe income losses even when they were reemployed. Podgursky's analysis suggested that older male blue-collar workers were especially prone to longer spells of unemployment following displacement, with each additional year in age accounting for an increase of .314 weeks in the median spell of unemployment. The negative influence of age on unemployment duration was less pronounced for male white-collar workers and was even greater for female white-collar workers than for male blue-collar workers. Surprisingly, female blue-collar employees exhibited a negative influence of age on unemployment duration following displacement. Lower levels of education, more prevalent among older workers, also were associated with longer spells of postdisplacement unemployment.

Although the seniority system in the industries hit hardest by displacement in the early 1980s meant that older blue-collar workers were less likely to be displaced, greater seniority also is associated with greater losses in income once displaced workers are re-employed. Since income losses in re-employment are even more strongly associated with the duration of joblessness following displacement, which is correlated with age, older displaced workers are doubly vulnerable. Higher losses in income associated with re-employment also are associated with a higher probability of losing health insurance coverage, suggesting yet another risk for the older displaced worker.

Another cause for concern about the effects of new technology on older workers stems from the high probability that these technologies will increase the importance of good basic skills. As was noted above, higher levels of educational attainment were associated with short spells of unemployment following displacement in Podgursky's analysis. To the extent that older workers, especially production workers, have less education, their basic skills are likely to be weaker, and the probability of lengthy unemployment following displacement will be higher. Moreover, other evidence on the characteristics of the workers displaced in the early 1980s suggests that deficiencies in basic skills are widespread within the production work force in such industries as steel and automobiles. Marc Bendick (1982) found that 34 percent of the workers from declining industries who were unemployed for eight weeks or more did not have high school diplomas. Within this population of displaced high school dropouts, 49 percent were functionally illiterate. Other evidence suggests that basic skills deficiencies within the employed work force, a group that will constitute more than 75 percent of the U.S. work force in the year 2000, are significant. The U.S. General Accounting Office (1987), citing unpublished data from the 1984 displaced workers survey, reported that 32 percent of the displaced workers unemployed as of January 1984 were high school dropouts and thus were likely to have serious basic skills deficiencies.

In other words, an unknown but almost certainly significant share of the population of older workers currently employed in U.S. factories and offices have significant weaknesses in their basic skills that will make it more difficult for them to adapt to the new technologies. Moreover, these workers suffer longer spells of unemployment and more serious income losses if they are displaced for any reason. A final reason for concern over the potential effects of technology on the older worker is the absence of public programs to support improvement in the basic skills of the employed or displaced worker. The major federal program of training assistance for the unemployed, the Job Training Partnership Act, provides little or no support for basic skills training. Moreover, very few state-level programs for training and retraining of the displaced (or potentially displaced) worker provide resources for basic skills improvement.

### The Retirement Behavior of U.S. Workers

It is worth repeating our admonition that historical trends in retirement behavior may prove to be inaccurate predictors of future behavior. Indeed, while some informed speculations can be made about the retirement behavior of the U.S. work force over the next several decades, an important theme of this section is that this behavior in the future remains in no small degree "endogenous." We as a society can influence such behavior by workplace organization, broadening part-time employment options and the like for older workers, using new technologies in ways that can adapt to the skills of older workers, providing training to displaced older workers, and providing incentives through Social Security benefits and federal and state tax code laws to encourage older workers to stay in the work force.

Over the next half-century, the U.S. population will experience a profound shift in its age structure. In 1990, there were twenty-one individuals aged sixty-five or older for each 100 individuals between the ages of twenty and sixty-four. By the year 2030, this number is projected to increase to around forty, nearly twice as many individuals over sixty-five per younger worker. This change in the age profile of the U.S. population is likely to increase the demand for older workers.

Not only will the large influx of entrants into the U.S. work force that has marked the past quarter-century slow down greatly, but the large increase in the labor force that has resulted from greater participation by married women also will slow down. The share of married women in the labor force increased from 15 percent in 1940 to 54 percent by 1985. The proportion of married women in the labor force may be reaching a peak, as women's labor force participation rates converge with those of men.

Further increases in labor demand are unlikely to be met by this group in the same manner. A cessation of growth in women's labor force participation may thus also increase demand for older workers.

The effects on any future growth in demand for older workers on the actual employment of older Americans will be influenced as well by factors affecting the labor pool of older people. Individuals reaching traditional retirement ages are in better health, on average, than was the case in previous generations. They have both the capability to remain employed and, because of greater life expectancy, a potential need for income over a longer period of time.

Social norms sanctioning continued labor force participation beyond the ages of sixty-five or seventy have been encouraged by the abolition of mandatory retirement ages in most industries. Other public policy changes have increased the attractiveness of remaining in the labor force after the age of sixty-five. For instance, the 1983 Social Security Act has increased the loss in benefits associated with early retirement, beginning in 2003. In addition, since 1986, years worked after age sixty-five have counted toward future Social Security benefits.

These recent changes in Social Security and mandatory retirement may well be extended as a result of potential political confrontations between older citizens and younger workers in the future. Younger workers, called upon to support a greater and greater proportion of retired Americans through Social Security and other public pension systems, may support efforts to reduce the real pension and benefit levels, or to tax them at higher levels than at present. Any such decrease in benefits will provide additional inducements for older Americans to remain in the labor force.

Future growth in the labor force participation of older workers, however, would represent a significant reversal of historical trends. Over the past fifty years, U.S. workers have retired at increasingly earlier ages. In 1930, over 50 percent of males older than sixty-five were in the labor force while at present fewer than 15 percent of males over sixty-five are. For males between fifty-five and sixty-four, labor force participation has declined from 89 percent in 1954 to 67 percent in 1989.

As the real wealth of older Americans has risen, as private pensions have become more common and better funded, and as Social Security benefits have increased, older Americans have chosen to retire earlier. Indeed, Social Security benefit levels have tripled in real terms between 1945 and today. The ratio of monthly benefits to preretirement earnings of the average worker retiring at age sixty-five increased from 19 percent in 1950 to over 51 percent by 1980.

Not only has the real level of Social Security benefits increased markedly, but several features of Social Security continue to actively discourage working past sixty-five. Earnings from wages and salaries count against Social Security benefits in determining tax liability, even though investment income does not. In addition, since 1986, employers of Medicare-eligible workers have been forced to assume primary financial responsibility for health insurance benefits disbursed by company health plans. This change in the costs of medical insurance may discourage an employer from hiring or retaining an older Medicare-eligible employee. Private pensions, which are available for about 30 percent of retirees today and will be available for an increasing proportion of retirees in the future, also frequently penalize workers for working beyond normal retirement age. Moreover, about 60 percent of defined-benefit pension plans allow an individual to retire before age sixty-five with full benefits.

Other important influences on the retirement behavior of older Americans are more difficult to assess. The increase in wealth of potential retirees since the 1950s has been an important influence on reduced labor force participation for those over sixty-five (and even for those over fifty-five). However, as Frank Levy and Richard Michel (1991) point out, those born in the 1950s are likely to have substantially less wealth than their parents around the year 2020, as they approach retirement. This decline in relative wealth may eventually reverse the historical trend for older Americans to seek earlier retirement.

## CONCLUSIONS

Concerns that new technologies will have a sharp and profound impact on the ability and propensity of the majority of older Americans to remain in the work force, because of deficiencies in their job-specific skill levels, appear to be unfounded. The effects of new technologies on skills, employment, and the workplace are complex. The skill effects of new technologies also are quite sensitive to managerial decisions concerning their implementation. Identical technologies may have different effects on skill requirements in different organizations.

Moreover, new technologies generally diffuse gradually across industries and firms and, as they do, they evolve and are molded into particular organizational settings. They generally become easier to use and require less specific training. In information technology, for instance, as more intelligence is embedded in the computer-based hardware and software employed in the country's offices and factories, users are likely to require less in the way of computer literacy.

Still, this does not mean there is no cause for concern about the impact of new technology on some groups of older workers. Available evidence suggests that the jobs of the future *will* increasingly demand a strong foundation in basic skills. While available evidence about basic skills of different age groups is very limited, the basic skills preparation of older workers in the United States gives some cause for concern about their adaptation to new technologies. Current public concern over the preparation of entrants to the U.S. labor force is well founded. Such concern, however, overlooks the demographic factors that indicate that the vast majority of the work force of the first two decades of the next century is *currently in* the work force. New training policies and institutions, involving public and private financing, training in basic and job-related skills, and the involvement of state, local, and federal government agencies, are badly needed.

Technological change is only one of several influences on the labor force participation of older workers. Many nontechnological forces also will influence the propensity of older workers to remain in or to reenter the work force. An aging population will make employers increasingly interested in retaining or hiring older workers. On the other hand, the recent increases in the financial security of potential retirees have underpinned a steady decline in retirement ages and in the labor force participation of older workers. Retirement ages are likely to continue to decline through the early years

of the century, but demographic, economic, and political factors may combine to reverse this trend by the second or third decades of the twenty-first century.

We opened this chapter with a disclaimer about predictions concerning the impact of new technologies on the aging U.S. work force. As we have seen, many of the most important influences regarding the impact of technology on employment and on the retirement behavior of older Americans are not well understood or well measured. Moreover, such evidence as does exist on the impact of technology on employment and on future retirement behavior suggests that public policy and business actions influence the outcomes in so many ways that predictions are treacherous.

Our discussion has focused on information technologies, including computer-based technologies of office and factory automation, telecommunications, advanced-information storage and retrieval technologies, robotics, computer-aided design, and computer-integrated manufacturing. This cluster of technologies will be particularly important during the next half-century and thus is especially salient in considering the role of older Americans in the labor force of the future. Nevertheless, much of this analysis applies equally to other technologies that will affect firms and industries in the U.S. economy in the decades to come. Thus, this chapter may provide an important starting point for more detailed consideration of the effects of new technologies on older workers.

## NOTES

1. Much of this discussion draws on the more extensive treatment of the topic in Richard M. Cyert and David C. Mowery (1987), especially Chapter 2; and Cyert and Mowery (1989).

2. John L. Enos (1962) found that the period between the invention of a new process or product and its *initial* application averaged fourteen years for one sample

of innovations, while Edwin Mansfield (1963) concluded that, for nine of twelve innovations, adoption by all of the large firms in the coal mining, railroad, brewing, and iron and steel industries took more than ten years.

3. For additional discussion, see Paul Osterman (1989).

## REFERENCES

Ayres, R. U., & Miller, S. M. (1983). *Robotics: Applications and social impacts.* Cambridge, MA: Ballinger.

Bendick, M. (1982). The role of public programs and private markets in re-employing workers dislocated by economic change. Unpublished manuscript for the Urban Institute, Washington, D.C.

Carnivale, A. P., & Goldstein, H. (1983). *Employee training: Its changing role and an analysis of new data.* Washington, DC: American Society for Training and Development.

Congressional Office of Technology Assessment. (1990). *Making things better: Competing in manufacturing.* Washington, DC: U.S. Government Printing Office.

Cyert, R. M., & Mowery, D. C. (Eds.). (1987). *Technology and employment: Innovation and growth in the U.S. economy.* Washington, DC: National Academy Press.

Cyert, R. M., & Mowery, D. C. (1989, May). Technology, employment, and U.S. competitiveness. *Scientific American*, 54–62.

Edquist, C., & Jacobsson, S. (1988). *Flexible automation.* New York: Basil Blackwell.

Enos, J. (1962). *Petroleum: Progress and profits.* Cambridge, MA: MIT Press.

General Accounting Office, U.S. Congress (1987). Dislocated workers: Local programs and outcomes under the Job Training Partnership Act. Washington, DC: U.S. Government Printing Office.

Kelley, M. (1986, November). Programmable automation and the skill question: A reinterpretation of the cross-national evidence. *Human Systems Management*, 6(3), 223–241.

Levy, F., & Michel, R. C. (1991). *The economic future of American families: Income and wealth trends.* Washington, DC: Urban Institute Press.

Lusterman, S. (1977). *Education and industry.* New York: The Conference Board.

Mansfield, E. (1963). The speed of response of firms to new techniques. *Quarterly Journal of Economics*, 77, 290–311.

Osterman, P. (1989). New technology and the organization of work: A review of the issues. In D. C. Mowery & B. Henderson (Eds.), *The challenge of new technology to labor-management relations.* Washington, DC: U.S. Department of Labor.

Podgursky, M. (1988). Job displacement and labor market adjustment. In R. M. Cyert & D. C. Mowery (Eds.), *The impact of technological change* (pp. 3–41). Cambridge, MA: Ballinger.

Spenner, K. I. (1988). Technological change, skill requirements, and education: The case for uncertainty. In R. M. Cyert & D. C. Mowery (Eds.), *The impact of technological change on employment and economic growth* (131–184). Cambridge, MA: Ballinger.

Tierney, M. L. (1983). Employer-provided education and training in 1981. In R.

Zemesky, *The impact of public policy on education and training in the private sector*, submitted to the National Institute of Education by the Higher Education Finance Research Institute, University of Pennsylvania, Philadelphia, PA.

Walton, R. E., & McKersie, R. B. (1989). Managing new technology and labor relations: An opportunity for mutual influence. In D. Mowery & B. Henderson (Eds.), *The challenge of new technology*. Washington, DC: U.S. Department of Labor.

# 6

# Is Unretirement Unprecedented?

## W. Andrew Achenbaum and Malcolm H. Morrison

A major labor force development in the United States during the period immediately ahead will be the aging of the work force amid a continuing trend toward early retirement. Over the past half-century, public and private pension policies have developed to assure a reasonable retirement income for most workers. These policies, initially designed to provide minimal economic protection for elderly persons no longer able to work, now permit and encourage many "older" workers in the labor force to leave their long-term employers anywhere between the ages of fifty-five and sixty-five (and sometimes earlier). The early departure from the labor force of large numbers of mature, trained, and experienced employees, however, can exacerbate personnel problems. It is costly because of the long periods during which health and pension benefits must be paid to retired workers. Retiree health benefit costs are generally unfunded and must come from current operating revenues of firms. Pension benefits are often prefunded, but in recent years many firms have ceased doing business and often pensions have not been fully paid to their retirees. Recent economic cycles have demonstrated, moreover, that changes in the economy and in the work force can often interact to product unanticipated consequences for American businesses in meeting labor force requirements.

In order to consider the implications of the aging of the work force and retirement costs for employers, much more information is needed about human resources. What is the effect of various employee benefit policies on employees? How do the organizational factors influence these policies? What role do cyclical movements in economic activities play in creating part-time opportunities for older workers? What kinds of practical steps can be taken by firms to alert job seekers to employment opportunities? Will corporate management increasingly seek to link the experience and expertise of an increasing retired population with business needs and requirements? Will a growing number of firms view older workers as a potential resource, as a part of the increasing diversity of the work force (Bureau of National Affairs, 1987)? Will people who seek postretirement employment have access to new training initiatives and a wider variety of new human resources policies (to support and accommodate certain life-style requirements) analogous to child care, flexible schedules, eldercare, health promotion, and personal leave?

Business cannot ignore the aging of the work force because of the related benefit costs and effects on employment needs. As corporate pension plans mature, more and more older workers are retiring at a reasonable standard of well-being. If recent patterns persist, these retirees probably will not return to work; instead they will receive both pension and health benefits that represent direct costs to organizations. Does it make sense for firms to ignore the productive potential of a growing retiree population at a time in which many human resource managers worry about their ability to recruit qualified, dependable workers? Are there steps that private firms can take to use the skills and experience of older persons—to create "unretirement" policies that augment the older-worker labor-supply pool?

The idea of maintaining public and private human resource policies and programs based on age-specific categories increasingly is being challenged. Gerontologists have long demonstrated that older people do not have uniform and predictable attitudes and behavior. We suggest that historical trends become malleable when demographic, social, economic, and institutional factors warrant change.

Retirement policies are dynamic. Rules have been changed in the past to expand or contract the pool of older workers in the marketplace. Virtually every corporation modifies and sometimes restructures employment and retirement policies over time. Therefore, it is important to consider the historical development of early retirement policies in this country since its present policies are based on prior circumstances and conditions. "Unretirement," or postretirement, options will be linked to prevailing retirement patterns. If and when these options become more acceptable to employers and employees alike, they will serve as an independent variable influencing retirement behavior.

## HISTORICAL RETIREMENT TRENDS

Table 6.1 summarizes three major developments in the employment behavior of older American men during the past forty-five years. First, besides the net decline in the percentage of males over sixty-five still working, there has been an overall drop in the labor force participation rates of men between the ages of fifty-nine and sixty-four. This early retirement trend is

Table 6.1
Employment Patterns of Older Men

| Survey of Retired Men | Percentage Employed | Percentage Full-time | Percentage Part-time |
|---|---|---|---|
| 1944 Ohio Survey[a] | 55 | 32 | 23 |
| 1946 Boston Survey[a] | 24 | 15 | 9 |
| 1949 Philadelphia/ Baltimore Survey[a] | 24 | 16 | 8 |
| 1951 National Survey[a] | 34 | 19 | 15 |
| 1957 National Survey[a] | 36 | 19 | 17 |
| 1963 Survey of Aged[a] | 30 | 13 | 17 |
| 1968 Social Security Survey[b] | 35 | 21 | 14 |
| 1973 Social Security Survey[c] | 34 | 12 | 22 |
| 1976 Social Security Survey[d] | 27 | 9 | 18 |
| 1979 Social Security Survey[e] | 27 | 9 | 18 |
| 1984 Social Security Survey[f] | 22 | 7 | 15 |

Sources: [a]Wentworth, p. 40.
[b]Demographic & Economic Characteristics of the Ages, p. 89.
[c]1973 Social Security Annual Statistical Supplement, p. 41.
[d]1976 Social Security Annual Statistical Supplement, p. 53.
[e]1981 Social Security Annual Statistical Supplement, p. 63.
[f]1986 Social Security Annual Statistical Supplement, p. 77.

characteristic of most advanced industrial economies (Johnson, 1989; Kohli, 1988). Second, despite the increasing exit from the marketplace in late life, there always has been a significant minority of men—more than a fifth of the population canvassed—who choose to work beyond the "official" retirement age. Third, elderly men's work schedules have changed over time. In the 1940s and 1950s, those who worked past sixty-five were likely to be employed in full-time positions. Since the late 1960s, older workers have tended to be engaged in part-time activities.

Caution must be exercised in assessing these data. Table 6.1 is not based upon successive panels of a single longitudinal survey; it has been pieced together with data from eleven separate cross-sectional surveys. Data that appear comparable prove not to be because of divergent sampling criteria and nuances in defining key terms. Only Social Security beneficiaries were interviewed in the earliest six surveys; later surveys were not limited to OASDI (Old-Age Survivors and Disability Insurance) recipients, which elevated the proportion of people listed as employed. Surveys from 1944 through 1957 focused on "employment and ability to work." That people are able to work does not signify that they are doing so. The last five surveys merely asked respondents if they "worked"—interviewers apparently did not specify the number of hours employed or another work-related item as a criterion for inclusion.

The gross trends reported in Table 6.1 are reliable, but the figures (for a variety of reasons) are slightly higher than data compiled by the Bureau of Labor Statistics (BLS), which consistently applied a more stringent definition of "labor force participation." According to the BLS, only 16 percent of noninstitutionalized men over sixty-five participated in the labor force in 1985. Perhaps more significantly, age sixty-five no longer signals *the* critical turning point in behavioral patterns. For men, the average age of retirement declined from nearly seventy in 1945 to under sixty-two in 1985. By 1980, nearly a fifth of those who retired with pensions did so prior to their sixtieth birthday. The relationship between chronological age and the act of retiring, in other words, is hardly fixed.

Defining *retirement* always has been problematic because it has meant different things to distinctive sets of historical actors at various points in time. The institution of retirement developed in the United States a century ago as a way to create a more efficient work force, to aid in the transfer of employment opportunities from one generation to the next, and to help stabilize the existing social order. "Among the largest and most efficient corporations, pensions are now regarded as good business," Burton Hendrick has observed (1908, p. 118). He continued, "They largely solve one of their most difficult problems—how to get out of a large labor force the most efficient service" (see also Graebner, 1980; Gratton, 1985; Haber, 1983; Hannah, 1982).

Scholars disagree about the extent of retirement between 1875 and 1935. Some claim that people began to "retire" in progressively significant numbers after 1900; others claim that retirement rates for men were about the same in 1870 as in 1930—possibly as high as 35 percent (Achenbaum, 1978; Gratton & Haber, in press; Moen, 1987; Ransom & Sutch, 1986; Streib, 1988). Resolving the debate is partly complicated by functions served by retirement other than those related to old age. Elderly men out of the labor force were not necessarily "retired." Some were sick or disabled. Others were temporarily or permanently unemployed. Still others were laid off because their skills became obsolete or their firms were shut down. A few entered into nonincome-generating exchanges with family members. Fewer still could rely on independent savings. Many factors shaped "retirement" in its formative stages, but not everyone so affected would be considered "retired" by current definitions, largely because they were not guaranteed a lifetime pension upon leaving their jobs.

Fuzzy arrangements that might be construed as retirement persisted well into the twentieth century. A report by the National Industrial Conference Board (1925) noted that transferring older workers into easier, routine jobs so that they could earn a partial wage was the oldest, most traditional manner of dealing with superannuated employees. Murray Webb Latimer's definitive *Industrial Pension in the United States and Canada* (1932) differentiated among "voluntary superannuation retirement," which allowed an employee to choose the time of retirement (and permitted partial retirement); those options determined by an employer on a discretionary or compulsory basis; and incapacity retirements. Retirement under Social Security, claimed Wilbur J. Cohen (1958), was designed to be flexible, permitting an admixture of employee options, incentives, and disincentives for working. Other scholars stress its usefulness for keeping unemployment rates down (Myles, 1984; Quadagno, 1988).

While acknowledging "a certain degree of vagueness and lack of clarity as to its meaning," Wilma Donahue and associates described retirement as "the creation of an economically non-productive role in modern societies which are capable of supporting large numbers of persons whose labor is not essential to the functioning of the economic order" (1960, pp. 330–331). Post–World War II commentators have described retirement both as an individual life stage and as a social pattern possible only in a progressive, affluent era. "Retirees" in the 1950s were "a new American group, and a new word to most" (Flexner, 1982, p. 48; see also Friedman & Havighurst, 1954; Streib & Schneider, 1971). But how many older men actually had joined the "unproductive" class? If the measure of retirement was less than year-round, full-time work, according to Erdman Palmore (1964b), 87 percent of all men over sixty-five were retired in 1962. If the indicator was "not usually at full-time job (among men who have worked at full-time jobs for 6 months or more within the preceding 5 years)," then only 54 percent were retired. Significantly, the dichotomy was drawn between work (implicitly full-time, or at least regular) and leisure. Actual and subjective retirement might just as plausibly have been associated with continuities or changes in behavior after the initial receipt of a pension (Murray, 1979).

A growing number of experts have begun to question the assumption that employment for older people must mean *full-time* remunerated work. Evidence has been found of people who have "retired" but still work, often part-time. Even though this partial retirement phenomenon characterizes a relatively small number of older persons, in retrospect it appears to be a long-standing trend that only now is attracting attention:

For those who are not forced out of their main job by poor health or by mandatory retirement provisions, or those who are not attracted away from their jobs by pension provisions, partial retirement both within and outside the main job is still found to be an important phenomenon. The numerical importance of partial retirement outside of the main job for this group calls into question results based on models that make no allowance for this phenomenon. (Gustman & Steinmeier, 1984; see also Honig & Hanoch, 1985)

Historically, partial retirement, like the retirement process itself, has taken many forms. For some, it entails cutting back on the number of hours previously devoted to a career. For others, it signals self-employment. For a few, the "unretired," it involves a shift—after collecting a pension—to a new job with flexible hours and varying wages.

Retirement, therefore, is not necessarily a single transition in a person's life course. It is a dynamic process consisting of several stages. Yet *only* pensioners can "unretire." Elements of the components of postretirement employment have long existed, but their dynamic interconnections have changed during the past half-century. This means that unretirement as a formal stage of an older worker's career (and as an institutional arrangement to be negotiated by corporate managers) is an unprecedented phenomenon. Though it has historical antecedents, "unretirement" can be correctly understood as an emerging trend. Retirees going back to work on a part-time, part-year basis may become an increasingly important, adaptable phase of retirement, which itself has proven to be a dynamic institution. In part, this is because the roles of older workers have changed their composition over time.

## THE CHANGING PROFILE OF OLDER WORKERS

The proportion of older workers gainfully employed tends to decline with advancing years—with two exceptions. One exception is among married couples when a shift occurs from two-worker to single-worker units, with the wife assuming a greater share of work responsibility outside the home as her spouse leaves the labor force. The second exception relates to the slight increase at age seventy-three in the number of male pensioners employed in full-time jobs year-round. The elimination of the Social Security earnings test at age seventy-two probably accounts for this rise (Jaffe, 1971; Palmore, 1964a; Thompson, 1974). These exceptions, however, have little effect on the overall early retirement trend, with nearly two-thirds of all people now accepting Social Security benefits at age sixty-two.

Deteriorating health, not surprisingly, always has reduced the likelihood of people seeking or keeping a job. A 1944 statistical analysis found a stronger association between ability to work and employment than it did between age and work. One-third of the retirements occurring between 1966 and 1981 and three-fifths of those occurring before age sixty-two in the same period were attributable to poor health (Motley, 1978; Parnes, 1985; Wentworth, 1968). Despite recent declines in morbidity rates and mortality differentials, poor health encourages permanent retirement.

The relationship between working in retirement and financial need, in contrast, is not as straightforward as might be expected. In the early years of Social Security, most beneficiaries reported that they had returned to work whenever they needed the income and could find a job. Conversely, those in good health who had adequate retirement incomes typically were not interested in working (Bixby et al., 1968; Wentworth, 1968). Yet it does not follow that only older people in extreme need choose to work. Based on data from the 1960s, researchers confirmed earlier findings that the working retired were more likely to have higher incomes than the nonworking. But they went on to point out that adequacy of retirement incomes was not "an important discriminating variable" in predicting employment behavior. Furthermore, many retirees took on tasks having a lower status than their preretirement jobs, like the former owners of small businesses who became part-time janitors (Fillenbaum, 1971; Jacobs, 1978). Differences in decisions concerning employment after retirement cannot be explained by referring simply to objective, monetary considerations.

Indeed, a bimodal distribution arises when unretirement is correlated with occupation. An elite group—usually better-educated men previously leaders in their field—tends to seek out postretirement opportunities, especially if these individuals can serve as senior advisors or in some self-employed capacity. Many elderly poor, in contrast, work in retirement because they have no choice. Economic conditions impel them to pursue extrinsic rather than intrinsic rewards, often through low-paying, dead-end tasks (Barresi, 1974; Jaffe, 1972).

It is harder to generalize about the demographic characteristics of unretired people who do not fall into either income or occupational extremes, but reviewing life histories of older people who may be potential employees offers clues. Attitudes and behavior after retirement are often conditioned by mid-life experiences. Consider mobility patterns. Workers over forty-five have tended to be less flexible than younger workers in their willingness to relocate to find new jobs. Not surprisingly, since most older people would prefer to "age in place" among friends and kin, few of the unretired choose to move in order to secure employment (Sobel, 1972). The elderly mainly consider jobs that are conveniently located nearby.

There are racial differences in unretirement. The gap between blacks and whites has narrowed as a result of greater investments in education and policy interventions, but disparities persist (Farley, 1987). Higher percentages of black men have tended to withdraw from the labor force at earlier ages than white men because of reported poor health or unfavorable labor force conditions. Because of the proportion of black men on disability rolls, some researchers claim that becoming "unretired-retired" may occur for blacks more often than whites (Gibson, 1986); that is, black retirees who work are likely to be employed in their previous occupation. Black women over sixty-five have been less likely during the twentieth century to work for pay than elderly black men. Historically, however, a greater proportion of older black women than older white women have been in the labor force. What does this indicate about the role that gender plays in unretirement behavior?

Perhaps the most striking demographic trend in recent American history has been the growing proportion of gainfully employed women. Only 18 percent of the total labor force was female in 1900; there is near parity between the sexes today. A fifth of all women over sixteen were in the labor force in 1900; in 1985, 54.5 percent were in the labor force (Baxandall, Gordon, & Reverby, 1976; Rix, 1989). Older women, however, always have been less likely than men in their cohort to be in the labor force. At least until very recently, the spheres of work and family in the United States have been "at odds." Around the turn of the century, for instance, families chose to have their children work, thus enabling wives to stay at home. If the primary breadwinner became disabled or died, or if the household budget was seriously reduced, then older women did work for pay—more often than not, keeping boarders and lodgers or doing piecemeal tasks and services in a domestic setting (Abramovitz, 1988; Degler, 1971; Fraundorf, 1979; Rotella, 1981). Today, however, labor force participation by older women is quite low and is not growing.

Despite the overall increase in female employment, the proportion of women over sixty-five in the labor force overall has declined slightly from 1900 (8.3%) to 1987 (7.1%). Actually, there has been considerable fluctuation with a low in 1940 (6.1%) and figures in the 9 percent to 10 percent range during the 1960s and early 1970s (Rix, 1989; U.S. Department of Commerce, 1975). Several factors contribute to low participation rates. Sex discrimination persists in the marketplace. Women's relative lack of gainful work experience, because of care-giving responsibilities, has reduced their employability. Historically, the fact that few women during their careers "earned" vested rights to adequate pensions for their later years induced some to work in retirement (Iams, 1986; McEaddy, 1975). Yet concurrently, the rising value of cash benefits over time increasingly has influenced the decision of women as well as men to retire and not return to work.

Gender differences in unretirement behavior, in fact, may have been eroding during the past decade. Labor force activity of aged Americans is becoming increasingly similar for men and women (Tuma & Sandefur, 1988, p. 70). The employment rates of elderly men are falling to an extent that makes it reasonable to forecast that they will "catch up" to women. And as women are encouraged to pursue career opportunities, more may elect to postpone retirement or take advantage of unretirement options. Surveys from Europe report that older women are more work oriented even though older men are more likely to work. Both sexes are seeking jobs in "peripheral" sectors of the economy, where there is greater flexibility than found in permanent full-time positions (Dale & Bamford, 1988; Ricardo-Campbell, 1988; Skoglund, 1979; Smirnov, 1977). Thus it is important to determine why older people work and what the objectives are that they seek through employment. Given the socioeconomic, gender, and race differences related to working at older ages, it is difficult to generalize about the reasons for unretirement. Predicting who will work after retirement is quite difficult because multiple factors influence unretirement decision making.

In terms of the proclivities to work or not to work, older people fall into two camps. Since the 1950s, those who have expressed satisfaction with retirement manifest little interest in returning to a job. Conversely, those who view retirement unfavorably find it difficult not to be working. Claiming that it takes a long time to become adjusted to leisure, the latter group are markedly predisposed to seek new employment opportunities. Among the potential pool of pensioned employees, the propensity to work is generalized, not job specific—a pattern confirmed in cross-cultural studies (Fillenbaum & Maddox, 1974). Even those who retire with hefty benefits resent restrictions on their employment (IBM, 1981; Stagner, 1979). That those who change jobs shortly before retirement are the most likely to work afterward (Holden, 1988) underscores that unretirement is part of a repertoire of adaptive behavior in later years.

Part-time employment always has been a (often *the*) favorite option among retirees who work. There have been notable increases in recent years in year-round, part-time positions. As noted earlier, the percentage of older people engaged in part-time, part-year jobs has grown slightly (see also Best, 1980; Borus, 1988). While most analyses of part-time employment deal with trends at the national level (Iams, 1986, 1987), case studies of older workers across occupational lines suggest that part-time work has broad appeal to retired state bureaucrats as well as to blue-collar workers (Golub, 1985; Palmore, 1964a, 1964b). Based on existing evidence, it is impossible to determine whether employment constraints relegate retired workers to marginal jobs or, *ceteris paribus*, the elderly truly prefer part-time arrangements after retirement. Is Jeremiah Driscoll, the seventy-six-year-old captain of a refueling tanker, who now works as a deck hand for the new captain, an anachronism or a pioneer (Zwingle, 1986)? After all, working part-time demonstrably has costs. Workers usually earn less pay and fewer benefits in jobs having less status than their previous employment. Arranging part-time schedules is difficult (Kaplan, 1981; McConnell, 1981; Sandell, 1987).

So the verdict on part-time work in retirement is mixed at best. Nevertheless, in his review of labor force participation of older, self-employed workers, Joseph Quinn (1980, 1981) hypothesizes that more wage-and-salary workers might choose a transition period of partial retirement if more part-time employment opportunities were available. Canadian studies support this prediction (McDonald & Wanner, 1982). Here, then, is an unretirement vehicle—if management perceives part-time work to be advantageous to its interests. Of the documented older-worker programs in the United States, the great majority provide part-time employment for unretired older workers.

## EMPLOYERS

Less is known, historically or contemporaneously, about the demand side than the supply side of the unretirement equation. Researchers have not focused in depth on shifts in employers' attitudes toward older workers or how the unretirement/retirement options they control actually operate within the corporate milieu. Only a few (Hirshorn, 1988) have studied how companies deal with mature employees. Nonetheless, three (obvious) trends have persisted over time. First, the corporate goal is to stay in business and make profits, not perform good works. The ways in which corporations respond to upswings and downturns in the economy is bound to affect their commitments to older workers. Second, managers often achieve their objectives by minimizing risks and maximizing control over their workers. Third, employers rarely have paid much attention to older workers' needs and desires. Relatively few in numbers, the aging usually become marginal within a firm; their preferences minimally affect procedures governing hiring, training, and firing (Achenbaum, 1989).

Hence, from a historical point of view, ambivalence has characterized employers' images and treatment of older workers. This ambivalent attitude also has characterized union organizations which must balance the interests of younger and older workers. Usually this balance has been achieved by supporting higher and earlier retirement benefits for older workers. But, particularly before Social Security, managers have resisted the enactment and enforcement of categorical old-age policies that would require the withdrawal of valued older employees who might otherwise have stayed in the labor force (American Management Association, 1930; Latimer, 1932).

Steeped in such ambivalence, the retirement policies of employers in the United States did not evolve in a straightforward manner. In the late nineteenth century, promising a pension to someone for years of faithful service was not intended just as a reward to the old. The intent was also to prevent earlier turnovers, limit work sharing, and ensure room at the top for middle-aged workers. To effect such disparate goals at an affordable price in a seemingly impartial manner, companies began to design elaborate eligibility criteria based on chronological age and years of service. Retirement initially was not automatic; requests from the capable were routinely rejected. A pension was a gratuity, not an earned right. Some companies forbade work after a superannuitant collected a pension. Others permitted a pensioner to work—but only for a different employer. Still others enabled their valued workers to retire voluntarily, to continue on a part-time basis, or to assume a less demanding job (National Industrial Conference Board, 1925).

An analogous ambivalence and tentativeness characterize current efforts by employers to create part-time employment opportunities for retirees. An available labor pool is needed to meet temporary increases in work loads (McConnell, 1981); still, employers worry about the administrative problems, pension and health benefit costs, and possible hidden costs associated with this arrangement (Coberly, 1984). Managers typically underestimate the extent of interest in part-time jobs among older workers, despite the fact that 40 percent of older managers sampled report that *they* would like to work a little after retirement (Gray & Morse, 1980). Furthermore, in contrast to the premium placed on training younger employees, scant attention has been paid to developing innovative training programs for the aging (Golub, 1985).

Why does such ambivalence persist? Is it mainly due to ageism? Do employment and retirement policies reflect an (unintentionally) insidious bias against older workers? Are these retirement policies thus considered to be the most functional approach to retirement? Do the continuing early retirement incentive programs reflect an underlying stereotype of the older worker as "superannuated"? Or is it possible that public and private policies, once set in place, have a life of their own and continue to exercise an independent influence—often in terms of structural lag—on both the supply and (perhaps more important) the demand side?

## POLICIES AS AN INDEPENDENT VARIABLE

Companies began to design retirement policies in the latter decades of the nineteenth century. But after six decades of experimentation only an eighth of all workers were potentially eligible for private pensions. The 1935 Social Security Act serves as the real stimulus for policy innovation in this area. Corporate plans (though not the Federal Civil Service Retirement System or programs for state bureaucrats) were adjusted to meet Social Security criteria for its fledgling Old Age Insurance scheme. Its sixty-five-year-old baseline for "normal" retirement became the accepted norm.

Researchers often exaggerate the influence of Social Security guidelines on retirement policymaking. It is worth bearing in mind, for instance, that the first Social Security retirement benefit under Title II was not paid until 1940. Before 1952, fewer senior citizens received support from old-age insurance than accepted old-age assistance. (Average benefits under Title II pensions were smaller, too.) There was a lag, in short, between when various Social Security provisions were enacted and when they may have had an impact on employer, or employee, attitudes and behavior (Wentworth, 1968).

Distinguishing actual from perceived policy influences on either the supply or the demand side, moreover, is difficult. It is commonly believed, for example, that the Social Security earnings test has diminished older people's penchant for work. Some research corroborates this view (Ginsburg, 1985; Gray & Morse, 1980; Tuma & Sandefur, 1988). Others discount its significance independent of other factors (Holden, 1988; Jaffe, 1970). Economic theory and cross-cultural comparisons neither prove nor disprove causal connections (Aaron, 1982; Morrison, 1979; Tracy, 1978, 1982). In a situation where both public and private pension policies encourage relatively early retirement and few if any policies provide incentives to work after pensions are accepted, marginal incentives may have little effect on behavior.

Therefore, the impact of federal policymaking on older-worker options usually cannot be measured directly, because it has been so intertwined with private-sector decisions during the last half-century. The original Social Security Act was based on insights and experience from both industrial and commercial sectors. Existing and projected assumptions about the private sector thus were used in designing the original national plan. Sometimes the pattern of influence was reversed. Court rulings made pensions part of collective bargaining. Private plans after World War II, therefore, were related to public models—often with a new twist, which transformed existing options. For example, Social Security's architects eschewed attempts to force older workers to retire. Private plans, however, typically made retirement mandatory at sixty-five (or an earlier age, pegged at Social Security eligibility ages). As a result, retirement policies overall before World War II became more rigid than they originally were intended to be. And the popularity of early retirement pensions has grown over time so much that today a pensioned retirement is a social expectation for nearly all workers (even if it is not achieved).

Perhaps the crucial point hinges not on establishing how much impact policies really have on attitudes and behavior but on understanding what people believe reality to be. Consider the pervasiveness of age discrimination in public and private policies. Strict upper age limits were used in early twentieth-century hiring and promotional procedures. Basically, these limits were justified on the grounds of efficiency in a marketplace geared to the young. Sometimes a paternalistic rationale—about the need to protect the dignity of the seasoned veteran—was made (AAOAS, 1928; Maryland, 1930; *Monthly Labor Review*, 1932; Smith, 1929). Ageism became more virulent in the United States during the Great Depression (Markowitz & Rosner, 1987), though it is important to note that age discrimination is hardly unique to America (Boglietti, 1974). Any effort to develop unretirement as an older-worker option must reckon with this historical animus against age which today may be covered over by structured early retirement policies.

But attitudes have changed over time, particularly as scientific evidence undermines stereotypical images of the place of the elderly within the labor force. Especially during the past two decades, there has been an effort to reduce ageism in the marketplace. Beginning with the 1967 Age Discrimination in Employment Act (which ironically protected only those workers between the ages of 40 and 65 until 1977), the drive culminated in 1987 with the virtual elimination of mandatory retirement. Expert witnesses stressed the benefits of the act to older people, to the nation's human resource pool, and to Social Security financing. Significantly, they also minimized the impact of such action on employment opportunities for minorities, youth, and women. Note the ambivalence: the symbolic politics of fighting age discrimination, advocates predicted, would on balance change very little in terms of increasing employment opportunities for older persons.

Indeed, since the late 1970s, experts doubted that officially ending mandatory retirement would significantly increase labor force participation rates among the elderly; it may slightly increase the retention of people over sixty-five but not slow the rate of early retirement (Borus, 1988; Burkhauser & Talley, 1978; Levine, 1980; U.S. Department of Labor, 1982). Some tempered the seemingly negative implications of this projection by stressing how federal policies were to be reinforced and made more effective by broad state and local interventions (Golub, 1985). Nonetheless, personal accounts and systematic surveys attest to the difficulties elderly people have in finding desirable jobs (Bland, 1973; Schulz, 1974). Two Harris polls (1975 and 1981) found that 80 percent of all Americans believe that employers discriminate against older workers. Employers claim they have quite positive assessments of older workers, but the financial arrangements and opportunities most personnel offices have created to encourage early retirement have suggested otherwise (Rhine, 1984). Is the incessant concern over age discrimination diverting attention from other factors that make it difficult to advance postretirement employment? Can legislation designed to protect the employment rights of older persons through prohibiting discrimination have any significant effect on aggregate hiring by employers or on retention policies?

## BROADER ECONOMIC AND CULTURAL FACTORS

The viability of unretirement as a policy option to either the supply or the demand side is affected by broader economic and cultural factors:

Age discrimination, the culprit in many individual cases, does not seem to be the primary cause of employment difficulties that many older Americans face. The solutions to their employment difficulties include improved economic conditions, training and retraining, and improved job search. These are similar to policies that have proven to be successful for persons with labor market problems, regardless of age. (Sandell, 1987)

The thrust of this statement seems plausible until it is tested historically. How, for instance, might "improved economic conditions" assuage the elderly's "employment difficulties"? Workers unquestionably enjoy more opportunities in an expanding marketplace. And as we have seen, a subset of the older population always has chosen to work because they needed money. But the replacement ratio of average wages in manufacturing by old-age benefits for single workers rose in the United States from 29 percent to 44 percent between 1965 and 1980; for couples, the replacement ratio increased from 44 percent to 66 percent (Ricardo-Campbell, 1988). Has economic security risen so much that older people think any extra income to be gained from working is not worth the effort? If so, then why have some retirees with high incomes persisted in expressing an interest in working? Nor can training or retraining alone be counted on to produce an increase in employment opportunities for older workers. Employers still seem content to lose many highly trained older employees through early retirement while taking few steps to encourage their return to work. Will the Supreme Court's ruling in the *Betts* case (U.S. House of Representatives, 1989), which declared that employee benefit plans were exempt from Age Discrimination in Employment Act (ADEA) protection, indirectly add incentives for postretirement employment? Might this interest in postretirement opportunities be a distinctly American phenomenon, where the work ethic is so deeply ingrained? Why has there been so little interest in "unretirement," in West Germany and other Western European countries, where there are greater percentages of older workers available and a longer tradition for public policy innovation in labor market adjustments?

A certain paradox emerges. Some global trends may be so sweeping in scope that they mask fluctuations along the historical timeline and variations within either the supply or the demand side. The paradox cannot be resolved, but our analysis suggests an important lesson concerning policymaking as it applies to older workers. It is precisely the malleability of structural, behavioral, and attitudinal patterns in changing historical circumstances that makes "unretirement" a promising older-worker strategy. However, if this strategy is to be applied effectively, both older persons and employers will have to view unretirement as a viable approach for satisfying labor demand—at least in terms of particular labor force requirements; that is, both will have to accept the possibility of changing and modifying structure, behavioral, and attitudinal patterns and develop policy modifications that accommodate changing needs.

## A RESEARCH AGENDA

Effecting a balance between older workers' needs and corporate demands has been difficult to achieve and to maintain in the United States. The pool of potential employees always has been diverse; the relative importance of various factors (such as a desire to earn money to survive) has shifted over time. Managers' perceptions of the productive capacity of people in later life and their willingness to use older workers have varied according to prevailing economic conditions. Business decisions and hiring policies reflect present and projected needs of the organization. Seemingly minor adjustments (such as eliminating an upper-age hiring limit or liberalizing the earnings test under Social Security) usually have only a marginal impact since few people premise their choices and behavior exclusively on policy guidelines. Economic factors patently influence decisions and expectations, but older people and business organizations are likely to act in response to their (not necessarily compatible) understanding of economic requirements and policies rather than on the basis of an objective measure of economic reality.

Two major conclusions emerge from this review. First, unretirement, the decision to return to work on at least a part-time basis after receiving a pension, has few historical antecedents. Elements of the phenomenon—which can be viewed as a stage in the retirement process—are familiar, but it is the "blips" in the historical record that merit reflection. These indicate that some older people have *always* worked, irrespective of public and private retirement policies. However, there has never been a meaningful recognition of unretirement as a social norm. On the demand side, many firms, especially in times of emergency (such as wars) or seasons in their business cycle when they need people with certain skills, have been eager to use the talents of older workers. Through policymaking it has always been possible to influence, if not wholly regulate, older people's work patterns. What is novel about conditions of the 1990s is that the prospects for unretirement have never been so sanguine on both supply and demand sides or in the realm of policymaking. Gerontologists have demonstrated that many older people have the cognitive resources and personality traits that make them highly desirable in the marketplace. Surveys of older people reveal a persistent desire on the part of at least a quarter of those interviewed to work on a part-time, part-year basis. Faced with declining numbers of younger recruits and impressed by older workers' recent performances, more and more employers have begun to reappraise their views of age. The elderly, it is said with increasing frequency and conviction, can play a positive role. However, unretirement will not develop simply because there may be labor demand for competent and consistent employees.

For example, in a survey by the Travelers Insurance Company it was revealed that over a five-year period (1982–1987) 17 percent to 23 percent of company retirees reported that they were still working. Most of these "unretirees" worked for economic reasons but they also valued the social and psychological benefits of employment. And, most who worked were concerned about their economic and health benefit requirements but were in good health. Policies that limit the number of hours of employment or that reduce pension benefits (because retirees remain employed) do reduce the work effort, or the incentives of individuals. In general, then, these findings indicate that older persons who "unretire" may be a highly self-selected group with unique characteristics (The Travelers Companies, 1989).

Second, the key variable appears to be employer action on the demand side. It is unlikely that the characteristics of the labor pool in this country will change dramatically in the near term. A further increase in the number of older people willing and able to work is not expected. Instead, conditions are conducive for better utilization of a resource—older people—that has been relatively untapped. Managers and workers alike need greater options to work as retirees. Based on limited evidence (because of the newness of the phenomenon), it appears that the corporate culture itself may prove to be the most important factor affecting the dynamics of unretirement. If employers view older workers as contributors to the larger enterprise, and if these workers are also needed, then it may be possible to attract older workers who are capable of meeting corporate needs while simultaneously satisfying their own requirements.

Human-resource managers should be sensitive to covert and overt ageism in employment policies. The cafeteria-style approach to benefits, increasingly demanded by younger two-wage-earner families, should become a feature of benefit options for older workers. In suggesting that employers' actions could significantly affect the supply of older workers, this analysis differs from others on the subject. Many researchers identify the availability of public and private pension benefits as the most important factor influencing labor-force participation by older workers. Despite the dramatic effects of institutional rules in creating and sustaining the early retirement trend, there is evidence that significant numbers of older persons are interested in working *after* retirement if certain conditions can be met (U.S. Department of Labor, 1989).

As findings from The Travelers Companies retiree survey indicate, a certain sub-group of retirees will "unretire" even though they are receiving pension benefits. The particular conditions that are most likely to encourage unretirement are not completely understood, but they are clearly related to corporate views and personnel policies regarding older workers. To a considerable extent, most organizations hold certain values and beliefs regarding their employee pools and their expected lengths of service with the firm. These types of expectations (which also include the overall retirement policy of the firm) become a part of the corporate culture and thus pervasively influence the policies *proposed*, as well as adopted, by the organization. If personnel managers signal strong expectations for early retirement and few opportunities are offered as a matter of policy for workers in their later years, the prophecy of discrimination will be fulfilled. The rigidity of current retirement and employment policies makes it very difficult to gain access to the potential supply of retired workers who could assist in meeting employment demands. The challenge is to examine how supply and demand can be better matched through possible modifications in corporate policies, taking into consideration public and private policies that have introduced barriers between the supply of and demand for older workers. The degree to which unretirement can be enhanced depends on the extent to which corporate policies are designed to be more effective in increasing the employment of older workers.

# REFERENCES

Aaron, H. (1982). *Economic effects of Social Security.* Washington, DC: Brookings Institution.

Abramovitz, M. (1988). *Regulating the lives of women.* Boston: South End Press.

Achenbaum, W. A. (1978). *Old age in the new land.* Baltimore, MD: Johns Hopkins University Press.

Achenbaum, W. A. (1989). History of business involvement in aging needs. *Generations, 13*(13), 7–10.

American Association for Old Age Security (AAOAS). (1928)). *Old age security.* New York: American Association for Old Age Security.

American Management Association. (1930). *Personnel series.* New York: American Management Association.

Barresi, C. M. (1974). The meaning of work. *Industrial Gerontology,* (1), 4–29.

Baxandall, R., Gordon, L., & Reverby, S. (Eds.). (1976). *America's working women.* New York: Random House.

Best, F. M. (1980). *Flexible life scheduling.* Westport, CT: Praeger.

Bixby, L. E., et al. (1968). *Demographic and economic characteristics of the aged.* Washington, DC: Social Security Administration, Office of Research and Statistics.

Bland, D. (1973). Retirement... and rehirement. *Perspectives on Aging, 2,* 15–17.

Boglietti, G. (1974). Discrimination against older workers and the promotion of equality of opportunity. *International Labour Review, 110,* 351–365.

Borus, M. E. (1988). *The older worker.* New York: Industrial Relations Association.

Bosworth, T. W., & Holden, K. C. (1983). The role part-time job options play in the retirement timing of older Wisconsin state employees. *Aging and Work, 6,* 31–36.

Bureau of National Affairs. (1987). *Older Americans in the workforce: Challenges and solutions.* Washington, DC: Bureau of National Affairs.

Burkhauser, R. V., & Talley, G. (1978). Older Americans and market work. *The Gerontologist, 18,* 449–453.

Coberly, S. (1984). Incentives for hiring older workers—Are employers interested? *Aging and work, 6,* 31–36.

Cohen, W. J. (1958). *Retirement under Social Security.* Berkeley: University of California Press.

Dale, A., & Bamford, C. (1988). Older workers and peripheral workers: The erosion of gender differences. *Ageing and Society, 8,* 43–62.

Degler, C. N. (1971). *At odds.* New York: Oxford University Press.

Donahue, W., Orbach, H. L., & Pollak, O. (1960). Retirement: The emerging pattern. In C. Tibbetts (Ed.), *Handbook of social gerontology.* Chicago: University of Chicago Press.

Farley, R. (1987). *Blacks and whites.* Cambridge, MA: Harvard University Press.

Fillenbaum, G. G. (1971). The working retired. *Journal of Gerontology, 26,* 82–89.

Fillenbaum, G. G., & Maddox, G. L. (1974). Work after retirement. *The Gerontologist, 14,* 418–424.

Flexner, S. B. (1982). *Listening to America.* New York: Simon & Schuster.

Fraundorf, M. N. (1979). The labor force participation of turn-of-the-century married women. *Journal of Economic History, 39,* 401–417.

Friedman, E. A., & Havighurst, R. J. (1954). *The meaning of work and retirement.* Chicago: University of Chicago Press.

Gibson, R. J. (1986). Outlook for the black family. In A. Pifer and L. Bronte (Eds.), *Our Aging Society* (pp. 181–197). New York: Norton.

Ginsburg, H. (1985). Flexible and partial retirement for Norwegians. *Monthly Labor Review, 108,* 33–43.

Golub, C. (1985). *Older worker employment comes of age: Practice and potential.* Washington, DC: National Commission for Employment Policy.

Graebner, W. (1980). *A history of retirement.* New Haven, CT: Yale University Press.

Gratton, B. (1985). *Urban elders.* Philadelphia: Temple University Press.

Gratton, B., & Haber, C. (in press). *Aging over time.* Bloomington: Indiana University Press.

Gray, S., & Morse, D. (1980). Retirement and re-engagement: Changing work options for older workers. *Aging and Work, 3,* 103–111.

Gustman, A. L., & Steinmeier, T. L. (1984). Partial retirement and the analysis of retirement behavior. *Industrial and Labor Relations Review, 37,* 403–415.

Haber, C. (1983). *Beyond sixty-five.* New York: Cambridge University Press.

Hannah, L. (1982). *Inventing retirement.* Cambridge, England: Cambridge University Press.

Hendrick, B. J. (1908). Superannuated man. *McClure's Magazine, 32,* 118.

Hirshorn, B. A. (1988). Organizational behavior regarding older workers: Prototypical responses. *Journal of Aging Studies, 2,* 199–215.

Holden, K. C. (1988). Physically demanding occupations, health, and work after retirement. *Social Security Bulletin, 51,* 3–15.

Honig, M., & Honach, G. (1985). Partial retirement as a separate mode of retirement behavior. *Journal of Human Resources, 20,* 21–46.

Iams, H. M. (1986). Employment of retired-worker women. *Social Security Bulletin, 49,* 5–13.

Iams, H. M. (1987). Jobs and persons working after receiving retired-worker benefits. *Social Security Bulletin, 50,* 4–18.

IBM. (1981). What IBM retirees think of retirement. *Aging and Work, 4,* 191.

Jacobs, R. H. (1978). Re-employment and unemployment in old age. *Journal of Geriatric Psychiatry, 11,* 79–80.

Jaffe, A. J. (1970). Men prefer not to retire. *Industrial Gerontology, 5,* 1–24.

Jaffe, A. J. (1971). Has the retreat from the labor force halted? *Industrial Gerontology, 9,* 1–23.

Jaffe, A. J. (1972). The retirement dilemma. *Industrial Gerontology, 14,* 75–85.

Johnson, P. (1989). The labour force participation of older men in Britain, 1951–1981. *Work, Employment & Society, 3,* 351–368.

Kaplan, B. H. (1981). Alternative work options for older workers—The union and professional association view. *Aging and Work, 4,* 146–159.

Kieffer, J. A. (1983). *Gaining the dividends of longer life.* Boulder, CO: Westview.

Kohli, M. (1988). Ageing as a challenge for sociological theory. *Ageing and Society, 8,* 367–394.

Latimer, M. W. (1932). *Industrial pensions in the United States and Canada.* New York: Industrial Relations Counselors.

Levine, M. (1980). Four models for age/work policy research. *The Gerontologist, 20,* 561–574.

McConnell, S. (1981). Alternative work options for older workers—The managers' view. *Aging and Work, 4,* 81–87.

McDonald, L., & Wanner, R. A. (1982). Work past age 65 in Canada: A socio-economic analysis. *Aging and Work, 5,* 169–180.

McEaddy, B. J. (1975). Women in the labor force: The later years. *Monthly Labor Review, 98,* 17–24.

Markowitz, G., & Rosner, D. (1987). *Slaves of the depression: Workers' letters about life on the job.* Ithaca, NY: Cornell University Press.

Maryland, State of. (1930). *The older worker in Maryland.* Annapolis, MD: Commissioner of Labor and Statistics.

Moen, J. (1987). The labor of older men: A comment. *Journal of Economic History, 47,* 761–767.

Monthly Labor Review. (1932). Hiring and separation methods. *Monthly Labor Review, 35,* 1005–1017.

Morrison, M. H. (1979). International developments in retirement flexibility. *Aging and Work, 2,* 221–234.

Motley, D. K. (1978). Availability of retired persons for work. *Social Security Bulletin, 31,* 3–21.

Murray, J. (1979). Subjective retirement. *Social Security Bulletin, 42,* 20–24.

Myles, J. (1984). *Old age in the welfare state.* Boston: Little, Brown.

National Industrial Conference Board. (1925). *Industrial pensions in the United States and Canada.* New York: National Industrial Conference Board.

Palmore, E. (1964a). Work experience and earnings of the aged in 1962. *Social Security Bulletin, 27,* 3–14, 44.

Palmore, E. (1964b). Employment patterns among men. *Social Security Bulletin, 27,* 3–10.

Parnes, H. J., et al. (1985). *Retirement among American men.* Lexington, MA: D. C. Heath.

Quadagno, J. (1988). *The transformation of old age security.* Chicago: University of Chicago Press.

Quinn, J. (1980). Labor-force patterns of older self-employed workers. *Social Security Bulletin, 43,* 17–28.

Quinn, J. (1981). The extent and correlates of partial retirement. *The Gerontologist, 21,* 634–642.

Ransom, R., & Sutch, R. (1986). The labor of older Americans: Retirement of men on and off the job, 1879–1930. *Journal of Economic History, 46,* 1–30.

Rhine, S. (1984). *Managing older workers.* New York: Conference Board.

Ricardo-Campbell, R. (1988). Women and retirees. In R. Ricardo-Campbell & E. P. Lazear (Eds.), *Issues in contemporary retirement* (169–187). Stanford, CA: Hoover Institution Press.

Rix, S. E. (1989). *The American woman, 1988–89.* New York: Norton.

Rotella, E. (1981). *From home to office.* Ann Arbor: University of Michigan Press.

Sandell, S. (Ed.). (1987). *The problem isn't age.* New York: Praeger.

Schulz, J. (1974). Economics of mandatory retirement. *Industrial Gerontology, 1,* 3–12.

Skoglund, J. (1979). Work after retirement. *Aging and Work, 2,* 103–111.

Smirnov, S. (1977). The employment of old-age pensioners in the U.S.S.R. *International Labor Review, 116,* 87–94.

Smith, E. D. (1929). Employment age limitation. *Bulletin of the Taylor Society, 19,* 223–224.

Sobel, I. (1972). Older worker utilization patterns. *Industrial Gerontology, 13,* 6–25.

Stagner, R. (1979). Propensity to work. *Aging and Work, 2,* 161–181.

Streib, G. (1988). Discussion. In R. Ricardo-Campbell & E. P. Lazear (Eds.), *Issues in contemporary retirement.* Stanford, CA: Hoover Institution Press.

Streib, G. F., & Schneider, C. (1971). *Retirement in American society.* Ithaca, NY: Cornell University Press.

Thompson, G. B. (1974). Work experience and income of the population aged 60 and older, 1971. *Social Security Bulletin, 37,* 3–16.

Tracy, M. B. (1978). Flexible retirement features abroad. *Social Security Bulletin, 41,* 18–25.

Tracy, M. B. (1982). Removing the earnings test for old-age benefits in Canada: The impact on labor supply of men ages 65–69. *Aging and Work, 5,* 181–189.

The Travelers Companies. (1989). *The Travelers 1988 retiree survey: Retirees views of work and retirement.* Hartford, CT: The Travelers Companies.

Tuma, N. B., & Sandefur, G. D. (1988). Trends in the labor force activity of the elderly in the United States, 1940–1980. In R. Ricardo-Campbell & E. P. Lazear (Eds.), *Issues in contemporary retirement.* Stanford, CA: Hoover Institution Press.

U.S. Department of Commerce. (1975). *Historical statistics of the United States,* Part 1. Washington, DC: U.S. Government Printing Office.

U.S. Department of Labor. (1982). *Report to Congress on studies conducted under the Age Discrimination in Employment Act.* Washington, DC: U.S. Government Printing Office.

U.S. Department of Labor. (1989, January). *Labor market problems of older workers.* Washington, DC: U.S. Government Printing Office.

U.S. House of Representatives, Select Committee on Aging. (1989, July 7). Aging Committee chairman announces intent to introduce legislation to remedy supreme court decision in Betts Case. Press release.

Wentworth, E. C. (1968). *Employment after retirement.* Research report no. 21. Social Security Administration; Office of Research and Statistics. Washington, DC: Social Security Administration, Office of Research and Statistics.

Zwingle, E. (1986). The golden door. *National Geographic, 100,* 17–41.

# Part III

## Volunteering and Long-Term Care

# 7

# Formal Volunteer Work among Older Americans

## A. Regula Herzog and James N. Morgan

Volunteer work is a mainstay of American society, contributing in substantial ways to society's productive output. Many voluntary, service, and religious organizations depend in important ways on volunteers to accomplish their missions. In recent decades, these needs have become harder to fill because the women who used to do volunteer work as part of their traditional "at home" roles are instead entering the paid work force in record numbers. To offset this loss in potential volunteers, one particularly promising (and growing) group comprises the older, retired members of society. Because Americans are retiring at younger ages, and are in better health and better educated than earlier cohorts of retirees, they are very likely to have the time, skills, and energy to contribute to society through volunteer work.

In addition to benefiting society, volunteer work may benefit the individual who performs it. From the earliest controversies over the disengagement and activity theories, many have argued that in older age the loss of work and family roles and of other opportunities for meaningful and productive social involvement may lead to a loss of identity, self-esteem, and mental health. If that is so, then maintaining active involvement—for example, through volunteer work—should have a positive impact on health and well-being and mitigate some of the stresses of aging.

Unfortunately, the predominant view of older Americans as unproductive (Butler, 1975) has not helped in drawing attention to productive involvement among this particular group. One exception is a study by Louis Harris and associates (1977) as part of the larger study of *The Myth and Reality of Aging in America*, which produced the intriguing finding that 22 percent of people over sixty-five performed volunteer work, compared to 35 percent of those younger than sixty-five; it was subsequently analyzed more thoroughly by Susan Chambré (1987) as to factors related to volunteer work.

More recently, a nationwide survey of the elderly indicated that about 40 percent of them did volunteer work (Marriott Senior Living Services, 1991); a survey of Minnesota's older residents showed as many as 50 percent of them doing volunteer work and further examined factors affecting participation (Fischer, Mueller, & Cooper, 1991). But for the most part, we lack today a comprehensive documentation of the extent of volunteer work performed by older Americans and an understanding of the conditions under which such volunteer work can flourish. If older persons were viewed as a potential societal resource, we might begin to document the contributions they make through volunteer work today and attempt to identify circumstances that can facilitate further volunteer work.

The major questions addressed in this chapter, therefore, are (1) what contributions do older Americans make to this society in the form of formal volunteer work? (2) who among the elderly currently contribute? and (3) are there untapped propensities for volunteer work and, if so, how might they be tapped? These questions call for an assessment of a representative sample of older Americans and for measures not only of volunteer behaviors but also of factors that are likely to influence such behaviors. Because behaviors such as volunteer work are always a function of the individual as well as the environment within which the individual operates, a broad range of environmental as well as individual factors must be considered, and an articulated conceptualization of the causal processes must guide the multivariate data anlayses.

## THE AMERICANS' CHANGING LIVES SURVEY

The data set that we chose to address these questions is the Americans' Changing Lives (ACL) survey, a survey conducted in 1986 designed to assess the paid and unpaid productive contributions among American adults. One crucial component of the assessment was volunteer work, defined as work without pay in a formal organization such as a church, hospital, or school. The assessment further included informal help to friends, neighbors, and relatives; housework; maintenance work; and paid employment. Compared to many of the other productive activities that were measured and that more directly benefit the individual and his or her immediate family, formal volunteer work has a more purely altruistic or philanthropic character, and we therefore focus on formal volunteer work. We are aware, however, of proposals that also include informal help to others in the definition of volunteer work (Fischer, Mueller, & Cooper, 1991).

In the ACL survey we measured formal volunteer work in the following way. We first asked each respondent a series of five questions about whether during the past twelve months he or she had done volunteer work (1) for a church, synagogue, or other religious organization; (2) for a school or educational organization; (3) for a political group or labor union; (4) for a senior citizens group or related organization; or (5) for any other national or local organization. Respondents who answered any of these questions in the affirmative were then asked, "About how many hours did you spend on volunteer work of this kind during the last twelve months? Would you say less than 20 hours, 23 to 39 hours, 40 to 79 hours, 80 to 159 hours, or 160 hours or more?" For analytical purposes, the answer categories were assigned the midpoints of the hour range.

The ACL survey used a multistage stratified area probability sample of persons twenty-five years of age or older living in the coterminous United States. Relative to the sampling rate for non-blacks under sixty years of age, the sampling rate for blacks aged sixty and over was 4:1, and 2:1 for blacks under sixty years of age and for non-blacks aged sixty and over. A total of 3,617 respondents were interviewed in their homes by interviewers of the University of Michigan's Survey Research Center (SRC), reflecting a response rate of 70 percent among sampled households and 67 percent among sampled individuals (more than one individual being interviewed in some households). The interviews were conducted between May and October of 1986 and lasted, on average, about eighty-five minutes. Nonresponse did not vary substantially by age, race, or other known respondent characteristics. In 1989, 2,867 of the respondents were reinterviewed. Weights are used in all analyses to adjust for variations in probabilities of selection and in response rates across sample areas. Significance calculations for the regression coefficients were computed with the OSIRIS.IV program REPERR, which adjusts for the design effect in the data resulting from the clustered and weighted probability sample. The analyses presented in this chapter were based only on respondents who were fifty-five years old or older in 1986, resulting in a sample of 1,896 persons for the following analyses to be described below.

### The Volume of Volunteer Work by Older Americans

According to the 1986 ACL study, 36 percent of all Americans fifty-five years old or older had engaged in some formal volunteer work over the previous twelve months. Twenty-four percent of all adults fifty-five and older had done some volunteer work for church groups. Fewer older volunteers had worked in senior citizens groups (10 percent), political organizations (6 percent), and educational groups (6 percent). Some of the older volunteers offered their services to more than one type of organization. About one-quarter of them had performed volunteer work in two types of organizations, about one-fifth in three or more types. The remaining half had served only one type of organization. Altogether, these findings indicate a limited breadth in beneficiaries of volunteer work.

The magnitude of the contributions by older Americans can be gauged by the number of hours they spent in all types of formal volunteer work.

Table 7.1
Hours Spent in Formal Volunteer Work during Past Year, by American
Volunteers Fifty-five Years of Age and Older

| Number of hours | Percentage |
| --- | --- |
| <20 | 30% |
| 20-39 | 21% |
| 40-79 | 18% |
| 80-159 | 12% |
| 160+ | 19% |
|  | 100 % |
| n | 655 |

Among those older persons who had done any volunteer work, 19 percent
had spent 160 hours or more during the past year, 30 percent had spent
less than twenty hours, and the remaining 51 percent fell in between (see
Table 7.1). Over the span of one year, an average of seventy-two hours of
work was performed by each older volunteer.

The formal volunteer work by older Americans may be compared to the
magnitude of other productive behaviors. For instance, 68 percent of all
Americans fifty-five years and older had helped friends and relatives in
various informal ways, and these people had spent an average of seventy
hours per year in this way. Ninety-three percent of older Americans had
performed housework, spending an average of 865 hours per year, and 33
percent had worked for pay at an average of 1,629 hours per year. (For
more detail on the magnitude of other productive activities, see Herzog,
Kahn, Morgan, Jackson, & Antonucci, 1989.)

Of course, not everyone's contributed hours have the same worth. One
way of estimating the dollar value that a person "contributes" while volunteering is to take the wage that he or she could have earned working for
pay instead. Economists refer to this method as the "opportunity cost"
method. For volunteers who do not work for pay at all, and who therefore
do not command a wage, a wage can be estimated based on personal characteristics. If an hourly wage is attached to each hour of volunteering using
such an opportunity cost approach, in 1986 an average of $428 was con-
tributed in the form of volunteer work by each older volunteer. Another
way of attributing productive value to these quantitative estimates is to ask

respondents either about the amount of money that the volunteer organization saved by "employing" them without wages or about the benefit more broadly defined that accrued to other people because of the volunteer work. Both methods were used in the ACL survey. While more detail is provided elsewhere (Herzog & House, 1991; Herzog & Morgan, in press), suffice it to say that both indicators suggest that formal volunteer work and paid work can be viewed as equally productive.

All of these figures suggest a substantial contribution by older Americans, documenting their productivity in just one specific area—formal volunteer work. Nevertheless, the figures also suggest that there is room for additional volunteer work.

### Unmaterialized Potential for Volunteer Work

Quite clearly, 64 percent of all Americans over the age of fifty-four did not engage in any formal volunteer work during the twelve months preceding the 1986 survey. Obviously, they represent a group that might be targeted as potential volunteers. Also, quite obviously, among the 36 percent of older Americans who did perform volunteer work, only a relatively small proportion spent large numbers of hours in volunteer work, while about two-thirds spent less than eighty hours per year or less than two hours per week this way. These latter groups might be willing to increase the level of their volunteer work. To explore these possibilities, the nonvolunteers and volunteers were asked in the 1989 ACL follow-up survey, respectively, whether they would like to do some volunteer work or whether they would like to do more volunteer work. Close to 40 percent of the nonvolunteers indicated that they would like to perform *some* volunteer work; 20 percent of the volunteers answered that they would like to do *more* volunteer work.

The question then becomes: Why have so many older Americans not volunteered their efforts, despite the fact that many of them say they would like to? And why have those who have volunteered contributed only a relatively small number of hours? Are they not healthy enough? Do they lack necessary skills or other resources? Is there no demand for their services? We can get a sense of what accounts for older Americans' volunteer work by investigating how volunteers differ from nonvolunteers.

### Characteristics of Volunteers

Volunteer work, like most other behaviors, is a function of the person and his or her environment. The environment is often characterized by its physical and its social-structural aspects, the person by his or her relatively stable personal characteristics or personality traits. Social-structural characteristics—like age, gender, race, and socioeconomic class—define an individual's position in the social structure. Social-structural positions, in turn, prescribe functions and roles in society and imply differential access to society's resources and opportunities. Personality traits are thought to describe an individual's basic approach to life and as such to be related to life-style preferences and behavior choices. Because many behaviors are a function of role prescriptions, of life-style preferences, and of opportunities and resources to perform them, social-structural characteristics and personality traits are expected to be related to volunteer behavior. The ACL survey is well suited for an examination of the personal characteristics and social-structural aspects of the volunteer environment; this is where our discussion begins. The physical characteristics of this environment are considered more briefly.

As shown in Table 7.2, the participation in volunteer work dropped significantly after the age of seventy-five, but the number of hours that volunteers spent doing such work remained rather stable. Of course, ACL data at this point are strictly cross-sectional and thus confound age changes with cohort differences. Moreover, correlates of age confound the age comparisons, and different roles, resources, and life-styles might mediate the age effect. So we must further explore possible explanations of these age patterns in the following multivariate analyses. Gender differences are rather small and not statistically significant. Racial differences also are small and nonsignificant.

Socioeconomic status is one of the strongest and most consistently replicated social-structural correlates of volunteer participation. Educational attainment, for example, repeatedly has been found to relate to volunteer work (Fischer, Mueller, & Cooper, 1991; Harris & Associates, 1977; Morgan, Dye, & Hybels, 1979). It is suggested that better-educated adults face more interesting opportunities than those less educated because they are capable of designing more interesting activities for themselves and are offered more challenging tasks than less-educated adults. In addition, more highly educated adults may find it easier to master the information required for taking on new activities than those less highly educated. Occupational status, related to education, may provide additional skills and create interests which, in turn, facilitate volunteer involvement. Finally, income, which is of course related to educational attainment and occupation and represents another component of socioeconomic status (SES), also facilitates volunteer work (Gallup Organization, 1990; Morgan, Dye & Hybels, 1979). Suggestions are that higher income makes it possible for people to pay for miscellaneous expenses associated with unpaid work such as transportation, necessary clothing, health and accident insurance, and so forth. Higher income also should reduce the need to work long hours for pay or to seek paid work beyond one's regular job to supplement low income.

In the ACL data, older Americans with higher educational attainment, higher incomes, and professional, sales, and clerical occupations were more likely to do volunteer work than those with less education, lower incomes,

Table 7.2
Social-Structural, Environmental, and Personality Correlates of Older Americans'
Volunteer Work

| | Percent volunteering[a,b] | Unweighted n | Annual hours spent by volunteers[c] |
|---|---|---|---|
| Age | | | |
| 55-64 | 41%** | (685) | 65.1 |
| 65-74 | 40% | (765) | 78.2 |
| 75+ | 26% | (446) | 74.6 |
| | | | |
| Gender | | | |
| Male | 34% | (629) | 69.0 |
| Female | 37% | (1267) | 74.1 |
| | | | |
| Race | | | |
| Non-Black | 36% | (1326) | 72.2 |
| Black | 31% | (570) | 69.9 |
| | | | |
| Education | | | |
| High   (16+ yrs ) | 60%** | (164) | 78.4 |
| Medium (9-15 yrs) | 39% | (1115) | 71.3 |
| Low    (0-8 yrs.) | 19% | (617) | 68.3 |
| | | | |
| Income | | | |
| High   ($25000+) | 45%** | (425) | 67.0 |
| Medium ($10000-$24999) | 38% | (658) | 77.7 |
| Low    (< $10000) | 23% | (813) | 70.2 |
| | | | |
| Current or former occupation | | | |
| Professional | 50%** | (421) | 74.4 |
| Sales/clerical | 43% | (372) | 75.6 |
| Craft | 26% | (154) | 65.6 |
| Labor/Service | 25% | (808) | 70.7 |
| Never Worked | 21% | (130) | 48.0 |
| | | | |
| Religious preference | | | |
| Protestant | 38%* | (1413) | 69.5 |
| Catholic | 32% | (369) | 82.3 |
| Jewish | 28% | (30) | 63.2 |
| None | 21% | (76) | 65.5 |

Table 7.2 (continued)

| | Percent volunteering[a,b] | Unweighted n | Annual hours spent by volunteers[c] |
|---|---|---|---|
| Region | | | |
| Northeast | 30%* | (383) | 94.4* |
| Central | 40% | (502) | 73.1 |
| South | 32% | (733) | 58.5 |
| West | 43% | (278) | 72.7 |
| | | | |
| Urbanicity | | | |
| Metropolitan | 33% | (607) | 75.7 |
| Suburban | 37% | (674) | 76.5 |
| Rural | 36% | (615) | 62.9 |
| | | | |
| Access to community | | | |
| Yes | 37%* | (1692) | 72.2 |
| No | 26% | (204) | 69.4 |
| | | | |
| Extraversion | | | |
| Highest | 52%** | (330) | 82.0* |
| . | 39% | (458) | 78.2 |
| . | 32% | (618) | 68.0 |
| Lowest | 25% | (490) | 53.8 |
| | | | |
| Neuroticism | | | |
| Highest | 27%* | (477) | 65.5 |
| . | 35% | (441) | 87.3 |
| . | 36% | (449) | 71.5 |
| Lowest | 43% | (529) | 65.7 |
| | | | |
| Self-efficacy | | | |
| Highest | 39%* | (464) | 67.7* |
| . | 41% | (457) | 83.2 |
| . | 36% | (470) | 77.5 |
| Lowest | 27% | (505) | 56.2 |

* $p < .05$          ** $p < .01$

[a] Percentages are based on weighted ns.
[b] Significance levels are based on Chi-Square tests for each set of subgroups.
[c] Significance levels are based on Anovas.

and craft and labor occupations, or no occupation (see Table 7.2). Interestingly, however, the number of hours spent volunteering differs little between volunteers of higher and lower SES. From this, it appears that SES is related to participation itself but not to the quantity of the participation. Again, many interpretations of the SES effect are possible, and we will have to return to the interpretation in the multivariate analyses later in the chapter.

Religious preference is yet another social-structural characteristic that may be significant in facilitating volunteer work. Religious belief systems of the Judeo-Christian tradition include an ethos of altruism and community service. While it has been maintained that these orientations are particularly strong among Protestants and Jews but somewhat less among Catholics, most recently such differences seem to have disappeared (Chambré, 1987). As the ACL data indicate (Table 7.2), there is a significant difference in volunteer participation between older adults with different or no religious preferences.

Characteristics of the physical environment that we were able to investigate using the ACL data were, for example, the region of the country and the urban or rural character of the residence that the volunteer lived in. For a variety of reasons, such as economic and cultural differences or differences in climate and predominant industries, one might expect regional differences in the levels and forms of volunteering. Likewise, one might expect urban-rural differences in volunteer behavior because of the level of complexity of the labor market, the level of social integration and connectedness, and the level of services. While urbanicity does not seem to be a factor, using the ACL data, region does relate to mere participation in volunteer work as well as to the hours spent in volunteering. Northeasterners and Southerners were less likely to do volunteer work than people from the Central and Western regions of the country; volunteers in the Northeast spent the most time as volunteers, while those in the West spent the least (see Table 7.2).

We further reasoned that the difficulty an individual experiences when trying to access his or her community, presumably because of lack of transportation, would act as a barrier to volunteer work. And, indeed, whether or not respondents felt that they could get to any given place in their community was related to their participation in, but not to the hours they spent, volunteering.

Finally, we examined the relatively stable personality traits of extroversion, neuroticism, and personal efficacy, because personality traits are thought to capture the core of a person and determine his or her unique approach to the world and as such to influence his or her behaviors and activities (George, 1978; Lawton, 1985). With regard to volunteer work, we might expect that people who are outgoing and gregarious are more likely to get involved than are withdrawn people and that they are more likely to persist in doing volunteer work. This is hypothesized because extraverted people may find satisfaction in volunteer work, which often takes place in social contexts. Likewise, people who feel competent and in control of their lives might be expected to be more likely to take the initiative and look for volunteer positions than people who feel incompetent and directed by external forces beyond their control. This hypothesis is predicated on the suspicion that very little recruiting for volunteering is directed toward older volunteers and that volunteering is therefore mostly a question of individual initiative. The prediction regarding neuroticism is less clear, but neuroticism is an important personality trait in its own right and is therefore included here.

We measured efficacy with six items, three of which were from the Rosenberg Self-Esteem scale (Rosenberg, 1965), and three from the Pearlin Mastery scale (Pearlin, Lieberman, Managhan, & Mullan, 1981); coefficient alpha for the older respondents was .65. Introversion-extraversion was measured by four items from the Eysenck Personality Inventory (Eysenck & Eysenck, 1963) that showed a coefficient alpha of .68 among older adults, neuroticism by five items from the same scale with a coefficient alpha of .74.

The findings (see Table 7.2) indicate that extraversion is very clearly linked to the mere participation in volunteer work as well as to the number of hours spent in such endeavors, suggesting that it is at least in part the social nature of volunteer work that attracts older extraverted people to it. Neuroticism is negatively related to volunteer participation, but not to the number of hours spent in it. In other words, older people who are more neurotic are more likely to shy away from volunteer work than are people who are less neurotic. Finally, the relationship with self-efficacy suggests that older people with a low sense of efficacy are less likely to volunteer and spend less time volunteering.

As we noted above, these social-structural, environmental, and personal characteristics are at least in part expected to impact on volunteer work by way of affecting roles, resources, and opportunities. Thus, we examined an individual's reported work and marital roles, his or her health status, and his or her social contacts and organizational participation in order to learn whether these things relate to volunteer work and whether they might mediate the effects of more stable environmental and personal characteristics.

We measured informal social contacts in the survey by asking how often respondents visited with others in person or on the telephone, and we measured formal organizational participation by asking how often respondents participated in meetings of formal organizations and in religious services. Both forms of social involvement are related to volunteer work (see Table 7.3). This relationship may be interpreted as supporting the effect of a socially active life-style on volunteer work. Whether individuals seek out opportunities for volunteering during social contacts or whether volunteer

Table 7.3
Roles, Competency, and Life-Style Correlates of Older Americans' Volunteer Work

| | Percent volunteering[a] | Unweighted n | Annual hours spent by volunteers |
|---|---|---|---|
| Paid work | | | |
| Full-time | 37%** | (302) | 55.1* |
| Part-time | 55% | (205) | 72.5 |
| None | 33% | (1389) | 77.6 |
| | | | |
| Marital status | | | |
| Married | 40%** | (1013) | 68.9 |
| Divorced/Separated | 26% | (192) | 63.4 |
| Widowed | 29% | (610) | 85.2 |
| Never Married | 25% | ( 81) | 96.0 |
| | | | |
| Informal social contacts | | | |
| Highest | 45%* | (465) | 77.7* |
| . | 39% | (511) | 80.0 |
| . | 37% | (412) | 73.0 |
| Lowest | 22% | (508) | 46.2 |
| | | | |
| Formal organizational participation | | | |
| Highest | 66%** | (560) | 85.5** |
| . | 45% | (357) | 62.4 |
| . | 25% | (543) | 49.2 |
| Lowest | 8% | (436) | 50.9 |
| | | | |
| Functional health | | | |
| Little or no impairment | 39%** | (1479) | 72.0 |
| Great deal of impairment | 20% | (417) | 72.4 |

\* $p < .05$          \*\* $p < .01$

[a] Percentages are based on weighted ns.

work is solicited within the formal organizational settings to which they belong cannot be determined from the ACL data, but the existence of the relationship is consistent with a study reported by Frances Carp (1968) and the investigations of Chambré (1987) with the data from the Harris survey.

Frequent social and organizational contacts do appear to facilitate volunteer participation among older Americans, but we identified certain personal barriers to such activity. One of the major barriers is bad health and difficulties encountered in physical functioning. Respondents who reported a great deal of functional impairment were only half as likely to participate in volunteer work as were those who reported no or little functional impairment, and the level of functional impairment is not related to the number of volunteer hours. Apparently, health status only affects whether persons can get to the site of the volunteer work, but not how much time they spend once there. We measured functional impairment by categorizing as greatly impaired all respondents who reported that they spent most of their day in a bed or chair or that they had considerable difficulty bathing, showering, walking, or climbing stairs.

Because the commitment to the role of work declines or stops entirely as people grow older, older people have more time and potentially more interest in other productive involvements. Likewise, following the death of their spouse, survivors may look for other outlets for their interpersonal needs and commitments. In gerontological research, the consequences of the age-related loss of major adult roles such as worker and spouse are thought to be a great deal of unstructured time, a lack of stimulation, feelings of uselessness, and generally sagging well-being (Rosow, 1985). New activities that can substitute for lost adult roles are often thought to provide the individual with new roles and associated behavioral guidelines. Volunteer work would appear to be a particularly appropriate substitute activity because its productive nature carries the connotation of usefulness (Romero, 1986).

Work status, we found, is indeed related to volunteer work. Those older individuals who are employed part-time are more likely to participate in volunteer work than those who are employed full-time, and those employed part-time spend more time volunteering than full-time employees (Table 7.3). These figures suggest strongly that full-time paid work presents a possible barrier to volunteer involvement, most likely in the form of time constraints. Nonemployed older individuals, on the other hand, are no more likely to do volunteer work than are full-time employees. But if they do volunteer work, they spend as much time on it as part-time employees and more than full-time employees. This second set of findings suggests that free time does not necessarily promote participation in volunteer work but may affect the number of hours spent by volunteers. Older age, poorer health, a lack of interest in all productive activities, or a generally less-active lifestyle may explain why nonemployed individuals do not necessarily participate in volunteer work. We will return to these issues in the multivariate analyses.

Marital status is not related to volunteer work in predicted ways. Those respondents who were not married (because of divorce, widowhood, or lifetime singlehood) were less likely to participate in volunteer work than those who were married. Whether this was the case because married persons tended to be younger and healthier than those who were not must be addressed by the multivariate analysis.

### Multivariate Analyses of the Participation in Volunteer Work

The bivariate analyses presented thus far have two major shortcomings. First, because of the interrelationship between the various predictors, the strength of the relationships is probably biased; multivariate analysis must be performed in order to arrive at an adequate estimate of the importance of each factor. Second, no causal sequence between the independent factors has been implied. We now propose a multivariate causal model in which environmental, social-structural, and personality characteristics are cast explicitly as relatively stable and thus probably distal causal factors affecting the participation in volunteer behavior. They might produce their effects directly or through roles (i.e., the work role), competencies and resources (i.e., health status), or life-styles (i.e., social relationships and behaviors). Therefore, we now describe the test of such a multivariate causal model, as displayed in Figure 7.1.

For testing the model we used regression analysis with dummy variables representing all categories. Logistic regression analysis was used for predicting participation in volunteer work, ordinary least squares regression for predicting hours of volunteer work. At a first stage (hereafter called Model 1), all environmental, social-structural, and personality characteristics were included as predictors of volunteer participation and of number of hours volunteered by those who do any volunteer work at all (coded as the number of annual hours). At a second stage (hereafter called Model 2), role occupancy, resources, and life-style were added as predictors to the regressions. The results in the form of unstandardized logistic regression coefficients for volunteer participation on predictor dummy variables are shown in the second and third columns (labeled "Net effects") of Table 7.4. For comparison purposes, results from regression analyses that contain only dummy variables for one particular predictor are shown in the first column (labeled "Gross effects" of Table 7.4. Because the predictors accounted for only a small amount of variance in the volunteer hours, those results are not shown in tabular form but are available from the authors.

Multivariate results for Model 1 (shown in column 2 in Table 7.4) indicate that most multivariate or net effects of environmental, social-structural, and personality predictors remain similar to those observed in the bivariate

Figure 7.1
Conceptual Framework for the Analysis of Volunteer Work

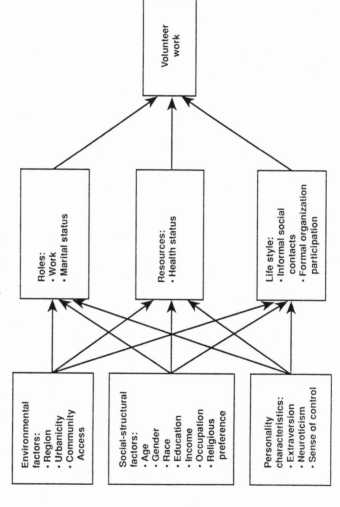

Table 7.4

Multivariate Analyses of Older Americans' Participation in Volunteer Work

| | Gross effects | Net effects for Model 1 | Net effects for Model 2 |
|---|---|---|---|
| <u>Age</u> | | | |
| 55-64 | .479* | .294 | .459 |
| 65-74 | .605** | .524** | .419 |
| 75+ | Omitted | Omitted | Omitted |
| | | | |
| <u>Gender</u> | | | |
| Male | Omitted | Omitted | Omitted |
| Female | .157 | .230 | .130 |
| | | | |
| <u>Race</u> | | | |
| Non-Black | .229 | -.351 | -.058 |
| Black | Omitted | Omitted | Omitted |
| | | | |
| <u>Educational attainment</u> | | | |
| High | Omitted | Omitted | Omitted |
| Medium | -.866** | -.463 | -.231 |
| Low | -1.836** | -1.015** | -.743** |
| | | | |
| <u>Family income</u> | | | |
| High | Omitted | Omitted | Omitted |
| Medium | -.308 | -.034 | .119 |
| Low | -1.021** | -.463 | -.338 |
| | | | |
| <u>Current or former occupation</u> | | | |
| Professional | Omitted | Omitted | Omitted |
| Sales/clerical | -.301 | -.295 | -.400 |
| Craft | -1.071** | -.665* | -.764* |
| Labor/service | -1.107** | -.744** | -.805** |
| Never Worked | -1.323** | -.809* | -.847* |
| | | | |
| <u>Religious preference</u> | | | |
| Protestant | .837** | .977** | -.301 |
| Catholic | .581 | .825* | -.476 |
| Jewish | .064 | .318 | -.333 |
| None | Omitted | Omitted | Omitted |

Table 7.4 (continued)

|  | Gross effects | Net effects for Model 1 | Net effects for Model 2 |
|---|---|---|---|
| Geographic region |  |  |  |
| Northeast | -.585** | -.477* | -.749** |
| Central | -.140 | -.071 | -.282 |
| South | -.497** | -.386 | -.611** |
| West | Omitted | Omitted | Omitted |
|  |  |  |  |
| Urbanicity |  |  |  |
| Metropolitan | -.129 | -.108 | -.043 |
| Suburban | .081 | .078 | .003 |
| Rural | Omitted | Omitted | Omitted |
|  |  |  |  |
| Community access |  |  |  |
| Yes | .552* | .222 | .089 |
| No | Omitted | Omitted | Omitted |
|  |  |  |  |
| Extraversion |  |  |  |
| Highest | Omitted | Omitted | Omitted |
| . | -.516** | -.357 | -.215 |
| . | -.814** | -.588** | -.453* |
| Lowest | -1.196** | -1.041** | -.681** |
|  |  |  |  |
| Neuroticism |  |  |  |
| Highest | Omitted | Omitted | Omitted |
| . | .364* | .231 | .307 |
| . | .381* | .229 | .105 |
| Lowest | .699** | .448* | .273 |
|  |  |  |  |
| Self-efficacy |  |  |  |
| Highest | Omitted | Omitted | Omitted |
| . | .089 | .304 | .112 |
| . | -.106 | .300 | .233 |
| Lowest | -.517** | .150 | .013 |

Table 7.4 (continued)

|  | Gross effects | Net effects for Model 2 |
| --- | --- | --- |
| Paid work | | |
| Full-time | Omitted | Omitted |
| Part-time | .744** | .615* |
| None | -.179 | .021 |
| | | |
| Marital status | | |
| Married | .696** | .297 |
| Divorced/Separated | .093 | .031 |
| Widowed | .210 | .048 |
| Never Married | Omitted | Omitted |
| | | |
| Informal social contacts | | |
| Highest | Omitted | Omitted |
| . | -.257 | -.145 |
| . | -.371* | .028 |
| Lowest | -1.084** | -.095 |
| Formal organizational participation | | |
| Highest | Omitted | Omitted |
| . | -.860** | -.798** |
| . | -1.782** | -1.937** |
| Lowest | -3.167** | -3.188** |
| | | |
| Functional health | | |
| Little or no impairment | Omitted | Omitted |
| Great deal of impairment | -.951** | -.650* |

* p < .05          ** p < .01

Note: Entries are unstandardized logistic regression coefficients from regressions in which participation in volunteer work was regressed on all dummy variables for one predictor (Gross effects), from a regression in which participation in volunteer work was regressed on all environmental, social-structural, and personality predictors (Net effects for Model 1) and from a regression in which volunteer participation was regressed on all environmental, social-structural, personality, role, resource, and life style predictors (Net effects for Model 2).

analyses (shown in Tables 7.2 and 7.3) or in the gross effects (shown in column 1 in Table 7.4), but they generally are somewhat weaker. Specifically, SES as indexed by educational attainment remains clearly related to higher likelihood of participation in volunteer work. A current or former professional or clerical/sales occupation also is related to higher volunteer participation than craft, service, and no occupation, net of its relationship with education and income. Age remains related, with a significant drop in volunteer participation between the ages of sixty-five and seventy-four and seventy-five and older. Protestants and Catholics are more likely to participate than those without a stated religious preference, and Northeasterners are less likely to participate than Westerners. The only social-structural predictors that fail to retain an independent relationship with volunteer participation are family income and community access. Apparently, older adults with higher incomes are more likely to participate only because they are better educated and have more prestigious occupations.

The personality traits that remain related are extraversion and, to a much lesser degree, neuroticism. The more extraverted individuals are more likely to participate than the less extraverted, and the least neurotic more than the most neurotic. The sense of efficacy does not retain an independent relationship with volunteer participation.

Adding the potentially mediating predictors to the model adds substantially and significantly to the explained variance, and the predictors that are responsible include work (those who work part-time are more likely to participate in volunteer work than those who work full-time), formal social participation (those who more frequently attend social clubs and/or religious services are more likely to participate in volunteer work), and health status (those with few or no functional impairments are more likely to volunteer). The finding that part-time employees are more likely to participate in volunteer work than full-time employees—even when age, gender, and health status are controlled—suggests that employment status is related to volunteer work independently of the compositional differences between full-time, part-time, and nonemployed older adults in terms of age, health, gender, and socioeconomic status. Likewise, the relationships between health status and volunteer work and between formal organizational participation and volunteer work remain statistically significant despite statistical controls. On the other hand, marital status and informal social participation do not retain an independent relationship with volunteer work. After statistically controlling compositional and other differences between those who are married and those who are not and between those who are socially active and those who are not, these groups do not differ in terms of volunteer work.

We now turn our attention to the potential mediating effects of role incumbency, resources, and life-styles by comparing the effects of the environmental, social-structural, and personality variables with and without controls for potential mediators (i.e., Models 1 and 2 in columns 2 and 3 of Table 7.4). The effects of most environmental, social-structural, and personality variables are partly explained by the mediators investigated here. This is clearly the case for religious preference, which is entirely explained by the higher frequency of formal organizational participation in the form of religious attendance. Protestants and Catholics attend religious services more often than Jewish people, and all three groups attend services more often than people without any religious preference. The higher religious organizational participation of these three groups relates in turn to their higher likelihood of doing volunteer work. Likewise, the effect of educational attainment is at least partly explained by organizational participation. The effect of age is explained by all the mediators. While the effect of neuroticism also is explained by social participation, this is only partly the case for extroversion. Finally, the effects of occupation and of geographic region remain largely unexplained by the potential mediators investigated here, as indicated by their largely unaltered regression coefficients when the potentially mediating factors are included.

## SUMMARY

A fair number of older Americans contribute to societal well-being through formal volunteer work. More specifically, 36 percent had done volunteer work in the past twelve months, and each of these volunteers contributed an average of seventy-two hours, or $428. This documents a definite productive contribution of older Americans that goes beyond their contribution through paid work. At the same time, it also highlights the possibility that older adults might be able to contribute more volunteer work and thereby might further benefit a society in need of person power. At the same time, they might forge useful and satisfying roles for themselves.

What are the factors that facilitate or impede volunteer work among older adults? Our partial answers to this question must be restricted to correlates of participation in volunteer work. While we examined correlates of the number of hours spent in volunteer work and the expressed desire on the part of older people to perform some volunteer work or more volunteer work than currently being done, we were not able to account for major variations in the answers to this question. The reason for this might be that we did not examine the most relevant correlates, or that we measured the number of volunteer hours less reliably than the mere participation. Moreover, our answers are limited by the cross-sectional nature of the data that we utilized for our investigations. Whereas relationships observed in such data are a necessary condition for a causal link, they are not sufficient to establish whether the link is direct or not and what the direction of causation is.

The likelihood of having engaged in volunteer work during the previous twelve months is clearly related to proximal factors of individual roles, resources, and life-styles. An older individual's social contacts—particularly the frequency with which he or she attends church services and meetings of other voluntary associations—are closely related to his or her participation. Although part of this relationship may be artifactual because participation in meetings and performance of volunteer work may be somewhat overlapping (as when the local senior citizens' group meets for bingo and afterward discusses the outreach program for shut-in elderly) and some voluntary organizations exist for the sole purpose of providing volunteer work (as in the examples of the Foster Grandparents program or the Service Corps of Retired Executives), we contend that part of the relationship reflects a true substantive link between organizational participation and volunteer work. After all, providing various volunteer services is often one of many functions of a formal organization—particularly a religious organization—and organizations rely on their members to provide such services. This link is further substantiated by data from the Gallup survey in which the reason for starting to do volunteer work that people cited most often was that they had been asked and been recruited through an organization to which they belonged (Gallup Organization, 1990).

As predicted, the likelihood of volunteering is related to employment status. However, the form of the relationship is not entirely what was predicted. While full-time employment indeed is related to lower likelihood of participation in volunteer work than part-time employment, full-time employment does not differ from full retirement in this regard. This interesting finding replicates a finding reported for the older adults in the Harris survey (Chambré, 1987) and for the entire age range in the Gallup survey (Gallup Organization, 1991). A possible interpretation of this finding is that full-time employment creates time constraints for other productive involvement. Such constraints are less severe in the case of part-time employment and therefore older individuals employed part-time are more likely to engage in volunteer work than those employed full-time. In fact, for the elderly employed part-time, volunteer work may fulfill a function similar to paid work, except for the income; volunteer work takes place in the context of an organization and affords social contacts, exercise of competence, and feelings of usefulness. At the same time, it is presumably less regulated and inflexible than paid work and thus lends itself as an ideal compensation for declining work activities. The lack of a significant increase in volunteering among fully retired older individuals, however, suggests that lack of constraints from full-time paid work does not necessarily imply higher volunteer participation. This lack of an effect cannot be explained entirely as a statistical suppression due to differences in socioeconomic and health status between the full-time working and the full-time retired older adults because it persists—albeit in weaker form—after controlling for health and socioeconomic status. Possibly some or many fully retired individuals never were positive enough about their work to miss it, or they found after they had retired that they simply liked "not working"; for these reasons, they may not have sought any compensation for its loss through either reemployment or volunteer work.

In conjunction with our other findings regarding formal organizational activities, these findings suggest that volunteer work may be part of an overall active life-style that unfolds primarily in the formal arena of work and organizational activities. The likelihood of volunteering also is related to physical impairments that presumably limit how easily an older individual negotiates traveling by private or public transportation to the site of volunteer work and possibly how easily he or she can perform the physical activities involved in performing volunteer duties and assignments.

A somewhat broader view of the individual in the context of his or her environment and his or her relatively permanent personality structure suggests that environmental and personality factors affect participation in volunteer work, partly directly and partly through the factors of roles, resources, and life-styles discussed previously. Thus, a major part of the relations among age, education, religious preference, and personality operates through social relationships. Individuals who are younger and more highly educated report more frequent social relationships, and those relationships, in turn, are related to volunteer work. Extraverted individuals are more likely to participate in social relationships and thereby are more likely to volunteer, although the entire relationship between extraversion and volunteer participation is not explained by the mediators. Likewise, as part of their religious association, Protestant and Catholic individuals are required to attend religious services which, in turn, are related to volunteer work.

Because a sizeable portion of volunteer work is for church-related organizations, we also performed the data analyses for volunteer participation in church-related organizations only to learn whether predictors might differ. The general pattern of predictors remained the same as when we examined volunteer participation in all kinds of organizations; minor differences were observed for the effects of educational attainment, occupation, and extraversion, which were somewhat weaker for volunteer participation in church groups only and for the effect of religious participation, which was somewhat stronger.

Other factors are not explained by roles, resources, and life-styles. For example, the relationship between geographic region and volunteer work persists. Thus, we do not know what it is about geographic regions that makes for differential involvement in individual volunteer work; we only know that it has nothing to do with roles, resources, and life-styles (nor with compositional differences in the populations).

The likelihood of engaging in volunteer work also is clearly related to current or former occupation, with professionals and clerical/sales employees being more likely to do volunteer work than individuals within any other type of occupation. This relationship is weakened somewhat but not eliminated when educational attainment and current income level are controlled. We know from previous research that people who are employed in professional occupations like their jobs better than those employed in other occupations. Most likely, current or former professionals are also able to garner more interesting and satisfying volunteer positions, and these opportunities might draw them into volunteer work. Such an interpretation is supported further by our finding that the effect of occupation cannot be attributed in its entirety to compositional differences in terms of race, gender, education, income, or personality between individuals employed in different types of occupations nor can it be explained by differences in health and other potential mediators that we investigated here. This leaves us with the hypothesis that professionals are more attracted to work and work-like activities because they have had more positive work experiences, and they probably also have more satisfying and interesting experiences in the kinds of volunteer work that are available to them.

We believe that differences in opportunities for volunteer work that exist between older adults with different occupational backgrounds explain part of the effect that can be attributed neither to compositional differences in individuals from a professional or sales/clerical occupation nor to individual roles, resources, and life-styles. Unfortunately, surveys are not well suited to assess the opportunity structure except as it exists in the perception of the individuals. Only a few such perceptions had been measured in the ACL survey. ACL respondents were asked how easy it would be for them to find another job and whether they were ever asked to volunteer their time (but not what kinds of paid work and volunteer work). Perceptions of opportunities for paid work and volunteer work, as measured by these questions, clearly differ according to the socioeconomic status of the respondent and thus lend further support to the hypothesis of opportunity differentials related to socioeconomic background.

In conclusion, our investigations document the significance of individual positions in the social and physical environment and of personality on volunteer behavior and specify some of the mechanisms of role, resources, and life-styles through which environmental and personality characteristics affect behavior. Our findings regarding social-structural factors show some surprising consistencies with findings from another large, representative database (Chambré, 1987), the Harris survey (Harris and Associates, 1977), and thereby provide a nice confirmation. Our findings expand Chambré's analyses of the Harris data by including additional factors of environmental and personality and further elaborating on the potential causal sequence. By the same token, both investigations leave much about volunteer work unexplained and are unable to address directly the role of opportunities for volunteer work in various communities and the nature of those jobs. Better information on these issues is needed if we are to understand more fully the volunteer behavior of older Americans, and this information can only in part come from surveys. Whereas surveys of the population can provide information about individual perceptions of opportunities for volunteer work, contextual information should be collected from surveys of companies and organizations. Both investigations rely exclusively on cross-sectional data to investigate a hypothesized causal model. Ultimately, longitudinal data would help to firm up our confidence in the hypothesized processes.

## NOTE

Funding for this research was provided by the National Institute on Aging (Grant No. P01AG05561); funding for preparation of this chapter was contributed by an anonymous donor.

## REFERENCES

Butler, R. N. (1975). *Why survive? Being old in America*. New York: Harper & Row.

Carp, F. M. (1968). Differences among older workers, volunteers, and persons who are neither. *Journal of Gerontology, 23*, 497–501.

Chambré, S. M. (1987). *Good deeds in old age: Volunteering by the new leisure class*. Lexington, MA: Lexington Books.

Eysenck, H. J., & Eysenck, B. G. (1963). *Manual for the Eysenck Personality Inventory*. San Diego, CA: Educational and Industrial Test Service.

Fischer, L. R., Mueller, D. P., & Cooper, P. W. (1991). Older volunteers: A discussion of the Minnesota Senior Study. *The Gerontologist, 31*, 183–194.

Gallup Organization. (1990). *Living and volunteering in the United States*. Washington, DC: Independent Sector.

George, L. K. (1978). The impact of personality and social status factors upon levels of activity and psychological well-being. *Journal of Gerontology, 33*(6), 840–847.

Harris, L., & Associates, Inc. (1977). *The myth and reality of aging in America* (4th printing). Washington, DC: National Council on the Aging.

Herzog, A. R., & House, J. S. (1991). Productive activities and aging well. *Generations, 15*, 49–54.

Herzog, A. R., Kahn, R. L., Morgan, J. N., Jackson, J. S., & Antonucci, T. C. (1989). Age differences in productive activities. *Journal of Gerontology: Social Sciences, 44*, 129–138.

Herzog, A. R., & Morgan, J. N. Age and gender differences in the value of productive activities. *Research on Aging, 14* (2), 169–198.

Lawton, M. P. (1985). Activities and leisure. In M. P. Lawton & G. L. Maddox (Eds.), *Annual review of Gerontology and Geriatrics* (Vol. 5). New York: Springer.

Marriott Senior Living Services. (1991). *Marriott Seniors Volunteerism Study*. Washington, DC: Marriott Senior Living Services.

Morgan, J. N., Dye, R. F., & Hybels, J. H. (1979). *Results from two national surveys of philanthropic activity*. Ann Arbor, MI: Survey Research Center, Institute for Social Research.

Pearlin, L. L., Lieberman, M. A., Managhan, E. G., & Mullan, J. T. (1981). The stress process. *Journal of Health and Social Behavior, 22,* 337–356.

Romero, C. J. (1986). The economics of volunteerism: A review. In Committee on an Aging Society (U.S.), *Productive roles in an older society.* Washington, DC: National Academy Press.

Rosenberg, M. (1965). *Society and the adolescent self image.* Princeton, NJ: Princeton University Press.

Rosow, I. (1985). Status and role change through the life cycle. In R. H. Binstock & E. Shanas (Eds.), *Handbook of aging and the social sciences* (2d ed., pp. 62–93). New York: Van Nostrand Reinhold.

# 8

# Caregiving and Productive Aging

## *Pamela Doty and Baila Miller*

Advancing age brings increased risk of chronic illness, disability, and the need for long-term care. At any given time, about a fifth of older Americans can be said to require long-term care, defined as human assistance with one or more basic activities of daily living (ADLs)—such as bathing, dressing, mobility, toileting, and eating—and/or instrumental activities of daily living (IADLs)—such as cooking, shopping, cleaning house, managing money, and taking medications. Over three-quarters of these functionally impaired elderly continue to reside in the community, where they depend on family caregivers for all or most of the assistance they receive with daily living tasks.

While the popular image of informal home care of the disabled elderly focuses primarily on caregiving by middle-aged children—especially daughters and daughters-in-law—recent research indicates that spouses, most of whom are themselves aged, are such caregivers. According to the 1982 National Long-Term Care Survey (NLTCS),[1] 35.5 percent of informal eldercare was provided by spouses as compared to 37.4 percent provided by adult children (Stone, Cafferata & Sangl, 1987; Stone & Kemper, 1989). Moreover, spouses typically act as primary caregivers, with children providing only supplemental or backup help unless the spouse caregiver dies or becomes incapacitated (Cantor, 1991). In keeping with these patterns, approximately a third of caregivers in the 1982 NLTCS were themselves aged sixty-five or older.

Moreover, projections based on demographic and health trends suggest that the role of older persons as caregivers—predominantly spouses caring for spouses but also "young-old" children caring for "old-old" parents—will become increasingly important in the next century. Over the next forty years or so the supply of spousal caregivers is likely to increase because of longer life expectancies and a narrowing of the gender longevity gap while, conversely, the availability of adult-child caregivers decreases as a result of declining fertility rates. In particular, increased rates of marriage among both men and women aged eighty-five and older and women aged eighty to eighty-four—because of decreased widowhood—are expected to more than compensate for an increase in the percentage of never-married persons as well as the effects of divorce on marital status in old age (Wade, 1988; Zedlewski, Barnes, Burt, McBride, & Meyer, 1990).

These caregiving patterns and trends suggest that more attention and recognition should be given to the prevalence of older persons as caregivers as well as care recipients. While the category of "older caregivers" includes some friends and neighbors, some "young-old" (aged sixty-five to seventy-four) children of "old-old" (aged eighty-five and older) parents, and some older persons who work as paid caregivers or as volunteers, the great majority of older caregivers are the husbands and wives of those they care for. Accordingly, the focus of this chapter is to explore the economic, social, and psychological significance of spousal caregiving as distinct from other informal eldercare. Our principal aim is to evaluate the positive and negative aspects of older spousal caregivers' experiences with respect to the concepts of "productive" and "successful" aging.

## PRODUCTIVE AND SUCCESSFUL AGING IN RELATION TO INFORMAL CAREGIVING

To encompass informal caregiving, the concept of productive aging must include unpaid work or service performed in the context of natural groupings and relationships—that is, family, friendship networks, neighborhoods, and communities. Once it is clear that productivity is not limited to the output of paid labor or formally organized volunteer efforts, there can scarcely be any doubt that informal caregiving is an economically and socially productive role for older as well as younger family members. Caregivers (of all ages) in the 1982 NLTCS reported that they spent an average of four hours daily on caregiving tasks over and above usual housework. This translates into over three billion hours of "free" care provided annually to those moderate to severely disabled elderly who require help with basic activities of daily living (the "ADL dependent" elderly). Moreover, this estimate does not even begin to count the unpaid assistance given to less disabled elderly who require help only with housework and other instrumental daily living tasks (the "IADL-only dependent" elderly). Health and social service professionals are acutely aware of what it would cost the public sector to finance formal services to replace even a significant fraction of informal family care. This is a major reason why policymakers tend to adopt a stance of anxious solicitude concerning the strength and stability of family caregiving patterns and frequently express interest in policy initiatives to support and sustain family caregivers.

This chapter examines various ways of defining and measuring the productivity of informal eldercare provided by older spouses. It also examines the negative side of informal care, as evidenced by the considerable attention given in the gerontological literature to issues of caregiver "stress," "burden," and "burnout" as well as conflict between caregiving and other economic and social roles. The question implicitly raised by the high level of professional concern about caregiver stress and burden is whether the productivity of informal care comes at too high a price to individual caregivers in terms of ill effects on their physical and mental health, earnings, and other aspects of well-being. Similarly, research interest in conflicts between caregiving and employment, parenting, or other aspects of family life reflects doubts about whether the economic savings realized from informal eldercare outweigh the costs of caregivers' decreased productivity in other socially and economically valuable roles.

The idea of successful aging as a composite well-being index seems most appropriate as a sociological concept; for example, as a means of measuring how well a given society or nation is doing in terms of improving the aggregate health status, economic conditions, and so forth, of its elderly population. With respect to caregiving, this leads us to ask whether—or to what degree and under what circumstances—society's traditional and ongoing reliance on informal care to meet most of the long-term care needs of the disabled elderly enhances or detracts from the physical and mental health, prosperity, and other aspects of well-being of older care recipients and caregivers.

In some quarters, there is genuine concern that successful societal efforts to improve the economic security and health status of older Americans and to foster positive perceptions of retirement have inadvertently created a privileged strata of retirees whose expectations concerning what government should and can provide for seniors has grown out of proportion to the working population's capacity to finance social insurance benefits.

Is our culture promoting either unrealistic or socially undesirable expectations about life in the retirement years? An example of an image to ponder was provided by a recent television commercial in which a vivacious older woman laden with shopping bags stands in front of a Parisian landmark. Smiling triumphantly, she brandishes her gold credit card at the viewer and says, "It's *my* turn now." The implied message seems to be that this woman has spent her life catering to the needs of others—that is, her family—and, now that she has reached her later years, she has earned and ought to exercise the right to put herself and her own enjoyment first.

The commercialism could scarcely be more blatant, but we do not mean to suggest that there is anything wrong with an older woman "treating herself" or treating herself well. The problem lies in the underlying implications that responsible adulthood consists of nose-to-the-grindstone, self-denial-for-the-sake-of-family behavior that eventually will be rewarded by an old age in which one will be free to be, if not "selfish," at least primarily self-focused. Is there a danger in creating a "retirement mystique" that tells people they can bank on the psychological deficits of a lifetime's worth of deferred gratification being paid back with interest—if they can just hold out until the magic age of sixty-five? Who or where is the "FDIC" that can make good on such a guarantee for those confronted with prevalent old-age adversities, including functional disability or the need to be a caregiver to a disabled spouse, parent, or sibling?

But what about the feminist allegation that family caregiving duties have been and continue to be inequitably imposed on women (Hooyman, 1990)? Obviously, the questions of whether individuals who perform (traditionally female and usually unpaid) nurturant roles and tasks, at any age, should view them as duty or privilege, drudgery or joy, drain on or enrichment to their lives, and whether men are doing or can be made to do their fair share is a matter of both ideology and emotion-laden debate in contemporary America. The very intensity of this debate, however, has resulted in relatively little attention paid to the question of whether or not the public sector (or, if you prefer, the private sector via employee benefits or new insurance products) realistically is capable of offering family members (male or female) significant release and relief from family caregiving—including eldercare—responsibilities. The issue is only partly one of whether or not society can afford the financial costs of paid services to supplement or to substitute for family care. It also is a question of effectiveness (to what extent and under what circumstances are paid caregivers "as good" as family caregivers?) and of values (by what standards do we judge the quality of caregiving by paid caregivers or family members)?

Would we want to set as a goal—even acknowledging it for the time being as utopian—a state of affairs in which eldercare is considered fundamentally the responsibility of the state, except insofar as family members elect to perform these tasks on a purely voluntary (or stipended) basis? Should older persons be allowed, even encouraged, to "retire" from family caregiving roles as they do from paid work? From the pragmatic perspective of formulating workable social policy, we must also ask whether or to what extent and under what circumstances paid services actually can offer family caregivers the relief from stress and burden, the mitigation of role conflicts, and the increased freedom to pursue autonomous goals.

With respect to prevailing attitudes toward family caregiving, it is important to bear in mind that opinion surveys of older persons suggest that the values, expectations, and aspirations of real people may be rather different from those embodied in advertising and other media images or those espoused as political ideologies by various groups claiming to represent "families," "retired persons," "older women," and so forth. A public opinion survey (Harris & Associates, 1982) asked older persons in five English-speaking countries what they most enjoyed about their lives right now. The most common response was "spouse or marriage," followed by "health," "children," "grandchildren," and "home." Hobbies, travel, or other activities ranked near the bottom of the list. Indeed, over half the respondents named family relationships as their main source of enjoyment, with one-quarter specifically citing spouse or marriage, compared to only 9 percent who said that activities, including hobbies and travel, were what they enjoyed most.

It seems likely that the caregiver role appears in a different light to an older person whose expectations and aspirations for a "good old age" are home and family centered in contrast to one who hopes for a retirement life-style that emphasizes individualism, outside activities (work, volunteerism, travel, sports, and hobbies), and freedom from family responsibilities. From the perspective of an older person whose life is family centered, a spouse's disability will be experienced as distressing; however, this is due primarily to the effects of disability on the disabled spouse's functioning, the couple's life-style, and the quality of the marital relationship rather than the requirements and limitations that caregiving imposes on the well spouse's autonomy. Spousal caregiving in this context becomes an adaptive mechanism: an attempt to defend and preserve the continuity of the marital bond against the threats posed to it by one partner's disability. Similarly, the degree to which caregiving seems likely to be perceived by spouses as more or less stressful and burdensome versus rewarding and satisfying depends on the likelihood of sustaining the essential character and quality of the marital relationship—a hypothesis confirmed by Aluma Motenko (1989) in her research with spousal caregivers.

Each life stage presents individuals with characteristic life events, tasks, opportunities, and challenges. Coming to terms with death is the most obvious old-age experience. Coping with ill health and disability, in one's self or in one's spouse, is not quite so inevitable or universal an experience, but it is certainly a very common one. Although there is no single "right way" to engage the issues, challenges, and choices posed by chronic illness and disability at older ages, everyone recognizes that some persons deal with them more successfully than others, even given the fact that aging perceptions of "success" versus "failure" may vary from individual to individual and across groups or cultures. This perspective on caregiving leads us to examine adaptive and maladaptive coping styles as well as normative expectations. What expectations do the spousal caregiver, the spousal care recipient, and others around them have for caregiving and how do the various parties feel about themselves and each other when these expectations are or are not fulfilled?

Marital vows include a commitment to the partner "for better and for worse, in sickness and in health." Clearly, caregiving is a normative expectation intrinsic to marriage—both in the religious, sacramental view of marriage and in terms of the secular, legal conception of marriage as a type of contract. The connotations of duty and obligation—albeit voluntarily assumed—are inescapable. We therefore would expect it to be very important to most married persons, in terms of maintaining self-respect and the respect of others, to accept when necessary the spousal caregiver role and to acquit themselves honorably in it. It is furthermore in both the individual's and society's interest that the spousal caregiver role be perceived as one that ordinary persons are able to manage successfully. The key social or policy issue with respect to the impact of caregiving on the caregiver is not whether the caregiver role is difficult and demanding (i.e., "stressful," "burdensome") but whether (for whom and under what conditions) it is excessively or overwhelmingly so. Arguably, no society can afford to let important social roles—whether in work or community or family life—evolve in such a way that average persons cannot (absent superhuman effort or intense personal pain) perform them to the expected standard, allowing them to feel satisfied or "successful" about their lives.

## MEASURING THE PRODUCTIVITY OF CARE PROVIDED BY OLDER CAREGIVERS

The overall social and economic productivity of informal care provided to disabled family members can be evaluated along two dimensions. One involves identifying preferable attributes and outcomes of caregiving and measuring the strength of the association between informal care and these desirable features. There is widespread agreement that preferable attributes and outcomes of eldercare include avoiding nursing home placement and associated public and private expenditures for nursing home care; making it possible for the disabled elderly to remain in their "own" homes and to maintain, to the fullest extent possible, their accustomed, predisability way of life; and ensuring that they have sufficient care to meet their needs.

The second dimension involves measuring negative consequences or their absence with respect to other types of productivity. These include lower labor force participation and lost productivity at work and lesser ability to fulfill other family responsibilities (e.g., child rearing, companionship, and support to one's spouse).

Research indicates that care from close family members—spouses and children—is more effective in preventing nursing home placement than is care from more distant relatives or formal (paid) caregivers. Thus, individuals without close family are at greatly increased risk both of being admitted to nursing homes and of having long stays. For example, never-married individuals have twice the lifetime probability of nursing home admission than persons who stay married throughout their lives (48 percent vs. 27 percent). Never-married persons have twice the lifetime probability of spending more than five years in a nursing home than widowed persons (29 percent vs. 16 percent); those who are married throughout their lives have four times less probability (7 percent) of such a lengthy nursing home stay than the never-married (Murtaugh, Kemper, & Spillman, 1991). Concerning the disabled elderly living in the community, Peter Kemper's (1989) analyses of National Long-Term Care Demonstration ("channeling") data indicate that those who received care from close relatives (spouses or children) received on average twenty-eight more hours of care per week than those who received care from more distant relatives or formal providers.

One interesting implication of these findings is that it would be a serious mistake to measure the productivity of informal care merely or even mainly in terms of the dollar cost of replacing informal with paid care at prevailing wage rates for domestic labor. Formal and informal care are not interchangeable equivalents. Although formal care may be a useful adjunct to or, under certain circumstances, acceptable substitute for informal care, the latter is, in fact, worth more because, judged by effectiveness in promoting desired goals, it is clearly of superior quality.

In addition, research results tend to support a judgment that informal caregiving by spouses as opposed to other family members is, as a general rule, "better" because of its greater effectiveness in preventing institutionalization as well as furthering other desired outcomes. Longitudinal analyses of 1982–1984 NLTCS data, measuring rates and correlates of nursing home admission over a two-year period, found that the disabled elderly who had spousal caregivers in 1982 were significantly less likely to be institutionalized during the subsequent two years, even controlling for age and disability (Miller & McFall, 1989; Kasper, Steinbach, & Andrews, 1990). Other studies using different databases and focusing particularly on cognitively impaired care receivers also concluded that individuals with identical health and disability statuses having spousal as opposed to other kin caregivers are less likely to be placed in nursing homes (Colerick & George, 1986; Lieberman & Kramer, 1991).

Recent research by Mary Elizabeth Jackson (1991) found that among elderly disabled respondents in the 1984 NLTCS, those with spousal caregivers reported significantly fewer "unmet" needs for care. (Needs were considered unmet when a respondent reported the inability to perform specific ADL or IADL tasks, such as independent bathing or meal preparation, and reported not receiving assistance with the task.) This may be true because other studies (Enright, 1991) indicate that spouses spend more time providing care for these individuals than do other types of family caregivers.

Caregiving by older retired persons is less likely to involve negative "side-effects" for the caregiver, such as interference with work or other family responsibilities. Analysis of the 1988 National Survey of Families and Households indicates that, among the working-age population, caring for disabled spouses or parents is associated with lower labor force participation, particularly for women. Similarly, caregiving was associated with reduced productivity among persons in the work force, with working caregivers more likely to work part-time or to take time off. (For the sake of perspective, it is worth noting that such productivity losses associated with eldercare were far lower than those associated with child care [McLanahan & Monson, 1990].)

In the 1982 NLTCS, only 9.4 percent of caregiver wives and 12.3 percent of caregiver husbands (all ages) were working, compared to almost a third of caregivers generally. There is some evidence, however, that caregiver spouses feel a greater obligation than other types of caregivers to resolve work/caregiving conflicts by leaving work. In the 1982 NLTCS, 13.5 percent of wives and 11.4 percent of husbands reported having quit work to become caregivers—higher percentages than among primary caregivers generally (10 percent). In addition, 12.7 percent of caregiver wives and 16.3 percent of caregiver husbands worked fewer hours, rearranged schedules, or took time off without pay to provide spousal care (Stone, Cafferata, & Sangl, 1987; Stone & Short, in press).

While all types of informal family care help to "normalize" the lives of disabled elderly persons by providing in-home care in accord with their preferences, spousal caregiving is especially effective as it permits the disabled elderly to remain in their "own" homes with a minimum of intrusion by persons who are not or would not otherwise be members of the household. Shared living arrangements greatly facilitate informal caregiving especially of the severely functionally disabled or the cognitively impaired who need substantial supervision. Spousal caregiving has the advantage of a preexisting shared living arrangement; that is, one that is presumably desired for its own sake rather than imposed by the requirements of chronic care. Independent living—which means living apart from children and not being institutionalized—is a very strong preference among older persons. According to the previously cited 1982 Harris survey, older persons in all five countries said not only that they would prefer to remain in their own homes if they became disabled but that they would rather enter a nursing home than move in with children or other relatives.

Another desirable feature of spousal caregiving relates to increasingly vocal criticism of "gender injustice" in caregiving roles. Research has found a disproportionately larger amount of eldercare provided by daughters and daughters-in-law versus sons and sons-in-law (Stone et al., 1987). This contributes to a widespread perception that—like housework and child care—eldercare is socially defined as "women's work," with the result that women who work outside the home are required to work a "second shift" when they get home, whereas men are expected only to "help out" to the extent that they feel so inclined. Research, however, also has found that there is much more gender equality with regard to spousal caregiving.

According to the NLTCS, four-fifths of parent care was provided by women, whereas one third of spousal care was provided by husbands to wives. Closer examination of the data reveal, however, that the gender balance in spousal caregiving actually is more or less equal once adjustments have been made for the longer life expectancy of women and the tendency of men to marry women several years younger than themselves, resulting in fewer older women having husbands still alive to care for them when they become disabled.

Among adult-child caregivers, the types of care provided have been found to follow stereotypical gender lines: sons and sons-in-law provide heavy chore, transportation, and financial management help, while daughters and daughters-in-law provide the much more time-consuming help with house-work, shopping, cooking, and related tasks as well as hands-on personal care. Among spouses, however, differences in the types of care provided by husbands and wives were comparatively slight. Husbands tended to care for wives who were on average more physically dependent; a slightly higher percentage of wives cared for husbands who were cognitively impaired. Both husbands and wives were heavily involved in providing personal care, although husbands reported providing somewhat more help with walking and with bed transferring, whereas wives reported providing somewhat more help with dressing and bathing. Wives did report providing more household assistance, although husbands claimed more "extra" hours spent on such tasks (suggesting that they may well have been conscious of giving more such assistance than they would have offered a nondisabled or less-disabled wife) (Miller, 1990).

## STRESS, SATISFACTION, AND COPING STRATEGIES

The gerontological literature on family caregiving has tended overwhelm-ingly to emphasize measurement of the negative aspects of caregiving—that is, the "stress" and "burden" involved (Pearlin, Mullan, Semple, & Skaff, 1990). Until recently, this perspective seems to have gone almost entirely unquestioned; however, a few researchers have begun to study caregiver satisfaction as well and to urge their colleagues to give more balanced attention to the positive rewards of caring for a loved one (Motenko, 1989).

With respect to spousal caregivers, a prime concern among stress-and-burden researchers has been hypothesized linkages between caregiving and worsening health status (Gaynor, 1990). Poor health is viewed both as a contextual variable, believed to make the performance of caregiving tasks more stressful for older spouses, and as a dependent variable, that is, a probable outcome of the intrinsically stressful nature of caregiving. Ac-cordingly, the professional literature is replete with studies attempting to measure the psychiatric symptoms and damaging physical health conse-quences of caregiving on spousal caregivers.

A major weakness of this field of research is that many of the studies do not adequately define or differentiate the nature of the stress stimulus (the causal agent, such as sudden disequilibrating change or chronic overload) that is hypothesized as responsible for the stress response (the attitudinal or behavioral indicator(s)—such as exhaustion, depression, physical illness—of individuals experiencing stress). For example, few studies have attempted to distinguish between the physical and emotional effects of spousal disability as a "stressful life event" (analogous to other negative events or conditions affecting one spouse that might be expected to be stressful to the other—including a spouse's death, a spouse being diagnosed with a life-threatening acute illness, a spouse's loss of a job) as opposed to stress that is more specifically generated by "being a caregiver" (having to provide hands-on assistance with various kinds of personal care and IADLS that the spouse previously could handle independently).

This is an important issue because the implications for intervention are quite different if the stress response (illness, depression) is viewed primarily as a function of the difficulty of adjusting emotionally to a spouse's disability or, alternatively, as resulting from chronic fatigue and burnout. Despite the ambiguity of most research results, the literature on negative physical and mental health consequences attributed to caregiving has contributed to the creation of a prevailing conventional wisdom that older persons who undertake primary caregiver roles do so at great peril to their own health unless they receive supplemental or backup assistance from younger family members or paid helpers.

The 1982 NLTCS does confirm that, of spousal caregivers, 43.5 percent of wives and 50 percent of husbands rated their own health as fair or poor. Whether poor health among spousal caregivers actually is related to being a caregiver or mainly is a function of independent factors such as age-related risk (the average age of the wives was sixty-nine and of the husbands was seventy-three) is impossible to determine from a cross-sectional survey. However, the NLTCS data clearly indicate that most spousal caregivers do not perceive caregiving as detrimental to their health. Only about one in five (12 percent) reported a problem with worsening health as a result of providing care—a percentage only slightly higher than that reported by adult children caring for elderly disabled parents (17 percent). On the other hand, almost half of spousal caregivers (48 percent) reported having a problem with giving care because they did not always feel well, compared to two-fifths (39 percent) of adult children who reported having this problem.

Table 8.1 displays the comparative percentages of spouses as opposed to adult-child caregivers in the 1982 NLTCS who reported having various caregiver problems. Spousal caregivers reported somewhat more financial burden (24 percent) than did adult children (18 percent). This is to be expected since married couples typically share resources and constitute a financial unit for tax and other legal purposes, whereas adult children and parents usually maintain separate finances. Indeed, it is somewhat surprising that the differential between spouses and adult children in reported financial burden was not greater since analysis of the 1982 NLTCS data makes clear

Table 8.1
Indicators of Burden by Caregiving Relationship

| Indicator | Spouse (N=554) | | Adult Child (N=386) | |
|---|---|---|---|---|
| | N | Percent | N | Percent |
| Personal Burden - Caregiver has problems with: | | | | |
| Social limitations | 255 | 46.0 | 232 | 60.0 |
| Need to provide constant attention | 203 | 36.6 | 121 | 31.3 |
| Worsening health because of care | 116 | 20.9 | 65 | 16.8 |
| Giving care when not feeling well | 264 | 47.7 | 151 | 39.1 |
| Care costs more than can afford | 135 | 24.4 | 69 | 17.9 |
| Emotional strain | 248 | 44.8 | 181 | 46.9 |
| Interpersonal Burden - Caregiver has problem with: | | | | |
| Older person forgetting things | 290 | 44.8 | 181 | 46.9 |
| Older person embarrassing him/her | 107 | 19.3 | 94 | 24.4 |
| Older person lapsing into senility | 114 | 20.6 | 121 | 31.3 |
| Older person yelling and becoming upset | 230 | 41.5 | 138 | 35.8 |

that most out-of-pocket expenditures for long-term care are made by the disabled elder (and spouse if there is one) rather than by adult children or other relatives.

Spouses also were somewhat more likely than adult-child caregivers to report having a problem with the need to provide constant attention (37 percent vs. 31 percent). However, spouses were considerably less likely than adult-child caregivers to report having a problem with social limitations because of caregiving (46 percent vs. 60 percent). Reports of emotional strain were quite similar for spousal and adult-child caregivers (45 percent vs. 47 percent). On four of the interpersonal burden indicators, spouses were substantially less likely to report having a problem than adult children, although spouses were somewhat more likely than children to report having a problem with the care recipient yelling and becoming upset. The lower levels of reported interpersonal stress among spouses may reflect greater tolerance on the part of spouses for difficult behaviors, but it also may reflect the fact that proportionately more adult children than spouses in the 1982 NLTCS were caring for cognitively impaired persons (who are more likely to be older and widowed). Nevertheless, fully half of spousal caregivers reported "having a problem with" the care recipient's forgetfulness.

Table 8.1 shows that sizeable percentages of caregivers, both spouses and adult children, find caregiving burdensome or stressful on at least one indicator. What the table does not tell us—and what is indeed very difficult to evaluate—is the severity of the stress or how the stresses experienced in connection with eldercare compare to similar stresses that are commonly experienced by many people in other situations. After all, stress is a fairly ubiquitous phenomenon. Cynthia J. Meyer (1987), for example, points out that "buying a first home and the subsequent relocation can be an extremely stressful event in the life cycle of a family" and goes on to draw implications for prevention and intervention strategies and issues for family-life educators and family therapists. Most anyone who has ever purchased a home intuitively would agree that it is a stressful experience for most people, yet almost no one, including Meyer, would leap to the conclusion that the stress engendered is beyond most people's normal coping abilities or that no one should buy a home without the supportive counseling of a family-life educator or family therapist! Thus, *any* kind of stress, including caregiver stress, ought logically to be subject to some kind of "threshold" test—particularly from a social policy perspective—to evaluate whether and at what point it is excessive and unmanageable.

How do we define *unacceptably high, unmanageable,* or *intolerable* levels of caregiver stress for spouses of the disabled elderly? Anecdotally, we know that some caregivers experience what certainly appears to be unmanageable stress with very disturbing consequences; examples that spring immediately to mind include several highly publicized and widely discussed cases of husbands who shot and killed their wives with Alzheimer's disease, ostensibly in response to the wives' pleas to end their suffering. On a less sensationalistic level, the literature on family caregiving cites numerous cases of individual caregivers living "lives of quiet desperation"—exemplified by husbands and wives who tell researchers that they consider nursing home placement to be a fate worse than death and therefore continue to provide care at home while wishing constantly that their disabled spouses would die.

There have been some interesting recent attempts to develop good measures of caregiver distress and the specific characteristics or behaviors of care recipients that give rise to these feelings (Vitaliano, Russo, Young, Becker, & Maiuro, 1991) as well as the kinds of incidents and situations ("caregiving hassles") that are especially likely to provoke frustration among caregivers

(Kinney & Stephens, 1989). To our knowledge, however, the designers of nationally representative surveys have not attempted to measure—other than very superficially—the prevalence and severity of feelings of despair or frustration specifically associated with caregiving.

The NLTCS does, nevertheless, include several measures that could serve to gauge the prevalence of unacceptably high or intolerable stress among a nationally representative sample of caregivers. One is derived via comparison of self-reported stress and satisfaction ratings. Caregivers in the NLTCS were asked to rate their subjective feelings of stress and satisfaction: How many points would you give to show how good it makes you feel to help your (spouse, parent, etc.)? The better it makes you feel, the bigger the number. How many points would you give to show how much stress it causes you to do all of the things you do to help your (spouse, parent, etc.)?

Baila Miller (1989) compared stress and satisfaction ratings among adult-child caregivers. For the great majority of respondents, satisfaction was reportedly greater than stress. Global stress scores were highly correlated with reported problems (social limitations, emotional strain, etc., as well as difficult behaviors on the part of the care recipient). Unexpectedly, however, higher satisfaction and higher stress scores were also found to be positively correlated. Miller repeated the analysis for spousal caregivers and obtained essentially the same results.

These findings suggest that most family caregivers—whether spouses or adult children—view the problems they encounter in caregiving as challenges that can be successfully met and that coping successfully with stresses produces feelings of accomplishment and satisfaction. An additional, and by no means contradictory, way to interpret the association between high stress and high satisfaction is that both high stress and high satisfaction are a reflection of deep emotional bonding between caregivers and care recipients. Viewed from this perspective, caregiver stress is more a function of "care" than of "giving"—that is, the greater the feelings of closeness, intimacy, love, and mutual interdependence between caregiver and care recipient, the more the caregiver is likely to identify with the care recipient's feelings. In other words, if the care recipient feels discomfort, pain, anger, frustration, or depression in regard to his or her disabilities, the caregiver will tend to share these feelings. Being a caregiver may generate compensatory satisfaction by helping family members cope with their distress about a spouse or parent's deteriorated or deteriorating health; in particular, the performance of caregiving tasks may help one overcome feelings of powerlessness in the face of adversity that might otherwise be more overwhelming.

Another measure of "unacceptably high," "unmanageable," or "intolerable" stress levels is the rate at which respondents in the NLTCS chose to terminate informal caregiving. Variables associated with the decision to terminate informal caregiving, especially in favor of institutional placement rather than a change in the informal caregiver, can be viewed as indicators of the kinds of conditions or circumstances that give rise to levels of caregiver stress as defined as "intolerable" by the caregivers themselves. It has long been a prevailing assumption among long-term care professionals that stress leads to burnout, which in turn results in avoidable institutional placement, had there been recourse to coping strategies or outside interventions (such as referral to and payment for formal services).

Judith Kasper and associates (1990) examined decisions to terminate caregiving in the 1982–1984 NLTCS. Such decisions were comparatively rare: 6.8 percent in the short-term and 12.8 percent over the full two-year study period. In this study, decisions to terminate caregiving that occurred during the eight-month period between the 1982 NLTCS care recipient interviews and the Informal Caregiver Survey (ICS) were labeled "short-term" decisions. In only about half these cases was the termination of the caregiver relationship associated with institutionalization. Almost one-fourth of ex-caregivers said that they terminated caregiving because the family member was "getting other care," and 15 percent said that they were "unable" to continue providing care. Decisions to end caregiving over the long term referred to institutional placements that took place over the two-year period between the 1982 NLTCS and the 1984 follow-up survey. When univariate analyses were performed, only cognitive impairment and a non-spousal caregiver were found to be statistically related to both short-term and long-term decisions to end caregiving. For ending caregiving in the short term, a multivariable analysis found the statistically significant variables to be nonspousal caregiver, being unable to leave the care recipient alone, and feeling that the stress of caregiving outweighed the satisfaction. For ending caregiving in the long term, variables found to be statistically significant in a multivariable analysis included providing help with more ADL tasks and experiencing caregiving as "emotionally hard."

An analysis of the 1982–1984 NLTCS by Miller and Stephanie McFall (1989, 1991a, 1991b, 1992; Miller, McFall, & Montgomery, 1991) examining the relation between dimensions of caregiver burden, changes in caregiving networks, and institutionalization found that a higher reported "interpersonal burden" (forgetfulness, yelling and becoming upset, senile lapses, and embarrassing behavior on the part of the care recipient) was statistically associated with a higher probability of institutionalization over time. However, a higher reported "personal burden" (social limitations, having to provide care when not feeling well or despite worsening health, financial concerns) was associated only with increased use of supplemental formal help.

This suggests that use of formal helpers to provide supplemental or respite care may be an effective strategy for coping with some forms of stress or burden but not others. A reasonable interpretation of these results might be that formal help is more useful to caregivers when it fulfills instrumental functions—filling in for caregivers when they need to attend to other activities or when they are sick or incapacitated, providing night or "respite" coverage so that a caregiver of someone who requires round-the-clock attention can sleep or take time off, and providing help with specific tasks (bathing, transferring, heavy cleaning, and chores) that the caregiver may lack the physical strength to perform. In contrast, formal help may be much less useful to those who suffer from emotional burnout that has its source in a difficult relationship with the care recipient.

One implication of the finding that, for most caregivers, feelings of stress are more than balanced by feelings of satisfaction is that the decision to terminate caregiving in favor of institutionalization may not result from feelings of stress per se but rather from lack or loss of compensatory feelings of caregiver satisfaction. The fact that, on the interpersonal burden scale, mental and behavioral problems of the care recipient are reported as "being a problem for" the caregiver may indicate that the quality of the relationship between the caregiver and care recipient is deteriorating in the direction of no longer generating sufficient positive feedback for the caregiver. If this is, in fact, the nature of the dynamic that may lead to institutionalization of the care recipient, then it is readily apparent why recourse to formal helpers would not likely prove effective in changing caregivers' motivations for seeking institutional placement.

Regression analyses of the NLTCS respondents' self-rated satisfaction with caregiving failed to explain the sources of the variance in scores (with the single exception of a finding that higher satisfaction scores among husbands who were caregivers correlated with higher involvement; i.e., more hours spent performing caregiving tasks). We infer from this that the factors responsible for variation in caregiver satisfaction went largely unmeasured in the 1982 NLTCS.

The gerontological literature on caregiver satisfaction is smaller than that addressing caregiver stress and mostly emphasizes qualitative rather than quantitative research methods. In general, these studies suggest that future surveys seeking to give greater attention to satisfaction and its correlates would need to include measures of the following: the degree of love and affection, closeness, and intimacy between caregivers and care recipients; caregivers' assessments of their past relationships with care recipients (e.g., the quality of the marital or parent/child relationship over time); basic values (such as the importance to caregivers of maintaining family relationships and continuity in family relationships and the desire or sense of obligation to reciprocate past services performed by the care recipient for the caregiver); and personality characteristics of the caregiver (e.g., optimistic versus pessimistic).

What sustains informal caregiving when there is little positive reinforcement for the caregiver from the quality of the relationship—that is, when caregiving does not promote greater closeness; when the care recipient shows little or no appreciation or gratitude or responds to the caregiver's efforts with criticism, paranoid suspicion, or anger and emotional abuse? For some (perhaps many) family caregivers, enough satisfaction to motivate continued caregiving can be generated from a sense of moral duty, or "doing what is right." Note that we are not referring here to "duty" in the sense of legally imposed requirements (e.g., military service, court-enforced child support, etc.), but rather to the sense of duty internalized in the caregiver (albeit inculcated and reinforced by societal norms).

Rhoda Montgomery and Karl Koslowski's reanalysis of data (1991) from a respite-care demonstration to measure the correlates of greater or lesser likelihood of institutional placement found that both affection for the care recipient and a sense of duty or obligation to provide care were statistically significant predictors. The likelihood of placement increased as the level of affection or duty decreased among both adult-child and spousal caregivers. The authors note, however, that societal norms set higher standards of duty and obligation for spouses than for children, which may help to explain why spousal caregiving patterns evidence spouses' greater reluctance to access institutional alternatives to home care.

Montgomery and Koslowski's research also found that religious participation was a strong predictor of continued family caregiving. Clearly, a main function of religion is to help believers come to terms with and find meaning in suffering. Religiosity is often given as an explanation as to why certain ethnic groups—especially blacks and Hispanics—have lower rates of nursing home use than the population average (Hernandez, 1991; Walls & Zarit, 1991). The main point we want to make, however, is that a variety of social institutions and structures (other than government) are influential in establishing and sustaining the values and norms that individuals use to guide their family caregiving behavior and to interpret their caregiving experience (including perceptions of both burden and reward).

## POLICY ISSUES

Published studies of stress and burden among family caregivers of the disabled elderly very frequently—almost ritualistically—conclude with recommendations for more publicly funded formal services to assist and provide respite for overburdened family caregivers. Typically, such recommendations are not based directly on the research being reported, most often concerned with stress and its correlates. Rather, they reflect a generalized faith—no doubt to be expected among researchers mostly trained in the service professions of medicine, nursing, and social work—in the efficacy of formal services as a means of reducing caregiver stress and burden and a belief that mitigating them will result in lower rates of institutional placement of the disabled elderly.

Demonstration projects conceived to test such public policy initiatives using controlled experimental designs have, however, provided at best only modest support for the hypothesis that supplemental formal services can significantly decrease caregiver stress and achieve corresponding reductions in the use of institutional care (Lawton, Brody, & Saperstein, 1989). In the National Channeling Demonstration,[2] family caregivers as well as care recipients reported high levels of satisfaction with supplemental services provided. Yet there were no statistically significant reductions in caregiver stress—as measured through a variety of subjective and objective burden indicators—save one: family caregivers in the experimental groups that received enhanced formal services did express significantly lower levels of anxiety concerning whether their disabled elderly relatives were receiving enough assistance with dependency needs (Christianson, 1988).

A Health Care Financing Administration–sponsored respite-care demonstration in Washington State (Montgomery, 1988) compared service use and impacts on institutional placement between an experimental and control group. The investigators considered one of their most important findings to be the reluctance among many family caregivers to use respite services or to use them in recommended amounts, particularly among those family members whom case managers judged to be most overburdened and "in crisis." Even after agreeing to participate in the project, almost one-third of families eligible for respite did not use any services, and those who did used less than two-thirds of the funds for which they were eligible. Comparison of institutional use patterns found that use of respite services was associated with slightly less use of nursing home care by elders being cared for by their adult children and slightly higher nursing home use among elders being cared for by their spouses. The results indicated that respite services altered the behavior of adult-child caregivers—but primarily to delay rather than prevent or deter nursing home placement. In contrast, use of respite services appeared to encourage recourse to nursing home care by spousal caregivers.

A recent reanalysis of these data (Montgomery & Koslowski, 1991) concluded that "the results suggest a need to evaluate the goals of respite programs for caregivers of frail elders":

An implicit goal of most of these programs is to reduce the rate of institutionalization. This assumption was not supported by the present data. In fact, the reverse was true. . . . On the other hand, the fact that respite may increase the likelihood of placement is a reasonable, perhaps even a desirable outcome. Indeed, one of the functions of formal service providers may be to encourage caregivers, especially spouses, to "let go" of the elder before they become in need of care themselves.

A number of policy implications potentially flow from the proposition that, for a certain segment of the long-term care population, formal home and community-based care services are not a detour from but a "way station" on the road to nursing home placement. In this view, family caregivers must sometimes be helped to accept the inevitability of nursing home care, whether because of the disabled person's care needs or the need to safeguard the health of caregivers and allow families to "get on with their lives."

One policy implication is that efforts to decrease the supply of nursing home beds relative to the elderly population's size and growth—even if home care services are correspondingly increased—threaten to make it harder and harder for family caregivers to "let go," if that is what they need to do. That is, policymakers' well-intentioned efforts to eliminate or drastically reduce residential placements in favor of home care risk bringing about the unintended consequence of obligating families to provide informal home care (absent a public sector commitment to finance formal home care sufficient to meet all dependency needs, up to and including twenty-four-hour services). Paradoxically, an internalized sense of obligation is an inherent motivational factor in family caregiving. Note, however, that it is grounded in choice.

The nature of this dynamic is best understood in terms of what Carol Farran and associates (1991) term the "existential" paradigm of caregiving (they apply it to caregivers of dementia sufferers but it seems equally applicable to all family caregivers). They report that even though caregivers would not intentionally seek out their particular circumstances, they often say, "I choose to make the best of this situation." In theoretical terms:

In order to freely choose caregiving responsibilities, the caregiver must first entertain the possibility of not being a caregiver. However, while entertaining this option the caregiver may be confronted by existential freedom on the one hand and existential guilt on the other. Existential freedom may confront the caregiver with a "terrifying new series of choices" and may be reflected in "a fear of unwelcome possibility." (Farran et al., 1991, p. 484)

Caregivers experience existential guilt if they do not care for the impaired spouse, but they may also feel guilty or frustrated if they do not move on with their own lives. The challenge to caregivers is to act out of "true choice" as opposed to fear. (Farran et al., 1991, as cited in Levine et al., 1984, p. 220)

Family members are able to exercise "true choice" in providing care only so long as an alternative exists. Although formal home and community-based services are often characterized as providing "alternatives" to nursing home care, the statistics on nursing home use and research into the attitudes and behavior of family caregivers make it clear that it would be more accurate to describe nursing home care as a last-resort alternative to predominantly informal home care. Public policy (government action) and social policy (a broader term encompassing not only private- and voluntary-sector initiatives but also the social "consciousness") can intervene to either constrict or enlarge the possibilities for family caregivers to exercise "true choice." That is, family members may act out of fear rather than true choice if residential care alternatives either are or are portrayed as being of poor quality or worse ("prisons," "warehouses," "total institutions," "God's waiting rooms"), if residential care is structured so that it severely restricts continued family involvement (giving caregivers and care recipients the sense that placement equates with family "abandonment"), or if residential care alternatives are unaffordable literally or because recourse to means-tested public financing is stigmatized as "shameful."

Long-term care policy is so frequently characterized as "in crisis" that it would be easy to overlook the many developments currently under way that are enlarging the scope of true choice for the disabled elderly and family caregivers. The decade of the 1980s saw significant growth (albeit highly uneven across states) in public funding for formal home care services. Because research has found that formal home care is only marginally effective in preventing and postponing nursing home placement, it is more important to point to changes taking place not only in the financing but in the character and quality of residential services. New types of residential care are emerging. "Assisted living facilities" provide a level of care similar to the old "intermediate care" nursing home designation, but with more amenities and attention to resident autonomy and other quality-of-life concerns. "Adult foster care homes" along the model pioneered in Oregon offer a small, family-style, board-and-care situation without the welfare connotations traditionally attached to this type of facility. "Continuing care retirement communities" provide a supportive living arrangement that allows married couples to access varying levels of either formal home care or nursing home care when necessary—enabling the well spouse to choose a level of caregiving involvement that is neither the "all" of traditional home care nor the "nothing" of traditional nursing home placement. It is probably no accident that these "non-nursing homes" are developing largely in response to a private-pay market demand created by several decades' worth of improvement in the economic position of the elderly. The rapid growth of the private long-term care insurance market since 1985 will likely further stimulate the growth of higher-quality services across the continuum from nursing home to other residential and home-delivered care.

While the availability of Medicaid-certified nursing homes accessible to persons dependent on public funding is contracting, the quality of such care is being improved as a result of advocacy (e.g., the National Citizens Coalition for Nursing Home Reform) and research (the 1986 Institute of Medicine report), as well as legislative and regulatory initiatives (the 1987 Omnibus Budget Reconciliation Act reforms and associated revisions in federally mandated nursing home requirements). In addition, the changes in Medicaid spend-down requirements for spouses of nursing home residents enacted in the Medicare Catastrophic Coverage Act of 1988 (which were not affected by the repeal of the Medicaid provisions) now make it possible for the disabled elderly who are married to access nursing home care without endangering the well spouse's ability to maintain a decent standard of living in the community. These so-called "spousal impoverishment" protections are of particular interest because they reflect a delicate balancing act of opposing principles. On the one hand, they reduce the financial penalty (and implied social stigma) on spouse caregivers who make the difficult decision to seek institutional care for their mates. On the other hand, and equally important, they do not make the placement decision too easy by allowing the noninstitutionalized partner to appropriate all the couple's funds, making the other a ward of the state. Neither do the spousal impoverishment rules "insult" the institution of marriage by denying that marriage partners ought properly to assume a reasonable level of financial obligation to support one another's care in a nursing home.

## FUTURE DIRECTIONS

As we have said earlier, the prevailing focus of gerontological research on family caregiving has been on caregiver stress and burden and service interventions to prevent burnout leading to institutional placement. Not surprisingly, this perspective has done little to encourage the conceptualization of informal eldercare as a positive as well as productive social role for well elders. Indeed, by emphasizing negative experiences and outcomes associated with informal care, the stress/burden paradigm probably has fostered—albeit inadvertently—a judgment that the social and economic productivity of informal care costs too much in terms of deleterious effects on the well-being of informal caregivers.

Gerontologists need to rethink this paradigm and replace it with a theoretical perspective that permits more recognition of the intrinsic rewards of caregiver satisfaction in motivating and sustaining family caregiving. In addition, aging services professionals, health policymakers, senior citizens, and the public at large may need to develop lower, more realistic expectations about what increased use of, and public funding for, formal home and community-based services can and cannot accomplish. More research focusing on outcomes other than alleviation of caregiver stress and reduction in nursing home use is needed. The main value of formal home care may prove to be that of improving care recipients' quality of life, or—more precisely—what Francis Caro and Arthur Blank (1988) have termed "quality of circumstances"—the ability of the disabled elderly to obtain help not merely to stay "in the community" but to live there under what prevailing societal standards would define as at least "decent" or "adequate" conditions of comfort, safety, and dignity. If this allows family caregivers to do their best and feel that their best is "enough," caregiver satisfaction should likewise be enhanced.

There is a need for greater recognition that much of what is labeled "caregiver stress" is something of a misnomer. Only a portion of the stress experienced by family caregivers is reflective of the time, physical effort, and financial or opportunity costs of performing specific caregiving tasks. Perhaps the major factor is emotional distress that is essentially a grief response to a loved one's disabilities and associated losses. For spouses, such losses may include those of an accustomed way of life; of shared activities; of companionship; of help the ill spouse used to give the well spouse; of hopes, expectations, and plans for the future; and of the anticipated loss of the spouse to death. Grief may be particularly acute for spouses of persons with Alzheimer's disease and related dementias because by impairing the mind, these disorders cause a death of personality long before physical death occurs. Spouses of dementia sufferers, in particular, must struggle with painful emotions and wrenching decisions that have more to do with the changing character of their marital relations than with the stresses and strains of being informal care providers. As an example of spousal stress unrelated to caregiving tasks, several recent publications have discussed well spouses' conflicted feelings about sexual relations with their mentally impaired partners.

A theoretical paradigm that carefully distinguishes family members overburdened by the demands of caregiving tasks from those struggling with grief and other relationship issues can more readily discern the possibilities and limitations of formal services as opposed to other supportive coping mechanisms and more readily discern the appropriate role for government vis-à-vis other social institutions (religion, the extended family). To draw an analogy, everyone understands the value of having life insurance, Medicare, and prepaid burial plans to defray the expenses of terminal illness and death. Similarly, everyone appreciates that paid funeral directors, clergy, and devoted family and friends can be extremely helpful in arranging funerals and providing some emotional support to the bereaved. But no one expects, or would want, a sizeable life insurance policy or an expensive funeral or even the most sensitive of pastoral counseling to truly make it easy to accept a spouse's death. How much can we really expect support services to alleviate emotional distress related to a spouse's functional decline? Fundamentally, individuals must rely primarily on their own inner psychological and spiritual resources to meet this life challenge successfully.

Finally, researchers in aging need to show greater awareness of the fact that among the existential choices for family caregivers of the disabled elderly is that of using "life's lemons to make lemonade," as the saying goes. When older spousal caregivers realize this possibility—and according to their reports that caregiver satisfaction outweighs caregiver stress, the great majority do—then caregiving becomes a component not only of "productive" but also of "successful" aging.

## NOTES

1. This chapter relies on data from the 1982 National Long-Term Care Survey (NLTCS), a nationally representative survey of the functionally disabled elderly living in the community, and its companion Informal Caregiver Survey, in which caregivers of a representative sample of NLTCS respondents requiring help with basic activities of daily living (ADLs), including bathing, dressing, transferring, toileting, and eating were surveyed. Also referenced in this chapter are longitudinal analyses of the rate of nursing home use among the original sample members over the succeeding two years, based on a 1984 National Long-Term Care Survey, which included follow-up interviews with 1982 sample members. Both surveys were sponsored by the U.S. Department of Health and Human Services.

2. The National Channeling Demonstration was a large-scale social policy experiment carried out in the early 1980s testing two models of case management and enhanced public funding of home and community-based long-term care services in twelve different sites across the country.

## REFERENCES

American Association of Retired Persons. (1991, March). *America's aging workforce*. Issue Brief #3. Washington, DC: AARP Public Policy Institute.

Cantor, M. H. (1991). Family and community: Changing roles in an aging society. *The Gerontologist, 31*, 337–346.

Caro, F. G., & Blank, A. E. (1988). Quality impact of home care for the elderly. *Home Health Care Services Quarterly, 9*(2/3), 1–204.

Christianson, J. B. (1988, April). The evaluation of the national long-term care demonstration: 6. The effect of channeling on informal caregiving. *Health Services Research, 23*(1), 99–118.

Colerick, E., & George, L. K. (1986). Predictors of institutionalization among caregivers of Alzheimer's disease. *Journal of American Geriatric Society, 34*, 493–498.

Enright, R. B. (1991). Time spent caregiving and help received by spouses and adult children of brain-impaired adults. *The Gerontologist, 31*, 375–383.

Farran, C. J., Keane-Hagerty, E., Salloway, S., Kupferer, S., & Wilken, C. (1991). Finding meaning: An alternative paradigm for Alzheimer's disease family caregivers. *The Gerontologist, 31*, 483–489.

Gaynor, S. E. (1990). The long haul: The effects of home care on caregivers. *Journal of Nursing Scholarship, 22*, 208–212.

George, L. K., & Clipp, E. C. (Eds.). (1991, Winter). Aging well. *Generations, 15*, 1–80.

Harris & Associates, Inc. (1982). *Priorities and expectations for health and living circumstances*. A survey of the elderly in five English-speaking countries. Study No. 824006. Conducted for the Commonwealth Fund. New York: Harris & Associates.

Hernandez, G. G. (1991, April). Not so benign neglect; Researchers ignore ethnicity in defining family caregiver burden. *The Gerontologist, 31*, 271.

Hooyman, N. (1990). Women as caregivers of the elderly: Implications for social welfare policy and practice. In D. E. Biegel & A. Blum (Eds.), *Aging and caregiving: Theory, research, and policy.* Newbury Park, CA: Sage.

Jackson, M. E. (1991). *Prevalence and correlates of unmet need among the elderly with ADL disabilities.* Study carried out for the Office of the Assistant Secretary, U.S. Department of Health and Human Services. Contract Report No. HHS-100–88–0041. Lexington, MA: SysteMetrics/McGraw-Hill.

Kasper, J. D., Steinbach, U., & Andrews, J. (1990, February). *Factors associated with ending caregiving among informal caregivers to the functionally and cognitively impaired elderly population.* Final report to the Office of the Assistant Secretary of Planning and Evaluation, Department of Health and Human Services. Grant #88, ASPE 209A. Washington, DC: U.S. Government Printing Office.

Kemper, P. (1989, December). *The use of formal and informal home care by the disabled elderly.* Paper presented at the annual meeting, Allied Social Sciences Association, Atlanta, GA.

Kinney, J., & Stephens, M. A. P. (1989). Caregiving hassles scale: Assessing the daily hassles of caring for a family member with dementia. *The Gerontologist, 29,* 328–332.

Lawton, M. P., Brody, E. M., & Saperstein, A. R. (1989, February). A controlled study of respite service for caregivers of Alzheimer's patients. *The Gerontologist, 29*(1), 8–16.

Levine, N. B., Gendron, C. E., Dastoor, D. P., Poitras, L. R., et al. (1984). Existential issues in the management of the demented elderly patient. *American Journal of Psychotherapy, 38*(2), 215–223.

Lieberman, M. A., & Kramer, J. H. (1991). Factors affecting decisions to institutionalize demented elderly. *The Gerontologist, 31,* 371–374.

McFall, S., & Miller, B. (1992). Caregiver burden and nursing home admissions of frail elderly persons. *Journals of Gerontology/Social Sciences, 47*(2), S73–79.

McLanahan, S. S., & Monson, R. A. (1990, December). *Caring for the elderly: Prevalence and consequences.* National Survey of Families and Households Working Paper No. 18. Department of Sociology, University of Wisconsin, Madison, WI.

Meyer, C. J. (1987, April). Stress: There's no place like a first home. *Family Relations, 36,* 198–203.

Miller, B. (1989, September). Adult children's perceptions of caregiver stress and satisfaction. *Journal of Applied Gerontology, 8*(3), 275–293.

Miller, B. (1990). Gender differences in spouse caregiver strain: Socialization and role explanations. *Journal of Marriage and the Family, 52,* 311–322.

Miller, B., & McFall, S. (1989, November). *Caregiver burden and institutionalization, hospitalization, and stability of care.* Final report to the Office of the Assistant Secretary of Planning and Evaluation. Department of Health and Human Services. Grant #88, ASPE 207A. Washington, DC: U.S. Government Printing Office.

Miller, B., & McFall, S. (1991a). Effect of caregiver burden on change and formal task support of frail older persons. *Journal of Health and Social Behavior, 32,* 165–179.

Miller, B., & McFall, S. (1991b). Stability and change in the informal task support networks of frail older persons. *The Gerontologist, 31,* 735–745.

Miller, B., McFall, S., & Montgomery, A. (1991). The impact of elder health, caregiver involvement, and global stress on two dimensions of caregiver burden. *Journal of Gerontology, 46,* S9–19.

Montgomery, R. J. (1988). Respite care: Lessons from a controlled design study. *Health Care Financing Review,* 1988 Annual Supplement, 133–138.

Montgomery, R. J., & Koslowski, K. (1991). *Secondary analyses of effects of intervention on family caregivers: Correlates of nursing home placement.* Final report to the Health Care Financing Administration, HCFA–90–0435. Detroit, MI: Wayne State University.

Motenko, A. K. (1989). The frustrations, gratifications, and well-being of dementia caregivers. *The Gerontologist, 29,* 166–172.

Murtaugh, C. M., Kemper, P., & Spillman, B. (1991). The risk of nursing home use in later life. *Medical Care, 28*(10), 952–962.

Pearlin, L. J., Mullan, J. T., Semple, S. J., & Skaff, M. M. (1990). Caregiving and the stress process: An overview of concepts and their measures. *The Gerontologist, 30,* 583–591.

Stone, R., Cafferata, G. L., & Sangl, J. (1987). Caregivers of the frail elderly: A national profile. *The Gerontologist, 27,* 616–626.

Stone, R., & Kemper, P. (1989). Spouses and children of disabled elders: How large a constituency for long-term care reform? *Milbank Quarterly, 67*(3–4), 485–506.

Stone, R., & Short, P. F. (1990). The competing demands of employment and informal caregiving to disabled elders. *Medical Care, 28*(6), 513–526.

Vitaliano, P. P., Russo, J., Young, H. M., Becker, J., & Maiuro, R. D. (1991). The screen for caregiver burden. *The Gerontologist, 31,* 76–83.

Wade, A. (1988). *Social Security Area population projections, 1988.* SSA Pub. No. 11–11549. Baltimore, MD: Social Security Administration, Office of the Actuary.

Walls, C. T., & Zarit, S. H. (1991). Informal support from black churches and the well-being of elderly blacks. *The Gerontologist, 31,* 490–504.

Zedlewski, S. R., Barnes, R. O., Burt, M. R., McBride, T. D., & Meyer, J. A. (1990). *The needs of the elderly in the 21st century.* Urban Institute Report 90–5. Washington, DC: Urban Institute Press.

# 9

# The Political Economy of Productive Aging: Long-term Care

## Laura Katz Olson

This chapter seeks to address the concept of productive aging within the context of growing numbers of functionally disabled, or frail, older people in need of long-term care. An underlying concern is the lack of adequate formal services to care for those living at home. Current home services are assessed in relation to the political economy overall and to various sectors of society in particular.

Political leaders and corporate executives have blamed the "inability" of the United States to provide effectively and fully for the functionally impaired older population on such factors as our decreased economic growth, budget deficits, rapidly shifting demographics (especially among the oldest groups of the elderly), and a weakening of family responsibility.

This chapter contends that these factors are not the fundamental causes of our inability to care adequately for our frail elderly. Rather, it is American cultural values, U.S. business practices, and the public policies that support them that have failed to serve the needs of the elderly, their families, and workers.

While the life span has been extended for large numbers of older people, U.S. policies have not fostered the social conditions in which these additional years might be lived in a meaningful way. Instead, American sanctities of individualism and self-reliance, the privatization of human services and corporate values prioritizing short-term goals, the maximization of profits, and shareholder rights have precluded successful aging for the vast majority of the frail elderly. These values, practices, and policy measures also explain the underdevelopment of formal home care services.

In the face of faltering economic growth and increasing numbers of frail people in need of aid, U.S. policy has been to cut the costs of publicly financed long-term care. This has intensified family burdens, particularly those imposed on wives and adult daughters. Such a strategy has had and will continue to have deleterious effects on the ability of those giving care to age productively.

Corporate values and priorities have been adopted by the growing service sector of the economy. As a result, productivity in the field of human services tends to be measured in market terms. But the quantitative approach ignores the qualitative aspects of long-term care. Given the difficult working conditions and low wages characteristic of home care agencies and nursing homes, it is unlikely that those who work for them will either age productively themselves or contribute to quality aging among the frail elderly.

## LONG-TERM CARE: ALTERNATIVE VALUES AND PRACTICES

After World War II until the late 1960s, the U.S. economy experienced unprecedented economic growth. Industrial firms were predominant in the international economic order, producing almost 50 percent of the world's manufactured goods. Since the early 1970s, other nations have captured growing market shares in nearly every industry worldwide. By the 1980s, the U.S. manufacturing sector had declined substantially, and productivity growth lingered behind that of nearly all other industrialized nations (Bluestone & Harrison, 1982).

In contrast, the U.S. service sector rose both in absolute and relative terms, representing the vast majority of jobs created since 1970 and most of the new job growth since 1980. Currently, 75 percent of all U.S. employment is in the service-producing sector, compared to 59 percent in 1950. Health services account for 27 percent of service jobs, with long-term care representing the fastest growing part of the health care industry (Brown, 1986; Kane & Kane, 1985, p. 265).

Concomitant with the decline of the manufacturing sector and a less productive society overall has been an abrupt demographic change that was, for the most part, unanticipated. Over the last several decades the admixture of a liberalized immigration policy, improvements in mortality at middle and older ages, and a sharp reduction in fertility have fostered both an increasing number of elderly and a markedly older (and feminized) age structure in American society. Currently, the average life expectancy at birth is 78.3 years for women and 71.3 years for men.

The fastest-growing groups are those in the extreme ages. Between 1940 and 1960 there was a 154 percent increase and between 1960 and 1980 a 141 percent increase in the number of people age eighty-five and over (Longino, 1988, p. 515). The seventy-five-and-over and eighty-five-and-over age categories accounted for twelve million and 2.8 million, respectively, of the 28.6 million people age sixty-five and over in 1985. The evidence suggests that population aging, particularly among the oldest sectors of society, will continue unabated; the number of people age eighty-five and over is expected to increase to approximately five million by the year 2000 (Stone & Fletcher, 1988).

Chronic diseases and the disabilities they induce are prevalent among the elderly, especially for those in the upper age ranges. In the United States, about one-third of all people age eighty-five and over need limited assistance, while another one-third require substantial aid in order to perform their daily activities (Rosenwaike, 1985). Increasingly, older age groups represent a greater number of functionally impaired individuals requiring various levels and types of long-term care. The Pepper Commission has calculated that the seven million older people currently requiring help with basic tasks will escalate to approximately 13.8 million by the year 2030 (Pepper Commission, 1990).

Expanding numbers of frail older people in need of support do not necessarily impose burdensome problems in a society. The impact of long-term care services on the productive capacity of a nation depends highly on societal values and the function of such services in the political economy. Similarly, attitudes toward and roles of these services generate differential effects on various sectors of society, including workers and older people and their families, as well as on the nature of the services themselves.

In most industrialized nations other than the United States, community support and care for the chronically ill are assumed to be inherent rights. Growing requirements for long-term care are viewed as a social issue, thereby inducing social solutions. Consequently, long-term care services tend to be publicly funded and delivered for those in need, regardless of income. These include community-based sources of support that are designed to allow older people to remain in their own homes for as long as possible (Kane & Kane, 1976, pp. 170–171).

In contrast to this communitarian approach to social welfare and long-term care, the United States stresses individualism, independence, and privatization. The perception in the United States that increased numbers of frail older people foster a long-term care "problem" appears to be rooted in these core values as well as in the social and economic structures and policies supporting these norms.

Accordingly, the United States has not developed a comprehensive governmental approach to long-term care. Chronic illness is viewed as an individual problem, with responsibility for care relegated to the functionally impaired person and his or her family. As Robert and Rosalie Kane (1976, p. 187) conclude, "Nowhere are the conditions for the elderly perfect and nowhere are planners complacent, but nowhere outside of the U.S. is such a burden placed on the elderly individual and his family."

The elderly in this country themselves value independence and individualism. Most frail older people strive to maintain their own residence despite functional impairments. Their primary goal is to sustain an independent life-style; they fearfully avoid the prospect of institutionalization. At the same time, the aged endeavor not to encumber their adult children. They also eschew social services, viewing dependency on public resources as a personal failure.

When the chronically impaired require help that they or their kin cannot perform, it is assumed that they are best served by the private sector. Human services overall and long-term care in particular have been increasingly privatized in the United States. There are severe limits placed on public support for long-term care services in general and community-based services in particular. The public sector is the provider of last resort, generally requiring a means test for individuals to qualify; eligibility for publicly funded long-term care is based on personal insolvency.

In the United States "long-term care" has been nearly synonymous with "nursing homes"; public funding for home care services is severely restricted in spite of the strong preference of the elderly to remain in their own homes (Koff, 1982).[1] Throughout U.S. history, the approach to most social problems, including poverty, has been some form of institutional treatment. Accordingly, institutional care has been the predominant mode of public support, available primarily to older people without family or other private support systems, those who have been poor their whole lives, and the newly impoverished.

The values of individualism and self-reliance have had particularly negative effects on the frail elderly poor. In the United States, the kind and extent of services a chronically disabled person is able to acquire is a function of who pays the costs rather than the person's needs. Since there is a difference between real needs existing in the community (demand) and the ability to pay for appropriate services (market demand), a large percentage of older people with limited incomes are not able to obtain home-based supportive services. Such individuals often find themselves one caregiver away from institutionalization. The Brookings Institution has estimated that long-term care costs probably will escalate faster than the cost of living; the elderly may be even less able to afford home-based services in the future (Rivlin & Wiener, 1988, p. 50).

## THE NONSYSTEM OF LONG-TERM CARE

The rapid growth in the number of frail older people in need of supportive services has coincided since the 1970s with lingering economic growth, rising deficits, and cutbacks in social programs overall. During the 1970s, and especially the 1980s, there were substantial reductions in federal support for community-based human services serving the working poor, women with children, and the disabled. For example, the real value of benefits provided under Aid to Families with Dependent Children (AFDC) declined 15 percent nationwide from 1970 to 1986 (Quinn, 1989, p. 838). Retrenchment in such programs became even more severe by the 1990s.

There also have been sharp decreases in state and local revenues, including reduced federal assistance for social services. Under the guise of power devolution to the states, New Federalism public policies in the 1970s and 1980s (revenue sharing and block grants) successfully diminished national financial obligations. When, for instance, the 1981 Social Services Block Grant (SSBG) replaced the Title XX program, there was a 21 percent reduction in federal support (Estes & Lee, 1985, p. 29). Consequently, most states have been concerned with controlling costs rather than expanding commitments.

As suggested earlier, concern over expenditures for institutionalization has intensified as well. Public support for institutional care under Medicaid began in the mid–1930s as a limited government responsibility to a relatively small older population requiring institutional care; demand and costs increased by 1970 far beyond what was anticipated when Medicaid was passed.

At the same time, nursing home charges increased dramatically, as did the public sector's share of these costs (Estes & Lee, 1985, p. 9). Growing numbers of older people began to rely on Medicaid for nursing home care, especially those in middle-income households who were forced to impoverish themselves in order to become eligible. As a result, state governments experienced an escalating fiscal crisis in their Medicaid programs. In fact, the latter had become the single largest item in many state budgets.

Accordingly, national and state political leaders began to search for alternative, less costly ways of providing for long-term care. Limited federal funding became available, primarily for home care demonstration projects under several programs, provided by amendments to the Social Security Act, Medicaid, and the Older Americans Act. For the most part, however, these community-based services were funded by channeling existing resources from established programs.

One of the earliest experiments set up to compare the effectiveness and costs of noninstitutional services with those of nursing home care was established during the 1970s under Section 222 of the Social Security Act. These demonstration projects included Wisconsin Community Care Organizations, the Georgia Alternative Health Services Program, and the Triage Program (instituted in Connecticut from 1974 to 1981). The latter, for example, was financed through Medicare and Medicaid waivers.

Similarly, Section 2176 of the 1981 Omnibus Budget Reconciliation Act (OBRA) allowed the Department of Health and Human Services (HHS) to waive certain Medicaid requirements so that states could finance noninstitutional long-term care for specified services, such as case management and homemaker programs.[2] Since the Section 2176 waivers were expected to encourage experimental programs, states were allowed to focus on a limited geographic area when initiating these new services. The goal was to demonstrate whether or not the cost of providing in-home or community services would be less than providing nursing home care. The costs and numbers of people served under Section 2176 waivers cannot exceed what they otherwise would have been for nursing home care. As a result, program limitations are assured; in 1986, only 79,000 aged or disabled people were served (Pepper Commission, 1990, pp. 97–99).

The New York State Nursing Home Without Walls, which began in 1978, provides in-home services to Medicaid-eligible older people who would otherwise be placed in a nursing home. Moreover, service costs cannot exceed 75 percent of the local average annual Medicaid expenditures on nursing home care. In Massachusetts, limited homemaker assistance is available, through Homecare, to the very frail elderly; service costs are based on income.[3]

In order to control costs through more efficient service management systems, Congress instituted the National Long-Term Care Channeling Demonstration Program from 1980 to 1985. Funding became available from the Administration on Aging (AOA) and the Health Care Financing Administration (HCFA) to establish a system of long-term care in ten local sites, utilizing a case management approach. This national channeling experiment focused exclusively on those elderly who not only were at risk for institutionalization but also could be expected to live independently in the community with some assistance. Unlike earlier programs, which included an expansion of services, the Channeling Demonstrations focused primarily on efficiency of performance (Eustis, Greenberg, & Patten, 1984, p. 107).

Overall, most national and state efforts have focused on coordination among existing home care programs. However, many administrative obstacles have hindered program expansion. For example, new projects often must seek various funding sources, each with different criteria for such factors as eligibility and allowable services. Additionally, efforts to control costs by directing services toward those frail older people who otherwise would be institutionalized have proven difficult.

While nearly all of the limited efforts to expand or coordinate noninstitutional types of care over the past two decades have focused on the Medicaid-eligible frail elderly, several recent congressional proposals have attempted to promote some form of coverage for all older people.[4] Nearly all of these proposals also have attempted to offer a comprehensive long-term care system that incorporates both institutional and home care.[5] Such legislation includes the Medicare Long-Term Home Care Catastrophic Protection Act (the Pepper bill), proposed in 1988; Lifecare (the Kennedy bill); the Long-Term Care Assistance Act of 1988; Elder-Care Long-Term Care Assistance Act; and the Chronic Care Medicare Long-Term Care Coverage Act of 1988.[6] At the end of 1990, another approach was suggested by the Pepper Commission (1990, pp. 119–134). It is unlikely, however, that advocates of national long-term care will be able to garner sufficient political support for passage of such proposals in the near future.

Moreover, although there are continuing attempts to curtail nursing home costs, public funding continues to be focused primarily on institutional care. According to the Pepper Commission, five states, with only one-third of the older population in the United States, account for approximately two-thirds of all in-home and community-based expenditures (Pepper Commission, 1990, p. 97).

By 1989, only 3 percent of Medicare's $96 billion program and 1.5 percent of Medicaid's $61 billion program were providing for community-based or in-home services (Margolis, 1990, p. 111). Family-focused services such as respite and day care have been particularly underfunded. There also has been a failure to institutionalize successful in-home service pilot programs. In many localities where money has been available for demonstration projects, continuous funding tends to be tenuous; a significant number have been dismantled.

National long-term care proposals have not been received enthusiastically by policymakers, nor has home care significantly replaced nursing homes because of a number of factors. First, concern over costs, particularly given the continuation into the 1990s of slow economic growth; seemingly intractable budget deficits; and reductions in human services overall have prevented serious consideration of new programs entailing potentially sizeable federal funds.

Second, the evidence is mixed on whether home care programs actually save money (Benjamin, 1985, p. 200). For example, it is unclear if, and to what extent, home care services delay or prevent institutionalization. One recent analysis of the Channeling Demonstrations noted that home care services were utilized by extremely functionally disabled older people. However, a significant percentage of the recipients would not have entered a nursing home even without the benefits (Kemper, 1990).

Policymakers also are concerned over the issue of substitution; that is, whether publicly provided home care replaces informal care. If in-home services substitute for family and friends, decision makers fear that latent demands will emerge, thus escalating costs. Although studies of demonstration projects indicate that formal services tend to complement rather than to replace informal care, total program costs may, in fact, increase (see, for example, Caro, 1986; Edelman & Hughs, 1990; Pepper Commission, 1990; Stephens & Christianson, 1986).

Third, funding for programs serving the elderly has been escalating dramatically. Social Security, Medicare, and Medicaid together accounted for over one-third of the entire federal budget by the late 1980s. The resistance of older people to bearing the expenses of catastrophic medical coverage themselves forced Congress to repeal the Medicare Catastrophic Coverage Act even before its implementation, and it generated even more wariness about promoting or enacting new, potentially costly public programs for long-term care (OMB Watch, 1990, p. 16).

Fourth, provider advocacy associations, such as the National Home Caring Council, have not achieved the formidable power of other eldercare groups, such as the American Hospital Association, the American Medical Association, or the American Association of Homes for the Aging. Philip Brickner and colleagues (1987, p. 19) maintain that since there is no major industry or substantial profit to protect, there have not been serious lobbying efforts by trade associations for home care, day-care centers, or respite services.

Finally, long-term care programs have been proposed during a period of increasing privatization. Since the late 1970s, the federal government has been disengaging itself from specific kinds of market responsibilities and restricting publicly produced services. At the same time, a contraction in the role of government in addressing social needs has coincided with long-held American views about care of the elderly. Thus, the ethos of individual and family responsibility, imbued in the attitudes of policymakers, the general public, and even caregivers themselves, has further weakened political support for comprehensive, publicly financed long-term care.

## PRODUCTIVE AGING: THE FRAIL ELDERLY

The vast majority of the frail elderly have been productive for most of their adult lives, whether within the formal market economy or within the home. They have contributed substantially to their families, the workplace, and society overall. Vernon Greene (1989) asserts that the productive capacity of our nation has depended primarily on the knowledge, skills, and values provided younger generations through the efforts and sacrifice of their elders. Such massive investment in "human capital" during earlier periods of their lives entitles older people to claim a portion of current societal wealth.

I would argue that the functionally disabled older person, who can no longer contribute socially or economically to society, has earned the right to age successfully. A focus on successful aging entails a concern with the welfare of the individual. Thus, despite the fact that most frail older people no longer can be productive, societal resources must be available so that they can live a quality life and reach their maximum human potential. As Brickner and colleagues (1987, p. 171) denote, "[H]uman beings are most fulfilled when they are able to use all their personal resources—strength, intelligence, drive, and life experience."

With the increase in longevity, the period in which individuals are incapacitated has grown in the United States. This has occurred primarily because we have not provided the appropriate environment for those suffering from chronic ailments. While aging is a universal phenomenon, the way we age is linked to the social context.

Chronic diseases do not necessarily entail dependency; their debilitating effects can be understood and ameliorated only within the context of the interrelatedness of social, environmental, and economic conditions. As Theodore Koff persuasively argues,

Problems of changing neighborhoods, inadequate housing, limited income, and inadequate health assessment, services, or education, are among the forces that can ultimately lead to the need for long-term care—either institutional or noninstitutional. (1982, p. 6)

In order to engender successful aging, affordable supportive services and programs also must be available to enable physically frail and dependent older people to capitalize on their capabilities and opportunities. The availability of appropriate home-based and community services as well as quality institutional care for all older people in need provide the socially created settings in which successful aging can take place.

For the frail elderly, support services should help maintain, restore, and compensate for the losses incurred as a result of chronic disabilities. They should do so while protecting the dignity and self-respect of the recipient (Daniels, 1988, p. 107).

Consequently, as suggested by Elaine Brody (1990, p. 13), a successful long-term care system provides a continuum of care "on a sustained basis to enable individuals whose functional capacities are chronically impaired to be maintained at their maximum levels of health and well-being." This includes the provision of opportunities for the frail aged to maintain old relationships or discover new ones and to develop skills and talents despite functional impairment.

In the United States, aging itself is viewed as an inevitable biological decline, independent of social structure. Consequently, a significant number of the partially disabled elderly who, with appropriate supportive services, would be able to maintain their life-style and live fulfilled lives are unable to do so. Norman Daniels claims,

People with only mild disabilities, who could maintain normal patterns of living if they had modest help, cannot find or finance the home care and social support services they need. Ultimately, millions of elderly are forced into premature and inappropriate levels of dependency on their families or institutions. (1988, p. 8)

It is one of the ironies of U.S. public policy that though we promote individualism and independence, our structural arrangements tend to foster dependency.

For many older people, the emphasis on individualism also means social isolation. Gordon Streib and colleagues, in their study of shared living for the elderly, contend that in many instances such arrangements are preferable from a socialization point of view to bringing support services into the individual's home. They argue further that an overemphasis on independence for older people may be counterproductive (Streib, Folts, & Hilker, 1984, pp. 245–246).

Quality aging among the frail elderly cannot take place without the provision of public support as a right, which would allow older people to have maximum choice in their living arrangements. A sense of control over one's life is essential for maintaining personal integrity and should be supported by public policy to the fullest extent possible.

Impoverished nursing home residents have no resources with which to exert any control over their lives or even their care. While institutional care may be necessary and even beneficial in some cases, it must be seen as an alternative to community supports and not the other way around (Landsberger, 1985, p. 219). Just as important, as pointed out by Jeanie Schmidt Kayser-Jones (1981), care in institutions must be provided in such a way as to show the residents that "we value them as human beings." In my view, a profit-making environment is unsuitable for the development of such facilities.

## PRODUCTIVE AGING: THE CAREGIVERS

A substantial majority of policymakers in the United States view the escalation of the frail elderly population as evidence of an "aging crisis." They tend to argue that because of declining productivity in the manufacturing sector, and slower economic growth overall, the nation cannot afford the growing service needs of older people. The prevalent assumption appears to be that there is competition over scarce public resources for human services and that the elderly are taking an increasingly disproportionate share.

Rather than focus on the root causes of escalating nursing home costs and abusive institutional conditions, policymakers increasingly have attempted to encourage alternative, less costly home-based care. Concomitantly, they have systematically reduced funds for supportive social services and other forms of community aid.

Consequently, "privatization" of the "problem" of a growing older population has meant increasing expectations of help provided by family members and increasing burdens on the family. Social policies and politicians are effectuating caregiving arrangements in ways that reduce public budgets without measuring the personal economic, emotional, and other costs. These are largely borne by women, who often have limited options when "choosing" a caregiving role. As Elaine Brody asserts,

Belatedly, "alternatives" to institutional care are now being advocated, the "natural or informal support system" has been discovered, and the "family" is being cheered on in its caregiving role. But it has become clear that such words and phrases are only euphemisms for adult daughters (and daughters-in-laws), who are the true alternatives. If the impaired older person has a spouse, the vast majority of services are provided by the spouse together with the adult daughters or daughters-in-law. (1981, p. 474)

Women represent more than 70 percent of all caregivers, including adult daughters (30 percent), wives (23 percent), and other relatives, many of whom are daughters-in-law (20 percent) (Brody, 1990, p. 35). Elderly males generally are cared for by their spouses, while older women rely primarily on their adult children for care. Susan Stephens and Jon Christianson (1986, p. 25) note that "the general caregiving scenario consists of a woman . . . as the primary provider of services to an older, female relative."

Research shows that the American family always has maintained its frail elderly members, delivering about 80 percent of all long-term care, mostly without publicly supported aid. Institutionalization is sought "reluctantly, as a last resort, and only after considerable personal sacrifice and various alternative solutions have been attempted" (Dunlop, 1980, p. 515). In fact, studies show that the death, illness, or exhaustion of a caregiver is the most common reason for institutionalization.

Since the 1980s, national policymakers concerned with cost containment have enacted legislation imposing additional burdens on the elderly and their kin. Diagnostically Related Groups (DRGs), for example, have been incorporated into the Medicare program, fostering "sicker" and "quicker" hospital discharges. More stringent eligibility standards, caps on reimbursement levels, and a slower growth in the supply of available services also have served to cut costs, while shifting long-term care responsibilities to the family.

The family is expected to provide even more caregiving in the 1990s and beyond, but this pressure has been generated at a time when the family is least able to provide this care. The issue may not be the willingness of families to care for their disabled elderly kin in the future but rather whether they are capable of doing so.

There are unique features of contemporary society that contribute to such prohibitive conditions. First, the growth in the oldest age group, along with prolonged periods of chronic ailment, has meant that increasing percentages of the population will be facing caregiver roles. Similarly, there has been a substantial growth in the number of frail older parents each individual or family potentially will need to care for. The emergence of the four-generation family further compounds the problem.

Second, not only do more people require care but there has been a substantial change in the nature and duration of such care. There is greater frailty, including a larger number of older people experiencing dementia, as well as a relatively longer period of adult dependency on their families.

Moreover, chronic diseases often are progressive, requiring increasing amounts of care and responsibility.

Third, while the "problem" of eldercare has been relegated to the ever-increasing domain of women's work, contemporary women have decreasing amounts of time available for caregiving. They are expected to meet multiple demands that social observers have labeled the "double day." Many are single parents, participants in the paid labor market, and providers of other household and family services.

Indeed, middle-aged women, who are generally responsible for care of the aged, are the fastest growing sector of women entering the paid labor force. Currently, about 60 percent of all such women work; this rate is expected to increase steadily. As Brody (1981, p. 478) reminds us, even if men and women shared domestic tasks, "the combination of women at work and parent care means not a redistribution of existing tasks, but a larger package of responsibilities to be redistributed."

Fourth, the emergence of new and diverse family structures because of the dramatic increase in divorce and remarriage has blurred the lines of responsibility. Fifth, high divorce rates, along with a decline in the size of nuclear families, suggest that women are likely to face the financial, emotional, and physical responsibilities of caregiving alone.

Nearly half of all caregivers are in the labor force, attempting to balance their work and caregiving responsibilities. In fact, about a third of all working people, primarily women, are providing some help to a frail older person (Brody, 1990, p. 214).

The evidence suggests that caregiving can hinder significantly a worker's performance and productive capacity. In a recent study, for example, 40 percent of the caregivers studied reported that parental responsibilities interfered with their work. In fact, 12 percent had chosen their particular job based on their parental duties (Scharlach & Boyd, 1989).

Both employers and employees confront greater worker absenteeism and job turnover as well as unanticipated interruptions in work routines and plans. A large number of caregivers in the paid labor force reduce the number of hours worked, rearrange their work schedule to accommodate their ailing kin, or take unpaid time off (Brody, 1990, p. 35; Burnley, 1987, pp. 258–259). Some employees are forced to sacrifice professional opportunities and career advancement as well. Because of the demands of caregiving, workers may seek less exhausting (and lower-paid) employment. A significant number of caregivers are forced to quit their jobs, leaving many of them in dire financial need. Brody (1990) found that about 28 percent of nonworking women had left the paid labor market to care for an older parent.

Nancy Kane (1989) warns that the private sector will be increasingly affected by the caregiving requirements of workers. She argues that the situation will worsen because of the diminishing availability and affordability of in-home services relative to a growing frail elderly population. She predicts "major disruptions for productive workers with elderly relatives at home."

Research provides evidence that primary caregiving entails up to six hours a day, and many individuals assist seven days a week (see, for example, Stephens & Christianson, 1986, p. 50; Stone, Cafferata, & Sangl, 1987, pp. 7–8). Care of an Alzheimer's disease patient requires even more intensive effort. Moreover, the burden intensifies over time as the patient becomes increasingly disabled. Many caregivers are isolated in the home by themselves, without relief. They often relinquish their own needs and social activities. Marjorie Cantor (1983, p. 601) shows that caregivers experience substantial personal deprivation.

According to one study, about half of all caregivers suffer moderate to severe stress, from 15 percent to 33 percent are physically strained, and another 15 percent to 20 percent face financial problems. A high percentage of caregivers experience increased tension with family members, including the care recipients. Where the caregiver and parent share a household, strain is even greater (Brody, 1990).

The majority of caregiving daughters are over the age of fifty. According to one source, 30 percent of all spouses providing long-term care are age seventy-five and over. Since the age of the caregivers themselves has increased, many of these individuals have experienced health problems even before taking on the caregiving role. Moreover, many are struggling financially; a disproportionate number live in poverty or near poverty conditions (Abel, 1987, pp. 5, 29–30).

Given these conditions, it would appear that caregivers face serious obstacles in their efforts to age productively. They are unpaid, often sacrificing their job, job advancement, health, current income, future pensions, and other aspects of their well-being. Consequently, caregivers tend to be victims of the chronic physical and mental disabilities of old age in the United States.

Increasing pressures on adult children to personally take care of their frail relative's every need is socially irresponsible (Brody, 1985, p. 27). Since the emotional, physical, and economic costs are so considerable, private individuals, especially women, should not be expected to shoulder the entire burden of care of another individual. As noted by Gillian Dalley (1988), there is a tendency for Americans to equate caring about and caring for. This has both been internalized and built into the social structure.

For productive aging to take place among middle-aged and older women in the 1990s and beyond, U.S. social policy must address the needs of caregivers as well as those of the chronically ill population. The community should be responsible for relieving families of eldercare either fully or partially. Potential caregivers must have both greater publicly supported and delivered services when caring for a chronically ill relative and the option not to provide such care. As Dalley has stated perceptively,

It is the recognition of dependence and interdependence as facets of all human relationships that validates the collectivist approach to the issue of caring. By the collective taking on responsibility for the provision of care, the tensions, burden and obligation inherent in the one to one caring relationship, which are the product of the family model of care, are overcome. Particular individuals are not forced into particular caring and cared for roles, dictated by their social and biological relatedness; for it is in those relationships that dependence becomes a warped and unhealthy pressure on the actors involved. In collectively shared relationships of caring, the burdens are dispersed and fewer pressures arise. The individuals who are being cared for are not forced into dependence on certain other individuals with whom they might have other kinds of relationships (of love, dislike, intellectual partnership, parenthood, siblings, and so on). (1988, p. 115)

In addition, the market value of unpaid caregiving increases drastically every year, representing billions of dollars. Since family maintenance of the frail elderly contributes to society significantly, such work should be compensated.

The United States tends to place a heavy emphasis on employment in the formal workplace as a measure of worth and the only acceptable means of economic support. A recent study conducted by the Public Agenda Foundation (1988, p. 121) asserted that the "formal, monetarized market sector has come to monopolize the provision of material well-being, social status, and individual integrity or self-esteem." Direct payment to families for rendering care would offer recognition to caregivers, as well as alleviate financial strains, thus enhancing their well-being.

A few states have experimented with family-care payments. California's In-Home Supportive Services program, for example, reimburses family members to a limited extent for rendering care to relatives. However, given the fiscal crises confronting state governments and the fact that Medicaid prohibits such payments, political leaders tend to be concerned over the potentially high costs of these programs. As noted by Nathan Linsk, Sharon Keigher, and Suzanne Osterbusch (1988, p. 211), all of the state efforts to pay family caregivers "emphasized the principle of not supplanting other sources of support and most emphasized not making payments for existing levels of unpaid care."

The federal government also provides dependent care tax credits but on a very restricted basis. Relatively small annual amounts are available to caregivers if the older person resides in their home, but only when everyone in the household works. Moreover, these tax credits tend to benefit more affluent families rather than those who need them the most (Longino, 1988). A few states, such as Oregon, Arizona, Idaho, and Iowa, utilize income incentives to encourage care. According to Rivlin and Wiener (1988), however, these subsidies are extremely low and few families take advantage of them.

## PRODUCTIVE AGING: WORKERS IN THE
## SERVICE SECTOR

As the service sector increasingly has supplanted manufacturing as a source of employment in the United States, its economic role has become essentially indistinguishable from that of big business. Corporate values prioritizing profit maximization, short-term goals, shareholder rights, and efficiency have been adopted gradually by the social services. Consequently, productivity in the service sector tends to be measured by quantitative manufacturing criteria.

While some service-producing industries such as those in finance, transportation, and distribution are linked to technological developments, manufacturing, and economic growth overall, more consumer-oriented services play a less obvious role in modern industrial society. Such services cannot and should not be gauged comparably. The pursuit of productivity in the manufacturing sector is, in part, both to reduce human labor and to increase output; greater productivity in services depends largely on the effectiveness of workers.

In long-term care, for example, productivity is best evaluated by how employees contribute to the well-being of the frail elderly. It is personnel who are most significant in the type of long-term care supplied by home-based agencies or nursing homes. The quality of the practitioner-client relationship is of utmost importance. Moreover, rapport tends to be linked to worker satisfaction, a factor that plays a lesser role in manufacturing (Macarov, 1982, pp. 118, 178).

Just as important, greater efficiency in the service sector may not generate superior results. As Robert Butler advises, we must reconceptualize or humanize our concepts of productivity to include qualitative as well as quantitative measurements (Butler & Gleason, 1985, p. 11).

The transformation of the American economy from manufacturing to technical and social services has affected workers unevenly, contributing to growing income inequalities. There has been a serious transfer of income between the classes in the United States rather than between generations. Robert Reich (1989) points out that routine personal-service workers, including those employed in long-term care, account for 30 percent of jobs in the United States. Although this sector has expanded rapidly since the 1970s, the work tends to be poorly paid, with limited benefits.

And though the quality of long-term care is dependent to a large extent on the personnel, nursing homes and home-care agencies tend to be employers of last resort. Women, African-Americans, and ethnic minorities comprise the overwhelming percentage of workers in the long-term care industry. Nearly 90 percent of nurses aides, orderlies, and attendants in nursing homes are women.

It is unlikely that workers in the long-term care sector will contribute to quality aging among the frail elderly. It is just as improbable that such workers will age productively. As Rosalie Kane notes,

[T]he decades-long debate about the cost-effectiveness of nursing home care compared to home care ignores a key point: The costs of both community-based and institutional long-term care are predicated on a poorly-paid, poorly-benefitted, and poorly-trained labor force. (1989, p. 291)

Long-term care employers rely on unlicensed and untrained people. In fact, there is no other health field in the United States that has such a high percentage of unskilled workers, comprising about 75 percent of the total (Johnson & Grant, 1985, p. 123).

Wages also are extremely low. Nursing aides, for example, averaged less than $4.00 per hour in 1986 (Margolis, 1980, p. 162). The Service Employees International Union (SEIU) recently found that many of the 110,000 U.S. workers employed in the $2 billion Beverly Enterprises (one of the largest nursing home operators in the country) qualified for food stamps and Medicaid. Although aides, orderlies, and attendants are projected to be among the fastest-growing job categories over the next several decades, wages will remain under the poverty line for a family of four (SEIU, 1989, p. 18). Added to this, employees in long-term care generally are denied health care benefits and pension plans.

Consequently, except during recessions, there is a shortage of personnel both in home care organizations and nursing homes. These industries also experience a high rate of turnover, absenteeism, and vacancies. In nursing homes, the turnover rate often reaches 75 percent annually.

Workers in nursing homes and home health agencies tend to confront a contradiction between their concern for the frail elderly and the realities of their own working conditions. Dalley (1988, p. 136) claims that such individuals have the following choices: make the best of a bad job; experience mental or physical illness themselves; or adhere to the job description, ignoring the real needs of their patients. Employees who are exploited and dehumanized themselves will have great difficulty in treating their patients in a caring, dignified manner.

CONCLUSION

This chapter has attempted to address some of the structural barriers both to productive aging among family caregivers and long-term care service workers and to successful aging among the frail older population. I have argued that such American cultural values such as individualism, privatization of human services, and maximization of profits, as well as the policy measures supporting them, have failed to serve the real needs of these sectors of society. These values and social policies also have encouraged the emergence of a costly, long-term care nonsystem.

Enhanced economic growth will not necessarily foster the conditions for productive aging. Rather, the United States must redefine both the goals of a productive society and the means for achieving them. Such changes must incorporate newly conceptualized views on the nature of economic growth, and the linkages to human and community needs.

In a truly productive society, decent employment is available for any individual who wants to work, including older people of all ages. A productive society also seeks and is able to provide the following: (1) economic security for all of its members, including the retired and frail elderly; (2) rising living standards for both workers and retirees; (3) an equitable distribution of wealth and income; (4) enhanced living and working environments; and (5) conditions allowing individuals to meet their maximum capabilities. Productive aging and quality aging can take place only in such a society today.

## NOTES

1. Although only 5 percent of all older people reside in an institution at any one time, about 25 percent of all those eighty-five and over live in an institutional facility. Moreover, about one-quarter of men and half of all women in this age category live alone (Koff, 1982).
2. In 1987, OBRA continued the waiver program and broadened allowable services.
3. In 1989, program costs, which served 44,000 people, amounted to $87 million (OMB Watch, 1990).
4. Some of the proposals include other age groups as well.
5. Only the Pepper bill was geared exclusively toward home care.
6. For details on these bills, see OMB Watch (1990).

## REFERENCES

Abel, E. K. (1987). Love is not enough: Family care of the frail elderly. Washington, DC: American Public Health Association.
Benjamin, A. E., Jr. (1985). Community-based long-term care. In C. Harrington, R. Newcomer, & C. Estes (Eds.), Long-term care of the elderly: Public policy issues (pp. 197–211). Beverly Hills, CA: Sage.
Bluestone, B., & Harrison, B. (1982). The deindustrialization of America: Plant closings, community abandonment and the dismantling of basic industry. New York: Basic Books.
Brickner, P. W., Lechich, A. J., Lipsman, R., & Scharer, L. (1987). Long-term health care: Providing a spectrum of services to the aged. New York: Basic Books.
Brody, E. M. (1981). Women in the middle and family help to older people. The Gerontologist, 21, 471–480.

Brody, E. M. (1985). Parent care as normative family stress. *The Gerontologist, 25,* 19–29.

Brody, E. M. (1990). *Women in the middle: Their parent-care years.* New York: Springer.

Brown, L. (1986, July–August). Taking in each other's laundry—the service economy. *New England Economic Review,* 25–34.

Burnley, C. (1987). Caregiving: The impact on emotional support for never-married women. *Journal of Aging Studies, 1,* 258–259.

Butler, R. N., & Gleason, H. P. (Eds.). (1985). *Productive aging: Enhancing vitality in later life.* New York: Springer.

Cantor, M. (1983). Strain among caregivers: A study of experience in the United States. *The Gerontologist, 23,* 597–603.

Caro, F. (1986). Relieving informal caregiver burden through organized service. In K. Pillemer & Rosalie Wolf (Eds.), *Elder abuse: Conflict in the family* (pp. 283–296). Dover, MA: Auburn House.

Dalley, G. (1988). *Ideologies of caring: Rethinking community and collectivism.* London: MacMillan Education.

Daniels, N. (1988). *Am I my parent's keeper?* New York: Oxford University Press.

Dunlop, B. D. (1980). Expanded home-based care for the impaired elderly: Solutions or pipe dream. *American Journal of Public Health, 70,* 514–519.

Edelman, P., & Hughs, S. (1990, March). The impact of community care on provision of informal care to homebound elderly persons. *Journals of Gerontology, 45*(2), 574.

Estes, C., & Lee, P. (1985). Social, political, and economic background of long-term care policy. In C. Harrington, R. Newcomer, & C. Estes (Eds.), *Long-term care of the elderly: Public policy issues* (pp. 17–39). Beverly Hills, CA: Sage.

Eustis, N., Greenberg, J., & Patten, S. (1984). *Long-term care for older persons: A policy perspective.* Monterey, CA: Brooks/Cole.

Greene, V. L. (1989). Editorial: Human capital and intergenerational justice. *The Gerontologist, 29,* 723–724.

Johnson, L., & Grant, L. (1985). *The nursing home.* Baltimore, MD: Johns Hopkins University Press.

Kane, N. M. (1989). The home care crisis of the nineties. *The Gerontologist, 29,* 24–31.

Kane, R. A. (1989). Editorial: Toward competent, caring paid caregivers. *The Gerontologist, 29,* 291–292.

Kane, R. L., & Kane, R. A. (1976). *Long-term care in six countries: Implications for the United States.* Washington, DC: U.S. Department of Health, Education and Welfare.

Kane, R. L., & Kane, R. A. (1985). *A will and a way: What the United States can learn from Canada about caring for the elderly.* New York: Columbia University Press.

Kayser-Jones, J. S. (1981). *Old, alone, and neglected.* Berkeley: University of California Press.

Kemper, P. (1990). Case management agency systems of administering long-term care: Evidence from the Channeling Demonstration. *The Gerontologist, 30,* 817–824.

Koff, T. H. (1982). *Long-term care: An approach to serving the elderly.* Boston: Little, Brown.

Landsberger, B. H. (1985). *Long-term care of the elderly: A comparative view of layers of care.* New York: St. Martin's Press.

Linsk, N., Keigher, S., & Osterbusch, S. (1988). A state's policies regarding paid family caregiving. *The Gerontologist, 28*(2), 204–212.

Longino, C. F. (1988). Who are the oldest Americans? *The Gerontologist, 28,* 515.

Macarov, D. (1982) *Worker productivity: Myths and reality.* Beverly Hills, CA: Sage.

Margolis, R. J. (1990). *Risking old age in America.* Boulder, CO: Westview.

OMB Watch. (1990, April). *Long-term care policy: Where are we going?* Boston: Gerontology Institute, University of Massachusetts at Boston.

Pepper Commission. (1990, September). *A call for action.* Final report, U.S. Bipartisan Commission on Comprehensive Health Care. Washington, DC: U.S. Government Printing Office.

Public Agenda Foundation and the Aspen Institute for Humanistic Studies. (1988). *The world at work: An international report on jobs, productivity, and human values.* New York: Octagon Books.

Quinn, J. (1989). Poverty in the extremes: The young and the old in America. *The Gerontologist, 29,* 838.

Reich, R. B. (1989, May 1). As the world turns: U.S. income inequality keeps on rising. *The New Republic,* 23–28.

Rivlin, A. M. & Wiener, J. (1988). *Caring for the disabled elderly: Who will pay.* Washington, DC: Brookings Institution.

Rosenwaike, I. (1985). *The extreme aged in America: A portrait of an expanding population.* Westport, CT: Greenwood Press.

Scharlach, A. E., & Boyd, S. (1989). Caregiving and employment. *The Gerontologist, 29,* 382–387.

Service Employees International Union. (1989). *Solutions for the new work force.* Cabin Johns, MD: Seven Locks Press.

Stephens, S. A., & Christianson, J. B. (1986). *Informal care of the elderly.* Lexington, MA: Lexington Books.

Stone, L. O., & Fletcher, S. (1988). Demographic variations in North America. In E. Rathbone-McCuan & B. Havens (Eds.), *North American elders: United States and Canadian perspectives* (pp. 9–36). Westport, CT: Greenwood Press.

Stone, R., Cafferata, G., & Sangl, J. (1987). *Caregivers of the elderly: A national profile.* Washington, DC: U.S. Public Health Service.

Streib, G. F., Folts, W. E., & Hilker, M. A. (1984). *Old homes—new families: Shared living for the elderly.* New York: Columbia University Press.

# Part IV

## Mediating Institutions

# 10

# Lost Traditions and Horizons Reclaimed: Religious Institutions and Productive Aging

## W. Andrew Achenbaum

"I doubt whether man can ever support at the same time complete religious independence and entire political freedom," Alexis de Tocqueville mused in *Democracy in America*. "And I am inclined to think that, if faith be wanting in him, he must be subject; and if he be free, he must believe" (1835, pp. 151–152). De Tocqueville accurately gauged the place of religion in the American experiment. Waves of immigrants have come in search of religious liberties, political freedom, and economic opportunity. Protestantism (in all of its denominational varieties) has been the dominating spiritual force, but the nation's religious heritage has been enriched by the Greek Orthodox; Italian, Irish, and Polish Catholics; Hasidic and Reform Jews; Hindus, Buddhists, and Taoists; Huguenots; Mormons; Occultists; and a wide array of evangelical and sectarian groups (Ahlstrom, 1972; Marty, 1970; Niebuhr, 1937). Bigotry and intolerance have festered here, to be sure, but public sentiment, reinforced by the First Amendment, has considered most beliefs and disbeliefs private matters.

More than 150 years after de Tocqueville wrote these words, despite evidence to the contrary, citizens in the world's oldest democracy still claim to be a religious people. In 1981, over 80 percent of all Americans (including 93 percent of those over age sixty-five) said that they believed in the divinity of Jesus; most agreed when asked by pollsters that "God loves me even though I may not always please Him." Five years later, 81 percent of those surveyed under the age of thirty considered religion at least fairly important in their lives; 90 percent of those over sixty-five agreed (Moberg, 1990). Faith appears vital among men and women of advanced age. A case study of 700 centenarians revealed that an overwhelming majority considered religion "very important" to them (Beard, 1969).

While survey researchers are capable of eliciting considerable support for religiosity among Americans, it was not altogether clear what respondents meant by "religion" in the survey. As Williams James noted in *The Varieties of Religious Experience* (1901, pp. 40–41), "at the outset we are struck by one great partition which divides the religious field. On the one side of it lies institutional, on the other personal religion." Americans find it easier to articulate what they mean by the former than the latter. More than nine out of ten declare a religious preference, a statistic basically unchanged since the 1970s. But "the fact that religious interest and involvement are high," observes pollster George Gallup (1984, p. 9), should not blind us to the reality that Americans' actual "commitment is low." Since the peak-attendance years of the late 1950s, there has been a marked decline in affiliation among mainline Protestant churches. Less than 40 percent of the population attend religious services weekly; people under thirty evince the greatest disinterest. Such data suggest a shift in institutional dynamics.

Despite the attenuation of religious attendance among the young, surveys repeatedly reveal strong participation by the elderly. Those over sixty-five currently are twice as likely as those under thirty to read the Bible daily and to be involved in a prayer or meditation group; sixty-six percent of the older population claim to have at least a fairly high spiritual commitment compared to 34 percent of those under thirty (Moberg, 1990). Does such evidence indicate that people become more religious as they age (Burgess, 1952; Orbach, 1961; Payne, 1977)? Insufficient longitudinal data preclude a firm answer (Blazer & Palmore, 1976). Nonetheless, if the expression of piety were just a cohort phenomenon, there should have been a decline in religiosity found among successive surveys of the elderly during the twentieth century.

Indeed, the membership of America's religious institutions is aging at a faster rate than the population as a whole. In 1984, 42 percent of all Protestants, 34 percent of all Catholics, and 39 percent of all Jews were over the age of fifty; in the Gallup survey, 19 percent of the Protestants, 13 percent of the Catholics, and 18 percent of the Jews were at least sixty-five (Gallup, 1984). The graying of mainline denominations is even more apparent. Every fifteen minutes another Presbyterian reaches the age of sixty-five. The number of senior citizens in that denomination increased by 23 percent during the 1980s; the number over eighty-five by 67 percent.

In light of such population trends and social indicators, one might expect that scholars would pay considerable attention to religion and aging. Curiously, academic interest in the topic has waned as the numbers of elders in churches and synagogues has increased, though religion was considered a "hot" topic in gerontology's formative years. Paul B. Maves and J. Lennart Cedarleaf (with the help of Clare DeGruchy, Lawrence Frank, Ollie Randall, and Edward J. Stieglitz) published *Older People and the Church* in 1949. The volume helped to fill a "surprising" gap in the research agenda Otto Pollak (1948, p. 161) compiled for the Social Science Research Council. During and after the 1950 National Conference on Aging, Maves aided ministers and other delegates in translating his research into policy. He contributed his then most recent work on "aging, religion, and church" in a fifty-one-page chapter in Clark Tibbitts' *Handbook of Social Gerontology* (1960). Significantly, four separate chapters in James Birren's companion volume (1959) also dealt with late-life religiosity. Matilda White Riley and associates devoted two separate chapters to religion and aging in their three-volume *Aging and Society* (1968–1972).

The recent trilogy of gerontologic handbooks, by contrast, devote little space to aging and religion. In the first edition of the *Handbook of Aging and the Social Sciences* (Binstock & Shanas, 1976), for instance, Jack Goody has only a column and a half on religion in preindustrial societies, Marjorie Fiske Lowenthal and Betsy Robinson discuss religious institutions' place in social networks in just one column, and Richard Kalish has half a column in a chapter on death. The index to the second edition directs the curious reader to a page in my chapter on societal perceptions of aging and the aged (Achenbaum, 1985a); the third edition has no reference at all to aging and religion—though in the third edition of the *Handbook of the Psychology of Aging* (Birren & Schaie, 1990), James Jackson and Toni Antonucci devote a paragraph to the importance of religion to ethnic groups. Analyses of articles in *The Gerontologist* and the *Journals of Gerontology* as well as abstracts from Gerontological Society meetings further suggest that the subfield is marginal. The *Journal of Aging and Religion*, first published in 1984, has fewer than 2,000 institutional and individual subscribers.

Academics hardly have been alone in choosing not to focus much on religion and aging. Some clerical and lay leaders, hostile toward academic research, have expressed a "fear of manipulation and the regulatory uses of research to control people in ways that might potentially demean them as human beings" (Cook, 1977, p. 9; for the larger context, see Lacey, 1989). A few theologians, dismayed that research on aging eschews developmental themes, have recommended a life span orientation that emphasizes greater attention to perceptions of religion in childhood than in old age (Cantelon, 1967). Princeton Theological Seminary's Seward Hiltner (1975) has pointed to a more pernicious reason for ageism. "The tendency to deny, evade, or otherwise fail to take seriously the confrontation of the aging process," claimed Hiltner, has precluded theological attempts to grapple with the meaning of late life (p. 97). "Perhaps the deepest question of all is whether the elements that dominate our society will continue their present ambivalent attitudes toward both aging and older people or whether the negative aspects of the present attitudes can be eliminated," Hiltner concluded. "It may be at this point that theology's greatest responsibility lies" (p. 101). Hiltner's goal is commendable, but he focused only on one theme— the role of values in shaping institutional norms—pertinent to this volume. Other issues merit attention.

This chapter argues that U.S. Protestant, Catholic, and Jewish organizations qua institutions have consciously or unwittingly forced elders out of the mainstream in all of the ways in which the editors of this collection have hypothesized this kind of discrimination happens. First, institutional ageism is rampant in the churches. "Hoary heads" rarely are honored either in the pulpit (unless the individuals are major leaders) or the pew (unless they wield power). "Middle management" tends to get pushed out by advancing youth. Second, American religious bodies suffer from cultural as well as structural lag. They have not adapted strategies in their respective traditions for ministering to the aged, taking into account what aging congregants say they want and need. Third, although women lately have gained new clerical responsibilities, churches and synagogues seem to have forgotten the vital roles that widows and other older women used to play in religious life. Fourth, by so sharply distinguishing between religion's private and organizational dimensions, churches and synagogues may unwittingly endorse an assumption, dominant in American society, that productivity depends on activity. Yet many "productive" religious activities are conducted in prayerful silence, in solitary contemplation disengaged from ordinary pursuits. Such obstacles to the incorporation of older people into the full range of productive aging as it applies to religion can be surmounted. Religious institutions can be innovators if they so desire. Ironically, their best way to broaden horizons in the 1990s is to recapture traditions lost to a modern era.

## "HONOR YOUR FATHER AND YOUR MOTHER"

"Honor your father and your mother," Moses was told on Sinai, "that your days may be long in number in the land which the Lord your God gives you" (Ex. 20:12). Thus the covenant between God and Israel stipulates generational ties bound to affect the quality of life for all age groups. The Torah elaborates a variety of promises and punishments associated with this Commandment (Gen. 15:15; Deut. 21:18–21, 27:16, 19; Lev. 19:32, 20:9). Proverbs (30:1–4, 11, 17) restates the theme in poetic form.

New Testament passages underscore the notion of reciprocity. Colossians (3:20), for instance, tells children to "obey your parents in everything, for this pleases the Lord," but adds in the next verse that fathers should "not provoke your children, lest they become discouraged." In hard cases, however, the elders seem to have the spirit of the law on their side. Christ dismisses as "hypocrites" those who "for the sake of your tradition ... have made void the word of God." He criticizes attempts to renege on care for the elderly because the only funds available are earmarked for the temple and its staff (Matt. 15:1–9; Mark 7:9–13). Reverence for God entails respect for age (for more on biblical images of age, see Harris, 1987; Sapp, 1987).

Even so, ageism has become a norm pervading modern American religious institutional life. Maves and Cedarleaf (1949, pp. 204–207) noted that a host of disagreeable traits—"meticulousness," "eccentricity," "overly responsive" expressions of love and gratitude, a "flood of repressed grievances," intransigence, insecurities—prompted clergy to keep interactions with older people "short and formal." Subsequent researchers confirmed that "while it appears that most churches are willing to *passively accept* the participation of older people in church affairs, few are willing or able to *actively solicit* the participation of ill, handicapped or isolated older people" (Atchley, 1980, pp. 335–336).

Elderly men and women often perceive themselves to be treated like "has-beens." Some aged members question their acceptance in churches and synagogues that stress "family ministries" and that make pleas for financial help that they no longer can support. Stairs, poor lighting, and small print pose barriers for them. So do hard benches and having to kneel when there are no handrails. Transportation to services can be problematic on weekends. Some older people feel embarrassed because they cannot dress up; others feel stigmatized when their annual financial contributions seem modest. Sometimes ministers, rabbis, and priests exacerbate the situation. Since clergy rarely receive formal gerontologic training and because many harbor gerontophobic fears, a cycle of mutual disengagement sometimes ensues (Cook, 1976; Gray & Moberg, 1977; Moberg, 1990; Thorson & Cook, 1977).

Older people occasionally believe that their advancing years per se should preclude service to the church. Red Barber, one of America's great sportscasters, was fired by the Yankees at the age of fifty-eight. Now eighty-two, he enjoys a cultlike following among listeners to National Public Radio's "Morning Edition," who tune in for his 3.5-minute conversation with forty-four-year-old Bob Edwards. Yet Barber did not hesitate to give up his lay reader's license in the Episcopal Church when he turned seventy. "I feel very strongly that the strength of the church depends on young people coming along and that old people should not be in their way," Barber observed. "If I'm up there reading the lesson or the Psalms, then a younger person is not" (Minzesheimer, 1990, p. 4).

Indifference to elders in religious affairs does not evolve just from contemporary prejudices and misunderstandings, however. Ancient canons have become invisible, older customs obsolescent. There are at least 250 different references to old age in the Old Testament alone, yet scriptural passages relevant to "productive" aging rarely are read. Devout Jews repeat the Fifth Commandment in the course of the annual reading of the Torah. But Roman Catholics as well as those Protestant and Orthodox churches that use the lectionary created by theologians after Vatican II will hear Exodus 20:12 only once every three years. Christians too often take the phrase "children of God" (John 1:12) literally. Most members are baptized and first receive communion before they become adults. There are no comparable sacraments for the aged besides the burial rite. For two out of three Protestants, Christian education ends around age twelve, when few are mature enough to learn about spirituality in aging (Capps, 1983; McManus, 1990).

Similar patterns obtain in Judaism. Orthodox Jews probably observe the most complete set of life-cycle rituals (including circumcision, *bar/bat mitzvah* ceremonies, and the groom's reading of the Torah at the Sabbath service preceding his wedding). But there are no services designed for elders, though funerals and rituals such as *Oneg Shabbat* can lend themselves to age specificity. Indeed, older Jews may be more inventive than others in creating late-life ceremonies. In Barbara Myerhoff's *Number Our Days* (1978), lower-income, secular, Yiddish-speaking members of a Venice, California, senior center staged an elaborate ninety-fifth birthday observance for Jacob Kovitz, their president. Like Moses, Kovitz died during the festivities. Participants saw much symbolism and meaning in the events they witnessed. But their understandings (as well as the ritual itself) should be interpreted as a specific, adaptive response to the finitude of life, a recognition of religion's role in helping people come to terms with death (Clements, 1981; Moberg, 1962; Myerhoff, 1978).

Are aging religious leaders exempt from the disrespect for elders in the pews? There is evidence to suggest a few are so privileged. "While men in their prime conceived the great religions," observed G. Stanley Hall (1922, p. 420), "the old made them prevail." About two-thirds of all papal tenure has been rendered by men over sixty-five (Lehman, 1953). John XXIII, chosen to be a caretaker, was seventy-eight when he convened the Vatican Council that liberalized the Roman Catholic church. U.S. history is full of examples of clergy who served as productive elders. Ebeneazer Gay in 1781 marked his sixty-fourth year as pastor of the first parish of Hingham, Massachusetts, by preaching on Joshua 14:10, "And now, lo I am this day four score and five years old" (Smith, 1978). All Mormon presidents—and most of their counselors—during the twentieth century have served past their eightieth birthday (Arrington & Bitton, 1979).

Yet the prospects for an aging cleric, who has not secured a leadership position or an affluent pulpit, have never been good. Rare is the individual tapped for high office past the age of sixty. If it is time for a minister to leave, his options usually include a call to a congregation on the decline, one looking for a part-time (i.e., less expensive) minister who will be accorded not much more status than a student pastor (Moberg, 1962). Although evidence remains anecdotal, it seems that older women qualified to serve as clergy face both age and sex discrimination in seeking suitable posts. The treatment of aged nuns in the Roman Catholic church is quite different than for superannuated priests.

The status of the elderly in black churches epitomizes how ageism affects even institutions renowned for their regard for older congregants and for the esteem bestowed on senior pastors. Blacks are more likely than whites to state that religion is important in their lives, and they are more regular in church attendance. More than 80 percent of all blacks indicate that the church has helped the condition of American blacks. Only 10 percent of all blacks report no current religious affiliation. With other avenues of upward mobility traditionally blocked, many of the ablest black men often have been attracted to the ministry. By virtue of their authority, moreover, black pastors have been able to effect health-related behavioral changes and risk reduction among members of their congregation by advocating preventive-medicine measures (Levin, 1986; Taylor, 1988; Taylor, Thornton, & Chatters, 1987).

More effectively than mainline Protestant denominations, black churches can sustain the commitment of adult members. Apathy must be battled, however, to the extent that certain familiar terms are used to characterize the situation. "Many black churches are senior citizens' homes," notes Cecil L. Murray, pastor of Los Angeles's booming First African Methodist Episcopal church. They do not attract young adults and youths (Kane, Monroe, & Simpson, 1990, p. 89). That the median age of black ministers has "reached a dangerously high 52" is represented as a source of concern to black churches; this has happened presumably because the clergy must compete more vigorously with politics, business, and the academy for recruits. Ageist assumptions lie behind such characterizations, which put a premium on youth and discount the cumulative assets of age.

## "DO NOT CAST ME OFF IN THE TIME OF OLD AGE"

Heeding the prayer of the old man in Psalm 71 to "forsake me not when my strength is spent," Jews and Christians for centuries have cared for their elderly sick and indigent in hospitals and almshouses. Ironically, the ways that religious institutions have fulfilled this venerable ministry may have impeded its efforts to encourage "productive aging." The elderly's needs are fit into models of dependency, not channeled into empowering relationships.

Most nineteenth-century, private, old-age homes in the United States were founded as sectarian ventures. The oldest home in Philadelphia, the Indigent Widow's and Single Women's Society (1817), provided a "Christian" atmosphere. Lutherans built a home for their own in 1859, followed by Jews (1865), Methodists (1865), Baptists (1869), Presbyterians (1872 and 1885), and Evangelicals (1888). Quakers erected a Home for Aged and Infirm Colored People in 1865; Catholics underwrote a Home for Infirm People of the Little Sisters of the Poor a few years later (Achenbaum, 1985a; Haber, 1983). The response of religious organizations to late-life need complemented other philanthropic impulses. A third of the country's benevolent institutions were church-related in 1903; lower-income people were prime beneficiaries (Moberg, 1962).

Synagogues and churches continue to provide vital institutional support for older people in need. Researchers frequently note that Jewish programs, especially in elderly housing, are among America's most extensive and imaginative. The ways in which staff have used religion to promote meaningful activity among the frail residents of Boston's Hebrew Rehabilitation Center, for instance, has become a model for others (Abrams, 1977; Biller, 1952; Palmore, 1985). Case studies in Hartford, Connecticut, and New Mexico indicate that Protestant ministries focus on calls to the homebound or hospitalized, prayer groups, and broadly mandated social-action initiatives. Bequests of $250,000 or more, such as one made to Trinity Cathedral in Little Rock to construct a senior center, are not uncommon (New Mexico, 1966; Roozen, McKinney, & Carroll, 1984; "By Will and Deed," 1990). Until recently, Roman Catholics operated independent networks under the auspices of the National Conference of Catholic Charities.

The 1971 White House Conference on Aging encouraged religious groups to broaden their scope. Delegates at the proceedings discussed obstacles to constructive action. Some discounted the potential for a senior adult ministry, noting that most older people were not institutionalized and did not seem to require (or want) special care. They recognized that "charities," which served mainly the middle-class, dependent, or disabled aged did not do enough. Still, religious leaders were concerned about forming yet another organization, one that might further isolate the aged. Financial and time constraints loomed large (Gray & Moberg, 1977; Kerr, 1980). Institutional inertia dampened creative thinking, particularly since there seemed to be no compelling need to alter the status quo.

To serve as a catalyst for fresh initiatives, the National Interfaith Coalition on Aging (NICA) was formed in March 1972. By mid-decade, more than 100 Jewish, Protestant, and Catholic organizations—occasionally in cooperation with the National Council on Aging and the American Association of Retired Persons—were sponsoring 1,577 programs in forty-eight states and Canada. But in NICA's opinion, more had to be done; religious bodies in the United States were said to exhibit a relatively low effort on behalf of the elderly (Cook, 1977, p. 94). Expanding institutional networks across denominations was not enough. Different approaches were necessary. Early in 1991, NICA affiliated with the National Council on the Aging (NCOA). The merger should put religious bodies in better touch with progressive views about how to provide a wide range of services to the aging.

Surprisingly, religious institutions have made little effort thus far to foster *intergenerational* programs. Churches serve appropriately as satellites in the geriatric health care arena (Hendrickson, 1986). With support from the Robert Wood Johnson Foundation (1989), Interfaith Volunteer Caregivers provide services for the frail elderly and disabled people in their homes. In light of the debate over age versus needs-based programs prompted by Bernice Neugarten (1983) among others, however, religious groups might function effectively by focusing their attention on the needs of low-income poor people. "It may well be one of history's greater ironies," suggests Phillip Hammond (1969, p. 323), "that, at the same time society becomes more differentiated, it produces larger proportions of aged persons whose needs appear to be for less differentiation. The gerontological strategy of the church should, it would seem, be directed toward easing the strains of that differentiation."

There is ample scriptural justification for promoting intergenerational complementarity (Joel 2:28; Malachi 4:6; Luke 1:17). Some congregations have established a "Ministry of Elders" that empowers the aged to attend to the needs of their peers and younger people, as a way to effect "liberation of ageism" (Hougland, 1974). NICA sponsors Project HEAD (Help Elderly Adults Direct) and broad-based preventive and rehabilitative programs (Clingan, 1975). Such initiatives would seem to get religious institutions closer to their goal to "let the church be a 'whole' church" (Culver, 1961, p. 137).

Fostering intergenerational arrangements, however, may prove to be a risky venture in ageist institutional cultures. It becomes all too easy for the elderly's specific needs to go unaddressed when their needs are pooled with other worthy causes. Program officers tend to fulfill their particular missions by "borrowing" funds from "general" categories. And why not? Religious organizations today operate like other large bureaucracies. The only way for churches and synagogues to escape this policy conundrum is to ensure that the needs and the talents of the aged are given high priority in programs that consider involvement a lifelong commitment.

## "LET A WIDOW BE ENROLLED IF SHE IS NOT LESS THAN SIXTY YEARS OF AGE"

The radical suggestion that in intergenerational programs potentially disenfranchised elders help others rather than simply be ministered to has roots in the early years of the Jesus movement. The Jewish custom of caring for legally defenseless widows and orphans (Gen. 38; Ex. 22:11; Deut. 14:29, 16:11, 14) provided a precedent for the "daily distribution" to widows mentioned in Acts 6:1. A letter of St. Paul to Timothy lays out guidelines for the arrangement: Christians were to "honor widows who are real widows." To be eligible for financial support from the community, widows had to be over sixty, monogamous, and without kin able to support them. Perhaps the most stringent requirement of this means test was that a recipient must be "well attested for her good deeds, as one who has brought up children, shown hospitality, washed the feet of the saints, relieved the afflicted, and devoted herself to doing good in every way" (I Tim. 5:9–10). Support in old age presupposed continuing a ministry of service that had begun earlier in life.

Older women were Mothers of the Church. Some, like Anna, functioned as prophets (Lk. 2:36–38). Others, like Melania the Elder and her grand-daughter in turn, devoted their widowhood to mortification and good works (Reuther & McLaughlin, 1979). Still others became deaconesses, a class of respected senior women analogous to presbyters. As ministers to other women, they visited the sick, baptized, and led prayer services. This order was suppressed in the West during the sixth century; it survived a bit longer in the East, eventually being absorbed into monastic life (McBrien, 1981). Increasingly, as nuns were expected to carry on earlier ideals, "the virgins were ranked above the widows" (Clements, 1981, p. 49).

Remnants of this older tradition were to be found, albeit in different form, in the American experience until recently. A dying cohort of Eldresses preserved the Shaker spirit (Achenbaum, 1985b). Mary Baker Eddy, who published *Science and Health* at age fifty-four, presided over the Christian Science faith until her death at eighty-nine in 1910. Ellen Harmon White remained a leader of the Seventh-Day Adventists until 1915 when she died at eighty-seven. It is worth noting that all three of these groups emphasize the connection between living well and doing good.

Particularly in light of changing demographics, religious institutions need to pay far greater attention to older women. As a group, they are more likely than younger ones to attend church and more likely than their male counterparts to participate in religious activities (Moberg, 1990; Riley & Associates, 1968). Aged women are not all alike, of course, and important variations have been noted. Black elderly widows report lower subjective religiosity and church attendance than elderly black married women (Taylor, 1986). While aging Mexican-American women tend to be faithful worshipers, church attendance appears to have diminishing significance over time for life satisfaction (Levin & Markides, 1988). Such evidence brings to mind the observations by de Tocqueville and William James that institutional forms of religion are not the only sources of spiritual well-being in old age.

## "YOUR OLD MEN SHALL DREAM DREAMS, AND YOUR YOUNG MEN SHALL SEE VISIONS"

Implicit in this chapter thus far has been the assumption that older people must *do something* in order to be exemplars of productive aging. This orientation is consistent with the underlying theme of this volume, which seeks to understand how various organizations (including organized religion) either promote or discourage the involvement of older people in their spheres and activities in the larger society. Yet the Bible states that the people of God must "know that man does not live by bread alone, but that man lives by everything that proceeds out of the mouth of the Lord" (Deut. 8:3; Matt. 6:25–26). Perhaps to a greater extent than any other organization, religious institutions must count as "productive" those who do nothing less (or more) than *be someone* in touch with the spiritual dimensions of human existence. To be faithful to a strand of Judeo-Christian tradition, we must go beyond the scope of this book and briefly suggest how life-stage changes in spiritual growth (suggested by this section's epigraph from Joel 2:28) relate to productive aging.

The Book of Job, for instance, might be interpreted as the story of a productive elder's struggle to get right his relationship with God. Beset with tragedy, Job removes himself to a dungheap to sit in silence. His spiritual journey is punctuated by exchanges with men his own age and the youthful Elihu before he encounters the Voice from the Whirlwind. His relationships with himself, others, and God are utterly changed by this experience: "I will be quiet, comforted that I am dust" (Job 42:6, trans. Mitchell, 1987). Spiritually renewed, Job intercedes for his friends; that action taken, God then restores his health, his wealth, and his *raison d'être* (Achenbaum & Orwoll, 1991).

If Job serves as a Jewish archetype of spiritual aging, St. Anthony of Egypt (A.D. 251–355) embodies the Christian analog. His ascetic life began at twenty; at age thirty-five he retreated to live alone on a desert mountain for two decades. He then organized a monastic order of hermits. Periodically, Anthony sallied forth to fight demons and heretics; he was nearly 100 when he traveled to Alexandria to preach against Arianism (*Encyclopaedia Brittanica*, 1985). Anthony's soul-making was enough to qualify him for sainthood.

The American experience offers a few examples of aging spirituality. Thomas Cole in the 1840s represented how "the chains of corporeal existence" fall away in old age, affording a glimpse of "the angelic Being of whose presence until now the voyager has been unconscious" (Cole, 1991; Noble, 1853). James Birren (1987, p. 3) updates the picture noting that "a shift toward an interior focus lends itself to a more spiritual outlook," one less analytical and more affective and interpretive. Those who study black religiosity confirm the pattern among the aged (Taylor, 1988b). For artists such as Käthe Kollwitz, manifestations of spirituality are graphic. She drew fifty self-portraits to facilitate her "pilgrimage toward self-knowledge" (Winkler, 1990, p. 43). Consider, too, the popularity accorded Thomas Merton's writings (not to mention the appeal of New Age and Pentecostal products). "The monk abandons the world only in order to listen more intently to the deepest and most neglected voices that proceed from its inner depth" (in Leech, 1977, p. 189). Standing deliberately at the margins, eschewing the arts of commerce and politics, Merton felt his sense of God come together: "Our real journey in life is interior. . . . Never was it more necessary for us to respond to that action" (in Mott, 1984, p. 543).

## AN AGENDA FOR RELIGIOUS INSTITUTIONS IN THE 1990S

When forced to retire from her job with the Presbyterian church on her sixty-fifth birthday, Maggie Kuhn launched a new career. As convenor of the Gray Panthers, she has advocated radical social changes to benefit young and old alike. Kuhn still believes that religious institutions are capable of responding to the needs and opportunities of an aging society:

Churches and synagogues have a tremendous opportunity in the last years of this century for creative new ministries, if they take seriously the experiences, skills, and human resources represented in older members of their congregations. The churches are acculturated like other institutions in Western society and still remain youth-oriented. I believe that this is a detriment to their ministry. It deprives the young of a holistic approach to life as a continuum. (1981, p. 238)

Kuhn argues that changes in individuals' life courses, and in aging societies, require an adaptation of institutional dynamics, including those of religious institutions. She is not alone in looking to institutional-level interventions. "Programmatic strategies of the past 20 years, in all likelihood, will be unresponsive to the dramatically changing needs of the population and to the political climate of the 1990s and beyond," claim the editors of *Diversity in Aging*. "Institutions will have to become knowledgeable, remain flexible, exercise creativity, and be prepared to make some hard choices" (Bass, Kutza, & Torres-Gil, 1990, pp. xiii, 176).

Demographic exigencies clearly impel religious institutions to rethink their missions. Congregations are growing older at a faster rate than America's population. Synagogues and churches still are addressing the needs of a relatively small proportion of their aged congregants—"those" whom "we" can plainly see require help. Yet the healthy aged also have needs. Some research suggests that religious attendance may be conducive to better health in later years (Levin & Vanderpool, 1987). But not only do the aged want something from religious institutions, they also have something to give them. The talents and wisdom that accrue with age are relatively unexploited human resources. "Americans who are over 50 are not immune to becoming inactive," write George Gallup and Richard Castelli. Churches should guard against complacency with their members in this age group (Gallup & Castelli, 1989, p. 147).

A shift in religious ideas, and not just about spirituality, might also broaden perspectives on productive aging. We Americans have become more attuned to the heterogeneity of our older population and the diversity of older people's backgrounds. At the same time, our religious institutions are in the midst of recovering their pluralist traditions. "We find ourselves with diverse religious classics among many religious traditions," University of Chicago theologian David Tracy (1987) asserts. "We find ourselves glimpsing the plurality within each tradition while also admitting the ambiguity of every religion: liberating possibilities to be retrieved, errors to be criticized, unconscious distortions to be unmasked" (p. 112). Churches and synagogues might be able to broaden their horizons if they are earnest about rediscovering lost traditions. The search for a usable past will not be daunting. Religious bodies, more than other institutions, appreciate the truth of Faulkner's observation that "the past is not really dead; it is not even past." By definition, religious traditions are there to be made lively.

How, then, might religious institutions promote productive aging?

- Rather than concentrating primarily on the religious education of the young, more effort should be made to develop a life-course strategy. To wit: campus ministries tend to operate as if colleges and universities were age ghettos. If faculty and staff could be drawn into its activities—with lectures and social events—they in turn probably would be more inclined to involve their students and trainees in the network. Elderhostel provides another underutilized vehicle for providing religious education for senior citizens.

- More to do with aging should be introduced into the liturgy. It has been easier for some to accept women as clergy as examples from the Bible become familiar. A similar tack might be used to justify a broadened ministry of elders: Naomi, Elizabeth, Paul, and Barzillai are good role models. And discussions of death should not be limited to funerals and Holy Week. Debility, dependence, and death are key features of human existence.

- Most aging programs should be transgenerational in scope, but funds for the aged to be used by them alone should be clearly earmarked in "general" allocations. Preventive health care programs fit this rubric.

- Senior laity should be encouraged to take on leadership duties in volunteer programs. Churches and synagogues might consider opening child care facilities staffed by members of their congregations to expand the options available to working mothers. Similarly, retired people might help the young and unemployed develop the skills they need to find employment.

- Religious institutions should revive the diaconate of service that older women used to fulfill. Not only could deacons serve in weekly worship, but they also could direct local outreach programs to the sick and to the poor. Some might also feel called to serve as representatives of the local congregation in ministries overseas.

- If "spirituality" is indeed a distinctive feature of religion, then churches and synagogues must resist the temptation to become "domesticated as sacred canopies for the status quo" (Tracy, 1987, p. 83). Productive aging is not just a matter of giving, but of doing. Sometimes it entails being silent, contemplative, and open to the possibility of transcendence. Religious pluralism must take account of diversity in productive aging.

Once religious institutions take their ministry to the aging seriously, as Maggie Kuhn (1981, p. 265) has anticipated, "a second Reformation waits in the wings!" Possibly, but this chapter ends on a more modest note. As Berkeley sociologist Robert Bellah put it, "[I]t is the middle course—maintaining group identities and group boundaries while remaining open to knowledge of and cooperation with others, including those of different faiths—that is authentically biblical and authentically American and that holds the greatest hope for our future" (Bellah & Greenspahn, 1987, p. 231).

The opportunities for productive aging challenge religious institutions to broaden their horizons by restoring some old customs and bringing them into their current modus operandi. To be true to our pluralist tradition and responsive to a future in which the needs of older congregants will grow only more diverse, there must be *many* ministries *to* and *by* elders. Such a tack is bound to create personal discomfort, bureaucratic messiness, and intramural rivalries. But if the purpose of religious institutions is to draw people into an inclusive community committed to doing what is understood (however dimly) to be God's will, there really is no other alternative.

## REFERENCES

Abrams, E. (1977). Religion in the rehabilitation of the aged. In J. A. Thorson & T. C. Cook, Jr. (Eds.), *Spiritual well-being of the elderly* (pp. 54–62). Springfield, IL: Charles C. Thomas.

Achenbaum, W. A. (1985a). Societal perceptions of the aging and aged. In R. H. Binstock & E. Shanas (Eds.), *Handbook of aging and the social sciences* (2d ed., pp. 129–148). New York: Van Nostrand Reinhold.

Achenbaum, W. A. (1985b). Religion in the lives of the elderly. In G. Lesnoff-Caravaglia (Ed.), *Values, ethics, and aging* (pp. 98–116). New York: Human Sciences Press.

Achenbaum, W. A., & Orwoll, L. (1991). The wisdom of Job. *International Journal of Aging and Human Development.*

Ahlstrom, S. E. (1972). *A religious history of the American people.* New Haven, CT: Yale University Press.

Arrington, L. J., & Bitton, D. (1979). *The Mormon experience.* New York: Vintage Books.

Atchley, R. C. (1980). *Social forces of late life* (3d ed.). Belmont, CA: Wadsworth Publishing.

Bass, S. A., Kutza, E. A., & Torres-Gil, F. (Eds.). (1990). Diversity in aging: The challenges facing the White House Conference on Aging. In S. A. Bass, E. A. Kutza, and F. Torres-Gil, *Diversity in aging: Challenges facing planners & policymakers in the 1990s.* (pp. xiii–xix). Glenview, IL: Scott, Foresman.

Beard, B. B. (1969). Religion at 100. *Modern Maturity, 12*(3), 1–4.

Bellah, R. N., & Greenspahn, F. E. (1987). *Uncivil religion.* New York: Crossroad.

Biller, N. (1952). The role of the synagogue in work with older people. *Jewish Social Service Quarterly, 28,* 284–289.

Binstock, R. H., & Shanas, E. (Eds.). (1976). *Handbook of aging and the social sciences.* New York: Van Nostrand Reinhold.

Birren, J. E. (Ed.). (1959). *Aging and the individual.* Chicago: University of Chicago Press.

Birren, J. E. (1987). *Spiritual maturity in psychological development.* Unpublished manuscript.

Birren, J. E., & Schaie, K. W. (1990). *Handbook of the psychology of aging* (3d ed.). New York: Academic Press.

Blazer, D., & Palmore, E. (1976). Religion and aging in a longitudinal panel. *The Gerontologist, 16*(1), 82–85.

Burgess, E. (1952, January). Family living in the later decades. *Annals of the American Academy of Political and Social Science*, 279.

By will and deed. (Advent-Epiphany 1990). *TAD (The Anglican Digest)*, p. 53.

Cantelon, J. E., et al. (1967). *Religion and aging: The behavioral and social sciences look at religion and aging.* Los Angeles: Rossmoor-Cortese Institute, University of Southern California.

Capps, D. (1983). *Life cycle theory and pastoral care.* Philadelphia: Fortress Press.

Clements, W. M. (Ed.). (1981). *Ministry with the aging.* San Francisco: Harper & Row.

Clingan, D. F. (1975). *Aging persons in the community of faith.* Bloomington, IN: Indiana Commission on the Aged and Aging, Institute on Religion and Aging.

Cole, T. R. (1991). *The voyage of life.* New York: Cambridge University Press.

Cook, T. C., Jr (1977). *The religious sector explores its mission in aging.* Atlanta: National Interfaith Coalition on Aging.

Culver, E. T. (1961). *New church programs with the aging.* New York: Association Press.

De Tocqueville, A. (1835). *Democracy in America.* Richard D. Heffner, Ed. New York: Signet Press, 1984.

*Encyclopaedia Brittanica* (15th ed.). (1985). Chicago: Encyclopaedia Brittanica.

Gallup, G. (1984). *Religion in America.* Princeton, NJ: Princeton Religion Research Center.

Gallup, G., & Castelli, R. (1989). Religion in America: A second look. *Christian Century, 45*, 23–25, 31.

Gray, R. M., & Moberg, D. O. (1977). *The church and the older person* (rev. ed.). Grand Rapids, MI: William B. Eerdmans.

Haber, C. (1983). *Beyond sixty-five.* New York: Cambridge University Press.

Hall, G. S. (1922). *Senescence.* New York: D. Appelton & Sons.

Hammond, P. E. (1969). Aging and the ministry. In M. White Riley, J. W. Riley, Jr., & M. E. Johnson (Eds.), *Aging and society* (vol. II). New York: Russell Sage Foundation.

Harris, J. G. (1987). *Biblical perspectives on aging.* Philadelphia: Fortress Press.

Hendrickson, S. L. (1986). Churches as geriatric health clinics for community based elderly. *Journal of Religion and Aging, 2*(3), 13–24.

Hiltner, S. (1975). Facts and needs: Present and future. In S. Hiltner (Ed.), *Toward a theology of aging.* New York: Human Sciences Press.

Hougland, K. (1974, March 27). Liberation from age-ism. *Christian Century*, pp. 341–342.

James, W. (1901). *The varieties of religious experience.* New York: Mentor, 1958.

Kane, P., Monroe, S., & Simpson, A. (1990, August 16). Black religion in the U.S. *Time*, pp. 25–31.

Kerr, H. L. (1980). *How to minister to senior adults in your church.* Nashville, TN: Broadman Press.

Kuhn, M. (1981). The church's continuing role with the aging. In C. LeFevre & P. LeFevre (Eds.), *Aging and the human spirit.* Chicago: Exploration Press.

Lacey, M. J. (Ed.). (1989). *Religion and twentieth-century American intellectual life.* New York: Cambridge University Press.

Leech, K. (1977). *Soul friend.* San Francisco: Harper & Row.

Lehman, H. (1953). *Age and achievement.* Princeton, NJ: Princeton University Press.

Levin, J. S. (1986). Roles for the black pastor in preventive medicine. *Pastoral Psychology, 35*(2), 94–103.

Levin, J. S., & Markides, K. S. (1988). Religious attendance and psychological well-being in middle-aged and older Mexican Americans. *Sociological Analysis, 49,* 66–72.

Levin, J. S., & Vanderpool, H. Y. (1987). Is frequent religious attendance really conducive to better health? *Social Science Medicine, 24*(7), 589–600.

McBrien, R. P. (1981). *Catholicism.* San Francisco: Harper & Row.

McManus, M. J. (1990, August 11). Why are so many Protestant denominations shrinking? *Ann Arbor News,* p. A8.

Marty, M. E. (1970). *Righteous empire.* New York: Dial Press.

Maves, P. B. (1960). Aging, religion, and church. In C. Tibbitts (Ed.), *Handbook of social gerontology* (pp. 698–752). Chicago: University of Chicago Press.

Maves, P. B., & Cedarleaf, J. L. (1949). *Older people and the church.* New York: Abingdon-Cokesbury Press.

Minzesheimer, B. (1990). The "old redhead" still has his flock. *Episcopal Life, 1,* 4.

Mitchell, S. (1987). *The Book of Job.* San Francisco: North Point Press.

Moberg, D. O. (1962). *The church as a social institution.* Englewood Cliffs, NJ: Prentice-Hall.

Moberg, D. O. (1990). Religion and aging. In K. F. Ferraro (Ed.), *Gerontology: Perspectives and issues.* New York: Springer.

Mott, M. (1984). *The seven mountains of Thomas Merton.* Boston: Houghton Mifflin.

Mountford, W. (1851). *Euthanasy.* Boston: Wm. Crosby and H. P. Nichols.

Myerhoff, B. G. (1978). A symbol perfected in death. In B. G. Myerhoff & A. Simic (Eds.), *Life's career—Aging: Cultural variations on growing old.* Beverly Hills, CA: Sage.

Neugarten, B. (Ed.). (1983). *Age vs. need.* Beverly Hills, CA: Sage.

New Mexico, Department of Public Welfare and Division of the American Association of University Women. (1966). *Ministries in Aging.* Santa Fe, NM: Department of Public Welfare.

Niebuhr, H. R. (1937). *The kingdom of God in America.* New York: Harper.

Noble, L. (1853). *Course of the empire, voyage of life, and other pictures of Thomas Cole, N.A.* New York: Cornish, Lamport.

Orbach, H. L. (1961). Aging and religion. *Geriatrics, 16.*

Palmore, E. (1985). Religious organizations. In G. L. Maddox (Ed.), *Encyclopedia of aging* (pp. 559–563). New York: Springer.

Payne, B. P. (1977). Religious life of the elderly: Myth or reality? In J. A. Thorson & T. C. Cook, Jr., *Spiritual well-being of the elderly* (pp. 26–41). Springfield, IL: Charles C. Thomas.

Pollak, O. (1948). *Social adjustment in old age.* Bulletin 59. New York: Social Science Research Council.

Reuther, R., & McLaughlin, E. (Eds.). (1979). *Women of spirit.* New York: Simon & Schuster.

Riley, M. W., & Associates. (1968–1972). *Aging and society* (3 vols.). New York: Russell Sage Foundation.

Robert Wood Johnson Foundation. (1989). Interfaith volunteer caregivers. *A special report* (no. 1). Princeton, NJ: Robert Wood Johnson Foundation.

Roozen, D. A., McKinney, W., & Carroll, J. W. (1984). *Varieties of religious presence.* New York: Pilgrim Press.

Sapp, S. (1987). *Full of years.* Nashville: Abingdon Press.

Smith, D. S. (1978). Old age and the "great transformation." In S. F. Spicker, K. M. Woodward, & D. D. Van Tassel (Eds.), *Aging and the elderly.* Atlantic Highlands, NJ: Humanities Press.

Taylor, R. J. (1986). Religious participation among elderly blacks. *The Gerontologist, 16*(6), 630–636.

Taylor, R. J. (1988a). Correlates of religious non-involvement among black Americans. *Review of Religious Research, 29*(4), 126–139.

Taylor, R. J. (1988b). Structural determinants of religious participation among black Americans. *Review of Religious Research, 30*(2), 114–125.

Taylor, R. J., Thornton, M. C., & Chatters, L. M. (1987). Black Americans' perceptions of the sociohistorical role of the church. *Journal of Black Studies, 18*(2), 123–138.

Thorson, J. A., & Cook, T. C., Jr. (1977). *Spiritual well-being of the elderly.* Springfield, IL: Charles C. Thomas.

Tibbitts, C. (Ed.) (1960). *Handbook of social gerontology.* Chicago: University of Chicago Press.

Tracy, D. (1987). *Plurality and ambiguity.* San Francisco: Harper & Row.

Winkler, M. G. (1990). Walking to the stars. *Generations, 14*(4), 39–44.

# 11

# Learning Productive Aging as a Social Role: The Lessons of Television

## George Gerbner

"Biology is destiny," but the course it takes is culturally shaped. Women and men, tall and short, skinny and fat, dark and light, gay and straight, disabled and able, young and old have not only physiological differences but also social and cultural distinctions that can confine and shame and hurt.

Age is one of these traps. Stereotyped roles of the life cycle are learned early and confirmed throughout life. Mass media are the most ubiquitous wholesalers of social roles in industrial societies.

Mass media, particularly television, form the common mainstream of contemporary culture. They present a steady, repetitive, and compelling system of images and messages. For the first time in human history, most of the stories are told to most of the children not by their parents, their school, or their church but by a group of distant corporations that have something to sell.

This unprecedented condition has a profound effect on the way we are socialized into our roles, including age as a social role. We learn to be children, pre-teens, adolescents, adults and parents, and old persons and to differentiate and often even segregate those roles from the messages and images around us. The world of aging (and nearly everything else) is constructed to the specifications of marketing strategies.

What is the contribution of television to the process of age-role socialization? More specifically, what does growing up and living with television have to do with productive aging, the central theme of this book?

We have studied age-role portrayals in television drama and commercials and their association with conceptions of aging (Gerbner, 1980; Gerbner, Gross, Signorielli, & Morgan, 1980, 1981, 1986). Our ongoing research project, called "Cultural Indicators," builds a cumulative database of systematic and reliable coded observations. The samples of programs and commercials from which the data for this chapter were drawn includes prime-time (6 PM to 11 PM) and weekend-daytime (children's) network television fictional programs in the late 1970s and the 1980s in this country and reflects trends through 1988. All speaking parts in such television programs were analyzed; major characters (those who portray leading roles) were given special attention. The analysis includes a total of 25,608 characters in dramatic programs (16,688 major characters) and 8,301 characters in commercials.

Sex, race, class, age, type of role (major or minor), and type of program were coded for all characters. Age was coded in terms of both chronological age and social age. Social age is a functional category scheme that was used to characterize life cycle as well as type of dramatic roles. The categories are children and adolescents, young adults (typically the age between adolescence and a more settled vocational and personal life and responsibilities), settled adults, and older adults. For major roles, we also coded various aspects of characterization including personality traits, success (whether or not the character achieves what he or she sets out to do or otherwise exhibits characteristics indicative of success), the type of role (comic, serious, or mixed) in which a character is cast, and a variety of other aspects of characterization. A reliability test was designed to insure that the observations did not reflect ambiguity in terms of our instructions or bias on the part of the observer.

Our analysis shows that age is a stable and strong determinant of who appears most and gains or loses most in the world of network television drama. In contrast to the distribution of age groups in the American population, the television curve demonstrates a pronounced central tendency; it bulges in the middle years and underrepresents both young and old people. Figure 11.1 shows the percentage age distribution in the actual population and in the "worlds" of prime-time television dramas and commercials. More than half of all television characters in both samples were between twenty-five and forty-five years of age. Those sixty-five and over, comprising almost 12 percent of the U.S. population, made up less than 3 percent of the fictional television population. Commercials tend to further exaggerate these inequities.

The skewed pattern of age distribution reflects not real life but power, particularly purchasing power. The age profile of television characters resembles the distribution of consumer income by age. (Women may do most of the buying and older Americans may have significant purchasing and investment clout, but men earn and the middle-aged groups spend most of the money in this country.) On the whole, marketing strategies reflect a "prime-time, prime-of-life" male orientation. Television's prime-time viewer population is seen as a mirror of the audience referred to in the industry as the "prime demographic market."

Figure 11.2 compares the percentage distribution of characters in week-

Figure 11.1
Age Distribution of U.S. Population, and Characters in Commercials and Dramatic Programs in Prime-Time

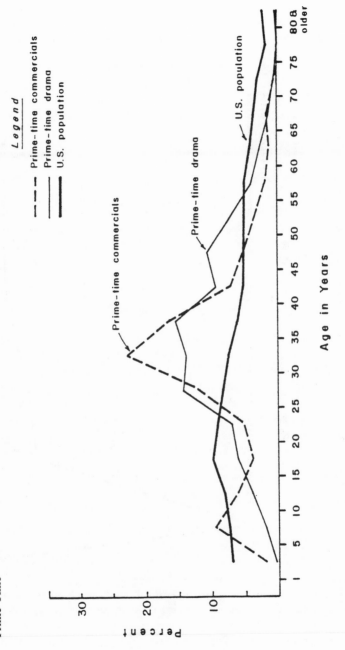

Figure 11.2
Age Distribution of U.S. Population, and Characters in Commercials and Dramatic Programs in
Weekend-Daytime

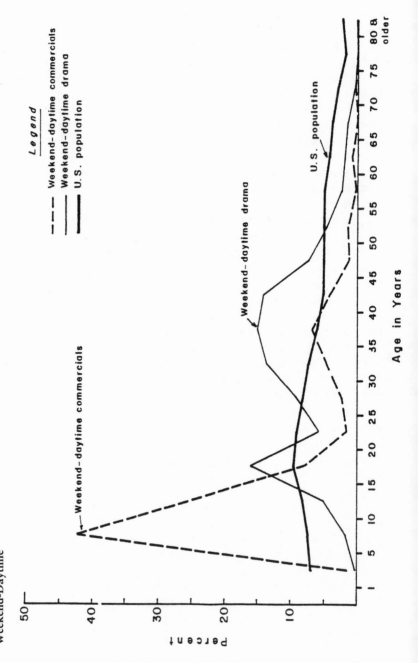

end-daytime dramas and commercials with the U.S. population distribution. Here we note the exaggerated overrepresentation of children and the virtual absence of older characters in children's programs and commercials. In children's programs, characters who are sixty-five years of age and older represented 1.4 percent of the fictional population. Characters in their twenties and early thirties, prominent in prime time, were reduced by half in children's programs and even more in the accompanying commercials. The age group of the parents of young children had a low profile, as did the age group of their grandparents. A significant portion of the larger group in their forties provided most of the villains.

In the world of prime-time television drama, as in most mass media, men outnumbered women about three to one. This fact has profound consequences for all that happens in that world, from patterns of aging and employment to sex and violence. Given such a cast, the stories that can be told best are stories of power and conflict, stories in which older characters (especially women) are most likely to end up as victims.

Gender differences can be seen in Figures 11.3 and 11.4. Figure 11.3 shows the percentage age distribution of male and female characters in prime-time dramatic programs and commercials. A larger percentage of women than men in their early twenties appeared in dramatic programs, when women's function as romantic partners and young housewives is supposed to peak, but then their numbers fall to four or five times below the number of men as their ages rise. (In commercials, there were more women than men in their early thirties.) As their usefulness in the world of television drama declined, their numbers shrank and their roles were constricted. While women were most concentrated—with almost a third of their total numbers—in the twenty-five to thirty-four years age bracket, men were most concentrated—also with almost a third of their numbers in the thirty-five to forty-four years age bracket.

The character population is structured to provide a relative abundance of younger women for older men, but no such abundance of younger men for older women. In other words, women age faster than men but both are barely visible in old age in the world of television. Television perpetuates an inequitable, if conventional, gender-age role pattern.

Figure 11.4 shows the gender pattern in weekend-daytime children's programs (mostly cartoons). Over half of all females were under twenty-one, but only twenty-eight percent of all males were under twenty-one. The most visible male age group was that between thirty-five and forty-five. Fully one-third of all men in weekend-daytime programs fell into that group. The pattern of aging reflected in prime time also is evident in weekend-daytime programs. Women over sixty-five, over 12 percent of the real female population, were 4 percent of the women in the world of children's television; older men accounted for only 3 percent of all male characters.

Weekend-daytime commercials showed a larger percentage of boys (71%

Figure 11.3
Age Distribution of Male and Female Characters in Commercials and Dramatic Programs in Prime-Time

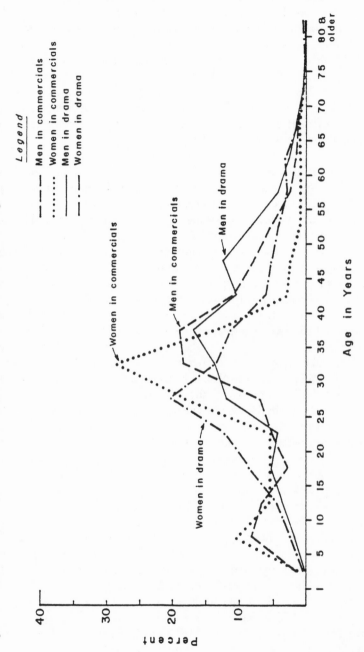

Figure 11.4
Age Distribution of Male and Female Characters in Commercials and Dramatic Programs in Weekend-Daytime

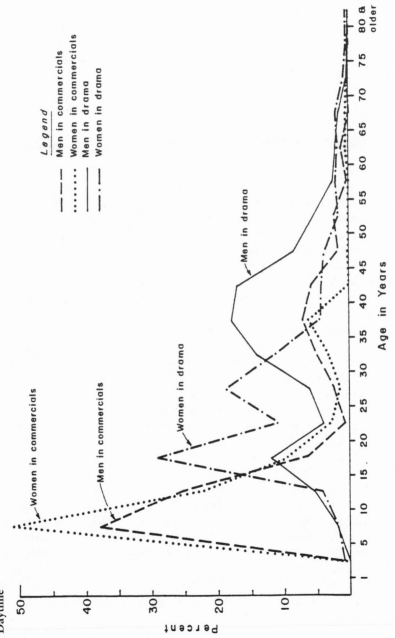

of male characters) as well as girls (85% of females) under nineteen years of age. But older characters hardly existed; less than 1 percent of both genders were sixty-five and over.

Representation is, of course, not just a question of numbers or of fidelity to census figures. It is a question of the variety of roles, opportunities, life chances, and images most people see in common from infancy on and as they grow old. Those underrepresented in the world of television are necessarily more stereotyped and limited. Visibility is privilege in the symbolic world. Symbolic annihilation is the price paid for aging in our (and our children's) entertainment.

Figure 11.5 compares the percentage age distributions of white and non-white men and women in prime-time drama. It shows that while white male characters dominated the age range between thirty-five and forty-five, both non-white men and all women tended to be younger than that. Minority males occupied an age-related power position between white males and all females. The pattern in commercials was a somewhat exaggerated version of the prime-time pattern. There were no characters sixty-five and over in weekend children's programs or commercials who were not white. Age as a resource cuts two ways for race as well as for gender. Those for whom the world of television has more use—with more jobs, adventures, sex, power, and other opportunities—are created and cast in greater numbers and more potent positions than those whose dramatic values are more restricted.

We have seen that women on television age "faster" than men. This means that mature female characters are more likely to be cast for older roles than male characters of the same chronological age. Through our "social age" classification of dramatic characters, we found that among characters from ages fifty-five to sixty-four, only 22 percent of the men and 33 percent of the women were cast as old characters with no professional or romantic possibilities, and rarely in a family setting. Among characters sixty-five and older, 72 percent of the men and 90 percent of the women were cast as "old" characters.

Personality profiles of male and female dramatic characters by social age were delineated on bipolar adjective scales. The mean ratings of older men were less "attractive," "fair," "rational," and "happy" than of other age groups. The mean ratings of women were less "potent," "smart," and "efficient." Older women were significantly more "repulsive" than women of other age groups and even somewhat more so than men (witches come from this group); but they also were more "peaceful," which, as we shall see, means that in a conflict they are more likely to be victimized.

Age-related chances for success also were unequally distributed in the world of television. The percent of successful men increased with age, but as women aged, their chances of success dropped. Overall, more older

Figure 11.5
Age Distribution of White and Non-White Male and Female Characters in Prime-Time Drama

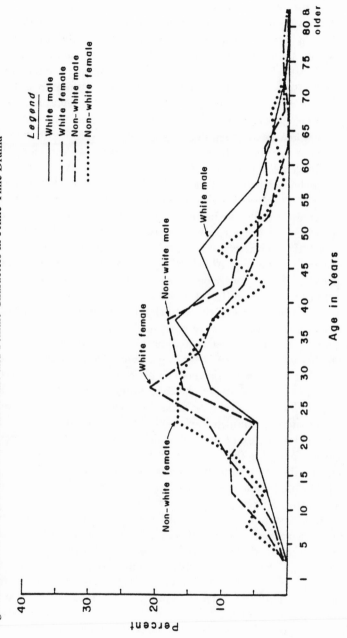

women were unsuccessful than were successful. No other age group of characters suffered such a fate.

Casting a character in a comic, serious, or mixed role also was related to age. Older characters were much more likely than younger characters to be cast in a comic role. Programs with older characters (especially women) were most likely to be comedies. But when older women were cast in conflict situations, they were more likely to be the victims than men of the same age, and both were more likely to be victimized than younger men. The gender-age victimization ratio works this way: For every ten violent characters in television drama, there were twelve victims. For every ten old male characters who were given violent roles, there were fourteen old male victims. For every ten old female characters who were violent, there were eighteen old women victims.

Major characters in a special sample of prime-time programs whose casts included older characters were rated on several personality attribute scales. These scales include whether characters are treated with disrespect or pity and whether they are portrayed as nuisances, stubborn, eccentric, or foolish.

More older characters were treated with disrespect than were characters in any other age group. About 70 percent of the older men and more than 80 percent of the older women were not held in high esteem or treated courteously, a very different pattern of treatment than that found for younger characters. Similarly, a much larger proportion of older characters than younger characters were portrayed as eccentric or foolish. A greater proportion of older women than older men—two-thirds compared to about one-half—were presented as lacking common sense, silly, or eccentric.

What are the lessons viewers derive from television about growing old in our society? To investigate the conceptions of age among television viewers, we used data from the National Council on Aging's Myth and Reality of Aging survey, conducted by Louis Harris and Associates in 1974. We constructed an index of the conception of older people from responses to statements asserting that the number, the health, and the longevity of older people are declining. A high score on this index would reflect a generalized belief that old people represent a diminishing rather than growing segment of American society.

There is a significant positive relationship between the amount of television viewing and scores on this index. The more people watch television, the more they tend to perceive old people in generally negative and unfavorable terms. Heavy viewers believe significantly more than light viewers that old people are a vanishing breed. The correlation is not reduced by controls for education, income, sex, or age, and it is much stronger for younger people. Thus, even with important demographic variables held constant, heavy viewers are more likely than light viewers to believe that old people are disappearing. Furthermore, those who watch more television are more likely to believe that people (especially women) become old earlier in life than those who watch less.

Other and later survey findings also show that heavy viewers are more likely than otherwise comparable groups of light viewers to think that older people are not open-minded and adaptable, are not bright and alert, and are not good at getting things done. All of these relationships are stronger among younger respondents, those between the ages of eighteen and twenty-nine.

We found similar patterns in studies of adolescents. When we asked about 600 sixth- to ninth-graders, "At what age does a man become elderly or old?" light viewers gave the combined average age as fifty-seven, while heavy viewers felt that people become old at fifty-one. Most of these adolescents believe women become old before men do.

We did not find watching television to be associated with *any* positive images of older people. Of course, there are notable exceptions of individual episodes and even series, such as the popular *The Golden Girls* (which, however, also conforms to the pattern of comedy format, age-sex humor, and the absence of normal family setting). But most viewers watch by the clock, not by the program, and heavy viewers watch more of everything. They cannot escape the overall portrayal of aging in the world of television, the composite view of which is revealed in our studies. Consequently, heavy viewers believe that the elderly are in worse shape both physically and financially than they used to be, not active sexually, close-minded, and not good at getting things done. At the same time, television is telling young people that old age, especially for women, begins relatively early in life.

The social goal of a medium that serves as the chief cultural arm of industrial society should be to mediate enlightened visions of aging, and of life in general, to the broadest and most diverse publics. However, the conflict between that goal and the function of efficient marketing tends to make productive aging and communication across age groups more difficult. Even with the proliferation of channels and the increasingly demographically targeted marketing strategies, the largest and most heterogeneous prime-time and weekend children's audiences share in common a vision of aging that is anything but productive. It cultivates conceptions that trap the elderly in limited and unproductive roles and it fails to promote the kind of vitality that is, in fact, characteristic of a growing number of old women and men. The overall television image resists rather than assists efforts to increase the scope and speed of productive aging.

These patterns are parts of a system of broadcasting and of storytelling with deep historical and commercial roots. They compose the cultural environment into which children are born and in which we all grow and learn aging as a social role, shifting much of the battle for productive aging to the cultural frontier.

Despite progress on many fronts, the overall patterns of the mainstream of the cultural environment have been very stable over the quarter-century that we have been able to track them. The prospects for significant change depend on change in the environment in which these patterns are embedded. We need a new environmental movement, a cultural environmental movement, to place the issue of television policy on productive aging on the national agenda. The need is not to regulate the image of aging—or anything else—on television but to loosen the existing constraints distorting it.

Consciousness of the dynamics of how one learns about aging in a mass culture is necessary for liberation from its constraints. Old people and their organizations have good reasons to be in the forefront of that liberation movement. It involves coalition and constituency building, including media councils in the United States and abroad; groups concerned with children and youth as well as aging; women's groups; religious and minority organizations; educational, health, environmental, legal, and other professional associations; consumer groups and agencies; associations of creative workers in the media and in the arts and sciences; independent computer network organizers and other organizations and individuals committed to loosening the constraints that now limit freedom and diversity on television.

Such a coalition will oppose domination of the airways by the limiting and exploitative formulas of marketing and work to abolish both concentration of ownership and censorship, public or private. It will expose use of the First Amendment only as a shield for power and privilege. It will seek to extend rights, facilities, and influence to interests and perspectives other than the most powerful and profitable. It will strive to include in cultural decision making the less affluent, more vulnerable groups which, collectively, are the majority of the population.

Waiting for advertisers to keep "discovering" the "age market," which they frequently do, is of limited use because it does not change the domination of the broad marketplace by the prime-time perspective. Productive aging as a social role is defined by the whole culture, not by the elderly or those who market to them. The best time to learn the meaning of productive aging is while one is growing up within a culture.

The cultural environment movement will support journalists, artists, writers, actors, directors, and other creative workers struggling for more freedom from having to present life in the most conventionally saleable packages. It will work with labor and other groups for diversity in employment and in media content. It will promote media literacy, media awareness, critical viewing and reading, and other media educational efforts as an essential educational objective on every level. It will place cultural policy issues on the social-political agenda. It will not wait for a blueprint; it will create and experiment with ways of community and citizen participation in local, national, and international media policymaking. A realistic democratic mechanism for broad public participation in cultural policymaking, unprecedented but ultimately inescapable, as that may be, is the way to make aging, starting with youth, as productive as it can be.

## NOTE

The studies on which this chapter is based have been conducted in collaboration with Larry Gross, University of Pennsylvania; Michael Morgan, University of Massachusetts; and Nancy Signorielli, University of Delaware. For more information about methodology and other details, see the publications listed in the References.

## REFERENCES

Gerbner, G. (1980). Children and power on television: The other side of the picture. In G. Gerbner, K. J. Ross, & E. Zigler (Eds.), *Child abuse reconsidered: An analysis and agenda for action*, (pp. 239–248). New York: Oxford University Press.

Gerbner, G., Gross, L., Morgan, M., & Signorielli, N. (1981, June). *Aging with television commercials: Images on television commercials and dramatic programming, 1977–1979*. Philadelphia: The Annenberg School of Communications, University of Pennsylvania.

Gerbner, G., Gross, L., Morgan, M., & Signorielli, N. (1986, September). *Television's mean world: Violence Profile No. 14–15*. Philadelphia: The Annenberg School of Communications, University of Pennsylvania.

Gerbner, G., Gross, L., Signorielli, N., & Morgan, M. (Winter, 1980). Aging with television: Images of television drama and conceptions of social reality. *Journal of Communication, 30* (1), 37–47.

# 12

# A Strategy for Productive Aging: Education in Later Life

*Harry R. Moody*

## IS LATE-LIFE LEARNING A SERIOUS CONCERN?

The most important observation about education for older adults in America is that the enterprise is not serious. Unless we get serious about late-life learning, we will fail to adopt appropriate means to promote productive aging in the years to come. The lack of seriousness in older-adult education is shown by almost any measure we adopt: numbers of students enrolled, money and other resources committed to the enterprise, level of sophistication in the delivery systems deployed. If continuing education for adults has long been a stepchild of higher education, then older-adult education must be considered an orphan or having a status still more remote than that (Ansello & Haslip, 1979). The literature on older-adult education clearly demonstrates what is possible (see, for example, Peterson et al., 1986; Lumsden, 1985; Lowy, 1984). Yet late-life learning languishes on the periphery of higher education, not in the mainstream, with a few rare exceptions to be noted later in this discussion.

But being an orphan is not the worst of the problem. Far worse is the fact that late-life learning is not taken seriously even by influential figures in the fields of higher education or gerontology. This remains true despite long-established evidence that it can contribute to productive roles.[1] The reasons are to be found in the political economy of higher education and aging services. Since older-adult education does not bring in grants for universities or offer career training paths, it tends to be ignored and not taken seriously (Peterson, 1987). Its current expansion is almost entirely a consumer enterprise, a species of leisure-time activity that does not command significant resources because it is not organized according to principles either of profit or social welfare. Older learners are almost invariably treated as passive consumers of learning[2]—as students to fill up seats or as paying customers in tuition-based programs—and rarely as capable of productive contributions to society based on the investment in their learning potential (Bass, 1986).

This nonproductive stance cannot be explained by the mere fact that late-life learning is peripheral to the higher education enterprise. That point is proved by the fact that programs such as Agricultural Extension or Executive Development also remain peripheral but are treated with great seriousness at institutions with strong ties to agriculture or corporations. Because these adult-education initiatives are tied to serious external constituencies, those educators who are in charge of them are constantly accountable—to produce results and to insure that investment in teaching and learning has consequences for productivity in the wider society. By contrast, older-adult education, even in those institutions where it flourishes on the margin, lacks any strong external constituency and, not surprisingly, lacks any solid foothold in the world of higher education (Peterson, 1983). The result is that late-life learning commands no serious attention by leaders in higher education, even at a time when the aging population is growing and the potential constituency of older learners is expanding.

One might think that gerontology, at least, would take late-life learning seriously. Indeed, within higher education, the field of gerontology itself has grown dramatically in the past two decades. But gerontology as an intellectual field is almost entirely dominated by what Richard Kalish called the "failure model" of old age; in recent years, gerontology itself has become, in Carroll Estes' terms, more and more heavily "medicalized." The most powerful external constituencies for gerontology are health care providers and social service agencies. These are the groups that provide the job market for graduates and that generate support for research and training funds from government at all levels. But these external constituencies tend to cast older people as passive "clients" or "patients," not as learners. The result is that gerontology, as a field, has almost no serious interest in older-adult education. It is organized, increasingly, as either a research enterprise seeking legitimation in mainstream higher education norms or as a career-training enterprise linked to social welfare norms.

By contrast, the most prestigious and influential adult continuing education programs are organized on a market basis. Courses are offered in response to consumer demand, either from individual customers or from corporations or government agencies. The curriculum is reorganized as a "product" that must meet the needs of customers, and fees are determined on the basis of what the market will bear. Profits either are retained by continuing education divisions or returned to larger sponsoring institutions. The largest, most sophisticated continuing education programs in the world of higher education, such as those of the New School (in New York City), New York University, and UCLA, have operated on this model for decades. They have proved skillful in finding ways to preserve high standards and a degree of collaboration with the central academic enterprise of their institutions, institutions still dominated by the research-driven model described in classic terms by David Riesman (Riesman & Jencks, 1968). At high-prestige institutions, therefore, no matter how financially successful any continuing education program may be, it remains at a distance from the "heartland" of academic power in the graduate professional schools and the arts and sciences. A similar pattern is repeated in less prestigious institutions. There is an abiding tension between the traditional model of academic prestige and the market-driven ethos of continuing education.

## OLDER-ADULT EDUCATION PROGRAMS ON CAMPUS

This broad picture is valid for research-oriented universities, whether public or private. The picture is more blurred when we move down the academic ladder to the vast number of public four-year state colleges and universities and community colleges, which together enroll the bulk of students in American higher education. No discussion of older-adult education can be illuminating without consideration of the financing system, or rather nonsystem, that supports the enterprise. In the public sector, more than 80 percent of states now have tuition-free, space-available policies in effect, and these programs continue to attract older people. However, it has long been clear that such policies are designed intentionally to keep the enterprise from becoming a serious one: legislators mandate tuition-free access but provide no funds to support older-adult programs (Long, 1982). Tuition-free programs for older people thus become an exercise in symbolic politics. They appear to offer benefits for older people but are designed in such a way that campus administrators have an interest in limiting the numbers of older people who enroll (Edelman, 1967).

In light of these conditions, it is not surprising that creative efforts at late-life learning in higher education have taken novel forms. Perhaps the most notable is Elderhostel, a liberal arts program now available on over a thousand U.S. campuses (Brady, 1983). Elderhostel is one of the most astonishing success stories on the higher education scene, and the secrets of its success are worth noting. It operates on a fixed-price, nonmarket pattern in which tuition is set at a level to cover (marginal) costs with no serious profit or overhead for the sponsoring institution. Elderhostel now enrolls over 200,000 participants each year and continues to grow. But, in fact, there are few campuses that enroll more than a few hundred Elderhostel students each year.

Part of the reason goes back to incentives built into the design of the program itself. The lack of profits or retained earnings means that administrators and faculty even at most successful Elderhostel campuses do not really take the enterprise seriously, in contrast, say, to Agricultural Extension or Executive Development programs. Leadership cannot afford to commit more than a modest level of resources to the enterprise. There will always be a minority of faculty and administrators who are enthusiastic about Elderhostel, and the benefits obviously exceed the low marginal cost enough to keep the program in operation. But lack of overhead, retained earnings, or public subsidy means that there is never enough money available for research or program development at the local level. Elderhostel remains successful as long as it is adopted at many institutions but, as a rule, on a limited scale.

A similar problem of scale and incentives crops up when we consider the political economy of older-adult education in the public sector. There are a few isolated institutions that have ingeniously designed ways to make late-life learning pay for itself and become institutionalized. For example, Saddleback College, located near Leisure World in Orange County, California, in recent years has attracted 20 percent of its 21,000 student body from retired persons in its Emeritus Institute. The college receives revenues for these students on an FTE (formula reimbursement) basis, so older-adult enrollment has become a significant part of its budget.

Despite spectacular successes like this, older-adult education programs around the country have come under serious threat of erosion because of deficits in state and local governments. In an atmosphere of fiscal constraint, older-adult education programs are the first items to be cut. Programs to teach pottery or philosophy to retired people look more and more like frills to legislators in a period when school budgets are defeated and funds for public higher education are cut. It becomes harder to defend the programs, no matter how successful they have proved. Tuition-free, space-available courses have proved to be overwhelmingly consumer-oriented, leisure-time activities, not serious investments in learning for productivity. The predictable result has been an erosion of political support for such programs at a time of broader economic crisis.

## CONSUMER STATUS: THE STRATEGIC ERROR

The thrust of the argument offered here is that our policy on older-adult education has taken the wrong strategic turn. The strategic error has both an economic and a social component. In terms of economic policy, older-adult education has favored consumption rather than production. Within the world of higher education, older-adult education operates at the margin, not the center, and it is constructed as a form of leisure-time activity, not human-capital investment. In terms of social policy, older-adult education has developed almost entirely separate from the "aging enterprise" activities of human services, including health care, social welfare, and the formal aging network. Late-life learning is perceived by gerontologists as a frill for the well-to-do, not as a fundamental strategy for solving problems of the less-advantaged elderly. This strategic orientation toward individual learning outside of social structure has had devastating results for older-adult education, depriving it of any wider legitimation. The concept of productive aging could offer a strategic alternative.

A prime concern of productive aging must be taking steps to improve job opportunities for older workers, not just people over sixty-five but "older workers" as defined by the U.S. Labor Department—namely, workers over the age of forty. Elsewhere in the American economy, education is linked to jobs. But older-adult education has never been organized, or even conceptualized, in relation to the substantial public initiatives of older-worker employment; specifically, Title V of the Older Americans Act and the older-worker set-asides of the Job Training Partnership Act (JTPA). The reasons for this neglect are not wholly on the side of higher education. In fact, the community-service employment approach, available on a means-tested basis, has been understood as a "jobs" program to support constituent organizations in the nonprofit sector which serve as sponsors (AARP, Green Thumb, NCOA) and at the same time to provide income support to elderly poor people.

Title V has been superbly effective in doing both of these things, and it has accomplished something more. It has achieved remarkable political support in Congress. Ironically, this very political success may make it harder to reform Title V to include a larger education and training dimension. Under Title V, unlike efforts within welfare in recent years, there has been no thought of providing education or serious older-worker retraining. The JTPA approach, by contrast, at least provides some training, but under the aegis of private industry. Neither public-service employment nor industrial retraining for older workers has developed links with the higher education sector. In general, worker retraining in the United States remains severely underdeveloped in comparison to that of our overseas competitors like Japan and Germany.

There are those who hold an optimistic viewpoint about older workers in the remainder of the 1990s. Some speak in glowing terms about a prospective "labor shortage" that will sharply increase demand for all workers and perhaps open up opportunities for older workers. Analysts point to the diminished number of young people entering the labor market during the 1990s, for example. There are historical precedents that support that optimism—for example, the dramatic change in attitudes toward women in factory jobs that took place in America during World War II when "Rosie the Riveter" became a popular image. Those opportunities, of course, were quickly reversed in the immediate postwar era. But it seems at least possible that employers might become more enthusiastic about hiring older workers if labor market conditions were right.

No one can predict the future, but the recession of the early 1990s has brought not a labor shortage, to say the least, but rather persistent unemployment. Another problem with the optimistic forecast about hiring or using older workers is that it omits consideration of other methods employers might adopt to combat shortages, such as relying on immigration. Immigrant labor has proved significant not only for low-wage jobs (e.g., building cleaning) but for some high-wage specialized functions (e.g., medicine and engineering). Widely touted demonstration programs, such as one at Travelers Insurance, or steps to put older workers in highly visible positions, such as senior citizens working at McDonald's, tell us very little about what is possible or likely in the event of a serious labor shortage. Still worse, none of the scenarios for the anticipated labor shortage envisage much of a role for higher education or older-worker retraining. This is especially unfortunate because the experience of workers of all ages during the 1991 recession was that education is a key element in employability for displaced workers. This fact should give late-life learning for productive aging a much higher priority as we think about aging policy in the 1990s and into the twenty-first century.

An analysis of strategic policy considerations will not, in itself, define directions for the future. To accomplish this, we will engage in "practical utopianism" and look more closely at some exemplary model programs that can give guidance about what is feasible.

*Gerontology for Older Learners.* The University of Massachusetts at Boston has long served as an urban counterpart to the rural land-grant university (in Amherst, Massachusetts). The university's Manning Gerontology Certificate program is unique in being committed to enrolling significant numbers of older people as students who are prepared through formal coursework and fieldwork for roles as advocates and service providers in the aging network. The University of Massachusetts also is distinctive in having a strong political and policy orientation to its professional training in gerontology. While engaged in academic research, the Gerontology program's leadership remains in close touch with political advocates working in Boston and throughout the state. The presence of large numbers of older people studying alongside younger people insures that education and training reflects the realities of aging and gives younger students tangible examples of productive aging in the skills and knowledge acquired by their elders.

*A New Vision of Creative Retirement.* In 1986, the North Carolina State Legislature authorized the creation of a Center for Creative Retirement at the University of North Carolina at Asheville. In the years since then, the Center for Creative Retirement has grown to become a network of programs offering liberal arts education, peer learning groups, health promotion, training of older volunteers, intergenerational programming, and engagement of senior citizens as mentors for career guidance of younger undergraduates. On the campus and in western North Carolina, the Center for Creative Retirement promotes gerontology research and links with the aging service network. But its special strength lies in developing innovative programs that cultivate the distinctive strengths of older people as both learners and teachers. The Center for Creative Retirement has attracted the attention of national media, and the center's leadership works to encourage replication of the model at other institutions.

The Boston and the North Carolina programs, though very different in their inspiration and program design, have certain common characteristics in terms of the broader political economy. Both were generated and sustained through the strong external political support of constituencies in the state legislature or the senior citizens movement rather than in academic departments on a campus. Both are legitimated around highly positive images of later life; they are constructed not around images of decline or need but on some ideal of productive aging. The University of Massachusetts model trains older people to become their own advocates and to take on paid employment in the aging service network. In this respect, it is similar to Agricultural Extension programs or Executive Development programs, where external constituencies help to shape the curriculum and provide leadership.

The North Carolina model also encourages strong ties between the campus and the wider community by training volunteers for local hospitals and schools and by demonstrating the importance of older people for regional economic development. Unlike some retirement-learning programs, the Center for Creative Retirement is not an island unto itself but is solidly anchored in the external environment and emphasizes not one but a variety of forms of productive aging. These ties to the wider environment are important in reinforcing the external constituency for the Center, which is supported by the state legislature partly because of the state's interest in promoting migration of retirees who can be attracted by the quality of life values embodied in the new retirement ethos of the Center. Thus, the idealistic values of self-actualization are balanced by a realistic politics of regional economic development which bodes well for the future. The "new older adult" inspired by the Center for Creative Retirement matches a broader social ideal of productive aging.

Both the North Carolina and the Massachusetts programs can be conceived under the rubric of a social-investment model, which differs from the private-market approach dominant in continuing education or the social-welfare approach dominant in today's aging service network.

A social-investment model differs from both the private-market model and the social-welfare approach inasmuch as it does not cast the elderly as a passive "consumer" of services rendered, regardless of how these services are financed, by marketplace or government. This is an important point because the passivity of older learners in the private-market and social-welfare models remains the same whether we charge a fee (and make a profit) on services rendered or provide the same service on a subsidized basis. The argument here is that the proper approach to developing older-adult education programs for the future is to be found in neither of these two models because both reflect a view of older people as essentially passive consumers. The affluent elderly are able to pay for late-life learning opportunities. Allowing older-adult education to develop on the basis of a fee-for-service mechanism would mean that programs will thrive only among the affluent, more or less the way alumni education programs do.

One problem with the social-investment model, as illustrated in the Boston and North Carolina examples, is that it so far has had few serious imitators around the country. It is possible that replication will come and the social-investment model of late-life learning is an innovation waiting to be diffused. An analogy here might be the Institute for Retired Professionals (IRP), a mutual-aid, peer-learning approach that began in 1962 but was widely replicated only in the past decade; there are now more than 100 Learning-in-Retirement (LIR) programs around the country (Hirsch, 1977–1978). The national Elderhostel organization has taken a lead in encouraging replication. These campus-based, learning-in-retirement programs might seem to be a positive example of productive aging where older people develop their own programs, supply their own leadership, and manage the enterprise on a nonmonetized basis largely outside the market system. Such programs are admirable and certainly to be encouraged. But the crucial difference is that the LIR model seems to flourish only among the more affluent elderly, and, even when it does flourish, it is largely cut off from the surrounding academic environment or wider community. It is not a social-investment vehicle but a kind of club for upscale elders who enjoy intellectual exploration.

A more plausible approach for expansion of the social-investment model would be the use of community colleges, a uniquely American institution. There is hardly a substantial town or county in the country that lacks a community college. Community colleges, moreover, combine a degree of academic orientation with much of the market ethos found in continuing education for adults. Community colleges typically are tied closely to the local economy and job market, and they pride themselves on ease of access. Older-adult education programs, linked to productive aging and the social-investment model, could establish a strong anchor in community colleges, which in turn might become the kind of constituency needed to sustain political support necessary for programs that cannot operate on a strictly fee-for-service basis. Two exemplary programs show what is feasible here.

*The Corporate Connection.*    Started in 1984, Mainstream, the Retirement Institute of Westchester Community College in suburban New York, helps older adults acquire new skills to return to the work force. In 1990, in collaboration with major local employers such as General Foods and Mutual of New York insurance company, Mainstream opened its Center for a Mature Workforce, offering training in areas such as substitute teaching, computers, and clerical skills. Its Customer Service Training Program enrolls students predominantly over fifty years of age. The program makes use of prior life experience and prepares graduates for a range of job opportunities.

*Job Training Partnership.* Grand Rapids Junior College and the Senior Employment Program of the U.S. Area Agency on Aging in western Michigan have developed a collaborative job skills program for retraining older people in their region. Funding from JTPA set-aside funds provides the program with stability and continuity. Specific curriculum elements include computer-based office procedures, computer-aided design and manufacturing, furniture manufacturing and finishing (important to the western Michigan economy), and building-maintenance mechanics. Most courses involve science and technology topics such as industrial mathematics, electronic spreadsheets, numeric control machinery, and electrical systems. Thus, the college is able to provide economically vulnerable older people with knowledge of up-to-date technology promising economic self-sufficiency in the future.

Both of these programs show why it is so important to overcome the gap between mainstream gerontology and older-adult education programs. It is significant that the Grand Rapids program involves ongoing, in-service gerontological training for all staff associated with the job-training program. This commitment serves to "gerontologize" the skilled job training and to differentiate it from that of other retraining programs. It insures that faculty will use the most effective methods of teaching older learners and will test and assess students' progress in ways that reflect both strengths and weaknesses of older learners. It means that the learning environment will be designed in such a way as to help older people grasp new technologies that might otherwise be threatening. Above all, it means taking the necessary steps to encourage self-esteem and foster successful job placement. Likewise, the Mainstream program in Westchester has modified the instructional format to allow a slower pace of instruction and take account of the various styles of older learners. Competency-based instruction permits the program to avoid the threat of grades while still insuring mastery learning to achieve instructional and occupational goals.

One problem with corporate-sponsored training is that it may foster narrow vocationally oriented programs, which limit the broad skills that students will require for the job market. The Grand Rapids and the Westchester programs deliberately have sought to avoid that narrowness. On the other hand, a special strength of corporate sponsorship is that programs are likely to reflect real-world skills. Thus, student motivation—the desire to get a job—probably will be high, and the external constituency for the programs should be strong. Productive aging, in the form of retrained older workers, contributes directly to the local economy and encourages off-campus support in times of cutbacks.

Programs like those in Grand Rapids and Westchester could be replicated in many other institutions, especially those in regions where the population is aging and younger workers are in short supply. In many institutions, funding from corporate sponsors follows a well-established pattern (Levin & Schutze, 1983; Powers et al., 1988). Older-adult education for productive aging could build directly on that pattern, a strategy that may prove increasingly important in a period when across the country states are restricting eligibility for older adults in noncredit courses.

The great advantage of community college models is that they reflect the realistic political economy of older-adult education and offer a hope that programs will not remain marginal or an exercise in tokenism and symbolic politics, as tuition-free, space-available programs have been. The basis for growth in the future is certainly there. Community colleges, like nontraditional programs in four-year institutions, increasingly enroll people in their twenties and thirties. These programs could be encouraged first to increase their enrollments to people in their forties and fifties—for example, by targeting displaced homemakers and mid-career workers forced to look for new jobs. The clientele could be extended gradually to people in their fifties and sixties. Late-life learning opportunities on this pattern could be one of our most effective tools for preventing impoverishment in later life.

At the same time, the community college models reveal some of the limitations of productive aging construed on a purely economic approach. The corporate connection holds not only a promise but also a danger of domination of higher education by narrowly drawn criteria of profit-making businesses (Eurich, 1985). It is just here where broader approaches, like the Boston and North Carolina models, are an important corrective. For example, the University of Massachusetts program is grounded in a solid understanding of the political basis of gerontology as an academic enterprise. The North Carolina Center for Creative Retirement offers a variety of ways in which older people can be productive, not only in paid jobs but through nonmonetized productivity and through intergenerational connections. Politics and intergenerational solidarity are correctives to the "single vision" of the marketplace. They must be essential elements in the agenda for productive aging in the future.

Productive aging offers a very hopeful basis for substantially revising the strategic basis of late-life learning in the United States. Taking older-adult education seriously will mean, at the very least, widening our vision of productivity while at the same time refashioning higher education institutions to encourage productive activity over the full course of the life span.

## NOTES

1. The literature here is substantial, beginning with Belbin and Belbin (1972).

2. For further discussion of the subject, see Chapter 2 in this book and Moody (1988).

# REFERENCES

Ansello, E. F., & Haslip, B. (1979). Older adult higher education: Stepchild and Cinderella. In H. Sterns et al. (Eds.), *Gerontology in higher education*. Belmont, CA: Wadsworth.

Bass, S. A. (1986). Matching opportunities with the able elderly. *Lifelong Learning*, 9(5), 4–7.

Belbin, E., & Belbin, R. M. (1972). *Problems in adult retraining*. London: Heineman.

Brady, E. M. (1983). Personal growth and the Elderhostel experience. *Lifelong Learning*, 7(3), 11–13.

Edelman, M. (1967). *The symbolic uses of politics*. Urbana: University of Illinois Press.

Eurich, N. (1985). *Corporate classrooms: The learning business*. Princeton, NJ: Carnegie Foundation for the Advancement of Teaching.

Hirsch, H. (1977–1978). Higher education in retirement: The institute of retired professionals. *International Journal of Aging & Human Development, 8,* 367–374.

Levin, H., & Schutze, H. (1983). *Financing recurrent education: Strategies for increasing employment, job opportunities and productivity*. Beverly Hills, CA: Sage.

Long, H. (1982). Analysis of research concerning free and reduced tuition programs for senior citizens. *Educational Gerontology, 8,* 575–584.

Lowy, L. (1984). *Education and the later years*. Boston: Lexington Books.

Lumsden, D. B. (Ed.). (1985). *The older adult as learner*. Washington, DC: Hemisphere.

Moody, H. R. (1988). *Abundance of life: Human development policies for an aging society*. New York: Columbia University Press.

Peterson, D. A. (1983). *Facilitating education for older learners*. San Francisco: Jossey-Bass.

Peterson, D. A. (1987). Who will fund education for older people? *Perspective on Aging, 16*(1), 10–12.

Peterson, D. A., et al. (Eds.). (1986). *Education and aging*. Englewood Cliffs, NJ: Prentice-Hall.

Powers, D. R., et al. (1988). *Higher education in partnership with industry: Opportunities & strategies*. San Francisco: Jossey-Bass.

Riesman, D., & Jencks, C. (1968). *The academic revolution*. Garden City, NY: Doubleday.

# Part V

## Implications for Special Populations

# 13

# Women's Lives, Women's Work: Productivity, Gender, and Aging

## Martha Holstein

Fifty years ago, sociologists Matilda White Riley (1985) and John Riley prophetically wrote, "[M]ature women no longer find a full life in the home, their traditional place. If we are ever to have a good society, wives as well as every other category in the population must have a place with ample opportunity for earning the social approbation which humankind so desperately need." The literary critic Malcolm Cowley (1980, p. 30), reflecting from the vantage point of eighty years, says "old people would like to have a clearly defined place and function in American life." And Simone de Beauvoir (1972) suggests that our existence, at all ages, derives its meaning from devotion to groups; to individuals or to causes; and to social, political, intellectual, or creative work.

Productive aging, in its noblest renderings, is a partial response to this urgent task of infusing life's last stage with personal meaning and social significance. Targeted at eliminating the "surplus dependency imposed on older people" (Cole, 1988), it would open opportunities for paid or voluntary work and stimulate self-help, lifelong learning, and social participation (Moody, 1988). Genuine improvement in older people's health and vigor, and their often passionately expressed wish to be involved, undergird productivity's positive pole.

But today's political mood can cast productivity in a much darker role—as a response to the problems created by an unproductive, selfish, and unfortunately burgeoning older population (Hewitt, 1986; Longman, 1987). Whether the crises this nightmare invokes are real or created, it has taken hold in the media and in the popular imagination, where productivity and social burden are often set at opposite ends of the social worth continuum.

Between these opposite poles—hopefully optimistic and darkly grim—lies the troublesome middle, where conflicting ideals, values, and goals can

easily become confused, shrouded in rhetoric, and ultimately severed from
the policies and practices that give them life. The problems with productivity—even its positive pole—therefore, rest less with its goals than with
who controls its interpretation, what negative consequences emerge, and
what important discussions it short-circuits. Older women, who are least
likely to be the "gatekeepers" of how productivity is defined and applied,
and who can benefit most profoundly from a reimagining of old age, will
be particularly vulnerable to the effects of these negative consequences.

In the end—though my discussion will recognize both its burdens and
benefits—I think the call for a productive aging society will truncate rather
than expand an older woman's chance to construct a meaningful last chapter
for her life, even though it may open the job opportunities so many women
want and need.

To ground this argument, we will look first at the impact of socially
constructed gender and age roles in contemporary society and then turn to
the chapter's core: an extended critique of productivity and suggestions for
a tentative but alternative vision to guide thinking about a meaningful old
age, especially for older women. The chapter will offer some ways that
women can contribute to society divorced from their reproductive role, their
physical appearance, and their economic productivity. It will, however, also
suggest some intermediary steps on this journey to a radically reformed
vision of a woman growing old.

## GENDER

There is now an extensive and important literature exploring gender issues
(see Benhabib, 1987; *Daedalus*, 1987; Epstein, 1988; Farganis, 1986; Levy,
1989; Markus, 1987) and an expanding literature that analyzes the combined effects of gender and age (see Garner & Mercer, 1989; *Generations*,
1990; Levy, 1989; Woodward, 1991). The scope of this chapter, however,
is narrow and necessarily brief. Two broad themes—the effects of socially
constructed and defined women's roles and the impact of male norms about
what is important, how one should think, and what the appropriate "standpoint" is vis-à-vis the world (which have also become societal norms)—help
inform our understanding of "productivity." They should make us profoundly skeptical that a noble intent—the creation of ways to acknowledge
the potentialities inherent in old age, particularly reflective of older women's
unique competencies—can be divorced easily from the power of the dominant culture.

In modern Western history, women's primary social location in the devalued private sphere of home and family has affected women's lives in
pervasive ways. Women's work as mothers or homemakers and the thinking,
values, and engaged vision of the world that arises from this work (caring,
nurturing, protecting, socializing), though often romanticized, have brought

them neither prestige nor power (see Gottlieb, 1989; Ruddick, 1989). Rather, when compared to the more public, product-oriented, and instrumental activities that are linked to monetary rewards, women's work has had a distinctly negative valuation, contributing to patterns of inequality within the family, and to women's social and economic marginalization, particularly if women become widowed or divorced. This separation of public and private also has limited women's power in the wider (to many, the "real") world. Despite generations of feminist activism and scholarship, most women have had little to say even about the central decisions that have affected their lives (Gottlieb, 1989). In Hannah Arendt's words, they have not "been seen and heard" (Markus, 1987). Women writers from Mary Wollstonecraft to Virginia Woolf, to the contemporary writers Adrienne Rich and Tillie Olsen, have personally and painfully recounted the stinging impact of their silencing. Women of color or poor women, who have always *had* to have a life outside the home, have been silenced because race and class generally have restricted their access to public power.

And as more women reach old age, it is becoming abundantly clear that age compounds a woman's already devalued status (see *Generations*, 1990). Many contemporary older women have internalized the norms that Cynthia Epstein's (1988) "gatekeepers of ideas" have imposed. Hence, when they feel attacked for their acceptance of a private life, often by the feminist movement itself, they become increasingly self-protective, reinforcing what may already be painful social marginalization. An older woman's gray hair, facial lines, and heavier body activate other negative assumptions about her capacity to work, to learn, or to make a significant intellectual contribution (Secunda, 1984). The consequence of their history of restricted roles also means that many older women simply lack the skills or the self-enhancing attitude to think of and be assertive about their needs (Gottlieb, 1989).

According to Maria Markus (1987, p. 106), "A demand for equality and even the legal guarantee of equal treatment do not seem to be sufficient either to transcend women's 'difference' or to transform it into their strength." History does not permit a neutral stance; it suggests that, despite their large numbers, women will not craft what will become a socially sanctioned definition of productivity or model new norms for living in old age. Instead, they face the risk that, once again, they will live by norms established by others.

## PRODUCTIVITY: A CRITIQUE

The central argument here focuses on the following themes. First, because of gender-based differentials in power and prestige as expressed in the public world, productivity is easily susceptible to a work-oriented interpretation. Such a narrow definition can defeat the best goals of its proponents. It can also be a confused blessing for older women. Second, productivity can become the captive of those who wish to delegitimate income-support programs if it is defined narrowly; it can be used politically to threaten the already tenuous economic status of older women, thereby reinforcing the structural inequities that historically have disadvantaged them. It also can impose new standards for the good life in old age. Third, such standards, albeit unintentionally, can negate an often invisible gift of age—the relative freedom to explore ways to flourish that are personally satisfying and socially significant. Fourth, a productive aging society, as a call to action, offers too few advantages over a simpler incremental reform strategy—for example, a push for job opportunities—to risk its negative consequences. Fifth, to affix an easily misconstrued label—as a symbolic cue as well as a practical guide—to an inherently complex time in human life can detract from a sustained and penetrating exploration into issues of dependency and interdependency, the impact of an aging society on the meanings of institutions such as work and the family; and cultural understandings of old age.

### A Narrow Interpretation

Like language in general, men and women will interpret *productivity* through their own filters. A feminist analysis of language has exposed the discrepant ways men and women use and understand language and, like gender biases in other areas of life, the male pattern is implicitly taken to be universal (see Lakoff, 1975; Tannen, 1990). Beyond gender biases, words and language also conjure up mental concepts that are neither objective and value-free nor ahistorical.

The language of productivity is no different. For example, in our common idiom, productivity's connection to paid work and to the work ethic, which recasts itself as the "busy" ethic in retirement (Ekerdt, 1986), seems firmly entrenched. For many, work is a synonym for productivity. Even when there is a commitment to a more inclusive definition of productivity, the conventional definition soon triumphs. In two recent discussions about productivity in old age (Morrison, 1986; Pifer, 1986), a newly formulated definition of productivity is proffered. Arguing from the perspective of both the older person and society, these observers advocate for rich new opportunities that include structured voluntary as well as paid work. Already limited in terms of options, paid employment receives primary attention, justified in large measure by social need. When the Committee on an Aging Society of the Institute of Medicine and the National Research Council (1986) undertook the task of considering productivity in noneconomic terms, they too discovered the difficulties of severing it from its traditional moorings. In another example of the seemingly ineluctable bond between productivity and paid employment, Social Security benefits are "earned" through productive work in the economy—that is, paid employment. The implications of this approach for women's economic status have been well documented.

At the most basic level, then, productivity is encumbered with a social definition that links it to paid employment. For older women, in particular, this link is a confused blessing. A work-oriented definition of productivity emphasizes the ends of production and its rewards—money and wealth—thereby reinforcing a masculine and youth-oriented conception of social status (Hess, 1990; Markus, 1987). Since an older woman's market value and her contribution to the system of economic productivity are already negligible, they can be further devalued if they remain outside the work culture. Yet, as discussed below, that very work culture may be unsupportive and reflect historical patterns of inequality. Moreover, if opportunities to work become *expectations* to work, the emphasis on productivity can discourage a vigorous exploration of alternative ways for women to achieve social recognition, utilizing their new freedom and their life experiences. It can easily become another vehicle to obscure diversity, negate personal choices for an existentially satisfying old age, and list heavily toward meeting someone else's vision of social and economic needs.

On the other hand, many women need and want jobs. Until (and if) their needs are erased by improved income-support programs or alternative ways to achieve social approbation and a sense of community, work will remain a critical option in a practical if not an optimal sense. Hence, linking a productive aging society to jobs, if it expands an older woman's employment opportunities, can be perceived as an advantage. But behind the opportunities lurk problems that at a minimum must be named, since the ambiguities embedded in the productivity-work interface may be sufficiently important to undermine the goals of a productive aging society. For this reason, it is useful to highlight some of these problems and propose a solution.

Despite three decades of legislation, women have not achieved equality in the work force. The primary economy remains stubbornly resistant to change. It is governed by patterns of male socialization and male role identification and is generally unable to nurture and respect women's particular strengths and values (Farganis, 1986). Decisions about how work ought to be done—for example, its hours, its stress on objective detachment, its "efficiency" achieved through bureaucratization—are rooted not in the "moral economy of the woman but in the traditions, customs and practices of men" (Kessler-Harris, 1990, p. 123). (See Grossman & Chester [1990] and Markus [1987] for an extended discussion of these biases.) To date, even the surge in the numbers of women who are entering previously male-dominated positions has not restructured the distribution of responsibilities in families (Hochschild & Machung, 1989) and has not resulted in a substantial public commitment to assistance with child or eldercare.

Perhaps even more intractable to change will be women's historic location in the secondary labor market, marked by low wages, few benefits, part-time employment, and little job security. Eighty percent of women's jobs are located within only twenty of the 420 occupations listed by the Department of Labor (Pateman, 1988). Because of the burgeoning growth of the service sector, the labor force participation of older women has been steadily rising (DeViney & O'Rand, 1988). Older women, who often need the income, probably will continue to take jobs that men, who have better pensions or other sources of income, would not take (Rodehaever, 1990). For many of these women, part-time work is involuntary, a symbol of their role as the "shock absorbers" of an economy marked by marginal working conditions (Nussbaum, 1990). It may be a "privilege" for older women to choose between this type of work or exclusion because of age, blunting efforts to assure an income sufficient for decency.

By hailing a productive aging society, its advocates may be offering tacit approval of work situations that reinforce patterns of inequality and allow the continued exploitation of women—emblematic of that troublesome middle ground where noble goals come to life as practical and somewhat baser policies. By conflating the availability of such low-wage work with a larger, value-laden goal, less sympathetic voices can transform an economic necessity into newly honored social norms. What is a coincidental—and perhaps transitory—juxtaposition between economic needs and women's experiences can shape new work expectations, particularly if policy shifts support such expectations.

Several threads of evidence should alert us to this possibility. The pivotal roles of business, government, and labor in the creation of and now the retrenchment from a commitment to the retirement wage (see Myles, 1989) signifies how this process can evolve. Further, our inability to achieve enough flexibility to encourage continued employment of older people without designing policies—such as raising the retirement age without modifying laws about disability—that penalize those who are either unable or unwilling to work provides another clue as to how tension between an individual choice and a social expectation model might be resolved. And, finally, today's political environment and the apocalyptic nightmare just described hints that the political uses of the social worth–productivity–work nexus can become a strategy for delegitimating income-support programs. We already have witnessed how the rejection of ageism, even in its most compassionate form, has been captured and transformed by interests that have given us the term "greedy geezer" to signify generalized disapproval of older people.

Because of its history, its connection to the work ethic, and its ability to serve those who might wish to undermine public support for older people, productivity can have the same fate. A decision that public support of society's oldest members, the poorer of whom are generally women, is no longer economically feasible or politically or morally necessary is a deeply troubling vision. If such a vision were to become reality without sharp modifications in the work environment, the inequalities older women already experience would be exacerbated. Hence, if it is jobs we are concerned about—and at least as an intermediate solution, we must be—then we should concentrate on an explicit job strategy. The rubric of a productive aging society confuses rather than serves a sustained effort to create better, more gender-sensitive jobs.

## Productivity, Cultural Meanings, and Old Age

Emphasizing a productive aging society may mask other more subtle but no less real issues about old age. Most generally, it provides an answer before we have systematically asked all the questions about its meanings. Since the idea of productivity seems so clearly a continuation of the values of the middle years, it begs the question as to whether old age is a unique time in human life, intrinsically valuable, and fundamentally different than the period that came before. An emphasis on productivity can easily, in the public consciousness and through the media, elevate one desirable model for growing old. Like its twin, the much maligned ageism, it can impose a negative value on those who are not productive in the traditional sense or who do not maintain youthful vigor and independence (Cole, 1988). It also can intensify the prejudice that already marks social attitudes toward the impaired elderly (Minkler, 1990). The unspoken assumption that an acceptable old age is simply an extension of middle age can do fundamental damage to the integrity of life's last stage.

An emphasis on productivity can devalue relational activities—often displayed in women's demanding roles as primary caregivers—that encroaching dependencies often demand and hide the creativity and moral integrity that are developed and realized in these relationships. A narrow understanding of productivity, especially when paired with the scapegoating of the old, can compound the psychological damage to female caregivers if the caregiving burden is not acknowledged and honored as part of productivity's meaning. A corollary risk is that those older women who do not conform to the new rosy image of a productive old age may blame themselves and not the underlying social conditions that influence so dramatically their experience of old age. In the most basic way, we must ask if productivity is at least one of the deepest goods we should wish for in old age. Only if that is true should we consider risking its negative consequences.

One risk is that the "productive aging" scenario might go as follows. Society will continue defining productivity in terms of work; simultaneously, it will retrench from the social welfare policies that have created the retirement wage. It will emphasize the productive capacities of the "healthy old," thereby forging new expectations that they should continue working. Opportunities to work will become expectations to work in whatever jobs become available. Social Security will be modified accordingly, unfairly discriminating against the unhealthy and limiting, rather than expanding, options (Crown, 1990). Women also will be expected to conform to these newly developed norms. They will maintain their primary caregiving roles and some will add new ones, such as the caring for the children of their drug-addicted daughters or sons. Such caregiving will not receive strong social recognition or public assistance. At the same time, the workplace will be unyielding in its maintenance of male norms of achievement, success, communication, and style (Fuchs, 1988; Kessler-Harris, 1990; Markus, 1987). Older women, at best, will be at the fringes of this gender-constructed workplace. The workplace will continue to reflect, as a microcosm, the place that women and older people occupy in society at large; it will be a primary area for understanding sexist and ageist social arrangements and in preventing or facilitating equal status and power (Stewart, 1990). Yet other ways in which one can contribute richly to society without being a part of the work force will be underestimated or unexplored. Individuals who are disabled, and so nonproductive by typical definition, will be even further marginalized.

In sum, a number of factors should alert us to the fact that productivity's best goals can be interpreted in ways that can harm older women, such as the following: (1) the impact and stubborn persistence of gender biases at work, (2) the almost instinctive linking of productivity to paid work and hence the devaluation of the "nonproductive" and their activities, (3) the contemporary consequences of historically imposed norms and privatization on women's lives, (4) the history of what and whose ends age- and gender-defined roles have served, (5) the nature of power—or gatekeeping—relationships, (6) the delegitimization of the old, and (7) the looming questions about cultural meaning. Using the analytical filter of the political economy of aging and the history of the silencing of women, I suspect that older women will be the last group with access to the definitional powers to convert a potentially harmful vision into a celebratory one. And more fundamentally, even if productivity were defined in a gender-sensitive, even feminist, way, is that a key value we wish to elevate as a fundamental marker of the good life in old age?

### Productivity Revisited

How then can I extricate myself from the dilemmas I've raised? If ageism and systematic denigrating of their ways of thinking and acting has silenced women; excluded many from playing a defining role in their own lives; and denied them full access to work, volunteer opportunities, or education and if a productive aging society is simply another trap to deflect and subvert meaningful roles for older women, what are the alternatives?

The emphasis on productivity points us in the correct direction. It reminds us that older people have been unnecessarily marginalized by a society that is unable to determine what, if anything, it wants from them. It reminds us that older Americans often exist in a permanent liminal state, exiting from one phase of life but often denied reentry into another phase that has an actual content. Destroying myths has not seemed to help very much in creating a space in which we can grow old in a culturally acceptable way. Raising the notion of productivity asks us to think about how older women can earn social approbation. It asks us to consider how to frame a mood that can serve as a symbolic cue for what is important and calls us, if need be, to action. A discussion of productivity helps us to think about, develop, and test a substantive image of what the last stage of life can and should be so that it responds to both individual and social needs. Raising the possibility of productive aging as a goal begs us to start a public conversation. Prior to that conversation, we may be unprepared to find the appropriate language to describe our goals for old age. A call for a productive aging society may prosaically have put the cart before the horse.

A few questions might guide consideration of what ends new symbolic language should serve. Does it encourage the development of new opportunities of personal growth and development, facilitate a more intense interiority and exercise of moral agency, stimulate participation in both formal and informal human interactions (Fahey, 1991)? Can it capture Malcolm Cowley's (1980) experience of "sitting like a snake on a sun-warmed rock? Can it embrace the Aristotelian concept of leisure—the doing of something good in itself? Can it simultaneously serve society and the older person? Can it support the relational values that women have so long acted upon in the private sphere, oriented toward process as well as outcome?

A few broad ideas and then a series of steps, from a feminist perspective, might facilitate movement toward positive responses to these questions. But one caveat is in order. Although a productive aging society does not serve the subjective or objective conditions of older women very well, except as it might create jobs for those who want and need them, we must be responsible to the immediate needs of contemporary women. Hence, a few public policy responses that primarily address interim solutions will be highlighted. As we test these intermediate steps, perhaps we will happen upon a felicitous and appropriate cue word or phrase.

If we could imagine transforming women's traditional "silence" into a grand uproar, assuring that they would be heard, we might see the following: (1) new uses for women's affiliative histories, their flexibility, and continued growth (Gottlieb, 1989); (2) women as our society's "moral entrepreneurs," exercising leadership roles as social critics (Jordan, 1989) based on a social acceptance of their styles and a robust respect for their wisdom nurtured by their diverse lifetime experiences; and (3) the testing, in larger spheres, of a woman's way of thinking, seeing, and acting so that women do not function as mechanisms of oppression but become part of the restructuring of the dominant culture (Markus, 1987).

For example, Elinor Lenz and Barbara Meyerhoff (1985) suggest that for women productivity often describes a process rather than an outcome. It is the bringing of order to chaos, repetitive doing and redoing. Rooted in cooperation, women's productivity often involves nourishing relationships to produce goods that serve the entire community engaged in a particular practice—for example, taking care of children or nursing the sick (Whitbeck, 1983). Because of this commitment to doing, many women have defined success not necessarily in terms of its external rewards but rather in terms of giving something to others: as the ability to be useful, to take care, to help (Markus, 1987). In her exploration of maternal thinking, Sara Ruddick (1989) emphasizes elements of protection, nurturing, and training for socialization as key practices for women. These attitudes suggest not only a different definition of productivity but also, even if applied to productivity's traditional forms, a radically altered way of working.

Through this new way of thinking, women would bring into public life those behavioral and emotional patterns that have been reserved historically for the private sphere. These would include the importance of personal (not only functional) relationships for life fulfillment, the value of work well done for its own sake, the norm of helpfulness to other, and an emphasis on caring and responsibility (Gilligan, 1982; Markus, 1987; Ruddick, 1989).

### Public Policy, Social, Media, and Other Responses

Ranging from the most immediate to the much longer range, the following public policy responses could begin to implement change.

1. Provide assistance for lower-income people to seek relief through the Age Discrimination in Employment Act; provide ample education and outreach to inform older women that they are part of a protected class and that legal assistance is available; allow for legal action based on combined age and sex discrimination.
2. Assure that formal caregivers receive adequate wages, benefits, and training so that they are elevated from their current level of exploitation.
3. Provide recognition for homemaking and child and eldercare in the calculation of Social Security and other retirement benefits so that women will not be forced to take whatever jobs are available in the market for reasons of financial necessity. Assure a minimum income, sufficient for decency.
4. Support training and retraining, particularly for the "displaced homemaker" and for others who wish to continue working or to reenter the labor force; if necessary, subsidize employment as long as that employment is nonexploitive.

5. Support the caring work of grandmothers, who have assumed the parenting role for their grandchildren, through respite and income support.

6. Help finance small work collectives, particularly on a neighborhood basis, committed to feminist ways of knowing and the ethics of caring; have older women manage and work at these collectives. Such localism also is important for enhancing psychological well-being and protecting the physical environment. It can forge a more organic sense of community and permit women to continue participating in community life while reducing their physical and emotional stress.

7. Establish "grandmother's dens" as a place for young people, mothers, and teenagers to have a sounding board. Grandmothers can be trained as formal mediators or informal discussants. Create "wisdom workshops" in schools, camps, and other places where younger people and parents gather in which older women can establish communities of memory and serve as guides to parenting.

8. Set up a series of public forums so that older women can describe the kind of work that they really want to do, rather than accept the conventional response that "they like to work as part-time bank tellers—that gives them time to travel and take off when they want to" (Beck, 1991).

9. Sponsor research that examines the more feminist approach to work that sustains those qualities of womanhood—nurturing, community, and relational abilities—that are likely to have been products of women's cultural and social roles but that have been traditionally devalued by the job market. Use these qualities not to romanticize a woman's past role but to adopt a more generative view of human life (Gilligan, 1982).

10. Sponsor research that critically examines and proposes recommendations concerning how to address the often conflicting needs of the broader society—for example, in regard to Social Security financing, the economy, and the needs or wishes of older people.

There are other kinds of approaches that need to be tried as well; some examples follow.

1. Create opportunities comparable to the "base communities" that emerged from liberation theology or the evangelical academies in Germany, which practice a commitment to the "politics of discussion." In such conversations, acclaim old age as a unique time in human life; explore its meaning; pose the question: What constitutes the good life in old age? Initiate discussions that challenge money and consumption as the measure of social worth or the assumption that working long and hard hours is an honorable "complaint" and often the key to workplace rewards. Determine where the "hurts" of society are and how women's particular experiences can help heal society.

2. Turn to the schools as a place to begin remodeling attitudes toward the old, starting with the youngest children. This is an essential and logical first step to assigning labels, such as productive aging, which are so easily open to conflicting applications.

3. Create new media images of older women that move beyond older people having "fun" (i.e., being just like middle-aged people) to older people learning to live well in spite of dependency and encroaching death. Readings from the poetry and journals of May Sarton or the journal of Florida Scott Maxwell are good beginning images.

4. Vigorously reimagine ways older women (and all older people) can gain in other ways some of the rewards that work offers—a sense of self-worth and purpose, meaningful social contact, and social approbation (Stewart, 1990).

## CONCLUSION

For today's older women, it is important to counteract the ageist, sexist stereotypes that have distorted their efforts to achieve a consistently satisfying sense of self-worth and social approbation without replacing these stereotypes with an alternative mandate of how women should lead their lives. For those who need to work, a constant effort must be made to chip away at the barriers to the kind of employment that they want and to not accept what will best serve the needs of business. At times, there may be synchronicity; at other times, there will be none. The fundamental challenge will be the construction of a new way to imagine work and life so false dichotomies that have seemed inevitable can be erased. However well intentioned, the move toward productivity as an important defining characteristic of a good old age, rather than helping this process, may be one more barrier to a rich—and feminist—appreciation of old age's gifts.

## REFERENCES

Beck, R. (1991). Personal communication.

Benhabib, S. (1987). The generalized and the concrete other: The Kohlberg-Gilligan controversy and feminist theory. In S. Benhabib & D. Cornell (Eds.), *Feminism as critique: On the politics of gender*. Minneapolis:University of Minnesota Press.

Butler, R., & Gleason, H. (Eds.). (1985). *Productive aging: Enhancing vitality in later life*. New York: Springer.

Cole, T. (1988). The specter of old age: History, politics, and culture in an aging America. *Tikkun, 3*(5), 14–18, 93–95.

Cowley, M. (1980). *The view from 80*. New York: Viking Press.

Crown, W. (1990). Economic trends, politics, and employment policy for older workers. *Journal of Aging & Social Policy, 2*(1/2), 131–152.

*Daedalus*. (1987, Fall). Learning about women: Gender, power, and politics, *Daedalus, 116*(4).

De Beauvoir, S. (1972). *The second sex*. New York: Vintage Books.

DeViney, S., & O'Rand, A. (1988). Gender-cohort succession and retirement among older men and women. 1951–1984. *Sociological Quarterly, 29*(4), 525–540.

Dolbeare, K. (1974). *Political change in the United States: A framework for analysis*. New York: McGraw-Hill.

Ekerdt, D. (1986). The busy ethic: Moral continuity between work and retirement. *The Gerontologist*, 26(1), 239–244.

Epstein, C. F. (1988). *Deceptive distinctions: Sex, gender and the social order.* New Haven, CT: Russell Sage Foundation.

Farganis, S. (1986). *The social construction of the feminine character.* Totowa, NJ: Rowman and Littlefield.

Fuchs, V. (1988). *Women's quest for economic equality.* Cambridge, MA: Harvard University Press.

Garner, D., & Mercer, S. (1989). *Women as they age.* New York: Haworth Press.

*Generations.* (1990, Summer). 14(3).

Gilligan, C. (1982). *In a different voice.* Cambridge, MA: Harvard University Press.

Gottlieb, N. (1989). Families, work, and the lives of older women. In J. D. Garner & S. Mercer (Eds.), *Women as they age: Challenge, opportunity, and triumph* (pp. 217–244). New York: Haworth Press.

Griffiths, M., & Whitford, W. (1988). *Feminist perspectives in philosophy.* London: Macmillan.

Grossman, H., & Chester, N. L. (Eds.). (1990). *The experience and meaning of work in women's lives.* Hillsdale, NJ: Laurence Erlbaum.

Hess, B. (1990, Summer). The demographic parameters of gender and aging. *Generations*, 14 (3), 12–16.

Hewitt, P. (1986). *Broken promises.* Washington, DC: Americans for Generational Equity.

Hochschild, A., & Machung, A. (1989). *The second shift: Inside the two-job marriage.* New York: Viking Press.

Institute of Medicine/National Research Council. (1986). *America's aging: Productive roles in an older society.* Washington, DC: National Academy Press.

Jordan, B. (1989). *The common good.* London: Oxford University Press.

Kessler-Harris, A. (1990). *A woman's wage: Historical meanings and social consequences.* Lexington: University Press of Kentucky.

Lakoff, R. (1975). *Language and women's place.* New York: Harper & Row.

Lenz, E., & Meyerhoff, B. (1985). *The feminization of America.* Los Angeles: Jeremey Tarcher.

Levy, J. (1988). Intersections of gender and aging. *Sociological Quarterly*, 29(4), 479–486.

Longman, P. (1987). *Born to pay: The new politics of aging in America.* Boston: Houghton Mifflin.

Markus, M. (1987). Women, success, and civil society. In S. Benhabib & D. Cornell (Eds.), *Feminism as critique: On the politics of gender* (pp. 96–109). Minneapolis: University of Minnesota Press.

Minkler, M. (1990). Aging and disability: Behind and beyond the stereotypes. *Journal of Aging Studies*, 4(3), 245–260.

Moody, H. R. (1988). *Abundance of life.* New York: Columbia University Press.

Morrison, M. (1986). Work and retirement in an older society. In A. Pifer & L. Bronte, (Eds.), *Our aging society* (pp. 341–366). New York: Norton.

Myles, J. (1989). *Old age and the welfare state* (revised). Lawrence: University of Kansas Press.

Nussbaum, K. (1990). Social insecurity: The economic marginalization of older women workers. In I. Bluestone, R. Montgomery, & J. Owen (Eds.), *The* aging of the workforce: Problems, programs, policies. Detroit, MI: Wayne State University Press.

Pateman, C. (1988). The patriarchal welfare state. In A. Gutman (Ed.), *Democracy and the welfare state*. Princeton, NJ: Princeton University Press.

Pifer, A. (1986). The public policy response. In A. Pifer & L. Bronte, (Eds.), *Our aging society* (pp. 391–419). New York: Norton.

Riley, M. W. (1985). Women, men, and the lengthening of the life course. In A. Rossi (Ed.), *Gender and the life course* (pp. 333–347). New York: Aldine.

Rodehaever, D. (1990, Summer). Labor market progeria. *Generations, 14*(3), 53–59.

Ruddick, S. (1989). *Maternal thinking*. New York: Ballantine.

Secunda, V. (1984). *By youth possessed: The denial of age in America*. Indianapolis, IN: Bobbs-Merrill.

Stewart, A. (1990). Discovering the meanings of work. In H. Grossman & N. L. Chester, (Eds.), *The experience and meaning of work in women's lives*. Hillsdale, NJ: Laurence Erlbaum.

Tannen, D. (1990). *You just don't understand*. New York: William Morrow.

Whitbeck, C. (1983). A different reality: Feminist ontology. In C. Gould, (Ed.), *From beyond domination: New perspectives on women and philosophy*. London: Rowman and Alloshild.

Woodward, K. (1991). *Aging and its discontents*. Indianapolis: University of Indiana Press.

# 14

# Cultural and Ethnic Contexts of Aging Productively over the Life Course: An Economic Network Framework

*James S. Jackson, Toni C. Antonucci,*
*and Rose C. Gibson*

The purpose of this chapter is to explore how life course, labor force participation, economic network involvement, and social support processes within different ethnic, cultural, and racial groups affect what is termed *aging productively* (Butler & Gleason, 1985). It is postulated that blocked opportunities contribute to very different economic experiences for racial and ethnic minorities in comparison to the majority population (Jackson, Antonucci, & Gibson, 1990a). Two theoretical propositions have dominated research on race and ethnicity in aging (Jackson, 1985). "Multiple jeopardy" holds that social, psychological, and economic disadvantages among ethnic and racial minorities in earlier periods of the life span have deleterious consequences in older age (Dowd & Bengston, 1978; Jackson, Antonucci, & Gibson, 1990a; Markides, Liang, & Jackson, 1990). "Age as leveler" suggests that the concomitant of old age neutralizes advantages that existed for nonminority individuals earlier in life. Some research supports "multiple jeopardy" while some does not (Gibson, 1989; Jackson, 1985; Markides, Liang, & Jackson, 1990).

Investigations of these competing hypotheses have been hampered by the lack of methodologically and substantively adequate, longitudinal panel data on nationally representative and racially, ethnically, and culturally diverse samples. We believe that the efficacy of these competing conceptual frameworks may be assessed by examining factors related to individual productivity, formal and informal support, and health and effective functioning among different gender, socioeconomic, sociocultural, and racial and ethnic groups. The chapter takes a life course perspective, stressing the importance of an individual's early experiences with the labor force as influencing later opportunities and type and level of productive activities (Jackson & Gibson, 1985).

## SOCIOCULTURAL INFLUENCES ON INDIVIDUAL PRODUCTIVITY

The productivity construct has important implications as a general framework for a number of continuing research trends on gender, socioeconomic status, race, and ethnicity in social gerontology. If the "productive years" are those during which an individual is employed for pay outside the home, the increase in life expectancy beyond the "productive" or employment years causes a major shift in the dependency ratio; that is, the ratio of employed people to those too young or too old to be in the labor force. The view suggests that people are productive only during their paid employment years and that those who are not employed for pay or who have intermittent work histories are less productive than those who have stable work-for-pay histories. The term *productivity* is used by economists to refer to the individual or collective creation of a product or service over a given unit of time. The National Plan on Aging (NIA, 1982) proposed that the definition of productivity be expanded to include paid work, unpaid work, organized voluntary participation, mutual help, and self-care. Practical reasons include recognizing how nontraditional forms of productive activity contribute to the society and valuing these contributions and their calculations in normal government policymaking activities. Both conceptual and practical problems become more acute as productivity is examined across the adult life span, and an effort is made both to compensate for productivity loss in traditional work areas and to provide support for what might be labeled hidden forms of productive activity.

This latter point is critical to a theoretical perspective on how gender, ethnicity, race, and aging affect productivity changes across the adult life cycle (Baily, 1986; IOM, 1986; Morgan, 1986). The use of nontraditional definitions, including the individual's enjoyment of activities, directly affects the overall assessment of productive behaviors, particularly certain subgroups of the populations, such as women, blacks, and older people. Thus, for example, defining individual productivity as work for pay suggests one rate of "productivity" for women, far below that of men. Using an expanded definition suggests that women contribute more, rather than fewer, hours of productive activity than men—although their pay for these activities remains far below that of men for similar or lesser *amounts* of work (see Antonucci, Jackson, Gibson, & Herzog, in press; Kahn, 1988). National statistics concerning employment differences among whites and other minority groups are available. Very little research, however, has attempted to explore and assess other types of productive activities or the long-term characteristics of these activities (Butler, 1985; Herzog, Kahn, Morgan, Jackson, & Antonucci, 1989). In our analyses of race and aging productively, we found that while blacks and whites do not differ significantly on the level of measures of individual aging productively, they do differ in the processes that underlie the relationship of our measures of productive involvement to individual well-being outcomes (Jackson, Antonucci, & Gibson, 1990b; Antonucci, Jackson, Gibson, & Herzog, in press). This finding is consistent with our general model of coping and adaptation (related to the issue of multiple jeopardy and age as leveler) which suggests that blacks may utilize different mechanisms than whites over the individual life course to maintain levels of productivity and well-being and effective functioning that are comparable to those of whites.

## REGULAR, IRREGULAR, AND SOCIAL ECONOMIC NETWORKS

At the core of the proposed productive aging framework is a model that postulates both life course continuity and discontinuity in individual participation in three distinct but interrelated economic networks. The first is the regular economy network. This is the one most frequently engaged in and is characterized by exchanges of labor for pay and an efficient government accounting and taxation system. The second also involves pay but does not include government oversight and regulation as in the regular economy. This one has been called the underground, illegal, or irregular economy.

The final economic network is a barter system that does not include exchanges of money. In this case, economic exchanges, largely among family and friends, are made without the explicit transferral of money. These three networks are interrelated and among racial and ethnic minority groups may be tightly interwoven. Participation in the three networks also is hypothesized to be integrally related to involvement in traditional familial and friend social and emotional support networks.

## NATIONAL ECONOMIC AND INDIVIDUAL PRODUCTIVITY

Problems related to the decline of productivity in the United States have received considerable attention in recent years (Baily, 1986; Baumol, 1989; Holzer & Nagel, 1984; National Research Council, 1979). Productivity refers to a set of national accounting assessments that generally are measured for the economy as a whole or for different large economic segments (National Research Council, 1979). Outputs are defined as goods and services produced, in dollar value, either counted or imputed, in the economy over a specified period. Inputs consist of such resources as labor, capital goods, and energy, usually measured in dollars (National Research Council, 1979; Rosen, 1984). Productivity is not measured directly but is determined as the ratio of outputs over inputs (Rosen, 1984).

A positive relationship has been found between paid productive activities (work) and social and psychological health (Herzog, Kahn, Morgan, Jackson, & Antonucci, 1989; Kahn, 1981; Kahn, 1986; Moss, 1979). The relationships of unpaid productive activities to the individual's health and well-being have gone largely uninvestigated (Jackson, Antonucci, & Gibson, 1990b), and these forms of productive activities do not enter into a national accounting scheme (Morgan, 1986). Thus, there may be a tendency to overemphasize the dependency of older adults (Morgan, 1986; Myers, Manton, & Bacellar, 1986; Siegel & Taeuber, 1986) and to impute improperly negative health and psychological consequences to the withdrawal from the paid labor force (Kahn, 1986; Morgan, 1986).

It has been proposed recently that the definition of productivity be expanded to include inputs from labor that reflect (1) paid work, (2) unpaid work, (3) voluntary organizational work, (4) mutual help, and (5) self-care (Kahn, 1986; Morgan, 1986; Myers, Manton, & Bacellar, 1986; NIA, 1982). Most attention has focused on understanding the effects of productive engagement on individual well-being, particularly in the latter stages of the life course (Kahn, 1986; Morgan, 1986; Institute of Medicine/National Research Council, 1986).

In the remainder of this chapter an economic and primary relationship network framework for understanding the context of individual productivity and productive aging is outlined. We present a set of processes hypothesized to occur within and among these networks and provide a brief discussion of the implications of the model for social and psychological well-being. We are especially interested in how these processes might be influenced by racial and ethnic status over the adult life course.

## THEORETICAL FRAMEWORK OF
## PRODUCTIVE ACTIVITIES

Productive activities occur within the larger context of economic exchange networks. The existence of three separate economic networks has been documented by a small but growing body of literature (Ferman, Berndt, & Selo, 1978; Ferman, Henry, & Hoyman, 1987; Lowenthal, 1975; Lowenthal, 1981; Smith, 1982). These three networks are bound together in mutual interaction in meeting individual and family economic needs (Henry, 1989). While in many communities the formal, regular economic network may be sufficient in addressing the subsistence needs of their members, in other more disadvantaged communities the irregular and social economy networks may provide supplemental structures for economic survival (Ferman, Berndt, & Selo, 1978; Stack, 1974). In order to comprehend the nature, correlates, and consequences of productive activities, each of these three different but interrelated networks needs to be examined.

We hypothesize that involvement in the same productive activity, whether paid or unpaid, may have different outcomes and consequences for the individual if performed in the different economic networks. Social and irregular economic exchanges may be of particular importance in the productive behavior of economically disadvantaged groups because they provide an alternative context for economic participation (Ferman, Berndt, & Selo, 1978; Ferman & Berndt, 1981; Lowenthal, 1975; Lowenthal, 1981). Economic necessity and relatively stable life opportunity restrictions may result in extensive intra-individual continuity across the life span in network participation and productive activities. For example, it is expected that because of differences in the past and immediate social environments, members of socially and economically disadvantaged groups may have distinctly different experiences across the life course than others regarding the nature, course, and consequences of productive activities (Kalleberg & Sorenson, 1979).

## Regular Economic Network

In the traditional market economy most Americans sell their labor (Cook, 1973; Godelier, 1980; Kalleberg & Sorenson, 1979; Lowenthal, 1975). The available literature reveals that many social groups (e.g., blacks) have been and continue to be blocked from full participation in regular economic activities (Anderson & Cottingham, 1981; Hill, 1981; Montagna, 1977). Numerous articles and aggregate data (Current Population Reports, 1980) document the disadvantaged economic position of different social groups in American society, and statistics show that the individual and family needs of many Americans are not met through participation in the regular market economy (Anderson & Cottingham, 1981; Cain, 1976; Hill, 1983).

## Irregular Economic Network

Many authors have pointed to the existence of networks other than the traditional market economy that may serve a subsistence function. While most have focused on the social, friendship, and kin networks as being of paramount importance (e.g., Stack, 1974), certain authors have proposed that a separate market economy operates in a parallel manner to the regular market economy (Ferman, Berndt, & Selo, 1978; Glutman, 1977; Smith, 1982; Witte & Simon, 1983). This network has been given a variety of names—the underground economy, the subterranean economy, the hidden economy. We prefer the designation of Ferman and associates (1978), and refer to these networks as the irregular economy.

Involvement within the irregular economic network concerns the receipt of pay for activities that are not recorded or monitored within the regular apparatus of the economy (Ferman, Henry, & Hoyman, 1987; Ferman, Berndt, & Selo, 1978; Ferman & Berndt, 1981). Much of the research on irregular economic activity has been concerned with gaining estimates of its

Achieving a Productive Aging Society

size in relationship to regular economic activity (e.g., Glutman, 1977; Smith, 1982; Witte & Simon, 1983). It has been proposed that it is 10 percent to 15 percent reported national income (Herzog, Kahn, Morgan, Jackson, & Antonucci, 1989; Smith, 1982; Witte & Simon, 1983). It is widespread throughout various levels of society (Henry, 1982; Henry & Brown, 1990), and the range of services and goods have been classified within the following broad categories: sale and/or production of goods, home-related services, personal services provided to consumers, "off-the-books" employment by regular establishments, rental of property, provision of entertainment, and criminal activities.

The irregular economic network seems to be most widely utilized for services that usually are not provided by regular firms or businesses. Ferman and associates (1978) also indicated that reasons other than price (previous contact, social convenience) might enter into the decision to use the irregular economic network. Although individuals would seem to prefer to work within the regular economic network, blocked opportunities as well as positive benefits other than economic ones may play a role in why people participate in irregular activities (Henry & Brown, 1990).

### Social Economic Network

The social economic network can be distinguished from the regular and irregular networks as encompassing economic activities that are not registered by the economic measuring methods of society and do not use money as a medium of exchange (Ferman, Berndt, & Selo, 1978; Lowenthal, 1975, 1981). Additionally, the economic exchanges often are embedded in and based upon the networks of social relationships that people maintain over time (Lowenthal, 1975; Stack, 1974). The provision of goods and services within the social, friendship, and kin networks has been the subject of much research with respect to the types of exchanges and activities that we are including under productive behaviors (Cantor, 1979, 1981; McAdoo, 1981; Martineau, 1977; Stack, 1974). Although the majority of these studies have been conducted for a variety of reasons, almost uniformly they point to the importance of the informal friend, neighbor, and kin networks in providing both economic and social support for their members. The work of Stack (1974) is exemplary in this respect:

I became poignantly aware of the alliances of individuals trading and exchanging goods, resources and the care of children, the intensity of their acts of domestic cooperation, and the exchange of goods and services among these persons, both kin and non-kin. Their social and economic lives were so entwined that not to repay on an exchange meant that someone else's child would not eat. (p. 29)

A number of studies point to the importance of community activities, embedded within these social networks, concerning the economic and social survival of their members. Martin Lowenthal (1975, 1981), however, indicates that there have been no systematic attempts to provide a theoretical orientation of how social economic networks fit with more traditional economic formulations. A. Regula Herzog and associates (1989) reported recently from a national study that approximately 83 percent of all respondents indicated participating in activities that we are including under the rubric of the social economic network. Of special importance to the elderly is the provision of care for both acute and chronic conditions. This care, particularly for the frail elderly, is becoming of greater importance as growing numbers of older people require care for an increasingly longer period of time (Soldo & Manton, 1985).

It is important to note that we draw a distinction between social economic networks and primary group relationships. The former refers to arrangements that involve the explicit exchange of goods and services, albeit without a monetary component. On the other hand, primary group relationships refer to the emotional, evaluative, or informational exchanges typically associated with the concept of social support (Antonucci, 1985, 1990; House & Kahn, 1985).

## SOCIOCULTURAL INFLUENCES, INFORMAL SUPPORT, AND INDIVIDUAL PRODUCTIVITY

In our research over the past few years we have explored the concept of social support in several ways. Among the most promising has been work on reciprocity (Antonucci, Fuhrer, & Jackson, 1991; Antonucci & Jackson, 1987, 1990). Beginning with the seminal work of Alvin Gouldner (1960), most social scientists have recognized the norm of reciprocity; that is, the give-and-take relationship in which norms can mandate certain exchanges. In our theoretical and empirical work we have argued that the concept or norm of reciprocity serves an important function in both maintaining and promoting productivity. Our analyses thus far have shown that people who believe that their relationships are reciprocal are higher on well-being measures than people who do not perceive their relationships as reciprocal (Antonucci & Jackson, 1987, 1990; Ingersoll-Dayton & Antonucci, 1988).

Several issues can be explored through the concept of reciprocity and exchanges. Reciprocity need not be contemporaneous, especially among long-term relationships. It has been noted that long-term exchanges that appear to be nonreciprocated are common in close social relations (Clark, Mills, & Powell, 1986; Wentowski, 1981). It is expected that these relations will eventually be reciprocal. This has important implications for the individual productivity concept since it serves as a motivator to maintain productive unreciprocated exchanges or to place deposits in what Toni Antonucci and James Jackson (1987) have called the "support bank," so that withdrawals might be made at some future time. It may be that one way older people are able to maintain reciprocal relations and feelings of productivity is by substituting reciprocity in kind (a ride to the store one week for a ride to the store the next) for reciprocity across kind (a ride to the store for babysitting). This latter form of reciprocity permits numerous possibilities for both maintaining productivity and being flexible and responsive to changing abilities and capacities of the elderly. The experience of these exchanges or reciprocity is seen as another form of productivity. Viewed in this manner, reciprocity serves both the function of providing to others and permitting one to maintain a personal sense of productivity by giving now and later having "deposits" from which one might "withdraw" when certain goods or resources are required to maintain individual productivity.

### Primary Group Networks and Individual Productivity

As we have discussed, a great deal of research points to the need to examine individual social behavior within family and friendship networks (Wellman, 1981; Wentowski, 1981). These networks have been most often studied within the area of social support. The social support literature, however, has not systematically related larger, macro social and economic opportunity factors to the functioning and effects of these primary networks. Much of the research on social support networks has focused on the nature of either primary groups or the principal caregiver and how they are structured and function to buffer or insulate individuals from the deleterious effects of stress (Conner, Power, & Bultena, 1979; Fischer, 1982; Kahn, Wethington, & Ingersoll, 1987; LaRocco, House, & French, 1980; Noelker & Zarit, 1983; Pearlin & Schooler, 1978; Thoits, 1982; Wellman, 1981).

The literature on the family/friend networks of older adults suggests that they serve an important function in both providing a context for productive activities and contributing generally to the well-being of the family itself (Chatters, Taylor, & Jackson, 1985; McAdoo, 1981). It is hypothesized that the regular, irregular, and social economic networks provide the larger context for the functioning of primary group relationships. Economic networks are assumed to affect and interact with primary group networks to influence individual functioning (Ferman, Berndt, & Selo, 1978). Participation in economic networks is hypothesized to be differentially and reciprocally related to interactions within smaller primary group networks. These relationships are critical since the work in social support clearly points to the mediating role of primary group ties to individual productive activities and social, health, and psychological well-being (Herzog, Antonucci, Jackson, Kahn, & Morgan, 1987). It is within this context of interaction among economic and primary group networks that opportunity structure variables operate to affect individual achievements and social and psychological behaviors.

It is of course likely that participation in the social economic network and primary group relationships will exhibit considerable overlap. We believe, however, that it is useful to maintain the distinction; the overlap is not absolute and there is a hypothesized independent role of each in individual productivity and subsequent independent contributions of each to well-being and effective functioning.

## HYPOTHESIZED PROCESS OF ECONOMIC NETWORK INVOLVEMENT

### Theoretical Overview

Central to the proposed process of economic network involvement is the fact that individuals, because of economic necessity, participate in a variety of different types of economic networks for individual and family survival (Hill, 1981). Socioeconomic position may play an important role in the qualitative and quantitative aspects of participation in the three economic networks (Cantor & Little, 1985). Other sociocultural distinctions (e.g., race), however, may also contribute to important differences between social groups in the rates, frequency, and type of participation. For example, differences between blacks and whites have been reported for such things as attachment to the labor force (Anderson & Cottingham, 1981), level of involvement in subjective experiences in regular economic participation (Ferman, Berndt, & Selo, 1978), and rates and types of participation in social or barter economies (Stack, 1974). Other data indicate differential sets of relationships and participation in primary social support group activities (Cantor, 1981; Taylor & Chatters, 1986). This suggests that more than socioeconomic factors may contribute to observed differences among social groups in productive activities (Ferman, Berndt, & Selo, 1978).

We propose that the involvement in productive activities begins early in preadult life in the irregular and social economic networks. This early participation may be dictated by a variety of motivating factors, but the overriding condition is that of economic necessity. We further suggest that this participation strengthens over the years. By mid-adulthood and old age, such participation has become well entrenched, and the individual has perhaps played a variety of key roles in the operation of the irregular economic and the social economic networks. We expect that similar types of parallel activities may have transpired in the regular market economy, though for many disadvantaged Americans this is not necessarily the case (Hamilton, 1975; Kalleberg & Sorenson, 1979; Montagna, 1977).

Economic necessity is predicted to have the strongest influence on involvement in irregular and social economic network activity. For example, economic necessity is predicted to be stronger in blacks than whites, and thus blacks should show greater involvement in the social and irregular economic networks than whites. It is predicted that socioeconomic status variables such as education and occupation will reduce the relationship between race and participation in social and irregular network economies.

Participative patterns within the social, irregular, and regular economic networks are viewed as interrelated. A person may participate in all three or two simultaneously or may participate in only one. Similarly, participation may be sequential or periodic. For example, a person with an episodic formal employment history may maintain an adequate level of individual productivity by moving between the regular and irregular economic networks as a function of general economic conditions but consistently maintain relationships and position within the social economic network. As indicated earlier, however, the nature and interpretation of participation in these economic networks may affect and be affected by the primary group relationships in which the individual is enmeshed (Moen, Kain, & Elder, 1983). The proposed connection in Figure 14.1 indicates our concern with the effects of participation within these economic networks on primary group relationships and how these relationships may affect productive activities and in turn social, psychological, and health outcomes.

Some productive behaviors will be more or less likely to occur as a function of the type of networks in which an individual participates. Thus, if an individual's network relationships are in the regular economy, the productive activity of prime importance is likely to be paid work. The person may also be engaged, however, in the full range of other activities. Whether these other activities are related to the regular economic network or not may be a function of the degree of connectedness to the irregular economic and social economic networks.

One of the major outcomes in conceptualizing productive behaviors as occurring within the nexus of these three different types of networks is the fact that the same productive behavior performed within different networks may differ qualitatively and quantitatively. For example, paid employment within the regular economic network may be important for securing a salary to help meet monthly bills and provide for the basic standard of living. Engaging in the same activities within the irregular network (even for less pay, perhaps) may be viewed as more enjoyable and self-satisfying because it occurs within a milieu of friends, neighbors, and kin.

We also propose that one set of the major outcomes of productive activities will be at the individual level. Some of the outcomes that we envision occurring in the elderly as a function of participating in these activities will be in the areas of coping, self-esteem, perception of control, health, and general well-being (Ferman, Berndt, & Selo, 1978). Further, we feel that positive outcomes derived from engaging in these productive activities will affect noneconomic incentives for further participation in these networks. One of the most common observations has been that involvement in the social, irregular, or even the regular economic network is dictated by

Figure 14.1
Antecedents and Consequences of Productive Activities: An Economic Network Framework

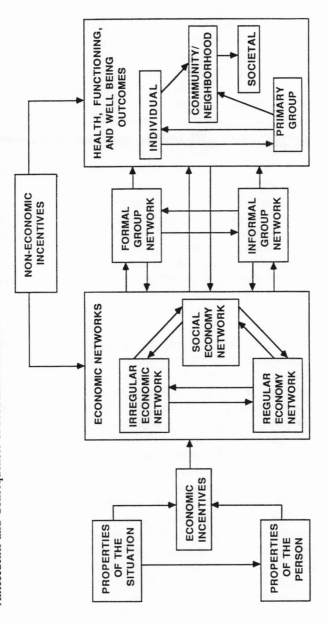

noneconomic considerations (Stack, 1974; Ferman, Berndt, & Selo, 1978; Lowenthal, 1975, 1981; Sarason, 1977). While we propose that economic necessity is the overriding consideration for participation in these networks at least initially (Oppenheimer, 1981), we believe that other incentives (e.g., altruism, religious motivation, group identity, etc.) may gain importance over time as a function of these individual outcomes.

We believe that participation in the social economic network, and to some extent the irregular economic network, is pervasive in some communities. In addition, we suggest that this involvement may have direct beneficial effects on the community itself by providing work and income. Several authors have reported on the importance of networks in maintaining the viability and integrity of the community (Ferman, Berndt, & Selo, 1978; Stack, 1974). In fact, Lowenthal (1975), commenting on community interactions, suggested:

These reciprocal arrangements are also important for the survival and integration of the community itself over time and help cement the social relationships themselves. The redistributional aspect of the social economy is particularly important in integrating groups in the community and assuring the permanence of the arrangement. The participants are able to derive a measure of security within a larger society in which they are considered marginal by wage-market standards. (p. 463)

Generally, we have predicted that different social groups may diverge significantly in their involvement and participation in different economic networks. More advantaged groups may be more likely to participate solely in the regular economic network and less advantaged groups may participate more in the social and irregular economic networks. As we indicated earlier, these are only working hypotheses. Little research has been conducted on these networks (Ferman, Henry, & Hoyman, 1987; Ferman, Berndt, & Selo, 1978), but we expect participation and productive activities to show continuity for less advantaged groups within the irregular and social economic networks and more sporadic participation, and perhaps entry later in life, for more advantaged members of society. The opposite is predicted for the regular economic network. These predictions suggest a different set of relationships over time among major network indicators as well as the types of activities engaged in within the networks.

We suggest that changes in status within the regular economic network should have less impact on the total productivity scores of disadvantaged group members than they will for others. This prediction is predicated on the belief that the former groups are much more likely to be involved in the other two networks and that more of their individual productivity is derived from these networks. We predict that the total productivity score for all social groups should be reduced with changes in regular economic network participation over time. This reduction should be greater and more debilitating for advantaged groups because of the disproportionate contribution of regular economic network participation to total productivity scores in comparison to less advantaged groups. Thus, loss of jobs, retirement, or disability should have the effect of disproportionately reducing individual productivity scores in advantaged groups, subsequently leading to greater reductions in well-being and health outcomes compared to less advantaged groups.

We further propose that the viability and integration of communities have some direct relationship to the well-being of the larger society. Obviously, activities within the regular economic network have direct and measurable effects on society through estimates of national income and the gross national product (Ferman, Berndt, & Selo, 1978; Institute of Medicine/National Research Council, 1986; Leichter, 1984; National Research Council, 1979; Rosen, 1984). We believe, however, that the contributions of productive behaviors in other economic networks have largely gone unrecognized in terms of their implications for individual well-being, as well as community survival and viability, which in turn has direct effects on the larger society.

## IMPLICATIONS OF THE PROPOSED FRAMEWORK

We believe that the proposed framework will aid in the study of productive behaviors of older Americans over the individual life course. The model emphasizes the importance of these networks for the productive behaviors at all life stages (Herzog, Antonucci, Jackson, Kahn, & Morgan, 1987). As McAdoo (1981) and others (Hamilton, 1975; Ferman, Berndt, & Selo, 1978), have indicated, these networks have particular value for disadvantaged groups in providing an avenue for engaging in activities that are of value to both the community and these groups. Commenting on the function of the irregular economy network, Ferman and associates (1978) have suggested that

The elderly on fixed incomes were often quite dependent on the irregular economy to supplement their monthly pensions and social security payment, particularly when they lived alone and had little help from their families. But *economic necessity* [emphasis ours] was often accompanied by other motivational factors, including feeling useful and needed, enjoying the work, and keeping active and busy. For some of our elderly informants, there was no financial necessity involved and the irregular economy served only these other functions. (p. 333)

While Ferman and associates (1978) did not do extensive analyses by race, they reported that blacks were slightly more likely to indicate using the irregular economy for services than other groups. In examining the social economic network, several researchers have commented on the importance of this network for poor and black elderly (Cantor, 1979; Lowenthal, 1975; Stack, 1974). Lowenthal (1975) states:

Gifts and various forms of assistance when a person has reached a certain age often fall within this category. A person who is considered incapable either physically or mentally may often be entitled to assistance from members of his social network because of his incapacity according to certain customs and traditions. An elder in a community may receive goods and services from people because of his age and status. (p. 464)

It may be true that black elders receive assistance from family and friends with no observable reciprocity. This may, however, be in keeping with a lifetime involvement with the social economic network and an extensive history of providing goods and services to other members of the community on the part of these elders. Finally, the very nature of what is considered to be productive behaviors may show significant shifts as people age. While declining physical abilities may severely limit certain forms of productive behaviors for elders, other behaviors may become more prominent. For example, counseling and advice of younger family members and friends may assume greater importance as productive activities for older as opposed to younger adults (Herzog, Kahn, Morgan, Jackson, & Antonucci, 1989).

## CONCLUSION

The theoretical framework presented in this chapter addresses the relationships among position in the opportunity structure, engagement in productive activities, and health and well-being across the individual life course. The increasing average life span, further lowering of the age of withdrawal from the labor force, and the potential increased consumption and dependency of older adults in the upper age range for long periods of time make an understanding of productivity and its antecedents and consequences of paramount importance. The policy issues and questions are pressing (Davis, 1986; Leichter, 1984; Rosen, 1984). By placing the relationship of individual productivity and well-being within an economic network context, differential predictions are possible regarding the same behaviors across settings and situations that may differ both qualitatively and quantitatively (i.e., regular market, irregular paid, and social barter situations). This aspect of the model also provides for a theoretical linkage to formal and personal and friend networks, which have been shown to have positive effects upon individual well-being. Finally, the model is important in providing independent assessments of productive activities separate from their predicted affects on individual well-being (Moss, 1979).

Two compelling factors provide a rationale for the proposed framework and approach to understanding how participation in these economic networks conditions and is influenced by racial, ethnic, and sociocultural factors. First, previous work on productive activities has not developed a theoretically meaningful definition of productive activities at the individual level. The proposed conceptualization of individual productivity (Rosen, 1984) includes traditional productivity measures of hours engaged or actual or imputed monetary value (Herzog & House, 1991; Herzog, & Morgan, 1989), but it also incorporates a broader set of activities as well as an assessment of the role of ancillary processes, notably process benefits and attributed benefits of the activity, as possible mediators of these traditional productivity indicators (Juster, Courant, & Dow, 1981). Second, the framework presented in this chapter provides a conceptual and theoretical life course approach to the empirical study of racial, ethnic, and cultural influences on the relationships of opportunity structure factors to processes and behaviors related to aging productively. These networks serve an important facilitating role, especially for ethnic and racial minority elders, by providing a context for engaging in activities that are of value to the community and to themselves (Hamilton, 1975; Ferman, Berndt, & Selo, 1978; Noelker & Zarit, 1983). We believe that the proposed life course economic network framework will facilitate new approaches to the study of gender, socioeconomic, racial, and ethnic factors related to aging productively.

## REFERENCES

Anderson, B. E., & Cottingham, D. H. (1981). The elusive quest for economic equality. *Daedalus, 10,* 257–274.
Antonucci, T. C. (1985). Personal characteristics, social support, and social behavior. In E. Shanas & R. H. Binstock (Eds.), *Handbook of aging and the social sciences* (2d ed., pp. 94–128). New York: Van Nostrand Reinhold.
Antonucci, T. C. (1990). Social supports and social relationships. In R. H. Binstock & L. K. George (Eds.), *Handbook of aging and the social sciences* (3d ed., pp. 205–226). Orlando, FL: Academic Press.
Antonucci, T. C., Fuhrer, R., & Jackson, J. S. (1990). Social support and reciprocity: A cross-ethnic and cross-national perspective. *Journal of Social and Personal Relationships, 7,* 519–530.
Antonucci, T. C., & Jackson, J. S. (1987). Social support, interpersonal efficacy and health. In L. L. Carstensen & B. A. Edelstein (Eds.), *Handbook of clinical gerontology* (pp. 291–311). New York: Pergamon.
Antonucci, T. C., & Jackson, J. S. (1990). The role of reciprocity in social support. In I. G. Sarason, R. Sarason, & G. R. Pierce (Eds.), *Social support: An interactional view* (pp. 173–198). New York: Wiley.
Antonucci, T. C., Jackson, J. S., Gibson, R. C., & Herzog, A. R. (in press). Age, gender, race, and productive activity across the life-span. In M. Stevenson, M. Kite, & B. Whitley (Eds.), *Gender roles through the life-span.* Muncie, IN: Ball State University Press.
Baily, M. N. (1986). What has happened to productivity growth? *Science, 234,* 443–451.
Baumol, W. J. (1989). Is there a U.S. productivity crisis? *Science, 243,* 611–615.

Butler, R. N. (1985). Health, productivity, and aging: An overview. In R. N. Butler & H. P. Gleason (Eds.), *Productive aging: Enhancing vitality in later life* (pp. 1–13). New York: Springer.

Butler, R. N., & Gleason, H. P. (Eds.). (1985). *Productive aging: Enhancing vitality in later life.* New York: Springer.

Cain, G. G. (1976). The challenge of segmented labor market theories to orthodox theory: A survey. *Journal of Economic Literature, 14,* 1215–1257.

Cantor, M. H. (1979). The informal support system of New York's inner city elderly: Is ethnicity a factor? In D. E. Gelfand and A. J. Kutzik (Eds.), *Ethnicity and aging: Theory, research and policy* (pp. 153–174). New York: Springer.

Cantor, M. H. (1981, November). *Factors associated with strain among families, friends, and neighbors, and neighbors caring for the frail elderly.* The 34th Annual Scientific Meetings of the Gerontological Society of America, Toronto, Canada.

Cantor, M. H., & Little, J. K. (1985). Aging and social services. In E. Shanas & R. H. Binstock (Eds.), *Handbook of aging and the social sciences* (2d ed.), (pp. 745–781). New York: Van Nostrand Reinhold.

Chatters, L. M., Taylor, R. J., & Jackson, J. S. (1985). Aged blacks' nominations to an informal helper network. *Journal of Gerontology, 41,* 94–100.

Clark, M. S., Mills, J., & Powell, M. C. (1986). Keeping track of needs in communal and exchange relationships. *Journal of Personality and Social Psychology, 51,* 333–338.

Conner, K. A., Power, E. A., & Bultena, G. L. (1979). Social interaction and life satisfaction: An empirical assessment of late-life patterns. *Journal of Gerontology, 34,* 116–121.

Cook, S. (1973). Economic anthropology: Problems in theory, method, and analysis. In J. J. Honigman (Ed.), *Handbook of social and cultural anthropology* (pp. 795–859). Chicago: Rand McNally.

Current Population Reports (1980). *The social and economic status of the black population in the United States: An historical view, 1790–1978.* Special Studies Series P–23 No. 80. Washington, DC: Bureau of the Census, U.S. Department of Commerce.

Davis, K. (1986). Aging and the health-care system: Economic and structural issues. *Daedalus, 115,* 227–246.

Dowd, J., & Bengston, V. (1978). Aging in minority populations: An examination of the double jeopardy hypothesis. *Journal of Gerontology, 33,* 427–436.

Ferman, L. A., & Berndt, L. E. (1981). The irregular economy. In S. Henry (Ed.), *Can I have it in cash?* (pp. 26–42). London: Astragal Books.

Ferman, L. A., Berndt, L., & Selo, E. (1978). *Analysis of the irregular economy: Cash flow in the informal sector.* A report to the Bureau of Employment and Training, Michigan Department of Labor. Institute of Labor and Industrial Relations, University of Michigan–Wayne State University.

Ferman, L. A., Henry, S., & Hoyman, M. (1987). Issues and prospects for the study of informal economies: Concepts, research strategies, and policy. *The Annals, 493,* 154–172.

Fischer, C. S. (1982). *To dwell among friends.* Chicago: University of Chicago Press.

Gibson, R. C. (1989). Guest editorial: Minority aging research: Opportunity and challenge. *Journal of Gerontology: Social Sciences, 44,* 2–3.

Glutman, P. M. (1977). The subterranean economy. *Financial Analysts Journal, 34,* 26–27.

Godelier, M. (1980). Anthropology and economics: The analysis of production, circulation, and consumption in economic goods. In I. Rossi (Ed.), *People in culture: A survey of cultural anthropology* (pp. 256–284). New York: Praeger.

Gouldner, A. W. (1960). The norm of reciprocity: A preliminary statement. *American Sociological Review, 25,* 161–178.

Hamilton,, R. N. (1975). *Employment needs and programs for older workers: Especially blacks.* Washington, DC: National Center on the Black Aged.

Henry, S. (1982). The working unemployed: Perspectives on the informal economy and unemployment. *Sociological Review, 30,* 460–477.

Henry, S. (1989). Can the hidden economy be revolutionary? Toward a dialectical analysis of the relations between formal and informal economics. *Social Justice, 15,* 29–60.

Henry, S., & Brown, J. (1990). Something for nothing: The informal economy outcomes of free market economics. In I. Taylor (Ed.), *The social effects of free market policies* (pp. 319–348). New York: Harvester Press.

Herzog, A. R., Antonucci, T. C., Jackson, J. S., Kahn, R. L., & Morgan, J. N. (1987). *Productive activities and health over the life course.* Paper presented at the Annual Meeting of the American Association for the Advancement of Science, Chicago, IL.

Herzog, A. R., & House, S. (1991, Winter). Productive activities and aging well. *Generations,* 49–54.

Herzog, A. R., Kahn, R. L., Morgan, J. N., Jackson, J. S., & Antonucci, T. C. (1989). Age differences in productive activities. *Journal of Gerontology, 44*(4), 5129–5138.

Herzog, A. R., & Morgan, J. N. (1989). *Age and sex differences in the value of productive activities.* Unpublished manuscript. Ann Arbor: Institute for Social Research, University of Michigan.

Hill, M. (1983). Trends in the economic situation of U.S. families and children: 1970–1980. In R. R. Nelson and F. Skidmore (Eds.), *American families and the economy* (pp. 9–58). Washington, DC: National Academy Press.

Hill, R. B. (1981). *Economic policies and black progress: Myth and realities.* New York: National Urban League.

Holzer, M. & Nagel, S. S. (Eds.). (1984). *Productivity and public policy.* Beverly Hills, CA: Sage.

House, J. S., & Kahn, R. L. (1985). Measures and concepts of social support. In S. Cohen and L. Syme (Eds.), *Social support and health* (pp. 83–108). New York: Academic Press.

Ingersoll-Dayton, B., & Antonucci, T. C. (1988). Reciprocal and non-reciprocal social support: Contrasting sides of intimate relationships. *Journal of Gerontology: Social Sciences, 43*(3), 65–73.

Institute of Medicine (IOM)/National Research Council. (1985). *America's aging: Health in an older society.* Washington, DC: National Academy Press.

Institute of Medicine (IOM)/National Research Council. (1986). *America's aging: Productive roles in an older society.* Washington, DC: National Academy Press.

Jackson, J. J. (1985). Race, national origin, ethnicity and aging. In E. Shanas & R. H. Binstock (Eds.), *Handbook of aging and the social sciences* (2d ed., pp. 264–303). New York: Van Nostrand Reinhold.

Jackson, J. S., Antonucci, T. C., & Gibson, R. C. (1990a). Cultural, racial, and ethnic minority influences on aging. In J. E. Birren & K. W. Schaie (Eds.), *Handbook of the psychology of aging* (3d ed., pp. 103–123). New York: Academic Press.

Jackson, J. S., Antonucci, T. C., & Gibson, R. C. (1990b). Social relations, productive activities, and coping with stress in late life. In M. A. P. Stephens, J. H. Crowther, S. E. Hobfoll, & D. L. Tennenbaum (Eds.), *Stress and coping in late life families* (pp. 193–209). Washington, DC: Hemisphere.

Jackson, J. S., & Gibson, R. C. (1985). Work and retirement among the black elderly. In Z. S. Blau (Ed.), *Current perspectives on the life cycle* (pp. 193–222). Greenwich, CT: JAI Press.

Juster, F. T., Courant, P. N. & Dow, G. K. (1981). The theory and measurement of well-being: A suggested framework for accounting and analysis. In F. T. Juster & K. C. Land (Eds.), *Social accounting systems* (pp. 23–94). New York: Academic Press.

Kahn, R. L. (1981). *Work and health*. New York: Wiley.

Kahn, R. L. (1986). *Productive activities and well-being*. Paper presented at the Annual Meeting of the Gerontological Society of America, Chicago, IL.

Kahn, R. L. (1988, October). *The forms of women's work*. Paper presented at the Conference on Women, Work and Health, Stockholm, Sweden.

Kahn, R. L., Wethington, E., & Ingersoll, B. N. (1987). Social networks: Determinants and effects. In R. Abeles (Ed.), *Implications of the life-span perspective for social psychology* (pp. 139–165). New York: Erlbaum Press.

Kalleberg, A. L., & Sorenson, A. B. (1979). The sociology of labor markets. *Annual Review of Sociology, 5,* 351–379.

LaRocco, J. M., House, J. S., & French, J. R. P., Jr. (1980). Social support, occupational stress, and health. *Journal of Health and Social Behavior, 21,* 202–218.

Leichter, H. M. (1984). National productivity: A comparative perspective. In M. Holzer & S. S. Nagel (Eds.), *Productivity and public policy* (pp. 45–70). Beverly Hills, CA: Sage.

Lowenthal, M. (1975). The social economy in urban-working class communities. In G. Gappert & H. M. Rose (Eds.), *The social economy of cities* (pp. 447–469). Beverly Hills, CA: Sage.

Lowenthal, M. (1981). Non-market transactions in an urban community. In S. Henry (Ed.), *Can I have it in cash?* (pp. 90–104). London: Astragal Books.

Markides, K. S., Liang, J., & Jackson, J. S. (1990). Race, ethnicity, and aging: Conceptual and methodological issues. In L. K. George & R. H. Binstock (Eds.), *Handbook of aging and the social sciences* (3d ed., pp. 112–129). New York: Academic Press.

McAdoo, H. P. (1981). *Black families*. Beverly Hills, CA: Sage.

Martineau, W. (1977). Informal social ties among urban black Americans. *Journal of Black Studies, 8,* 83–104.

Moen, P., Kain, E. L., & Elder, G. H., Jr. (1983). Economic conditions and family life: Contemporary and historical perspectives. In R. R. Nelson & F. Skidmore (Eds.), *American families and the economy* (pp. 213–259). Washington, DC: National Academy Press.

Montagna, P. D. (1977). *Occupations and society: Toward a sociology of the labor market.* New York: Wiley.

Morgan, J. N. (1981). Behavioral and social science research and the future elderly. In S. B. Kiesler, J. N. Morgan, & V. K. Oppenheimer (Eds.), *Aging: Social change* (pp. 587–612). New York: Academic Press.

Morgan, J. N. (1986). Unpaid productive activity over the life course. In Committee on an Aging Society, Institute of Medicine, & National Research Council, *America's aging: Productive roles in an older society* (pp. 73–109). Washington, DC: National Academy Press.

Moss, M. (1979). Welfare dimensions of productivity measurement. In National Research Council (Ed.), *Measurement and interpretation of productivity* (pp. 276–308). Washington, DC: National Academy Press.

Myers, G. C., Manton, K. G., & Bacellar, H. (1986). Sociodemographic aspects of future unpaid productive roles. In Institute of Medicine/National Research Council (Ed.), *America's aging: Productive roles in an older society* (pp. 110–148). Washington, DC: National Academy Press.

National Institute on Aging (NIA). (1982). *A national plan for research on aging: Report of the national research on aging planning panel.* Washington, DC: U.S. Government Printing Office.

National Research Council (Ed.). (1979). *Measurement and interpretation of productivity.* Washington, DC: National Academy Press.

Noelker, L., & Zarit, S. H. (1983). The integration of environment and network theories in explaining the aged's functioning and well-being. *Interdisciplinary Topics in Gerontology, 17.*

Oppenheimer, V. K. (1981). The changing nature of life-cycle squeezes: Implications for the socioeconomic position of the elderly. In R. W. Fogel, E. Hatfield, S. B. Kiesler, & E. Shanas (Eds.), *Aging: Stability and change in the family* (pp. 47–82). New York: Academic Press.

Pearlin, L., & Schooler, C. (1978). The structure of coping. *Journal of Health and Social Behavior, 19,* 2–21.

Rosen, E. D. (1984). Productivity: Concepts and measurement. In M. Holzer & S. S. Nagel (Eds.), *Productivity and public policy* (pp. 19–44). Beverly Hills, CA: Sage.

Sarason, S. B. (1977). *Work, aging and social change: Professionals and the one life-one career imperative.* New York: Free Press.

Siegel, J. S., & Taeuber, C. M. (1986). Demographic perspectives on the long-lived society. *Daedalus, 115,* 77–118.

Smith, J. D. (1982). *The measurement of selected income flows in informal markets.* Final report to the Internal Revenue Service. Contract No. TIR 81–28. Ann Arbor, MI: Institute for Social Research.

Soldo, B., & Manton, K. G. (1985). Changes in the health status and service needs of the oldest old: Current patterns and future trends. *Milbank Memorial Fund Quarterly, 63,* 286–323.

Stack, C. B. (1974). *All our kin: Strategies for survival in the black community.* New York: Harper & Row.

Taylor, R. J., & Chatters, L. M. (1986). Church based informal support among elderly blacks. *The Gerontologist, 26,* 637–642.

Thoits, P. A. (1982). Conceptual, methodological, and theoretical problems in studying social support as a buffer against life stress. *Journal of Health and Social Behavior, 23,* 145–149.

Wellman, B. (1981). Applying network analysis to the study of support. In B. H. Gottlieb (Ed.), *Social networks and social support* (pp. 171–200). Beverly Hills, CA: Sage.

Wentowski, G. J. (1981). Reciprocity and the coping strategies of older people: Cultural dimensions of network building. *The Gerontologist, 21,* 600–609.

Witte, A. D., & Simon, C. D. (1983). The impact of unrecorded economic activity on American families. In R. R. Nelson & F. Skidmore (Eds.), *American families and the economy* (pp. 145–182). Washington, DC: National Academy Press.

# 15

# Continuing Limits on Productive Aging: The Lesser Rewards for Working Women

*Karen C. Holden*

Data on incomes of individuals and families in the United States for 1990 do not present an auspicious picture for improvements in the economic well-being of the low-income population in future decades. The percentage of individuals most vulnerable to economic insecurity when they enter retirement is growing. Poor individuals, workers without pensions, and workers without employer-provided retiree health insurance are increasing as a percentage of the nonelderly. To the extent that these attributes predict financial vulnerability in later years, a growing percentage of elderly constrained in their work and retirement choices can be expected. But even for families who maintain living standards through the work of both husband and wife, higher total earnings may not translate into higher retirement income. For this segment of the elderly population, the productive alternatives to full-time work that are available to other elderly citizens who are well-protected by insurance against the financial consequences of retirement are at best a dream.

Current Population Survey (CPS) data released in March 1991 show that poverty rates in 1990 for both the nonelderly and elderly climbed above the previous year's rates (U.S. Bureau of the Census, 1991a). Among the nonelderly, this trend continues the slow upward climb that began in 1980. But for the elderly, the increase in poverty in 1990 suggests that, as has been true among the nonelderly, the population of the most vulnerable and the most economically constrained will grow.

In 1990, 13.7 percent of all individuals under the age of sixty-five were in families with income below the poverty threshold ($6,652 for a person living alone; $13,359 for a family of four), an increase from the approximate 12 percent who were poor during the 1970s.

Increasing poverty among the nonelderly in the 1980s contrasts with poverty trends during the 1970s, when the percentage of poor nonelderly held fairly steady, and during the 1960s, when it fell precipitously (Ellwood & Summers, 1986). It also contrasts with stability in poverty rates among the elderly (persons age sixty-five or older) that was maintained during the 1980s. By the end of the 1980s, these contrasting trends in poverty among the elderly and nonelderly left the elderly far less likely to be poor (11.4 percent of that group were poor in 1989) than the nonelderly (13 percent of them were poor in 1989). But in 1990, a higher proportion of the elderly (12.2 percent) were poor than had been poor in 1989.

The question arises as to whether the recent upturn in poverty among the elderly (after two decades of decline and slowly increasing poverty among the nonelderly) implies that poverty among the elderly may once again become a growing problem. Data from one year, of course, are insufficient to judge whether a true reversal of a twenty-year trend has taken place. This is not the first time poverty rates for the elderly have risen. In 1979–1980, a two-year increase in poverty among the elderly also began, to be followed by a steady decline, until an apparent low was reached in 1989. Thus, it is too early to tell whether poverty-rate stability has ended for this group as it did earlier for the nonelderly.

Nevertheless, this chapter argues that well-documented changes in family structure and diminished earnings growth, which have increased the chances of young families being poor, will produce higher percentages of economically distressed elderly in the future as current cohorts of younger families enter their retirement years. The essence of the argument is that because old-age income security in the United States is provided primarily through earnings-based private and public systems, increases in real wages and fringe benefits in the 1950s and 1960s contributed to steady improvements during the 1970s and 1980s in the economic status of successive cohorts of retired men and women and their surviving spouses. In contrast, recent increases in single parenthood (whether through divorce or unmarried parenthood), stagnation in real wage growth, and declines in pension coverage among the current working-age population suggest an increasingly insecure old age for this group. Some social commentators argue that increases in labor force participation of wives provide families with a means of counteracting the effect on retirement income of slow earnings growth. This ignores both the way in which the work of wives affects the Social Security benefits of a couple and the ability of pension-eligible workers to alter the division of pension income over the life of the couple and of the widow. The more likely result of slow wage growth will be increasing percentages among future cohorts of elderly for whom work and leisure choices will be severely constrained.

This chapter first reviews recent trends in earnings, Social Security benefits, and pension coverage. Next, through hypothetical examples of the relationship between earnings and retirement income, it illustrates how trends in earnings and pension coverage are likely to be played out in the

Table 15.1
Sources of Income: Elderly and Nonelderly Units,[a] 1988 (Percentage Distribution of Income by Source)

| Percentage of Income from: | Individual or family with householder | | | |
| | Sixty-five or older | | Under sixty-five | |
| | Nonpoor | Poor | Nonpoor | Poor |
|---|---|---|---|---|
| Earnings | 21% | 1% | 89% | 53% |
| Social Security & Railroad Retirement | 34 | 79 | 1 | 1 |
| Pensions | 18 | 3 | 3 | 4 |
| Interest/rents/dividends | 24 | 4 | 4 | 2 |
| Public assistance and other programs | 2 | 12 | 3 | 30 |
| Percent of all units | 85 | 15 | 86 | 14 |

[a] A unit includes individuals living alone or with nonrelatives only and multiperson families with householder of specified age.
Source: Social Security Bulletin (1990).

future in terms of changing circumstances of low-income families. The final section draws tentative conclusions about the future regarding the level and distribution of income for today's young adults upon their retirement as well as the implications for "productive" aging.

## EARNINGS AND RETIREMENT GAINS

The sources of income received by nonelderly families (the householder is under sixty-five) and by elderly families (householder is sixty-five or over) are quite different (Table 15.1). Among young poor families, a much lower fraction of their incomes compared to the nonpoor comes from earnings and a much larger from government transfers (Social Security and public assistance). Poor elderly are almost entirely dependent on Social Security, with a small fraction of this group receiving public assistance. The reasons for differences between the two age groups, and between the poor and nonpoor, are the result of complex relationships among age, disability, education, and work histories and economic outcomes. Some elderly are not yet poor because they are not yet retired; some nonelderly have withdrawn early from the labor force. Nevertheless, these gross statistics suggest that it is what other sources of income that are available when earnings cease that determines financial security for both old and young. For the elderly, what matters most is the level of Social Security and pension benefits for which they are eligible. Consequently, the economic status of elderly families is closely linked to the employment opportunities and earnings they had during their working-age years.

The rise in the relative economic well-being of the elderly has been labeled one of the most notable successes of U.S. social policy over the past few decades. Increased federal commitment to alleviating economic problems in retirement has certainly played a major role (Preston, 1984). At least equally important, however, has been expanded private pension coverage and rising real wages of workers which raised the wages upon which Social Security benefits are based and enabled greater retirement savings (Gottschalk & Danziger, 1985). The persistent increase in well-being among the elderly has led to predictions that such trends will continue and that those groups most likely to become poor in old age will diminish in size as pension coverage expands and women continue to move into the work force. Recent trends in earnings and pension coverage among the nonelderly suggest, however, that prior sustained gains in the standard of living of elderly families may not be matched in the future and that once again we will observe a rise in the proportion of economically vulnerable elderly.

### Earnings

Frank Levy documents changes in the earnings of individuals and families in the United States through the post-World War II period (see Levy, 1988; Levy & Michel, 1991). Between 1946 and 1973, real wages, per capita income, family income, and consumption expenditures rose at unprecedented rates. Sustained growth in productivity and wages enabled successive cohorts of new workers to achieve a higher standard of living than their parents at comparable ages. Productivity growth raised incomes across the entire income distribution.

Since then, however, growth in real wages has stagnated—income distribution is now more unequal as a result of income growth among families in the upper deciles together with no change in incomes of families in the lower deciles. Per capita and family income—the traditional measures of average family well-being—have continued to rise, but at a far slower rate and only through changes in family structure (e.g., fewer children) and the increasing proportion of women working. Higher earnings through greater labor force participation by prime-working-age women have enabled families to offset falling earnings among male workers.

### Social Security and Pensions

The unprecedented growth in wages and family income into the early 1970s occurred simultaneously with an expansion in Social Security and pension coverage which enabled families to enter retirement with unexpected greater income security. That is, those who retired during the 1960s and 1970s could not have planned on the higher Social Security benefits that were legislated or on the high rates of interest that resulted in high rates of asset growth both for individual savers and pension funds. During the 1950s, inflation-adjusted Social Security benefits paid to men increased by 50 percent; during the 1960s, they increased by 20 percent; and during the 1970s, by 34 percent. In contrast, since 1980 inflation-adjusted Social Security benefits have risen by an average of only 1.2 percent per year (Turner & Beller, 1989).

Ironically, expectations that incomes will continue to grow for the elderly are based on past changes in retirement income, which were in fact largely unexpected, resulting from one-time legislative changes. The growth in Social Security benefits has been slowed in part by the 1983 Social Security amendments, which, by introducing automatic inflation adjustment to benefits and imposing a benefit formula that fixed the percentage of real wages replaced, restrict future increases in Social Security benefits to those achieved through higher real earnings. In the future, changes in real Social Security benefits paid to elderly families will reflect only changes in the covered earnings of individuals and the distribution of earnings among family members.

Successive cohorts of retirees in the past also registered gains in income through improved pension coverage. While only 16 percent of persons age sixty-five and older received income from a pension in 1970, by 1984, 27 percent did (Turner & Beller, 1989). This percentage is expected to grow somewhat, based on the 34 percent of all workers who are now covered by a pension plan (Woods, 1989).

Coverage by pension plans always has varied across industries, and the shift in employment toward nonpension-covered industries has contributed to declining pension coverage for certain age groups. Pension coverage among full-time private-sector workers is highest in mining (63 percent covered in 1988[1]), durable goods manufacturing (64 percent covered)—two industries with declining employment—and transportation and public utilities (59 percent covered). Lowest rates of coverage are found in nonprofessional services (24 percent) and retail trade (29 percent)—two sectors that have experienced the most rapid growth in employment.

Table 15.2 presents pension-coverage rates of full-time workers for various years. Coverage rates for men fell from 54 percent in 1972 to 49 percent in 1988. While the decline has been small for older age groups, for the under–thirty-nine-year-olds, substantially fewer private-sector workers are now covered by pensions than were covered in 1979. Some current workers not now covered eventually will obtain pension coverage and eligibility prior to retirement, but declining pension coverage for younger age groups reduces

Table 15.2
Percentage of Full-time Private Wage and Salary Workers Covered by a Pension

| Age | 1972 | 1979 | 1983 | 1988 |
|---|---|---|---|---|
| | | Men | | |
| Total 16+ | 54% | 55% | 52% | 49% |
| Under 25 | 34 | 29 | 25 | 20 |
| 25-29 | 52 | 53 | 43 | 41 |
| 30-34 | 56 | 62 | 54 | 48 |
| 35-39 | 59 | 65 | 62 | 57 |
| 40-44 | 61 | 64 | 64 | 61 |
| 45-49 | 63 | 66 | 63 | 61 |
| 50-54 | 64 | 69 | 66 | 60 |
| 55-59 | 59 | 69 | 66 | 60 |
| 60 or older | 46 | 56 | 55 | 51 |
| | | Women | | |
| Total 16+ | 38% | 40% | 42% | 43% |
| Under 25 | 27 | 23 | 21 | 22 |
| 25-29 | 39 | 42 | 42 | 42 |
| 30-34 | 40 | 46 | 46 | 48 |
| 35-39 | 40 | 42 | 51 | 49 |
| 40-44 | 42 | 42 | 47 | 51 |
| 45-49 | 44 | 50 | 49 | 49 |
| 50-54 | 45 | 56 | 55 | 49 |
| 55-59 | 42 | 50 | 55 | 49 |
| 60 or older | 29 | 46 | 45 | 40 |

*Note*: Pensions include all private-sector employer-financed pension or retirement plans.
*Source*: Woods (1989).

the number of years during which contributions and service credits can be obtained.

For women, the outlook likely will be no expansion in pension coverage beyond the rates shown for them in Table 15.2. Employment opportunities that favor those industries in which pension coverage is less likely to be offered may leave no more than 50 percent to 60 percent of full-time female workers covered by pensions.

For retirees eligible for a pension, the size of their benefits determine the cushion provided against the loss of earnings in retirement. Here, too, no substantial gains have been made over the past decade; between 1976 and 1986, the inflation-adjusted median pension benefit amount paid to retirees declined by 15 percent (Turner & Beller, 1989).

## EARNINGS-BASED INCOME SECURITY

The effect on retirement income of slow earnings gains, changes in the distribution of paid work between spouses, and declining pension coverage depends on the way in which early earnings are translated into retirement income. Table 15.1 suggests that the translation is accomplished in large part through Social Security and pensions. Thus, the relative well-being of future cohorts of the elderly will depend on how changes in family earnings' levels and in the distribution of earnings between spouses are reflected in subsequent retirement income. The purpose of what follows is to illustrate that relationship for hypothetical families in which wives work and in which they do not and for a nonmarried female worker. While there is no doubt that increases in the number of years worked by women will assure that a higher percentage of women will be eligible for retirement income based on their own work histories, for some families the change in eligibility status may not lead to higher retirement income.

In defined-benefit pension plans, prior earnings directly affect retirement benefits because years of service and earnings—typically last or the highest—are included in the benefit formula.[2] Defined-contribution pension plans pay benefits that are roughly equal to an annuity purchasable with accumulated contributions plus interest; past contributions typically are based on the salary of workers in the year contributed and in some cases may rise with years of employment.

Social Security benefits are likewise, though less tightly, tied to earnings during one's working years. Working in covered employment for the equivalent of ten years now gains one eligibility for Social Security benefits based on average indexed monthly earnings (AIME) over thirty-five years.[3] A progressive benefit formula replaces a higher percentage of covered earnings for low- compared to high-income earners. Susan Grad (1990) estimates that low-income workers retiring at age sixty-five in 1982 had 64 percent of their earnings replaced compared to 29 percent of earnings for high-income workers. High-earning workers, however, always will be paid an absolutely higher benefit amount.

Under both employer-provided pensions and Social Security, individuals who have never worked cannot receive a benefit in their own right. But individuals may be eligible for a benefit based on the earnings records of current or deceased spouses. The Employee Retirement Income Security Act of 1974 and the 1984 Retirement Equity Act require that private pension annuities be paid out in a form that assures to a surviving spouse a benefit equal to at least 50 percent of the retiree's benefit.[4] A retiree's spouse must agree in a notarized statement to the election of a single-life benefit—that is, one paid out only during the lifetime of the retiree. Social Security pays a benefit to wives and husbands equal to 50 percent of the primary beneficiary's, and a benefit to surviving spouses that is equal to 100 percent of the primary beneficiary's.

There are two key features of Social Security and private pensions that should be described to make clear the protection these systems provide workers and their spouses. First, while employer-provided pension benefits typically are reduced when a worker chooses a joint-and-survivor benefit, Social Security benefits are not affected by the payment of benefits to other family members. The reduction in employer-provided plans is based on the notion that the choice of a survivorship option extends the period over which benefits will be paid. In pensions, the "financing" of the longer probable lifetime of survivors is incurred by the retiree through the lower benefit paid during his or her lifetime. The reduction in retiree benefits depends on the age of the worker and spouse, on the percentage that will continue for the survivor, and on the mortality experience of the fund. These reductions can be substantial. For example, under one state plan, benefits at age sixty-five are reduced by 20 percent when a retiree with a spouse aged sixty-two chooses a joint option that continues at 100 percent to the survivor.

The second key feature is the effect on benefits when both spouses are eligible for benefits based on their own work. Under an employer-provided pension plan, benefits paid to one person—as a retiree or survivor—are not affected by other pension benefits that person might receive, even if they are from the same plan. Under Social Security's dual entitlement provisions, individuals receive, in effect, only the higher benefit for which they are eligible. Thus, a survivor benefit amount will be offset by any retired-worker benefit amount for which the individual is also eligible.

These two features—and the different ways in which they operate between pension plans and Social Security—determine how changes in real wages and increasing work by women will influence the economic security of married couples as they age. This is illustrated with four hypothetical cases depicted in Tables 15.3 through 15.5.

The first sections in Table 15.3 and in Table 15.4 present dollar values for earnings and benefits. The second section in Table 15.3 and in Table 15.4 along with Table 15.5 show ratios where the comparison is to Case A.

The first case, Case A, consists of a single-earner couple (both spouses are age sixty-five); the husband is assumed to have earned near the maximum AIME in 1989 and the wife had no covered-earnings history. This couple's

Table 15.3
Earnings and Social Security Benefits (for Four Hypothetical Cases)

I.    Earnings and Benefits:  Dollar Values

| | AIME of | | Benefit at age 65[a] | | |
|---|---|---|---|---|---|
| Case | Husband | Wife | Husband | Wife | Widow |
| A | $4,000 | $__ | $1,194 | $597 | $1,194 |
| B | 2,666 | 2,666 | 993 | 993 | 993 |
| C | 4,000 | 2,666 | 1,194 | 993 | 1,194 |
| D[b] | __ | 2,666 | __ | 993 | 993 |

II.   Earnings and Benefit Ratios:  Comparison to Case A

| | Earnings | Benefits of | |
|---|---|---|---|
| Case | of Couple | Couple | Widow |
| A | 1.00[c] | 1.00[c] | 1.00[c] |
| B | 1.33 | 1.11 | 0.83 |
| C | 1.67 | 1.22 | 1.00 |
| D[b] | 0.67 | 0.55 | 0.83 |

[a]Benefits calculated based on 1991 benefit formula.
[b]Case D is for an unmarried woman. For ease of comparison, benefits are listed under "wife"
    and "widow" columns.
[c]Base case to which other values in column are compared.

AIME and Social Security benefits are presented in the first row of items in
Table 15.3. The husband's estimated monthly benefit is $1,194; his wife is
eligible for an amount equal to 50 percent of this when he is alive and 100
percent after his death. This couple is used as a standard against which to
judge the relative well-being of three other households.

The second case, Case B, consists of a couple each of whom earned an
AIME equal to two-thirds of the first couple (or combined, equal to 1.33
percent of Case A's AIME). This case represents those families consisting
of two relatively low-wage earners whose income stability is maintained
only because both work. While their combined AIME is one-third higher
than that of the first couple, the Social Security benefit paid to the wife and
husband combined is only 11 percent higher in this case, and the benefit
received by the wife as a widow is almost 20 percent lower.

The third couple, Case C, consisting of a husband with earnings equal to the husband in Case A and a wife with earnings equal to the wife in Case B, has an AIME almost 70 percent higher than the couple in Case A, but benefits as a couple only 20 percent higher and for the survivor not higher at all.

Finally, the last case, Case D, depicts that of a single woman earning two-thirds the AIME of the worker in Case A but receiving a benefit as an unmarried person that is just over half that of the couple in Case A and 80 percent of that for the widow in Case A.

A comparison of these four cases shows that changes over time in individual and family earnings will not be uniformly translated into proportional changes in Social Security benefits to the family. The progressive-benefit formula reduces the gains and losses in benefits as earnings grow or fall (i.e., "replacement rates" of 30 percent at an AIME of $4,000 but of 37 percent at an AIME of $2,666). The ability of a spouse to command a benefit solely because of marriage to an insured worker adds substantially to the relative well-being of single-earner couples. Note especially that when the wife in Case B is widowed, her Social Security benefits will be absolutely lower even though the couple in Case B prior to retirement reported higher Social Security covered earnings (an AIME one-third higher) and after retirement received slightly higher (by 11 percent) benefits than did the couple in Case A.

Table 15.4 calculates hypothetical pension benefits based on a stable, long-term work career for these same four cases. Coverage by a fairly typical defined-benefit plan is assumed. If we assume career-long pension coverage in all jobs, higher earnings translate directly into higher benefits paid to each worker. Here the assumption is that the benefit is lower by 15 percent when a couple chooses a joint-and-one-half survivor benefit; that is, one that pays a benefit to the widow equal to one half of the retiree's benefit after he dies. Greater protection from the pension for each retired couple and widow appears promised by the pension-covered work effort of wives. In the second section of the table, the standard for comparison is Case A with a joint-and-one-half benefit choice. The assumption of a uniform benefit formula applied across all earnings is the source of proportional increases in pension benefits as earnings rise. When a working wife is widowed (i.e., Cases B and C, last column), her own pension substantially improves her pension-income position vis-à-vis the widow in Case A, who by definition can receive only a survivor's benefit.

Finally, Table 15.5 combines the hypothesized Social Security and pension benefits and compares each case to the single-worker couple and widow (Case A) with a joint-and-survivor benefit. When the two-worker couples (Cases B and C) choose a single-life benefit, relative increases in family earnings translate uniformly into comparable increases in the couple's joint benefits, but the widows are left with only their own pensions and Social

Table 15.4
Pension Benefits (for Four Hypothetical Cases)

I. Pension Benefits: Dollar Values
(Formula = 0.2 x years of service x average earnings)

| Case | Single-life Benefit | | | Joint-life benefit[a] | | |
|------|---------|------|-------|---------|------|-------|
| | Husband | Wife | Widow | Husband | Wife | Widow |
| A | $2,400 | — | — | $2,040 | — | $1,020 |
| B | 1,600 | 1,600 | 1,600 | 1,360 | 1,360 | 2,040 |
| C | 2,400 | 1,600 | 1,600 | 2,040 | 1,360 | 2,380 |
| D[b] | NA | 1,600 | 1,600 | NA | NA | NA |

II. Pension Benefit Ratios: Comparison to Case A

| Case | Earnings[c] | Couple Benefit | | Widow Benefit | |
|------|-------------|-------------|-----------|-------------|-----------|
| | | Single-life | Joint-life | Single-life | Joint-life |
| A | 1.00[d] | 1.20 | 1.00[d] | NA | 1.00[d] |
| B | 1.33 | 1.57 | 1.33 | 1.57 | 2.00 |
| C | 1.67 | 1.96 | 1.67 | 1.57 | 2.33 |
| D[b] | 0.67 | 0.78 | NA | 1.57 | NA |

[a] A 15 percent reduction with a choice of the joint-and-one-half pension option is assumed.
[b] For this single woman, benefits are indicated in "wife" and "widow" columns, though no marriage is assumed.
[c] Repeats Table 15.3 Panel II, Column 1.
[d] Base case to which other values in column are compared.

Security. Only when the two-worker couples choose a joint-life benefit do increases in the couples' income continue for the wives into widowhood.

The hypothetical cases illustrate two important points. First, comparisons across married couples show that it is pension coverage that is most likely to translate gains in earnings, especially those of married women, into comparably higher retirement benefits. The combination of a progressive Social Security formula and the "dual entitlement" provisions—that offset survivor and spousal benefits by any retired-worker benefit received—reduces the additional contributions to Social Security retirement income from working wives. Second, comparison of the last two columns in Table 15.5 shows the importance of survivor benefits—even for women with their own pensions. While women with their own income are better off than nonworking women whose husbands choose a single-life benefit, without survivor ben-

Table 15.5
Earnings and Total Retirement Benefits: Ratios (for Four Hypothetical Cases)

| | | Combined Social Security and Pensions | | | |
|---|---|---|---|---|---|
| | Average | Couple Benefit | | Widow Benefit | |
| Case | Earnings | Single-life | Joint-life | Single-life | Joint-life |
| A | 1.00[a] | 1.09 | 1.00[a] | 0.54 | 1.00[a] |
| B | 1.33 | 1.35 | 1.23 | 1.17 | 1.37 |
| C | 1.67 | 1.61 | 1.45 | 1.26 | 1.61 |
| D[b] | 0.67 | 0.67 | NA | 1.17 | NA |

[a]Base case to which other values in column are compared.
[b]For this single woman, benefits are indicated in "wife" and "widow" columns, though no marriage is assumed.
Source: Combination of values in Tables 15.3 and 15.4.

efits they are only marginally better off than nonworking widows whose husbands chose a joint-and-survivor benefit.

## PRODUCTIVITY AND AGING

Income both reflects the productivity of individuals and enables future productive activities. Higher than sufficient income allows individuals to invest in their own better health, to engage in educational activities, and to seek the most economically advantageous employment. For workers who have low earnings, current choices as well as future opportunities are constrained. Thus, the growing incidence of poverty among younger families should be a major concern.

The review at the beginning of this chapter concerning what has happened to earnings, Social Security, and pension growth suggests that the gains achieved by the elderly during past decades are not likely to be duplicated by currently younger cohorts. This is in part because legislation that would raise Social Security benefits—a major source of growth in the past—is unlikely. Gains in retirement income for elderly cohorts in the future must come now from their improved earnings alone.

This limitation on the source of retirement-income gains coincides with declining real earnings among low-wage workers, lower pension coverage rates, and the growing prevalence of female-headed households. Economic opportunities for individuals with only a high school education have diminished. Female-headed families, whose poverty rates are high, account for a growing percentage of all families and a growing percentage of all poor families (see Table 15.6).

Tables 15.3, 15.4, and 15.5 illustrate why households that are composed

Table 15.6
Poverty of Female-headed Families

| Year | Percentage poor among All Families | Female-Headed Families | Percentage of Female-headed Families | Percentage of female-Headed families Among poor families |
|------|-------|-------|-------|-------|
| 1960 | 18.1 | 42.4 | 10.1 | 23.7 |
| 1965 | 13.9 | 38.4 | 10.3 | 28.5 |
| 1970 | 10.1 | 32.5 | 11.5 | 37.1 |
| 1975 | 9.7 | 32.5 | 13.3 | 44.6 |
| 1980 | 10.3 | 32.7 | 15.1 | 47.8 |
| 1985 | 11.4 | 34.0 | 16.1 | 48.1 |
| 1989 | 10.3 | 32.2 | 16.5 | 51.6 |
| 1990 | 10.7 | 33.4 | 17.0 | 53.1 |

*Source:* U.S. Bureau of the Census (1991).

of relatively low earners will be at a relative economic disadvantage in their later years compared to married single-earner couples with the same total earnings. Single-earner couples are relatively well protected by the combination of Social Security and employer pensions, and if they choose a joint-and-survivor pension benefit, the widows are also. Two-earner couples with the same lifetime earnings will have a lower percentage of earnings replaced by the combination of these retirement programs. Earlier, we described the rise in the number of families headed by single, low-income parents who are unlikely to have the fairly generous pension-coverage histories illustrated in Tables 15.4 and 15.5. Table 15.7 illustrates the more likely case of relatively low income workers not being eligible for pension coverage. Only the high earners (i.e., the husbands, as described in the examples) in Cases A and C, whose earnings are identical, are assumed to receive pension income.

What should be noted is the variation across these cases in how well they fare when earnings cease. Despite the higher total earnings of the two-earnings couple in Case B compared to Case A, benefits for the couple in Case B as well as for the wife as a widow in Case B are substantially lower. The much higher total earnings of Case C compared to Case A result in almost exactly identical income after retirement. Finally, the unmarried woman of Case D will receive an income that, even when adjusted for her lower consumption needs, reflects a much lower earnings replacement rate.

The critical factors in determining these outcomes, of course, are the absence of a pension benefit for lower earners and the fact that working

Table 15.7
Total Retirement Benefits: Ratios[a]

|  | | Combined Pension and Social Security | |
| --- | --- | --- | --- |
| Case | Average earnings | Couple Benefit | Widow Benefit |
| A | 1.00[b] | 1.00[b] | 1.00[b] |
| B | 1.33 | 0.52 | 0.45 |
| C | 1.67 | 1.10 | 1.00 |
| D | 0.67 | 0.26 | 0.45 |

[a]Assuming no pension coverage for the lower income worker of each couple.
[b]Base case to which other values in column are compared. Choice by the husband of joint-and-one-half pension option is assumed.

wives as widows gain no larger Social Security benefits. Both of these conditions are likely to become increasingly relevant as the percentage of low-earner, two-working couples among the population grows. Thus, it is likely that current trends in earnings of younger workers and pension coverage promise that the current level of economic vulnerability among the elderly is unlikely to diminish over time and, in fact, may increase.

What do these trends mean for the productive roles of the elderly in retirement? Only recently have we begun to understand the variety of activities in which the elderly engage during their "retirement" years, including continued participation in paid work (Burkhauser, Quinn, & Myers, 1990; Holden, 1988). Continued labor force participation is driven by financial considerations—particularly the changes in lifetime income that result from the delayed receipt of pension or Social Security income—as well as by the individual's health and family structure. Who engages in volunteer activities is less well understood but is surely dependent on these same factors. Thus, the growing percentage of low-income elderly presents a challenge to public policymakers interested in expanding the nonemployment, productive roles of elderly individuals. To the extent that this group's low income is a result of past low earnings owing to long-term health problems, lack of job skills, or poor work habits, members of this group will be relatively disadvantaged as they search for productive volunteer roles. To the extent that low incomes are the likely outcome of long careers that provided few retirement benefits, it may be less likely that the elderly will welcome nonearning "volunteer" roles. For these individuals, productive roles may have to be linked with income in cash or in kind.

Unfortunately, stagnating earnings growth may not be a short-term phenomenon. Until the nation solves its underlying economic problems—the low rate of domestic involvement, declining productivity growth, deteriorating job performance skills—it is unlikely to see a reversal in the rate of earnings growth and the number of children and families in poverty (Litan, Lawrence, & Schultze, 1988). The concern is not just how to encourage productive roles among the current elderly but how to insure that younger cohorts now of working age are being prepared to enter retirement with the economic security and work histories that will allow for productive work and volunteer opportunities.

## PRODUCTIVE AGING: POLICY IMPLICATIONS

This chapter has emphasized the retirement implications of slow earnings growth among low-income families in the United States. With hypothetical examples, it illustrates how growing proportions of low earners and increasing numbers of low-income families who maintain their standard of living through having two members at work eventually will produce greater inequality among the elderly than is observed for current elderly cohorts.

Our earnings-based retirement system makes this inevitable. Public policy efforts to enhance the productive roles of elderly individuals must take that fact and the sources of this inequality into account. Public policy that aims to enhance the chances for "productive aging" must consider the growing proportion of the elderly whose earnings histories and retirement income constrain their work and retirement options and whose skills and work histories relegate them to the bottom of the queue for volunteer roles. The fairly secure and skilled will respond to changes in the organization of work and volunteer roles as employers and nonprofit agencies find it worthwhile to alter work hours or structure attractive opportunities for them. For the less financially secure and skilled elderly, subsidies may be necessary that will provide them training or will encourage their volunteer placement. Thus, public policymakers may look to the experiences from job training programs in structuring programs that aim to enhance the job and volunteer activities for the least advantaged elderly.

## NOTES

1. Coverage is defined as participation in a pension plan offered by an employer.
2. The real value of those benefits will fall because of increases in prices between the time the worker left employment and the time when pension benefits were first received, since earnings typically are not price adjusted.
3. The average is indexed for increases in real wages between the time earned and the second year prior to the year the worker reaches age sixty-two, becomes disabled, or dies.
4. A joint-and-one-half option pays to the survivor half the benefit paid to the retiree under this option and will be less than half the benefit that would be paid under a single-life option.

# REFERENCES

Burkhauser, R. V., Quinn, J. P., & Myers, D. A. (1990). *Passing the torch*. Kalamazoo, MI: Upjohn Institute.

Ellwood, D. T., & Summers, L. H. (1986). Poverty in America: Is welfare the answer or the problem? In S. H. Danziger & D. H. Weinberg, *Fighting poverty: What works and what doesn't*. Cambridge, MA: Harvard University Press.

Employee Benefit Research Institute. (1990). *EBRI databook on employee benefits*. Washington, DC: Employee Benefit Research Institute.

Gottschalk, P., & Danziger, S. (1985). A framework for evaluation: The effects of economic growth and transfers on poverty. *American Economic Review, 75*, 153–161.

Grad, S. (1990) Earnings replacement rates of new retired workers. *Social Security Bulletin, 53*(10), 2–19.

Holden, K. (1988). Physically demanding occupations, health, and work after retirement: Findings from the new beneficiary survey. *Social Security Bulletin, 51*(11), 3–15.

Levy, F. (1988). Income, families, and living standards. In R. E. Litan, R. Z. Lawrence, & C. L. Schultze (Eds.), *American living standards: Threats and challenges*. Washington, DC: Brookings Institution.

Levy, F., & Michel, R. C. (1991). The economic future of American families: Income and wealth trends. Washington, DC: The Urban Institute.

Litan, R. E., Lawrence, R. Z., & Schultze, C. L. (Eds.). (1988). *American living standards: Threats and challenges*. Washington, DC: Brookings Institution.

Preston, S. H. (1984). Children and the elderly: Divergent paths for America's dependents. *Demography, 21*(4), 435–457.

Smeeding, T. (1990). Economic status of the elderly. In R. Binstock & L. George (Eds.), *Handbook of aging and the social sciences* (pp. 362–381).New York: Academic Press.

Turner, J. A., & Beller, D. J. (Eds.). (1989). *Trends in pensions*. Washington, DC: U.S. Department of Labor, Pension and Welfare Administration.

U.S. Bureau of the Census. (1991a). *Poverty in the United States: 1990*. Current Population Reports, Series P–60, No. 175. Washington, DC: U.S. Government Printing Office.

U.S. Bureau of the Census. (1991b). *Money income of households, families, and persons in the United States: 1990*. Current Population Reports, Series P–60, No. 174. Washington, DC: U.S. Government Printing Office.

Woods, J. R. (1989). Pension coverage among private wage and salary workers: Preliminary findings from the 1988 Survey of Employee Benefits. *Social Security Bulletin, 52*(10), 2–19.

# Part VI

## The Future

# 16

# Conclusion: Defining the Place of the Elderly in the Twenty-first Century

## Robert Morris

American society continues to celebrate the dramatic changes that have taken place in the past 100 years in our culture, economy, and social life. But one of the most dramatic and least understood changes has been the position of the elderly in American life, coming in an era in which not only their numbers have increased but also the health and vigor of the majority— who may now live into their eighties and beyond. As a class within the total population, people over sixty have moved from an active to a marginal role in the labor force, from being among the poorest in the nation to sharing the average national income with the rest of the population, and from being isolated with their medical problems to having equal access to medical care. Materially, conditions for our older citizens have improved, and the deficiencies they experience are no worse than for other groups in the population; some are in a better-than-average situation.

There remains an irony to these positive developments. As the nation has become more affluent, it also has moved its older citizens to the outer margins of society. The elderly (over the age of sixty, the age toward which retirement has been moving) are likely to spend at least a quarter of their adult years in a retirement that keeps them outside the mainstream of their world—even though most individuals are relatively healthy, vigorous, and alert into their eighties. Except for family ties, most of these later years are lived in a kind of limbo.

We have slipped into accepting this evolution without seriously asking whether, as a nation, we can or should abandon the energy and the accumulated experience, skill, and wisdom of our older citizens. If we pose this in the form of a question, we begin to consider our recently acquired, extended "retirement" for older people in a new light. We need to consider two interconnected issues: what enhances the life of the individual and what builds the strength of the collectivity—the community and the nation—on which individual well-being depends. We need to ask two questions. First, does our society *need* the contributions of all its citizens, at all ages, if it is to remain a healthy and vigorous society? And second, does a satisfying aging require socially meaningful roles as well as material comfort?

In asking such questions, we move from a view of retirement as a purely individual choice among limited options outside the mainstream of community life to a more complex and subtle view of social evolution in which a successful society and one's productive aging require each other.

At the risk of oversimplification, it can be said that the high value we place on early retirement has been shaped by conditions in the nineteenth century, when almost everyone worked until physically unable to do so, usually for long hours. In that era, retirement was hardly recognized as a standard except for a very privileged few or for the very sick. The voluntary withdrawal from work became a cherished goal that came to be embodied in public policy, legislation, and other practices of economic and voluntary institutions during the twentieth century. In the view that still prevails today, withdrawal from work is an earned right, made possible by modern production technologies and a retirement-income system.

## FILLING LIFE SPACE CREATIVELY OR MARGINALLY

Much of twentieth-century social thought has been devoted to how *individuals* use the time and increased resources newly available to them to accumulate goods and to satisfy the endless growth of individual physical, intellectual, and emotional appetites. Much less attention has been devoted to the concomitant public or collective effort to build an equitable and fair society, one in which individualization is reconciled with sharing for the common good. The continuous debate over whether we have too much or too little government, whether benefits and rewards are fairly open to all, whether the burdens of creating a fair society weigh too heavily on some classes, and whether family disorganization and crime and poverty and mental or physical dependency are created by flaws in individual character or by deficiencies in the social structure for opportunity is the industrial age's untidy way of trying to come to grips with how to make use of the opportunities that technology has opened up. We have not yet resolved whether or how to use our newfound resources and opportunities both to seek personal gratification and to create a society acceptable to multiple group interests.

We do make some provisions for the losers in life's competition, but reluctantly, lest individual choice for the winners become too constrained. For those age sixty and over, collective obligation is seen as satisfied by a modern Social Security system and a very incomplete private pension system. Beyond that, and with some exceptions, the public perception is that sometime around the age of sixty or sixty-five, most people want to, or should, withdraw from paid work, and the occupation of the life space for the next twenty years is primarily an individual and personal matter.

Public discussion about collective responsibility in the aging process has been constrained by a deeply held anti-age bias in our society. This ageism is seen in all the institutions of modern life and is fully revealed in the earlier chapters of this book. It is not consciously cruel or neglectful, only deeply negative. Those over sixty are often perceived through the "old" lens as being the slow, the halt, the hard of hearing, the bewrinkled; they are perhaps pitied but not welcome. They supposedly slow down youth—in walking, in driving, and in everything else.

At work, they are perceived as out of date, too slow, not sufficiently attractive. On television, they are often the objects of ridicule. Few people believe that the aged possess wisdom, have a function, or are creating something to fill a new life space.

Elders persevere in positions in the legislative and executive branches, but the recent campaign to limit terms of office as a way to invigorate government may be only partly a desire to open up the system. It is also, conceivably, an expression of distrust in survivors, and a desire to extend retirement to public life as well as to industry.

At one level, our faith in science leads us to concentrate on its promise of continued life extension and disease conquest; we dream not only of prolonging life but of defeating death. At another level, our individualistic past pushes us to assume that the blessings of the twentieth century are gifts that individuals should use as they wish. They are released from obligation to contribute to the general well-being either through paid work or through significant volunteer work to improve the community or the nation. Their future is for themselves.

As the twenty-first century draws closer, this social disengagement in combination with the anti-age undercurrent in our basic institutions begins to seem less satisfactory for several reasons. First, some of those who can choose to do nothing (except consume goods and leisure services) find it less satisfying than expected. Between one-quarter and one-half of the fully retired want to be actively engaged in something other than self-gratification, though they may not want to do exactly what they have done in the past (McNaught, Barth, & Henderson, 1989). But they find that major institutions have little room for them, little interest in their abilities. This is true for industry, business, and volunteer organizations. While many institutions have disavowed an age bias, their actions (with a few exceptions, which are a hint of the future) are not open or welcoming. Such attitudes ignore the sociological and psychological evidence that humans find their basic satisfaction in engagement with others, not in separation from them.

Within this book, Joseph F. Quinn and Richard V. Burkhauser, Martha Holstein, A. Regula Herzog and James N. Morgan, Harry R. Moody, and W. Andrew Achenbaum and Malcolm H. Morrison, in their several ways, document how earlier points of view persist in all of our institutions. These views remain in the workplace, among employers, and in voluntary associations. They also persist in popular attitudes about the role of women, even those who have moved into the job market and shed the basic homemaker, caretaker role to which so many women have historically been assigned. The gap between individual choice and opportunity is widening.

A few favorably placed individuals find satisfying activity in their later years with voluntary and public associations, but their involvement is usually limited to a few hours a month.

Second, at the same time, employing institutions (economic or voluntary) are finding it difficult to maintain their activities as productively as they would like with a younger work force. Demographic projections for the next twenty years make clear that the proportion of young workers will decline and that the labor force will be older. It is becoming clear that technology alone will not make it possible to perform all organization or business tasks with a reduced labor force.

Third, there is accumulating though still largely anecdotal evidence that an elderly retired or disengaged population is not satisfied with present choices. There are those who in numerous surveys say they are willing and able to work, those who volunteer (though the volume of people is insignificant), those who engage in unreported work at least part-time, and those who report being dissatisfied with a life devoted only to recreation or relationships with a scattered or distant family.

These developments are ushering in the twenty-first century, in which aging will be valued in a different way. We can see signs of this change in a number of areas: in the current promotion of increased opportunities for self-chosen leisure consumption, in the quest for greater family integration, and in efforts to remove age discrimination at work. These developments represent ad hoc efforts to open up more meaningful social roles for the elderly.

## STRATEGIC POLICIES AND PROGRAMS

Valuable as these efforts have been, as a transition they lack a sufficiently clear rationale or conceptual foundation and a strategic sense of where such action leads us. The focus remains fixed on increasing the variety of directions from which individuals can choose to realize their private aspirations.

What is lacking is consensus that everyone is needed, that being needed is as important as being free. The concept of productive aging depends finally on achieving such a consensus. To this end, two elements are lacking in the attempt to come to terms with and to adapt to the late twentieth century: (1) a wide public discussion about the way the rights of individuals to free choice, to retirement, and to nonwork are also dependent upon the level of responsibility assumed for society's strength, which makes these rights possible; and (2) studies made over time on how (if at all) individuals change their views about different kinds of retirement activity, especially those consisting only of leisure.

As we have widened our personal freedoms, we have not given equal legitimacy to the accompanying collective interdependency and responsibilities in the community upon which the individual rights are based. Despite the opening up of opportunities in the twentieth century, involvement in public life has decreased or diminished. Missing from the usual activity lists are work for pay, volunteering with significant effort for the well-being of one's community, or roles in the political or environmental life of the times. These activities may be no less significant as parts of life's mainstream than are family relations and hosteling.

The heart of an agenda for productive aging is agreement that everyone is needed. The authors of the earlier chapters in this book have, one by one, identified next steps that might be taken to create the conditions for a truly productive aging society. For instance:

1. Developing a national consensus that the aged can and should be considered as assets, with opportunities for those over fifty-five or sixty or sixty-five to continue, or to create their own roles in society.
2. Changing public anti-age discrimination.
3. Opening the doors of all institutions, whether proprietary, nonprofit, voluntary, or governmental, for significant opportunities for interested and capable elders.
4. Placing a value on many activities that are voluntary, or private, or unreported and thus fail to appear in our national accounts (the gross national product) even though these activities may concretely improve social and economic conditions. Examples include caring for others, helping to staff agencies or businesses or schools, improving the environment, grandparenting, and so forth.

Among the practical steps that can be initiated or expanded for public education, research, or policy advocacy are:

1. Developing and disseminating the available evidence that new technology is a mechanism to make use of older skills, not a bar to their use. The newest high technology may depend on a young work force at the start, but the number of workers who will require the most complex of advanced technical skills is relatively small; most workers in a new technological age will need better basic skills, not exotic new ones. Correcting the misconception that science makes basic skills obsolete is a first-order task in changing public perception.
2. Improving and disseminating the data about the labor force potential of older workers; that is, about the requirements that can be met with experienced people—which specific tasks can be better performed by seasoned older workers with minimum upgrading in basic skills and which require wholly new career training mainly for new job entrants.
3. Identifying a broader base of volunteer opportunities by enlarging the

data about tasks in communities and in the nation that need doing but are not being performed in the classic marketplace or in public bureaucracy models of organization.

4. Valorizing volunteer and social activity. Voluntary activity is accepted in our society but not given any significant place in public policymaking, which is governed by economic market models that measure narrowly the value of production of goods and services.

It would be extremely valuable if a mechanism could be developed that would link nonmarket volunteer or under-market-rate work with the dominant economic model. One approach would be to start with the smallest, most discrete example of the nonmarket world—the family. Can the family, as a unit (not as a collection of individuals) be viewed as a producing unit for society as much as an economic enterprise is? It may seem fanciful, but it *is* possible to see the family as having two main producing functions: (1) it produces children for the next generation, healthy and capable of creative contributions; and (2) it produces an intimate environment that nourishes and sustains its members through good and bad times so that they have a sound base for developing their own creative lives in relation to the larger world around them (cf. Becker, 1988).

In such a model, it is possible, without being crassly material, to place values on what family members do for one another and how they interact with the outer world from which the family secures food, education, income, and so forth. Extrapolated to other volunteer activities, such a model could provide the kind of concrete data for public policy guidance on many issues such as family responsibility vis-à-vis formal services, whether dependent families are always a burden on society or may in fact be making valuable but previously unmarked contributions, and so forth. The same could then be said about volunteering to aid the ecology, the environment, and human services. The cost of failures in family function could also be identified more systematically than is now the case in calculating gross national product and well-being.

Development of such a model is being considered by some groups, among them the United Nations Research Center in Vienna. A service-credit model is now being tested in the United States in a dozen sites (Cahn, 1988). Certain academic centers such as the Family Policy Center at Brandeis University and the Gerontology Institute at the University of Massachusetts at Boston have begun to explore the economics of voluntary work. What is suggested is the conceptual development of a social GNP model for volunteering and less formal "work" that can supplement the economic modeling of input-output analysis.

5. Producing a set of explicit niches in society in which the talents of able elders can be used more productively than is now the case and with greater satisfaction for older citizens.

6. Improving the ways the retired and the soon-to-retire can think about and express their views on how they would fit the next twenty years of their life into the life of their community. This is crucial if exploitation of the retired is to be avoided through the well-meaning but possible misguided choices made by those not elderly.

To repeat, step one is securing agreement that everyone is needed through-out their life span, needed for their personal well-being and for society's well-being. Then, institutions and organizations can begin to expand op-portunities to adults in the Third Age (Laslett, 1991) of living. Sweden already has announced this as a national aim. My wish is that by the year 2000 the United States may have done the same.

## REFERENCES

Becker, G. S. (1988, March). Family economics and macro behavior. *American Economic Review*, 78(1), 1–13.

Cahn, E. S. (1988). In R. Morris & S. A. Bass, *Retirement reconsidered: Economic and social roles for older people* (pp. 232–249). New York: Springer.

Laslett, P. (1991). *A fresh map of life: The emergence of the third age.* Cambridge, MA: Harvard University Press.

McNaught, W., Barth, M., & Henderson, P. (1989, Winter). The human resource potential of Americans over 50. *Human Resource Management*, 28(4), 455–473.

# Name Index

Aaron, H., 107
Abel, E. K., 179
Abramovitz, M., 104
Abrams, E., 196
Achenbaum, W. Andrew, 7, 9, 15, 21, 100, 106, 191, 195, 198, 199, 289–290
Ahlstrom, S. E., 189
Anderson, B. E., 253, 257
Andrews, J., 149
Ansello, E. F., 221
Antonucci, Toni C., 13, 122, 191, 249, 250, 251, 252, 254, 255, 256, 261, 262
Applebaum, E., 50
Arber, S., 63, 65
Arendt, Hannah, 237
Arrington, L. J., 194
Atchley, R. C., 193
Axinn, J., 8

Bacellar, H., 252
Baily, M. N., 250, 252
Bamford, C., 104
Barber, Red, 193
Barnes, R. O., 144
Barresi, C. M., 103
Barter, J., 77
Barth, Michael, 4, 10, 44, 55, 57, 289
Bass, Scott A., 4, 5–6, 10, 18, 21, 200, 222

Baudelaire, 35
Baumol, W. J., 252
Baxandall, R., 104
Beard, B. B., 189
Beck, R., 245
Becker, G. S., 292
Becker, J., 154
Bell, Daniel, 28, 33
Bellah, Robert, 201
Beller, D. J., 54, 273, 275
Belous, Richard, 51
Bendick, Marc, 89
Benecki, T. J., 71
Benhabib, S., 236
Benjamin, A. E. Jr., 173
Berger, S., 68
Berndt, L., 252, 253, 254, 256, 257, 258, 260, 261, 263
Best, F., 105
Biller, N., 196
Birren, James, 191, 199
Bitton, D., 194
Bixby, L. E., 102
Bland, D., 109
Blank, Arthur, 162
Blazer, D., 190
Bluestone, Barry, 168
Boglietti, G., 108
Borowski, A., 9–10
Borus, M. E., 105, 109
Boyd, S. L., 68, 178

# Subject Index

# About the Contributors

W. ANDREW ACHENBAUM is Professor of History at the University of Michigan and Deputy Director of its Institute of Gerontology. The author of *Old Age in the New Land*, he is currently working on a history of the emergence of gerontology as a field of scientific inquiry in the United States.

TONI C. ANTONUCCI is Research Scientist and Program Director at the Institute for Social Research at the University of Michigan. She holds appointments in the departments of Psychology and Family Practice. Her research has focused on social relationships over the life span.

SCOTT A. BASS (co-editor) is the Director of the Gerontology Institute at the University of Massachusetts at Boston and of its Ph.D. in Gerontology program. He is the Center Head of the university's Gerontology Department. The author of numerous articles, he is co-editor of *Retirement Reconsidered* and *Diversity in Aging: Challenges Facing Planners and Policymakers in the 1990s*.

RICHARD V. BURKHAUSER is Professor of Economics and Senior Fellow at the Gerontology Institute at Syracuse University. He has taught at Vanderbilt University and was a visiting scholar at the University of Wisconsin and the Netherlands Institute for Advanced Study. He has published widely on the behavioral and income distribution effects of government policy in the labor market.

FRANCIS G. CARO (co-editor) is the Director of the Frank J. Manning

Research Division of the Gerontology Institute at the University of Massachusetts at Boston. A sociologist and researcher on long-time care and urban policy, he was formerly director of research for the Community Service Society of New York. He has taught at Brandeis University, among other places, and has published extensively on evaluation design and research methodology. He edited *Readings in Evaluation Research*.

YUNG-PING CHEN (co-editor) holds the Frank J. Manning Eminent Scholar's Chair in Social Gerontology at the University of Massachusetts at Boston. He has taught at the University of California at Los Angeles and the American College in Bryn Mawr, Pennsylvania. An economist, he is co-editor of *Social Security in a Changing Society, Checks and Balances in Social Security*, and *Unlocking Home Equity for the Elderly*.

PAMELA DOTY is a Senior Policy Analyst in the Office of the Assistant Secretary for Planning and Evaluation, U.S. Department of Health and Human Services. She has worked previously for the Office of Legislation and Policy of the Health Care Financing Administration, the Congressional Office of Technology Assessment, and the New York–based Center for Policy Research. She specializes in long-term care for the elderly and disabled.

GEORGE GERBNER is Professor of Communication and Dean Emeritus of the Annenberg School for Communication at the University of Pennsylvania. He has directed U.S. and multinational communications research projects under numerous grants and contracts. His current major research is a comparative analysis of television in twelve countries, and he has written widely on the influence of the media.

ROSE C. GIBSON is Associate Professor in the School of Social Work and Faculty Associate at the Institute for Social Research at the University of Michigan. A former National Institute on Aging postdoctoral fellow in statistics, she participated in the first National Survey of Black Americans and is the author of *Blacks in an Aging Society*.

A. REGULA HERZOG is Adjunct Associate Professor in the Department of Psychology at the University of Michigan and Associate Research Scientist at its Institutes for Gerontology and Social Research. She has published numerous articles and has directed several research grants under the National Institute on Aging.

KAREN C. HOLDEN is Assistant Professor in the Department of Consumer Science, School of Family Resources and Consumer Sciences, and at the Robert M. LaFollette Institute of Public Affairs, University of Wisconsin/

Madison. Her research interests and publications cover social welfare policy, demography and the economics of aging, the economic well-being of older women, and program evaluation.

MARTHA HOLSTEIN is completing her interrupted doctoral studies at the University of Texas Medical Branch in the Program in Medical Humanities after a nearly twenty-year career in the field of aging. She was formerly Associate Director of the American Society on Aging and taught courses in ethics, aging, and health at the University of California at Berkeley and San Francisco State University.

JAMES S. JACKSON is Professor of Social Psychology and Public Health and a Research Scientist at the Institute for Social Research at the University of Michigan. He is Director of the Program for Research on Black Americans and the African-American Mental Health Research Center. He is co-author of *Hope and Independence: Blacks' Response to Electoral and Party Politics.*

MARK S. KAMLET is Professor of Economics and Public Policy and Head of the Department of Social and Decision Sciences at Carnegie Mellon University. He also holds an appointment in the School of Urban and Public Affairs and is Adjunct Assistant Professor in the Department of Psychiatry at the University of Pittsburgh. His research interests have focused on budgetary and health care policy.

BAILA MILLER is Associate Professor of Social Work at the University of Illinois at Chicago. Her research interests include the consequences of caregiver burden on long-term care options, race and gender differences in spouse adaptation of persons with dementia, and minority access to long-term care.

HARRY R. MOODY is the Deputy Director of the Brookdale Center on Aging of Hunter College, City University of New York. He is also an executive officer of the National Eldercare Human Resource Development Institute under the federal Administration on Aging. He is an adjunct faculty member in the Department of Philosophy at Hunter College and the author of *Abundance of Life: Human Development Policies for an Aging Society.*

JAMES N. MORGAN is Professor of Economics at the University of Michigan and Program Director of its Survey Research Center at the Institute for Social Research. He is a fellow of the National Academy of Arts and Sciences. He is the author of *Consumer Economics* and co-author of a number of other books.

ROBERT MORRIS is Senior Fellow of the Gerontology Institute of the

University of Massachusetts at Boston and Cardinal Medeiros Visiting Lecturer. Professor Emeritus of Brandeis University's Heller School for Advanced Studies in Social Welfare, he is a renowned pioneer in gerontological research. He is co-editor of *Retirement Reconsidered*.

MALCOLM H. MORRISON is the Director of Research and Information Services at the National Association of Rehabilitation Facilities in Reston, Virginia. Formerly, he was Director of the Division of Disability Program Information and Studies and National Vocational and Rehabilitation and Work Incentive Demonstration Projects for the Social Security Administration. He is an authority on disability, health, employment, and retirement policies and programs.

DAVID C. MOWERY is Associate Professor of Business and Public Policy in the Walter Haas School of Business at the University of California at Berkeley. He was Study Director for the Panel on Technology and Employment of the National Academy of Sciences and has served as a Council on Foreign Relations International Affairs Fellow. His research deals with the economics of technological innovation and the effects of public policies on innovation.

LAURA KATZ OLSON is Professor in the Department of Government at Lehigh University. She has been a Fulbright Scholar, Gerontological Fellow, and NASPAA Fellow at the Social Security Administration in Baltimore. She is the author of *The Political Economy of Aging: The State, Private Power, and Social Welfare*.

JOSEPH F. QUINN is Professor of Economics and Chairman of the Economics Department at Boston College. He has been a Visiting Professor at the Institute for Research and Poverty at the University of Wisconsin, the Graduate School of Public Policy at Berkeley, and the University of New South Wales in Sydney. He has published primarily on the economics of aging and is co-author of *Passing the Torch: The Influence of Economic Incentives on Work and Retirement*.

PHILIP TAYLOR is Research Fellow at the University of Sheffield, England. A psychologist, he has carried out research in the areas of the psychological impact of unemployment and organizational behavior and is conducting research with Alan Walker on the employment experiences of older workers.

ALAN WALKER is Professor of Social Policy at the University of Sheffield, England. He has researched and written extensively in the fields of social policy and social gerontology and is the author or co-author of ten books, including *Ageing and Social Policy* and *The Caring Relationship*.